The Virgin of Guadalupe
and the Conversos

LATINIDAD

Transnational Cultures in the United States

This series publishes books that deepen and expand our knowledge and understanding of the various Latina/o populations in the United States in the context of their transnational relationships with cultures of the broader Americas. The focus is on the history and analysis of Latino cultural systems and practices in national and transnational spheres of influence from the nineteenth century to the present. The series is open to scholarship in political science, economics, anthropology, linguistics, history, cinema and television, literary and cultural studies, and popular culture and encourages interdisciplinary approaches, methods, and theories. The series grew out of discussions with faculty at the School of Transborder Studies at Arizona State University, where an interdisciplinary emphasis is being placed on transborder and transnational dynamics.

Matthew Garcia, Series Editor, School of Historical, Philosophical, and Religious Studies; and Director of Comparative Border Studies

For a list of titles in the series, see the last page of the book.

The Virgin of Guadalupe and the Conversos

Uncovering Hidden Influences from Spain to Mexico

MARIE-THERESA HERNÁNDEZ

Rutgers University Press

New Brunswick, New Jersey, and London

Library of Congress Cataloging-in-Publication Data

Hernández, Marie-Theresa, 1952– author
    The virgin of Guadalupe and the conversos : uncovering hidden influences from Spain to
    Mexico / Marie-Theresa Hernandez
        p. cm.—(Latinidad: Transnational Cultures in the United States)
        Includes bibliographical references and index
        ISBN 978-0-8135-6569-9 (hardcover : alk. paper) — ISBN 978-0-8135-6568-2 (pbk.) —
    ISBN 978-0-8135-6570-5 (e-book)
        1. Christianity and other religions—Judaism. 2. Judaism—Relations—Christianity. 3.
    Crypto-Jews—Mexico—History—18th century. 4. Crypto-Jews—Mexico—History—
    19th century. 5. Espinosa de los Monteros, Manuel, 1773–1838. 6. Carvajal, Luis de, 1567?–
    1596. 7. Guadalupe, Our Lady of. I. Title.
        BM535.h458 2014
        261.2'60972—DC23   2013040662

A British Cataloging-in-Publication record for this book is available from the British Library.

Visit our website: http://rutgerspress.rutgers.edu

Manufactured in the United States of America

In Memory of John S. Broussard, C.S.B., 1919–2012

Contents

Acknowledgments

This book has traveled a winding road of narratives. It began with an interest in the racial and ethnic issues surrounding the Mexican Virgin of Guadalupe and Malinche, Cortez's translator, and their importance in the construction of the Mexican nation-state. Yet early on the research took an abrupt turn, as it often does, with my discovery at the New York Public Library of the writings of Manuel Espinosa de los Monteros. Monteros clarified something I had always wondered about, whether Guadalupe in some way had an association with the crypto-Jews who migrated to México during the colonial period. This book therefore transformed into a broad study of Catholics and Sephardic conversos, the monarchy in Spain and Colonial México, and the circulation of narratives as Sephardic conversos and *judaizantes* traveled across the Atlantic.

With these wide-ranging issues it was necessary to seek the consultation of a number of scholars. I thank Arturo Álvarez Álvarez and Elisa Rovira for their assistance with my research on the Virgin of Guadalupe in Spain; Brian Connaughton for graciously allowing me to see the galleys of his biographical writing on Monteros; Matt Goldish and Schulamith Halevy for their invaluable support regarding the history and traditions of the Sephardic diaspora; and Sergio Fernández López for his guidance on Hebraic scholars of Spain's sixteenth century.

My appreciation goes to colleagues Brian Riedel, Yolanda Godsey, Alessandro Carrera, Bernice Heilbrunn, Marc Zimmerman, and Hildegard Glass, who provided advice and ongoing support for what Marc Zimmerman called my "Da Vinci Code" project. Integral to the project was my colleague and friend Shannon Leonard for her critically important observations on the manuscript.

Friends often construct the core of support for the writing of a book. I thank Ana Burgoyne, Gail Gutierrez, Nestor Rodriguez, Charles Munnell, and especially Monica Villagomez, who listened (and commented) through all the twists and turns of the research and writing of this book. I deeply appreciate the support from my friend and colleague in Monterrey, Nuevo León, Federico Garza Martinez, especially his assistance in obtaining permission for the use of a particular (and strategic) image of Michael the Archangel from the Archive of the Basilica of Guadalupe.

I thank Ray Ramirez for his daily encouragement and support during the final stages of writing, which helped to make *The Virgin of Guadalupe and the Conversos* a reality.

Most important is my family. My children, Belen and Greg, have listened to the stories with great patience. I look forward to someday telling the new addition to our family, my grandson, Thomas, the stories about the two Guadalupes and the *judaizantes* who lived among the kings of Spain.

This book is dedicated to the memory of John S. Broussard—whose presence during my childhood left an indelible mark on my intellect and character.

Note on Text

While most of the texts cited in this book have been translated, there are a number of formal names and terms left in the original Spanish. For example, the name of the Spanish king Philip II remains in the original, as Felipe II. Ferdinand and Isabella, known as the Catholic kings, are listed as Fernando and Isabel, los Reyes Católicos—their name and description not being translated to English. In citing the work of Manuel Espinosa de los Monteros, I left his text in its original form. Monteros does not use the normally expected accents on certain vowels.

There is an ongoing dilemma regarding the publication of any issue regarding conversos (Jews converted to Catholicism during the early modern period). As mentioned in the book, the term "*marrano*" is avoided because of its connotation to the term "pig." There are also particular complications because not all conversos secretly practiced Judaism; secondly, many of the conversos who continued to practice Judaism privately considered themselves to be Jews. However, according to Rabbinic Law, this is incorrect, leaving us to decide between how a group identifies itself and whether they are identified by a legitimizing authority. The term *judaizante* (Judaizer) used in this book in its Spanish form is not ideal because it was a term used by the Inquisition for those newly converted Christians who were convicted and punished for practicing Judaism. Yet it appears to be the best option for now. It is not translated simply because it sounds less offensive in Spanish.

The Virgin of Guadalupe and the Conversos

Introduction

In the spring of 2006, while searching through the archives at the New York Public Library (NYPL), I experienced a jolt such as Ann Laura Stoler describes—"a sort of 'shock' of unexpected details that alters one's vision, 'pricks' one's received understandings of what counts as a history and what makes up people's lives."[1] This occurred when I found a large mass of writings by a Mexican priest named Manuel Espinosa de los Monteros, indicating that he was a crypto-Jew, or at the least, a Jewish Christian.[2] The papers are dated between 1825 and 1830. They are particularly important because in the last few years of his life he held a significant position at the Basilica of the Virgin of Guadalupe, the most important Catholic shrine in the Americas.

Monteros (1773–1838), the highly educated son of an economically challenged *criollo* (Mexican-born Spaniard) family in México City, led an obscure existence in the provinces until late in his career. His facility with indigenous languages, the overabundance of priests in México at the time (and perhaps other, unknown reasons) left him in positions at a number of indigenous parishes.[3] Finally, at the age of fifty-nine, he was appointed to the supremely important Basilica of Guadalupe in México City, where he remained from 1832 to his death in 1838. He was well respected in this position, and even in the present day, Basilica archives maintain a Web page detailing his contributions.

Monteros's appointment to what was called *la colegiata* of the Basilica was significant.[4] It was and has continued to be the heart of the Mexican nation, for both the religious and the secular. The late Guillermo Schulenburg, rector of the site for twenty-five years, told me in 2008, "Everything that happens in México passes through the Basilica."[5]

Before moving to the sanctuary, Monteros languished in different indigenous parishes, angry at what he perceived as the poor intelligence of the natives, and the manipulative ways of the *criollos*.[6] During his time of ministry in the rural parishes, he took occasion to write extensively. The documents I found amounted to more than five hundred pages of handwritten text.

These writings are within a collection that came to be known as *Monumentos Guadalupanos*, acquired by the NYPL in 1880. In the voluminous writings that Monteros produced, he took on the uncanny position of historical reporter and quasi-heretic, devotee of Christ and Philo-Semite who incessantly thought of the Virgin of Guadalupe and her association with the "Hebrew nation."[7] While showing his significant (and surprising) ambivalence for the Roman Catholic Church, he states the Virgin of "Guadalupe is wearing clothing that is typical of the Hebrew Nation restored to its ancient dignity as the Wife of the Lord, and absolutely has no reference to the Roman Church."[8] Monteros continues, "Among the family or house of Israel she among them is the most honorable and beautiful."[9]

This book is about Monteros and other priests before him who conserved a belief in a Jewish God while presenting themselves to the world as Christian clergy. Monteros's type of Jewish Christianity relates to the writings by sixteenth-century Italian and Spanish Hebraists. In the following centuries, while the Inquisition attempted to eliminate any type of Jewish-leaning Christianity, two Jesuits—the Portuguese Antonio Vieira and the Chilean Manuel Lacunza—continued to develop this thinking. These two important writers forwarded this philosophy around the world; Vieira worked in Portugal and Brazil during the seventeenth century and Manuel Lacunza in the eighteenth. Displaced to Italy, Lacunza's writings reached the Americas shortly before Monteros began his treatise.

Traveling Papers

There are reports that U.S. general Winfield Scott stole a number of documents from what is termed the Carlos Sigüenza y Gongora Collection, located in México City, during the Mexican War. The Mexican Church historian Mariano Cuevas wrote in 1921: "This group of precious manuscripts was taken to Washington by General [Winfield] Scott in 1847. It was placed in the archive of the Department of State, where, according to a letter located in the Archivo General de la Nación [the Mexican National Archives], it was seen by our Minister Luis de la Rosa. Our government made a claim to have the documents returned. The American government promised to return them, admonishing Scott for his actions. . . . yet nothing has been returned."[10]

Cuevas was concerned about the disappearance of the *Nican Mopohua*, a document from the Sigüenza collection, written in Nahuatl, describing the apparitions of the Virgin of Guadalupe. The *Nican Mopohua* is considered one of the most important texts in the national patrimony. It is not known if the Monteros papers were already part of the Sigüenza collection. What is known is that the *Nican Mopohua* was sold at auction in London as part of *Monumentos Guadalupanos* on July 8, 1880.[11]

Winfield Scott is implicated in the loss of the documents to this day. The Internet is saturated with sites that emphatically state that the *Nican Mopohua* came back to the United States with him. Yet the story is much more insidious.

Monumentos Guadalupanos is part of a group of documents collected by José Fernando Ramírez (1804–1871), who left México abruptly after the fall of Maximilian in 1865. Ramírez was born in northern México. An obsessive bibliophile since his youth, he held various positions of importance in the state of Durango. In 1842 he was elected to the Mexican Congress representing his home state, and later was appointed to various high-level positions within the executive branch.[12] In 1847 he was named secretary of exterior relations (*secretaria de relaciones*). During the U.S.-Mexican War he was instrumental in "saving the archive of the Secretaria de Relaciones and the objects of the National Museum, in addition to the National Archives."[13] As American forces approached México City, he is said to have "handed the Secretaria de Relaciones documents over to an official of that department, hid the objects from the museum in the houses of various friends, and placed the treasures of the Archive in thirty or thirty-one trunks, that were locked in the warehouses of Don José Maria Andrade,"[14] "a publisher and bibliophilist" later known for having "laid the foundation during the French Intervention, for what was intended by Maximilian to be the imperial library of México."[15] There is no mention in Ramírez's biography of when he returned the books. In a letter dated 1851 he describes his new house as having a salon of 29 *varas* (965.7 square feet) and a studio of 10 *varas* (333 square feet) that does not have enough space for all the books he has accumulated.[16] In 1856 he was appointed director of the National Museum and president of the executive board of the Academia de Bellas Artes (Academy of Fine Arts). Again he became a "rescuer" of libraries when he "intervened for the libraries of the former convents in México, saving from "rape and destruction a great many books and a multitude of ancient manuscripts that would have been lost forever."[17] It is assumed that what he saved was placed in the national collections. It is significant to note that in 1858 his personal library consisted of 8,178 volumes.[18] Ramírez was minister of exterior relations and president of the Cabinet during the reign of Maximilian, where he remained until 1866, when he sought refuge in Europe after it became clear that Maximilian's troops would be defeated.[19]

Ramírez died in 1871 in Bonn. Nine years later, his remaining books and documents were sold by the London agency Puttick and Simpson in an auction that lasted five days. *Monumentos Guadalupanos* was included in the auction, with *Nican Mopohua* part of those documents.[20]

Finding *Monumentos*

In the spring of 2006 the NYPL online catalog listed *Monumentos Guadalupanos* as part of the Obadiah Rich Collection in its archives. A few months later, while in New York, I visited the library and asked the reference desk staff about the collection. They looked through the catalog and were not able to find anything. One person sought the opinion of another, yet nothing could be found. After about an hour of searching, they suggested I look at a ten-foot-high wall of books across the room from the reference desk. They were bound volumes of photocopies of the old card catalog. Under the "Ms," we found the notation regarding *Monumentos*. I was directed to the archives and, producing my academic credentials, I was able to request microfilm reels of the documents.

Once I was sitting at the microfilm-reading machine, I went through the three reels slowly. The first thing I saw was the *Nican Mopohua*, for which Gen. Winfield Scott had been so widely maligned for its loss. I knew it was there because that is how I had found the documents in the first place. A number of publications on the Virgin of Guadalupe cite the *Nican Mopohua* and state that it is located at the NYPL. The description available for *Monumentos* stated that it contained sermons and various writings from the sixteenth to nineteenth centuries. As I began viewing the second reel, I found some unusual writings with a theme I had never seen before. I saw phrases such as "It is very possible that America is the foundation of a Millennial Empire of Israelites,"[21] and ". . . the Israelites will again exist as a sovereign nation."[22] It was a moment of shock for me, seeing so many pages written by this priest who was promoting the Hebrew Nation over the formation of his own very new nation-state.

Shortly after my visit, I purchased copies of the microfilm. Several months went by with no response. I contacted the library and they told me they could not find the master reels. Eventually the NYPL staff found the master, and six months after they were ordered they finally arrived. About the same time, I made a subsequent trip to New York and met with Michael Terry, director of the Dorot Jewish Division of the NYPL. He was greatly surprised when I told him about the information I found in the documents. After some negotiating with the archive department, they gave Terry and me permission to look at all the originals of *Monumentos*, except the *Nican Mopohua* because of its fragile state. I found a number of passages that convinced Terry that this was a major find for Jewish studies, even considering the manuscript was written by a priest.

In 2010 a scholar from a major university in México contacted me about *Monumentos*. He was looking for other material on the Mexican colonial period and had seen a reference to my research on Monteros. He had checked the NYPL website and had found nothing about *Monumentos*. In addition, he had been corresponding with the NYPL regarding the collection and had been told repeatedly that the documents were not there.

In the meantime I continued to do research regarding writers that Monteros cited. I went further and further back into history, finally stopping in the fourteenth century. Monteros's stories were connected every step of the way. Using the establishment of the sanctuary to the Virgin of Guadalupe in Extremadura, Spain, as an artificial starting point, I traced the Jewish influence on the Spanish clergy and their subsequent interest in the millennium from the fourteenth through the sixteenth century—traveling literally and metaphorically through Extremadura, Castilla–La Mancha, and Andalucia. I studied how these influences made the trans-Atlantic voyage to New Spain, and how, long before Monteros, they located themselves in México City's Basilica of Guadalupe, the same place where, two centuries later, he was to live and work.

Although most historians of Jewish history in the Americas search through Inquisition archives, for the most part I chose to avoid these types of documents. The idea of testifying under extreme duress removes credibility from what is said. I chose instead to search for sermons and religious writings. In this realm, the clergy told different types of stories. The only exceptions are the Inquisition records pertaining to the Hieronymite Order of Monks (los Jerónimos). While it is possible that the charges made against the converso or *judaizante* monks were either false or exaggerated, there is a large body of scholarship surrounding the secret identity of so many of them that corroborates the narratives from the Inquisition records.[23]

Ultimately I found one document in México City and others at Brown, Indiana, and the University of Texas. The text of interest at the University of Texas is a book published in 1648, *Imagen de la Virgen Maria de Guadalupe*, by Miguel Sánchez, a secular priest who lived in México during the mid-seventeenth century, the most active period of the Mexican Inquisition.[24] Sánchez's book has been reprinted numerous times, yet few people noticed the material that was removed when his book was severely edited in 1655. In 1648 it was a Jewish-Christian book with scores of citations from the Psalms, references to Guadalupe as a menorah, and oblique notations of the tension and duplicity surrounding the Inquisition. The edition of 1655 was only about the Virgin of Guadalupe.

In contrast, Monteros's writing located at the NYPL never made it to the publisher. As he states, he was careful about his citations, conferred with his colleagues, and ultimately awaited approval of the authorities.[25] Yet nothing came of his work. The documents most likely stayed with the author while he was living at the Basilica, yet sometime between his death and 1880, his writings entered the library of José Fernando Ramírez. Under normal circumstances it would not be likely that the Basilica would have officially sold the documents. In fact, the late Monsignor Schulenburg, the former rector of the Basilica told me he believed Ramírez stole the documents.[26] However, in light of their controversial nature, they might have been easy to let go. Could the change of hands also be attributed to a sacristan or priest who needed money? This occurred frequently in Nuevo León; Aquiles Sepulveda of Monterrey told me that in the late twentieth century he bought numerous religious artifacts and documents from people who came by his house wanting money.[27] Or could Ramírez have collected the documents while he rescued México City's archives from the Americans in 1848 and merely kept them after the occupation ended?

The Politics of Archives

As Ann Laura Stoler writes so aptly in *Along the Archival Grain*, state archives are an expression of "political rationalities" in which policies and practices are informed regarding what is appropriate information to distribute and or camouflage.[28] While not denying that many developing countries lose precious documents and artifacts, could there have been a special reason why the Monteros papers were quickly installed in a New York archive? Here they create an absent presence, hidden away for some curious researcher to rescue, a narrative so similar to the multitude of crypto-Jewish stories circulating in México.[29]

The politics and policies of the archives affect the document's availability, as does the political positioning of the scholar. As Michel de Certeau writes, the scholar has a "patron"—dissertation advisor, tenure and promotion committee, funding source, or publisher.[30] Monteros's writing on a Guadalupe that rescues the Jews would be greatly offensive to many in México, which is primarily a Catholic country. The idea of offense came to light in 2008 when I was asked to submit a paper regarding Monteros and Sánchez's writings on Guadalupe for the upscale Mexican journal *Literal*—only to be told that if they published the paper, the Mexican Church would shut them down.

While more recent narratives of this nature are dangerous, it is not difficult to write and publish on the seventeenth-century Inquisition history of México. The centuries have cleansed México's history of *judaizantes*. As numerous scholars have proposed, the *judaizantes* were all gone after the last major auto-da-fe conducted by the Mexican Inquisition in 1649. Yet problems surface once Guadalupe becomes involved. Any discussion that connects Guadalupe with the conversos conflates with issues of national identity, patriotism, and proper conduct. The story is complex. Strong national sentiments place her without question within the narrative of the Catholic Virgin Mary appearing to an indigenous man in early colonial México. Yet her genealogy is put into question if the *judaizante* narratives in Sánchez's book are acknowledged.

I have already seen the consequences of this in a number of conversations with ardent Guadalupe devotees, who believe that any type of converso connection would negate her importance to the Mexican identity. Moreover, the reaction has been a feeling of assault because the *original* story of the Mexican Guadalupe has been stolen. This somewhat compares to the issue of the genealogical origins of the Japanese emperor; according to national narratives his bloodline is purely Japanese, yet, as Marilyn Ivy notes, his long-ago ancestors were Korean, something unthinkable to most modern Japanese.[31]

Are historians' references to secret practices of *judaizantes* that they found in the archives politically impractical? Or are they just unimportant? The great circulation of Inquisition narratives creates an illusion of interest into the *judaizante* presence in Mexican colonial history. Presented under the rubric of the Holy Office, the texts are read in relation to traditions, beliefs, and identities that are seen by Catholics as transgressive and repulsive, at least officially.

To complicate matters, the *judaizante* references in Sánchez's and Monteros's writings are much more frightening than Inquisition records because they are written by high-level clergy and, more importantly, because they are about the Mexican Virgin of Guadalupe. *Imagen* (Sánchez's book) was sanctioned by the highest officials of the Mexican Church.[32] It was even commissioned by the viceroy.[33] Sánchez was a friend of several viceroys. He lived as a hermit yet consorted among the elite of the city. The question remains: what was he doing writing about a menorah during a time that *judaizantes* were being intensely persecuted? Yet, although his book has been circulated for centuries, only one scholar—Solange Alberro—noted his mention of the Inquisition. Even so, she concludes that Sánchez supported the work of the Holy Office and thought that people coming from foreign countries "were bringing heresy to México."[34] Perhaps this is an example of how conclusions can be made to suit the political climate. Indeed, a colleague of mine, Schulamith Halevy, at Hebrew University, who has interviewed dozens of families in northern México who claim to be of Jewish ancestry is often told the conversations have to remain confidential.[35]

The Monteros papers are in the same collection as the *Nican Mopohua*, which has been cited continuously during the past century. It is common knowledge that this document is at the NYPL. Yet no one has ever spoken of the Monteros papers. When I interviewed Monsignor Schulenburg, he said he had never heard of Monteros.[36] This seemed extremely odd because the ninety-year-old Schulenburg had a lifelong affiliation with the Basilica. With the most respected scholar of Guadalupe, David Brading, citing *Monumentos* yet not making note of the Monteros papers, I wonder if, previous to now, anyone has looked at the entire set of documents. Or, were the Monteros papers so heretical that they were simply ignored?

Writing Conversos and *Judaizantes* before Monteros

Michel de Certeau explains in *The Writing of History* that "religious history is a field of confrontation between historiography and *archeology*," and that it "allows us to analyze the relation between history and *ideology*."[37] It is at these intersections that religious history is often produced. Regarding the relationship between the Virgin of Guadalupe and the *judaizantes*, be it in Spain or México, doctrinal facts have consistently structured the resulting narratives. Thus, a Mexican text written in 1648, in the midst of the most significant and tragic phase of Inquisition activity, is read and analyzed as a masterpiece of typology that for the first time brought together narratives from the Old Testament, intertwining them with the Virgin's apparition in Tepeyac near México City.[38] Even more significant is how the Sánchez book was ultimately seen as a "foundation myth" of México. As David Brading notes in *Mexican Phoenix*, Guadalupe "provided . . . an autonomous, sacred foundation for their Church and *patria*," a likely "Mexican Ark of the Covenant, a sign that henceforth the Virgin Mary would act as a special protector of the Mexican people."[39] Situating Guadalupe in such a place is solidly correct, but what previous scholars have not addressed is the dramatic religious and political situation occurring as Sánchez was preparing his text.[40] The story is not complete unless the Inquisition is discussed. Yet the religious ideology of the seventeenth century and, inclusively, of the twenty-first does not allow a discussion regarding the *judaizante* influence on the Church in México (or in Spain for that matter) and their relationship to Guadalupe. It is the purpose of this book to address this narrative.

Trajectory

The Virgin of Guadalupe and the Conversos sits on the periphery between "lived meaning and designated fact."[41] It seeks to challenge the oft-repeated narrative of the disappearance of the *judaizantes* in Spain and the Americas. It tells of stories that lived inside narratives of accepted religiosity. In addition, it questions the "designated fact[s]" that have been neatly printed in books dealing with *judaizantes*—people of Jewish descent who continued to believe in "the law of Moses." It provides pieces of information—some large, some small, forming an amorphous body of knowledge regarding a group of people that were said to have left, disappeared, or were never present at all.

This book about conversos, *judaizantes*, and the Virgin of Guadalupe highlights a rarely discussed connection. Yet it is Jacques Lafaye who quietly opens the door to the hidden space of that relationship by mentioning the connection in the first paragraph of the first chapter of the canonical *Quetzacóatl y Guadalupe*, a book on the historical and mythical origins of México. He tells of many Portuguese situated in the court of New Spain's viceroy who were conversos. He also reminds his readers that the "Jews of Castilla were already in México" at the time of the mass Portuguese migration during the late sixteenth century.[42] He explains the context and reasoning for this interjection of information on Mexican conversos in New Spain, a colony full of religious and political tension. However, according to established history, the tension in 1531 (the year of the Guadalupe apparitions) was mostly related to the conversion to Catholicism of millions of indigenous people and was accompanied by a fierce struggle for power (among the Spaniards) in the new colony. When the Mexican Guadalupe appeared, there was still no official Mexican Inquisition.[43] El Santo Oficio (the Holy Office) did not officially arrive in México until 1571. Lafaye reminds his readers of the previous Guadalupe and her monastery in Extremadura and that the older Virgin is considered "the history of Spain from 1340 to 1541." He also notes that the Spanish Guadalupe's monastery was no "royal garden," citing Américo Castro's narratives describing Judaic rites practiced within the monastery by the Hieronymite monks of the king.[44] "The history of Guadalupe is tied to the inquisitorial persecutions against the Jews" in late fifteenth-century

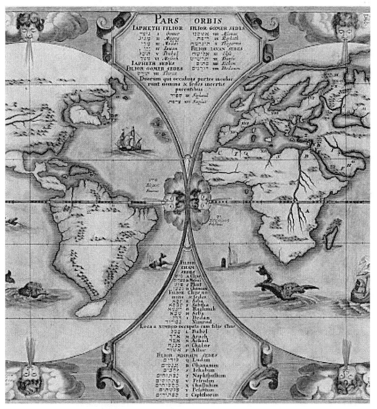

FIG. 1 Map of the World by Benito Arias Montano. From *The Antwerp Polyglot Bible* (Antwerp, 1572). Courtesy National Library of Australia.

Spain.[45] Lafaye is, as yet, the only scholar to make these associations between the *judaizantes* and Guadalupe.

The historiography surrounding *judaizantes* in Spain and México has focused on a theme of Inquisitorial confrontation. The famous riots of 1391 when thousands of Jews were killed in pogroms throughout Spain have been studied many times, as has the Spanish Inquisition. The Inquisition's foray into the *puebla* (village) of Extremadura, Spain, in 1485 has often been studied, with the self-destructive spiral of Hieronymite monk Diego de Marchena presented in detail, down to his execution by fire in front of the monastery doors.[46] In addition, numerous well-respected scholars have published significant works on the history of the Mexican Inquisition, including Solange Alberro, Seymour Liebman, and Nathan Wachtel.[47]

It is, however, Wachtel's *La fe del recuerdo* that propels scholarship on the Mexican Inquisition to a new level. He tells an engaging story about a number of conversos who still considered themselves Jews, describing their lives in Portugal and the Americas and their encounters with the Inquisition. He goes beyond what most others have done in terms of reaching deep into the circumstances and relationships of the people in question, providing readers with more than information about motivations, intrigues, relationships, and ultimately anguish as each person finds himself or herself in the Inquisition jails. Reading the pages of *La fe del recuerdo*, you can almost feel the insanity of the situation.[48]

Beyond What Can Be Thought

As I write the introduction of *The Virgin of Guadalupe and the Conversos*, I recall how Jules Michelet describes his writing of *History of France*: ". . . thus I roamed, from age to age . . . for thousands of years . . . I went, I wandered . . . I ran along my path . . . I went . . . as a bold voyager."[49] I found what some would consider a "strange dialogue," an Other dialogue belonging to the dead who spoke and thought those words that many scholars are sure they cannot say.[50]

The Virgin of Guadalupe and the Conversos belongs to that Other dialogue. It brings a different Guadalupe and traces the relationship among conversos and *judaizantes*, the Church, and the Spanish monarchy through five centuries, starting in the late Middle Ages and ending shortly after México achieves its independence from Spain.[51] Although there are individual stories relating to each location and time period, the continuous themes are of ambiguity, secrecy, duplicity, and dual allegiances at the highest levels of power. This incomprehensible scene has made serious scholarly analysis nearly impossible. It is the incongruence, inconsistency, and illogical trajectory amid the narratives of Monteros and his predecessors that informs this research. At the least, it can be said that their form of Christianity was not orthodox.

This study crosses six centuries as it tells of *judaizantes* and conversos (or their descendants') relationship with the two Guadalupes. The idea that a relationship between Guadalupe and the conversos, albeit in different forms and in different spaces, could continue for so many centuries led me to question the political and religious structures surrounding these narratives that were constructed in the centuries following the establishment of the Monasterio de Guadalupe (Monastery of Guadalupe), the monastery of the Jerónimos named for the Virgin of Guadalupe of Extremadura, considered to be the wealthiest in Europe during the fifteenth century.

Central to the study of the monastery is the work of Sophie Coussemacker and María del Pilar Rábade Obradó. Coussemacker produced an outstanding dissertation in 1994 on the Jerónimos, traveling from monastery to monastery analyzing their archival records as no one had done before.[52] With the information provided by Coussemacker's exhaustive study, the familial relationships between the Jerónimos and conversos in service of the monarchy during Spain's early modern period became clear. Rábade Obradó presents a number of detailed studies on the presence of Jews, conversos, and *judaizantes* among the nobility and closest circles surrounding the monarchs before and after the Expulsion.[53]

The theatrical works from the Golden Age of Spain provide an additional avenue for this study of devotion. Two *comedias* written about the Spanish Guadalupe—one by the *judaizante* Jesuit Felipe Godínez and a second attributed to Cervantes—present a Guadalupe that cleansed and forgave. They also address the ubiquitous problem surrounding *limpieza de sangre* (purity of blood) and the suspicion that entered each character's existence.[54] Guadalupe conversely cleansed her own judaizing monks as they practiced "Jewish rituals" within her sacred space. A poem attributed to Luis de Góngora y Argote comments on the Inquisition at Guadalupe by writing that heretics broke their heads at the feet of the virgin. He does not say, however, that the virgin cleansed their soiled blood. What the poet *does* indicate is the king's complicity in the matter. It is this junction of complicity within the realm of power that is central to *The Virgin of Guadalupe and the Conversos.* It is the intimate relationship between the conversos and the highest powers in Catholic Spain and its dependencies that prove to be the most paradoxical and intriguing aspect of this study, which leads to the ultimate question of just how Christian they were.

The Sacred and the Immaculate

The obsession in Spain that developed in the late fourteenth century regarding what came to be termed the Inmaculada (the Virgin of the Immaculate Conception) is significant to the trajectory of *The Virgin of Guadalupe and the*

Conversos. In a juncture of time that is more than coincidence, Iberia develops an intense interest in a representation of the Virgin Mary, mother of Christ that is known as la Inmaculada—the one without stain. The name itself provides part of the answer. The opposite of *"inmaculada"* is *"macula"*—a term used for people stained with Jewish or Moorish blood.[55] The monastery of Guadalupe places an Inmaculada in the choir loft of the sanctuary. Only the monks can see her, as they do several times during the day when they sing their hymns.

In a curious connection that has been repeatedly denied, the Inmaculada of the choir loft is said to be the model for the Virgin of Guadalupe of México, who appeared thirty-three years after the one in Extremadura was created by a Flemish sculptor. Yet there are uncanny resemblances between the monastery's Virgin and the one of México. They both are surrounded by a *mandorla* representing the rays of the sun. They both are standing on the sliver of a moon. They both wear a blue cloak adorned with stars. There are two significant differences, however. First: the monastery Virgin is holding the Christ child and the Mexican Virgin is pregnant. Second: the monastery Virgin is a white woman and the Mexican Virgin is dark-skinned.

Beyond the differences and similarities within representations of the Virgin Mary herself are those that resonate with Judaism. Arthur Green presents an extensive analysis of the relationship between the Shekhinah and the Virgin Mary, attributing this to cultural contact between Christians and Jews during the late medieval period. Indeed, a number of his examples are striking. The rays of light surrounding the Inmaculada could represent the flames of fire that do not burn and therefore related to the Shekhinah of the burning bush.[56] The concept of Mary and the Shekhinah as the mediators between man and God, along with both containing the feminine or erotic aspect of their religion's divinity, are difficult to deny.[57]

Genealogies of Learning

In a moment of openness within the Roman Catholic Church, a group of men in sixteenth-century Florence began studying the Jewish Kabbalah, making an effort to learn Hebrew. This initiated the *Hebraica veritas* movement, which sought divine truth through the Hebrew scriptures. The coincidental relationship between one of these men, Cardinal Egidio da Viterbo, with Emperor Carlos V and the monarch's orator, an Augustinian named Dionisio Vázquez, led to the a generational line of scholars who rescued Hebrew learning during the sixteenth century, a time dominated by the Spanish Inquisition.

Vázquez was taught by a converted Jew named Alonso de Zamora, who assisted in the production of the first major polyglot Bible produced in the early sixteenth century. It was published in Hebrew, Latin, Greek, and

Aramaic. Zamora and Vázquez were both teachers of Cipriano de la Huerga, a Hebraist and Christian Cabalist.[58] With the next generation came Luis de León and Benito Arias Montano, both known to be the greatest scholars of Spain's sixteenth century. Montano came to be pivotal in the monarchy of Felipe II, influencing governmental and religious policy as well as directing the production of the second great polyglot of the century, the *Antwerp Polyglot*.

Across the Atlantic

As the Inmaculada was taking hold of Spain—with representations of the Virgin multiplying constantly—the empire also expanded. The sixteenth century became the era of greatest migration from the peninsula to the Indies. Inclusive to this, the policies promulgated by the monarchy strongly affected the lives of those who emigrated from Spain and Portugal. The monarchy's interest in Hebraic studies created an ambiguous positioning that opened the possibility of other types of beliefs. This was particularly notable in the person of Benito Arias Montano, who was appointed *capellán* (chaplain) to King Felipe II in 1566.[59] While not the subject of many studies in the Americas, Montano is an object of fascination in Spain. Next to Cervantes, he is known as the most famous (and prolific) scholar and author of sixteenth-century Iberia. Part of the interest in Montano is his role in producing the Antwerp Bible. Commissioned by Felipe II at astronomical expense, the Bible is a marvel, written in five languages (Hebrew, Latin, Greek, Chaldean, and Aramaic). The Antwerp Bible and Montano's other works were banned by the Roman Inquisition in 1603. Even so, his writing continued to circulate with numerous copies located in colonial libraries.

In typical fashion of most texts concerning the presence of *judaizantes* (or conversos) in Iberia, there is constant debate whether Montano was the descendant of Jews. Historian David Gitlitz considers Montano a converso, and religious historian Stafford Poole states Montano "possibly was" a converso, yet three prominent scholars—Juan Gil, Gaspar Morocho Gayo, and Bernard Rekers—state there is not enough evidence to say that Montano was secretly a *judaizante* or was the descendant of Jews.[60] Yet Spanish scholar Sergio Fernández López notes that Montano's superior knowledge of Hebrew, his interests, his family history (or lack of it), and his writings as well as his intense interest in Jewish theology and scripture indicate the strong possibility of his having the upbringing of a *judaizante*.[61] Montano's poetry about the Torah speaks for itself. Priests were not known (or allowed) to write praising the Torah. Equally significant (and contrary to Church law) is that Montano signed a number of his letters "*el Talmid*"—one who studies the Talmud.[62]

The collaboration between the king and Montano produced the most striking statement made by Spain's sixteenth-century monarchy, the construction of Escorial, Felipe II's palace-monastery. Montano was responsible for the library, which allowed him to purchase a wide range of books and manuscripts from all over Europe. His unique position as Inquisition censor allowed him to obtain books that were questionable or even condemned by the Holy Office. Through his efforts, a large amount of information regarding the Jews of Spain (and Europe) was saved from the Inquisition pyres. His wishes are still seen in Escorial in the twenty-first century, in the Patio of the Kings, where he is said to have convinced Felipe to install the statues of the six kings of Israel. This act is significant in that the Patio of the Kings was originally the official entry to the palace—it would have been the first thing the visitor would see during the time of Felipe II. In addition, things are not the norm outside the gate. It is odd that in the palace of the "Catholic King" (as Felipe II is often called), the first thing the visitor sees when approaching the palace is a statue of San Lorenzo. There is no cross or virgin to be seen. Once inside, a medium-sized wrought-iron cross can barely be seen over the dome of the church.[63]

Montano's service to Felipe II included a number of striking roles. He was a consummate political consultant and negotiator, and was sent on numerous intriguing missions to England, Portugal, Italy, and the Low Countries. Montano had great influence during his time of service to the king. His closest friends included the president of the Consejo de Indias (Council of the Indias) and two extremely successful Sevilla merchant families—the Alcocers and the Tovars—known to be part of the Portuguese converso trade network. Through Montano's ability to obtain favors from his intimates, thousands of what could be considered questionable or censored texts were transported to the Indies, including his own Antwerp Bible. This was central to the transmission of Jewish thought across the Atlantic. As Wachtel notes in his studies of conversos tried by the Mexican Inquisition in the seventeenth century, all of the men could read and write, as could 50 percent of the women.[64]

México

When Spain took over the crown of Portugal in 1581, Portuguese *judaizantes* who left before and during the Expulsion were now considered citizens of the Spanish crown. This provided the opportunity for them not only to return to Spain but also to immigrate to the Indies. Even before Columbus, Portuguese traders "already had generations of experience in the African trades to Guinea and São Tomé, where they procured spices, gold and enslaved Africans, and in the northern and Mediterranean trades to Bruges, Antwerp, London, Genoa, and Venice, where grains and textiles were exchanged for olive oil, wine, African slaves, malagueta pepper, and gold."[65]

Quick to place themselves in the new market only nine years after Columbus landed on Hispaniola, the Portuguese established a trading post and warehouses in Sevilla. By the "first decades of the sixteenth century, reports began to filter back to Sevilla noting, with some alarm, the presence of Portuguese ships and traders throughout the Caribbean basin and in the Canaries."[66] By the mid-seventeenth century they had already established highly developed markets in New Spain that included México City, Oaxaca, Taxco, Guanajuato, Puebla, San Luis Potosi, Parral [Chihuahua], and Guadalajara.[67] *Judaizantes* lived openly in México City and Guadalajara. According to Seymour Liebman, there were fifteen synagogues in México City alone before the Portuguese rebellion of 1640.[68]

Support for the Portuguese community of *judaizantes* in México evaporated quickly after the revolt. The massive arrests began in 1642. The extreme tension continued until April 1649, the date of the Inquisition's last great *auto-da-fe*. It was during this time that Miguel Sánchez, a secular priest living at the Basilica of Guadalupe, wrote and published the first known book on the Mexican Virgin, *Imagen de la Virgen Maria de Guadalupe* (Image of the Virgin Maria of Guadalupe). Hailed as the most significant publication from the colonial period, the book is considered canonical in the history of the American Guadalupe.[69] Yet a significant subtext of *Imagen* has been ignored. While reciting a baroque history of the Virgin, it also appears that Sánchez was attempting to communicate with the *judaizante* community of México. He makes numerous inferences to the Old Testament, telling readers to "pray psalm 16 in secret so that God may save them," and he likens Guadalupe to a menorah.[70]

The writings of Miguel Sánchez and later writings by Manuel Espinosa de los Monteros, also a priest at the Basilica of Guadalupe (discussed in chapter 6), indicate the strong possibility of judaizing among the highest echelons of the Catholic Church in México in the mid-seventeenth century and in the first half of the nineteenth century.

Power and Religion

Michel Foucault notes in *The Order of Things* that "reason allows human beings to communicate ideas that can have a "plurality of meanings."[71] Thus, a conveyed meaning of a statement or pronouncement or a law may be totally different than what it appears to be. The ability to do this gives much power to the speaker, especially if he is the king, a cardinal, or a bishop.[72] There was no secret aspect in the proclamations and decisions regarding Church policy and the presence of *judaizantes* in Spain after the Expulsion. From Pedro I (*el cruel*) to Felipe II, powerful people appointed Jews or conversos to the highest positions, regardless of popular sentiment, the edict of Expulsion, or *limpieza de sangre* regulations. In the mid-fourteenth century, just as the Sanctuary of the Virgin of Guadalupe in Extremadura became popular, Pedro I's intense involvement with Jews spurred rumors that one of his Jewish advisors was his biological father.[73]

The favoring of the Jerónimos by a succession of monarchs is also curious considering the order was commonly known to have a large *judaizante*/converso population. During the early sixteenth century, the *Cisneros Polyglot* (also known as the *Complutense Polyglot Bible*), commissioned by los Reyes Católicos, Fernando and Isabel, used the services of a three recently converted Jews. As mentioned previously, Felipe II's choice of iconography at his palace, Escorial, belied his (and his *capellán*'s) deep affiliation with Judaism.

Regarding the Americas, regulations controlling the migration of people without *limpieza de sangre* certificates were commonly evaded, either by fraud or technicality.[74] Sometimes even the king openly changed his own rules, as in the case of the first governor of Nuevo León, Luis Carvajal y de la Cueva, in 1579. Carvajal brought in, with the explicit permission of the king, a group of families that did not have certificates.[75]

A Question of Identity

In *The Virgin of Guadalupe and the Conversos*, the term "*judaizantes*" is used to describe the descendants of Jews who continued to practice "Jewish rites" long after the Expulsion. In this introduction I have used the terms "*judaizante*" and "converso." While it is clear that not all conversos continued to practice Judaism secretly, there were a number that continued to be *judaizantes*. Scholars have used different terms. Some choose *marrano*, which has an unfortunate history. Many have continued to use the term "Jew" for descendants of conversos and actual *judaizantes*—as is seen in various citations throughout this book.

Returning to the term "*marrano*," although Wachtel states that the term is no longer offensive, I do not believe the negative connotations have disappeared.[76] Other scholars have used the term "Anusim," which is more neutral. Yet "Anusim" means "forced converts." Although there were many forced conversions in the early modern period, there were still a large number of people who converted without having the threat of death upon them. Lastly, the term "crypto-Jew," meaning "secret Jew" is also used. Yet even this term is not quite adequate because it suggests a person who still identifies completely, albeit secretly, as a Jew.

Not all conversos led the double lives so well described in Wachtel's *La fe del recuerdo*. The paucity of documented information regarding the history of *judaizantes* creates the impossible task of sorting through myth and inconsistent and oblique narratives to understand the story. Inquisition records provide a hint of those events in Spain and México when *judaizantes* were arrested, tried, and tortured, but there is no certainty as to their accuracy. Yet there were a number of *judaizantes* who continued to manifest intense interest in (their concept of) Judaism, leaving them out of sync with their current position within the Christian community. Montano was one of these persons, as he demonstrated an "unstable complexity" regarding his religious beliefs—those that appeared in his writings.[77]

It is so with the men described in *The Virgin of Guadalupe and the Conversos*. Benito Arias Montano, Miguel Sánchez, and Manuel Espinosa de los Monteros placed their ambiguous religious ideas into their writings. For the purpose of this text, I will use the terms "converso" or "*judaizante*," with full knowledge that they are insufficient regarding any proper identification. The lack of adequate nomenclature is indicative of how little we really know about those who placed themselves in between the two religions, indicating devotion and belief in Catholicism and Judaism, Christ and King David, Guadalupe and the Shekhinah.

1

Virgin of the Secret River

————————————●

Arturo Álvarez, director of the Guadalupe Monastery archive for twenty-five years, writes in his book on Guadalupe of Spain that "I lived in her shadow many years during which I had the opportunity to acquire the deepest knowledge about the past of her sanctuary. I developed a fascination and passionate love for this Virgin whose face is almost black."[1] Álvarez's devotion is representative of the village surrounding the monastery. Twenty-first century residents visit the Virgin several times per day, praying to her or simply meditating while sitting in the sanctuary. Tourists swarm the place on weekends, coming from different regions of Spain and numerous other countries. The shrine has been a significant pilgrimage site for seven centuries.

Yet, because the Virgin represents the soul of late medieval Christianity, the village of Guadalupe has an ambiguous history. As Álvarez finally told me after many hours of conversation, during the beginning centuries of the sanctuary, many of the villagers were Jews or conversos.[2] The association between the monastery and the Jews and conversos is alive in the twenty-first century. Local shops sell Judaica (Jewish religious objects) along with statues of the Virgin. Merchants occasionally display posters of geographic points that would be of interest to Jews. A number of local women wear the Star of David (while denying they are Jewish). Yet, according to historical narratives, all those who were secret Jews were either burned at the stake or banished in the late century. Guadalupe was repopulated by residents who were living on nearby lands owned by the monastery.[3]

The Guadalupe Monastery is in the heart of the Villuerca mountain range, a sanctuary of the Black Virgin of Guadalupe of Extremadura. It was considered the jewel of the Jerónimos—known to have a large number of

FIG. 2 Monastery of the Virgin of Guadalupe, Extremadura, Spain. Photo courtesy of the Monastery of the Virgin of Guadalupe.

conversos and *judaizantes*. A frequent story about the monastery and its monks is that the *judaizantes* heresy occurred at the foot of the Virgin.

Representing the Mother

The desire for mother is primordial. As described by Julia Kristeva, "the Virgin Mother occupies the vast territory that lies on either side of the parenthesis of language."[4] It is evident at birth when the infant cries for her mother's breast. The connection exists as an invisible filament that provides the requirements for physical and emotional survival. She gives life and retains an invisible cord with her offspring. The children of the mother retain the link to their original life-source—to her. Others expand this connection through devotion to the cult of a mother, such as the Virgin Mary, mother of Christ. Since late medieval times this Virgin has been mostly portrayed, at least in Europe, as a blond, blue-eyed young woman. In Latin America, she has been personified by a brown-skinned youthful adolescent girl in the form of the Virgin of Guadalupe of México (or Tepeyac). This Guadalupe has become the spiritual core of México. In the twenty-first century, her Basilica in México City is known as the most important Catholic shrine in the Americas.

Guadalupe of México's predecessor, the Virgin of Guadalupe in Extremadura, Spain, is no young virgin. She is in full adulthood, with the serious demeanor of a woman with the responsibility of the small child sitting on her lap. The baroque form of her dress, placed on her by the friars, covers her original bright polychrome. Known as a Majestic Virgin or enthroned madonna, she, in actuality, is a sitting woman holding a child, both formed in cedar in the style of the medieval period.[5] Her face is startling; she presents a stern and concentrated look. Yet she is also full of surprise. In contrast to her serious nature, her clothing is a celebration of red, royal blue, and gold, befitting a woman of nobility.[6] She has refined features and skin black as coal. She is known as a Black Virgin or a Black Madonna. She is one of many hundreds known to have existed during the late Middle Ages in areas surrounding the Mediterranean.

While the Virgin Mary, as we know her in the twenty-first century, is a stylized version of a beautiful northern European woman in full bloom of youth, the Virgin of Guadalupe from Extremadura is a dark, solemn *mater* (mother) with a past that travels far beyond early Christianity. Her antiquity alone situates her as a mother of the world. Her importance is related to her fertility (Black virgins are commonly associated with fertility) and the child on her lap. A cousin to Demeter and Isis, her pre-Christian past is not often acknowledged, and yet a number of scholars believe she is of Celtic origin.[7]

Whereas the Majestic Virgins proliferated throughout southern Europe, the specific name of Guadalupe is directly linked to the sanctuary in Extremadura and even more so to Tepeyac. The popularity of the Mexican Guadalupe has overshadowed the Black Virgin of Spain. Guadalupe of Tepeyac has been such a dominant force in Marian devotion (adherence to the cult of the Virgin Mary) that most of her devotees are not even aware of her precursor in Extremadura. The Spanish Nuestra Señora de Guadalupe (Our Lady of Guadalupe), a Black Madonna also known as La Morenita de las Villuercas, while being a mainstay of the nation's culture and history, is rarely mentioned outside of Spain.[8]

Arturo Álvarez writes that she is the "authentic" one, her sanctuary being established in the early fourteenth century, two hundred years before Tepeyac.[9] There is sentiment in Spain about this time difference, at least among some of La Morenita's devotees. Sebastian García, the present archivist at the Guadalupe sanctuary in Extremadura, tells a story about attending a conference on the Virgin of Guadalupe and finding himself very frustrated because everything focused on the Mexican Guadalupe.[10] He spoke in front of a large crowd of people, telling them that they were denying the importance of the first Guadalupe. He believes they did not understand the significance of what he was saying. His surprise at the slighting of La Morenita is reasonable considering that in 1520 Cortes, the conqueror of México, shipped a large quantity of silver to the Guadalupe Monastery and requested that three lamps be made in her honor.[11] Yet historians of the Mexican Church have all but obliterated narratives of the Black Virgin, making it seem that she never existed. Most Catholics have no knowledge of her.[12]

FIG. 3 Virgin of Guadalupe, Extremadura, Spain. Photo courtesy Archive of the Monastery of the Virgin of Guadalupe.

In 2006 I spent several weeks in the village of Guadalupe in Extremadura. Upon return I gave my parents a postcard of La Morenita. They were surprised to see a Black Virgin. Their parish priest was so incredulous when told that the statue is black that my father decided to take the priest a photograph to prove she existed. The color of the image confounded the already predominant notion that there was only one Guadalupe, who is brown, not black, and she is in Tepeyac, near México City.

Although radio carbon dating places the Extremadura statue from the thirteenth century, her origins (according to legend) date to the year 587 A.D., when Pope Gregory the Great gave her to San Leandro in Spain.[13] "En el tiempo que reinaba en España el rey Recaredo, que era de los godos de occidente" (In the time when Visigoth King Recaredo reigned over Spain[14]), the Church had rid all of Spain of the Arian religion. Arians were considered heretics because they did not believe in the Holy Trinity or the divinity of Christ. Recaredo himself converted to mainstream Christianity in 587, being influenced by his nephew, San Leandro, bishop of Sevilla (Seville). Leandro's siblings were the Abbess Florentina, and bishops Isidro (Isidore), and Fulgencio (Fulgentius)—all considered saints. Florentina's and Fulgencio's relics were buried near the monastery several centuries later.[15]

A short time before the pope sent the statue to San Leandro, there had been a great epidemic of the plague in Rome. After this, Pope Gregory the Great led a procession through the city that carried a small image of the Black Madonna, a black-skinned version of the Virgin Mary. For centuries, throughout Christian Europe and the Spanish and Portuguese dependencies, when there were epidemics or great calamities, clergy would lead processions through cities with a significant religious icon, hoping this sign of devotion would bring a miracle. Gregory's request was conceded and the city was soon miraculously saved from the pestilence. The phenomenon was attributed to this particular statue of the Virgin, which was normally kept in the pope's oratory.

Leandro's brother Isidro and a number of other Spanish clerics were said to have transported the gifts from Rome back to Spain. During their voyage they encountered a fierce storm in which they believed they were going to die. They took out the statue of the Virgin and knelt to pray in front of her. The storm then ceased and there appeared many lighted candles that illuminated the ship. The statue of the Virgin had saved them.[16]

La Morenita has an ancient story. It is said she was sculpted by San Lucas (Saint Luke).[17] La Morenita is made of cedar with black skin, a cloak of red that is trimmed in gold, and a dress of blue. Her face has a chiseled quality, her eyes are large, she has a direct gaze, and her cheeks are full and her nose narrow with a small mouth beneath it. Her hands are large, somewhat out of proportion to the rest of her body, considered to be the norm for Black Virgins. She is sitting on a chair with her knees apart and the Christ child on her lap. At the time of the statue's restoration in 1984, she measured 29 centimeters (11.41 inches) in height and weighed 3,975 grams (8 lbs., 7.6 oz.).[18]

Gregory's gift of the statue and other relics was a significant event for the history of premodern Spain. It emphasized the great feat of San Leandro and gave the Church of Visigoth Spain the necessary instruments to convey its legitimacy.[19] An ancient statue of the Virgin Mary was considered a relic. Since "the acquisition of relics" was one "of the major activities of the medieval church," holy relics were kept in sanctuaries throughout Christendom and were frequently given as gifts to monasteries and churches.[20]

According to Scripture, the Virgin Mary did not die; instead she ascended into heaven. There are no relics related to her body. Therefore "venerated images" of her likeness are considered as holy as any bodily relics would have been. According to medievalist Wilfred Bonser, the Black Virgins are the most revered of all of Mary's images.[21] In evidence of this, when the pope gave San Leandro a special gift, it included a small cedar statue of the Black Virgin along with a number of religious relics.[22]

Virgin of the Secret River

The story of the small statue of Guadalupe contains the motif of *inventio*—devotion toward an image that is miraculously found "after it had been lost or hidden away from infidels for centuries."[23] According to legend, in the early eighth century, as the region was being overrun by Moors, Guadalupe was buried in a cave high in the mountains west of Toledo.[24] Although Maria Isabel Perez de Tudela y Velasco reports there are no documents to substantiate the following narrative, allegedly "a number of holy clerics carrying relics, while escaping from Sevilla in advance of a Moorish invasion, reached a place that was close to the banks of the Guadalupe River." In the margins of a codex, an unidentified writer explains (with no date) that clerics encountered a small shrine where they found the relics of San Fulgencio.[25] Perez cites a different source stating the saint's relics were actually brought to that location by the fleeing clerics.[26] Sometime by the thirteenth century, the Virgin appeared to a cowherd named Gil Cordero and asked that a sanctuary be built in her honor at the spot where she said her statue would be found.[27] The sanctuary was constructed near the River Guadalupe, in Extremadura, an isolated region on the road between Toledo and Lisbon.

The image has remained at the center of Spanish culture and importance for seven centuries. The origin story (Cordero's vision) is repeated continuously. A number of scholars who have written about the Mexican Guadalupe attribute the name of the *original* Spanish Guadalupe to River of the Wolves—*guada* meaning river, *lupe* meaning wolves. Guadalupan scholar David Brading indicates that "'river of wolves' is a symbol of the Virgin conquering demons and idolatry," which correlates with Ecija's account of the statue being a gift to San Leandro for having conquered the heretics.[28] Yet, it is interesting that in 1599 Fray José de Sigüenza writes in the official history of the Jerónimos that "*lub*" or "*lupe*" in Arabic and Hebrew means heart, interior, or secret. Instead of River of the Wolves, he uses the term "*rio secreto*" (secret river).[29] More recently, Arturo Álvarez uses the term "*wa-da lubben*," meaning hidden water.[30] He has assured me that Guadalupan scholars in Spain no longer consider the "River of Wolves" story a valid thesis.[31]

It is interesting that no scholars from the Americas have mentioned that Spanish opinion has changed on the subject. Why do scholars of Tepeyac continue to define Guadalupe as "River of Wolves" when the Spaniards have clearly changed the definition of the river in Extremadura? Is there so much theoretical and geographic distance between the scholars of Spain and the scholars of the Americas? Or is it that the American scholars have so strongly paired the term wolf with evil that it cannot be extricated from the history of La Morenita? Clearly, the early Mexican evangelists saw the indigenous population as evil for worshipping false gods. What was considered evil (in terms of heresy) could easily be found in both Extremadura and New Spain. The Moors and Jews constantly threatened the cleanliness of Christian devotion in Spain, but the main object of cleansing in the Americas was the removal of the indigenous population who were seen as evil, and akin to the devil, according to the major narratives of the early colonial period.[32] The connection between the two, however, is that secrets are often considered evil or negative or demonic, even though Álvarez and his colleagues do not associate the secret with *maldad* (something wicked). In Spain, the secrets were both the pre-Christian antecedents of the Virgin, as mentioned previously, and the secrets of those who were not Christian but lived as monks inside the monastery walls.

The secret was much larger than Gil Cordero and a lost statue of a Virgin. Peter Linehan located a remarkable letter that indicates the supreme importance of the Guadalupe Shrine as early as 1326. The intention of the letter, signed "at Avignon by two patriarchs, two archbishops and fifteen bishops," was "designed to encourage the faithful to visit" the Guadalupe sanctuary in Extremadura.[33] It was given to Pedro Gomez Barroso (who would soon be cardinal) to oversee its administration. Gomez Barroso was already quite influential in 1326.[34] He was elevated to cardinal by Pope John XXII in 1328. Gomez Barroso was of Portuguese descent, from a highly regarded family living in Toledo. Linehan speculates that Gomez Barroso was likely to have been involved with Guadalupe at the time the letter was written.[35]

The letter found by Linehan highlights a number of inconsistencies in the early history of the Guadalupe sanctuary. First, only two of the prelate signatories to the letter were Spanish, raising the question, why would seventeen prelates from outside of Spain be interested in Guadalupe? Second, the letter is dated 1326, yet all other documentation places the monastery at least a decade later, when King Alfonso, in 1337, describes the Guadalupe sanctuary as "a very small house made of dry stones and green sticks."[36] The letter also shows evidence of what Linehan terms an "ecclesiastical trespass" in which the sanctuary is given to the Diocese of Palencia but was designated as part of the Diocese of Toledo in 1217.[37] Most unusual, Linehan found no trace of Guadalupe in the registers of John XXII's Avignon pontificate. Even in Toledo, there is no documentation concerning Guadalupe until 1382.[38] However important it was in 1326, by 1337 the sanctuary was a "total wreck."[39] The question remains: why was Guadalupe, a place that was extremely difficult to get to, with very few residents, with a sanctuary that was made of "dry stones and green sticks," so important for there to be a letter of support signed by nineteen prelates?

The Underground

The enigmatic Fulcanelli writes in his *Mystery of the Cathedrals* that in times "past, the large underground rooms of the temples served as a home for the statue of Isis, that were transformed after the introduction of Christianity into those *Black Virgins*, that in our day, are venerated by the masses with exceptional devotion."[40]

In Jerusalem, below ground inside the Church of the Holy Sepulcher is a dark area that appears to have walls and floor made of white and gray marble. At the center of a large niche stands a Virgin Mary made out of a coal-black substance. The style is late Renaissance. She is standing with no child in her arms. The color is unmistakably related to the more ancient-looking Virgin of Guadalupe in Extremadura and the other Black Virgins seen throughout Europe. Like the Black Virgin described by Fulcanelli, this tall, black figure stands isolated in a cool unlit space that has infrequent visitors.

The Black Virgin (or Dark Virgin, or Black Madonna) is a statue of the Virgin Mary with black skin that is seen with some frequency in France and Spain. In medieval times, devotion to her is evident in the existence of up to five hundred statues dispersed mostly throughout the southern regions. These statues, usually made of cedar, are generally about a meter in height. The virgins are often depicted sitting in a chair with the child in front. Black Madonnas are also known as Majestic Virgins because of the direct, powerful stance in which they are represented. Unlike the later Madonnas, the Dark Virgins do not exhibit tenderness or subservience. A recent description of a painting called *The Black Virgin* at the New Orleans Museum of Art portrays her as "stiff and eerily remote."[41] While some interpretations consider her demeanor as remote and inaccessible, others see her as a figure of power. The Dark Virgins, by virtue of their positioning as Majestic Virgins, exude strength. Using the words of Julia Kristeva, the Black Virgin, boldly sitting on her throne, child in hand, could be seen as taking "it upon herself to represent the supreme terrestrial power."[42] There is something special and unusual about the statues of Mary sitting on a chair with the Christ child. Ilene Forsyth uses the term "Majesties." They are "intimate in their relationship to the observer, yet hieratically aloof in style." They are "true cult statues," "rigidly majestic figures" that command "respect and veneration," and "retain their charisma to the present day."[43]

Scholars (who are not theologians) generally agree that her origins predate Christianity.[44] As Kristeva explains in her essay "Stabat Mater," "The history of the Christian cult of the Virgin is actually the history of the imposition of beliefs with pagan roots upon, and sometimes in opposition to, the official dogma of the Church."[45] A female deity transformed from the figure of Egyptian goddess Isis, she became Christian, fulfilling the role as mother of Christ. As Fulcanelli explains, "she is Isis, known as the '*Virgo paritura*,' meaning *the earth before conception*, that will soon be given life by the sun." She is the "primitive earth" the basic substance of all things.[46] She is part of the earth, related to magic, alchemy, and the dark. Fulcanelli, who is said to have been an alchemist, relates that the Dark Virgin's precursor, Isis, was titled "mother of the gods."[47] Even in the present, the aspect of fertility is prominent in her devotion. The village of Guadalupe, the location of her sanctuary, is mobbed every weekend by numerous couples and their families who travel to the remote area to be married. Having the marriage ceremony in front of the Black Guadalupe is said to promote fertility.[48]

A number of scholars direct her ancestry to the Druids and alchemy's search for the philosopher's stone.[49] As the narrator explains in the novel *Foucault's Pendulum*, "the ties between the Celtic virgins and the alchemist tradition" are evident if one closely studies the iconography of the gothic cathedrals.[50] "The black virgin symbolizes the prime matter that seeks employ in their quest for the philosopher's stone," known as *materia prima*, which is the "catalyst" that creates the change in the metabolism of the material, the most essential objective of alchemy.[51] The focus of those interested in alchemy was not only with transforming gold from lesser metals. The primary interest of alchemists had to do with the essence of life, mortality, and the search for the divine. Religious historian Mircea Eliade proposes that the idea of the alchemy and the stone is more than "the desire to counterfeit gold." It is "probably the old conception of the Earth-Mother, bearer of embryo-ores, which crystallized faith in artificial transmutation . . . the encounter with the symbolisms, myths," of those miners who first began experimenting with alchemy. "But above all it was the experimental discovery of the *living* Substance . . . felt by artisans . . . it is the conception of a *complex and dramatic Life of Matter*."[52]

A number of the synonyms used for "*materia prima*" are "water of youth," "heaven," "mother," "moon," "Venus,"[53] "the philosopher's stone," and even "God."[54] Over the course of the Dark Virgin's history, she has been associated with heaven, the mother, and the Egyptian goddess Isis. The Black Virgin of Guadalupe was buried in a cave during the sixth century and remained there for seven hundred years. Her underground tomb irrevocably affiliates her with the dark, the earth, fecundity, and primordial secrets. She came from the earth representing primary matter and life's innermost secrets. This intense relationship with secrecy, combined with her link to pre-Christian moments, set her apart and allowed her to be formulated as a container for the Other, whether it be the alchemist, the hidden *judaizante* or secret converso, or those who practice any remnants of Druid tradition; the Black Virgins were markers for the occult. As Forsyth attests, their following was (and is) massive.

The small sanctuary for the Virgin already existed when the *puebla* of Guadalupe was established by the end of the thirteenth century. Much of the population was Jewish, having migrated there as merchants who served the pilgrims who came to venerate the Virgin.[55] While the Spanish Guadalupe always pertained to the Christian religion, there was a continuous association with the Jews. This was either because of geographic proximity of the Jewish merchants living in the *puebla* or because of the many conversos and *judaizantes* who joined the Jerónimos and lived in the monastery.

In literature of the early modern period, there are references to the Old Testament that could be said to represent the expected relationship with Christianity. Yet, as Castro, Lafaye, and others consistently claim, the history of Sepharad (Jewish Spain before the Expulsion) is blended—at times almost invisibly—into the religion, culture, and the art of Spain. The question remains: how much is blending and how much is a type of counternarrative that explains beliefs that cannot be expressed openly?

In her recent book, *In the Shadow of the Virgin*, Gretchen Starr-LeBeau proposes that the exceptional relationship between the Virgin, the monks, and the people of the village lived an existence that "was supported both politically and spiritually by the religious devotions" of the time.[56] Starr-LeBeau notes that Queen Isabel promoted her own identification with the Virgin Mary. The concept of purity associated with the Virgin of Guadalupe and the Immaculate Conception only served to increase the popularity of both the queen and the Virgin during the popular reign of Fernando and Isabel, known as los Reyes Católicos (the Catholic monarchs).[57] "Pilgrims traveling to . . . Guadalupe" witnessed "the supernatural support of the Virgin for Isabel and Fernando's political agenda."[58] The repercussions of this are paradoxical. Although the monarchs are, on one level, exhibiting great force in expelling Jews and Jewish Christians, the message that Guadalupe purifies is broadcast throughout Spain and its dependencies. The power and riches of the monastery combined with the divine favor allocated to the miraculous statue of the Virgin created a geographic space of safety where heterodox behavior was permitted and at moments forgiven; everyone benefited from her divine grace. As Starr-LeBeau attests, "the Virgin of Guadalupe, by the very nature of her history, the kinds of miracles she was purported to carry out, and even the national and international nature of her cult, seemed to show more than generic assistance to people in need."[59] Julie A. Evans briefly mentions Fray Fernando de Vbeda (Ubeda): he was said to have told another monk in the mid-fifteenth century, "not only the monks donate, even more the Moors, Jews and Christians. Many donations are given at this door from people of the three laws [the three faiths]."[60] Unfortunately, neither Starr-LeBeau nor Evans explains how the Virgin provided "generic assistance" or why people "of the three laws" were more than willing to "donate" to the Virgin. Sophie Coussemacker notes that crypto-Judaic monks coordinated from the monastery donations for the rescue of Jews who had been kidnapped by Moors.[61]

This Virgin, with a non-Christian past that is tied to the Druids, the Greco-Roman deities, and to the Egyptians, has not been reified as a purely Christian icon. However much the Church has addressed her as its own, the populace knows she has a much varied past. Her darkness makes her identification as the usually blond Virgin Mary less certain. She herself is Other, allowing non-Christians to venerate her powers.

A Paean to the Virgin

The *autos* and *comedias* (theatrical dramas) or novels associated with the Virgin do not address the Inquisition and converso monks. Rather, they approach the question of conversos and *limpieza de sangre* in more subtle manner. The ones I discuss were written in the seventeenth century, a period when the monastery was no longer the prize of Spain, and traces of Judaism had gone further underground.[62] In the *Auto Sacramental de la Virgen de Guadalupe* by Felipe Godínez, and in volume 3, chapters 3–4 of the Cervantes novel *Persiles y Sigismunda*, the main objective is a discussion of the Virgin, along with her discovery inside a cave in the Villuercas by a cowherd and with a young woman who had involved herself in a sexual relationship outside of formal marriage. The woman had been stained and the Virgin cleanses the stain. In both texts, there is an attempted murder. In one case, the Virgin stops the stained woman's father from stabbing her.[63] In the other, the woman's lover murders a child and the Virgin brings a dead child back to life.[64]

The commonality in both stories is that there is a secret involved: an improper sexual relationship or marriage that cannot be sanctioned by the Church, a woman who is stained, and a murder. All of this is cleansed by the presence of the Virgin. These themes were a staple of monastery narrative. While the themes center on Guadalupe, they avoid any mention of the troubled narrative of "the grand and sumptuous monastery" and the *judaizantes* who were burned at the stake at the monastery's front gate in the year 1486.[65]

By the time the *comedias* and the *autos* were published, it was already more than one hundred years since the Inquisition held court in the monastery. Although Godínez and Cervantes do not directly mention the Inquisition at Guadalupe, they were well aware of what had happened, for it was one of the greatest scandals in Spain during the fifteenth century. Yet they are not completely ignoring what happened at Guadalupe, indicating this with a number of subtle references to the Virgin's divine powers regarding *limpieza de sangre*.

Godínez presents his subtext with the story of Isabel, a young woman who has fallen in love with Sancho, who appears to be an Old Christian (a Christian who is not descended from Jews or Moors). While he is of the nobility and she a cowherd's daughter, her suitor believes that if her father is a *godo* (Visigoth), she is indeed of "clean blood" and therefore marriageable.[66] His question indicates that her economic status is not as important. Isabel's father tells Sancho, "I cannot pass from being a peasant to a nobleman. I do not want nobility, if I would have to speak falsely. Because more is lost than gained when you commit fraud, so you will have the body of a noble and the soul of peasant."[67] Later, as Isabel notes how she feels about *limpieza de sangre*, she tells her father, "I do not know if I am well-born with what the world believes is clean blood and nobility. I know that I am the daughter of a father who has a clean conscience, and that is all that God recognizes."[68] Eventually Sancho and Isabel marry informally with the ghosts of two saints as witnesses (who are of Visigoth lineage).[69] Afterward Sancho tells his wife that the marriage has to be a secret, which devastates Isabel. Sancho adds to the disgrace by attempting to murder Isabel, thinking she has been unfaithful to him. But instead of injuring Isabel, he kills her young brother Juan. All seems lost, but later the Virgin appears to the dead child and brings him back to life. Isabel's father makes the Virgin an altar, and the Virgin subsequently thanks him by making his family of the nobility. Once this occurs, Sancho is able to publicly announce his marriage to Isabel. All is forgiven; Isabel is cleansed of her sin, demonstrating the Virgin's divine grace.

The alternate message in the *auto*, published posthumously thirty-eight years after the author's death, centers on the secret. The vows between the two lovers must remain occulted. The core of the polemic is Isabel's social status, her "impurity." Here the Virgin intercedes, corrects the problem, and Sancho no longer has any complaints. What does not change, however, is Sancho's vile personality.[70] Little Juan is brought back to life, Isabel is no longer a "fallen woman," and her family's lineage is now acceptable, yet there is no indication that Sancho has become less devious. He is happy that now he can publicly announce his marriage, but Godínez provides no clue as to his character.[71] Godínez could be indicating that marriage to an Old Christian with a malicious character is considered acceptable in order remove the *macula*.

Sancho wants to marry Isabel but has to be sure she is of the appropriate class. He is of the nobility and asks if Gil Cordero is at least *limpio de sangre* (of pure blood) when he asks if Gil is by chance a *godo*. Gil is not descended from the Visigoths and has concerns about misrepresenting himself, saying there is a price to pay for being false. Later Isabel also discusses her *limpieza* status, admitting that she is pure because her father is a good Christian and has a clean conscience. She does not say she has pure blood. This keeps Sancho from wanting to formally marry her. Eventually, however, the Virgin redeems Isabel and her family. Isabel is stained for bedding Sancho without formal marriage and for not being an Old Christian. The Virgin cleanses Isabel's sins, and all is well. However, Sancho's brutish behavior and his "unsuccessful" murder of little Juan remains inexplicable. Sancho appears to be forgiven and the Virgin shows herself to be all-powerful. She can bring the dead back to life, she can cleanse the sin of immorality, and the blood of an unclean person. She can even make a peasant into a nobleman.

The shamed woman in Cervantes's *Persiles y Sigismunda* is named Feliciana de la Voz. She is said to sing like an angel. In the novel, Persiles and Sigismunda are on a pilgrimage to Rome, although they have also decided to pass through the Monastery of Guadalupe in Extremadura. Before they enter the Villuercas, they find Feliciana, who just gave birth to a child and is hiding inside a tree. She accompanies them on their journey to the Monastery of Guadalupe. When the group arrives at the sanctuary, Feliciana begins to sing. Her father happens to also be inside the monastery. He is determined to murder her for having disobeyed him and for wanting to marry someone whom her father disapproves of, having shamed the family with a pregnancy outside of marriage. He is about to kill her when Guadalupe intervenes. The father of the child arrives and again all are forgiven and cleansed of their sins by the Virgin.[72]

Cervantes does not directly mention *limpieza de sangre*, as Godínez has done in the *auto*. Yet it is a facile conclusion once learning that Rosino, the wealthy noble who is the father of Feliciana's child, must have some type of significant stain since her father is forcing her to marry a less affluent noble who apparently is much more desirable (because of clean blood?) regardless of his economic status.

If guilt can be placed by association, the friends of Feliciana's lover, Rosino, are also implicated in stain. Rosino is accompanied by two men with famous names: Francisco Pizarro and Juan de Orellana. Cervantes does not identify them specifically as conquistadors, but their names are unmistakably recognizable as such.[73] In her comprehensive analysis of *Persiles y Sigismunda* and the Virgin of Guadalupe, Aurora Egido suggests that Cervantes's use of Pizarro and Orellana represents the significance of the Spanish Virgin of Guadalupe as a "fundamental symbol of American [New World] history."[74] Accounts of Columbus, Cortes, and other conquistadores requesting specific help from

Guadalupe are documented in a number of texts. Cervantes may have also had an additional motive for using Pizarro and Orellana. The occluded subtext of Feliciana's lover being a converso, therefore not being a desirable marriage partner (even though he was rich and noble), is supported by the identity of his companions. Cervantes's choice of names of Rosino's cohorts may not necessarily lead us to a concrete conclusion about Rosino's relationship to Judaism; however, it was often said that many of those who sailed to the Americas were conversos.[75]

Guadalupe, Santa de Moysen—Saint of Moses

In the play *Comedia de la Soberana Virgen de Guadalupe, y sus milagros, y grandezas de España* (Comedy of the Sovereign Virgin of Guadalupe, and Her Miracles, and Grandeur in Spain), attributed to Cervantes,[76] the usual narrative of the founding of the Virgin's statue is presented: the cow dies and is resurrected, and the child that also dies is resurrected. The legend is told in the usual manner, yet there are commentaries that do not fit the Christian theme.

When Alarico, a *godo* whose wife, Rosimunda, is presently being pursued by a Moor, enters the scene early in the play, he is carrying a sword with the statue of the Virgin under his arm. He calls to the Virgin for help in ridding the place of *el bárbaro Africano*, announcing himself as a Christian and a decent Visigoth: "I will take action and take them out of the Temple. . . . God rigorously punishes those who touch the Ark of the Old Testament, the Patriarch, Divine salvation for human beings, the most I can say is for him to bless us."[77]

A few scenes later, Alarico reminds his listeners that people of Castile are like the Jews in Egypt, when he references the origins of the Guadalupe statue and how Pope Gregory, the New Moses, found resolution with his prayer and saved the city of Rome from pestilence. Yet the most remarkable scene is when *el pastor* (the cowherd), known in other works as Gil Cordero, finds the statue of the Virgin and realizes she is speaking to him. He tells her, "A bush, Saint of Moses, that burns but does not incinerate."[78] The *pastor* is speaking from a certain perspective that is often associated with converso beliefs. The use of the word "saint" when speaking of Old Testament patriarchs is often seen in texts by *judaizantes*, and indicates the blending of the two religious belief systems.[79] The burning bush is believed by some Jewish scholars to be evidence of the Shekhinah's presence. God speaks to Moses through the burning bush, yet the flaming light also represents the light of the Shekhinah, who is said to be nearby. It is at this moment that the two religions intertwine. This is one of the many instances where Old Testament symbols have been used to describe the Virgin Mary.[80] Arthur Green, in "Shekhinah, the Virgin Mary, and the Song of Songs," presents a solid case for the relationship between Christianity and Judaism with regards to Mary and the Shekhinah. He notes the "complex intertwining of these two traditions as they were lived in greater physical and cultural proximity to one another than is often realized."[81] While I believe he is correct in his observation, my contention is that in many aspects of Spanish culture, especially between the fourteenth and eighteenth centuries, there was not just an "intertwining" but a concentrated voice of Jewish Christian existence that left its traces in all aspects of culture and tradition. In this particular *comedia*, the use of the phrase "a bush, Saint of Moses, that burns but does not incinerate" goes beyond (using Castro's term) "*convivencia*" (to coexist), when the three cultures of Spain (Christian, Jew, and Moor) are silenced and are holding on to a secret aspect of self that erupts in art and literature, where the eyes of the Inquisition do not scrutinize quite as heavily.

Thus we return to the *Auto Sacramental de la Virgen* by Felipe Godínez, who was arrested by the Inquisition and found guilty in 1624 of authoring a theatrical piece considered heretical.[82] We should read this posthumously published paean to the Virgin with close intent. Gil de Cacares (Cordero) speaks:

> What miracles can the Holy Virgin not do
> defeated the dragon and made him fall to the ground
> paralyzed him, made him deaf, blind, and dumb.
> Injured him as she pleased
> This mountain has received a great gift
> there can be no more evil in Spain,
> if the Virgin cures them in this way.[83]

What evil is there in Spain that has to be cured? Surely a Jesuit found guilty by the Inquisition is not referring to heresy. Since it is very probable that he wrote the *auto* after his incarceration, Godínez is referring to the likelihood that the Virgin will cure Spain of the evil of the Inquisition. Godínez's true objective in the *auto* can be understood by a reader who seeks out his contradictions. As Leo Strauss notes in *Persecution and the Art of Writing*, "There probably is no better way of hiding the truth than to contradict it."[84] As mentioned previously, Gil de Cacares admits he is not a *godo* and refuses to make false statements. Later, Isabel, his daughter, admits that her father has a "clean conscience" but does not state he has "clean blood." Yet toward the end of the *auto*, after King Juan has ordered Gil to establish a sanctuary for the Virgin, he pronounces Gil's family *hidalgos* and mistakenly says, "To this fortunate cowherd, even though without a doubt, his ancient ancestors were nobles, I dispense to him the name, Gil of Santa Maria de Guadalupe." The contradiction lies in the king's own words, that Gil is of ancient nobility; the king himself knows this is not correct. Yet Godínez includes this in the dialogue. Here is an example of the contradiction that Strauss references. The real truth is that many of the nobility of Spain were not of the ancient *hidalguia* (nobility) but had been pronounced such by the king. To speak thusly was to make it true.

The devotion to the Virgin of Guadalupe of Extremadura cleansed many "fortunate" people. Gil of Cacares only had to find the statue of the Virgin. The friars received this benefit from actually living inside the monastery, even if they did not take Holy Orders.[85] Others had to provide large sums of money to the monastery or to the king. This type of protection was at its height until the mid-fifteenth century. The reign of los Reyes Católicos, Fernando and Isabel, which began in 1474, brought a complicated chain of events that kept a select few from danger but broke the veneer of protection for the less fortunate. Having a clean conscience, such as the one espoused by Gil de Cacares (Cordero), would no longer be enough.

Una cañada al Escorial—A Line to Escorial

San Lorenzo de Escorial is the great monastery built by Felipe II in the sixteenth century just west of Madrid. The monarch specifically requested it to house Hieronymite friars. Many monks from Guadalupe transferred to the new location. With his newly favored palace/monastery, the king was no longer as supportive toward the sanctuary in the Villuercas. It is said that Guadalupe began its decline at this point. Yet the path from Guadalupe to Escorial is composed of Jerónimos. Felipe's request solidified the idea that they were the "monks of the king." The favor bestowed upon the Order by the monarchs extended into the grandest privilege of association with Escorial, considered the sixteenth century's wonder of the world.

Returning to Godíñez's and Cervantes's stories, the question of the *macula*—the stain associated with impurity often mentioned in the two *autos*—is also at the center of the Jerónimos' narrative. Questions of impurity and heresy dogged the clergy at Guadalupe and Escorial. The Inquisition's initial forays at Guadalupe continued a hundred years later, threatening a successive line of librarians and architects at Escorial. Central to understanding this conflict was the protection given by the monarch, preventing its most prominent residents from incarceration, torture, and potential death by burning at the stake.

The curious circumstances of Guadalupe's early existence have not been decoded. Yet Linehan's research provides a clue to the importance of the monastery and its relationship to the history of Spain. The line between the two monasteries consists of the king's favor initiated by the magic and religiosity surrounding Extremadura's Virgin of Guadalupe—yet the composition of those guarding La Morenita at the monastery is an open secret intimately tied to the foundational narrative of España. It is as if Linehan were writing an introduction to *The Virgin of Guadalupe and the Conversos* when he completes his essay with a cryptic comment; "a *cañada* [line] of a different sort, yet to be mapped, connects the shack in the mountains, with Philip II's establishment two centuries later of Madrid and of the Jerónimos at the Escorial, the body and soul of early modern Spain, the double centre of a great empire."[86] *The Virgin of Guadalupe and the Conversos* is an attempt to explore the line (or lines) that praise Guadalupe while occulting the *macula* on a particular road that starts in Extremadura and ends in México City.

2

The Monks of the King

Los Monjes del Rey

> I saw Don Juan [the king], affectionately ceding
> His king's crown to an eminent advisor;
> Surrender, I say, to the most religious prior
> The keys of his entire kingdom
>
> —Luis de Góngora y Argote,
> "Religion. Justicia"

There is a story from before the Expulsion, a learned Jew said that the Order of Jerónimos was established by decree of the king.

On what occasion would a king hand over his crown and the keys of his kingdom to an "eminent advisor," a "most religious prior"? What could be so immediate and secure that a king would dispose of his power and influence to such a relationship? What was this previous offering that meant so much to the king? The keys of the kingdom that Juan gladly gave to the Jerónimos meant more than the honor of having a close relationship with the monarchs. It was not the Church that gave the Jerónimos their fantastic privileges. From the time the pope in Avignon approved their order, the monarchs allowed the Jerónimos from Guadalupe the same freedom as laymen. Considering the wealth and power of the organization, the liberties the monks enjoyed led them to numerous adventures outside the monastery.

From the beginning, the Jerónimos had an intimate connection with the kings of Castilla. While their histories do not specify at what age the founders of the Jerónimos—Pedro Fernández Pecha and Fernando Yañez de Figueroa— entered the royal household of Alfonso XI, they are said to have been children. They were childhood companions of the future King Pedro I of Castilla, who was later known as Pedro el Cruel (1334–1369). Even though the king proved to be erratic and violent, he never completely turned against his two childhood friends. Once Pedro was reaching his end, Pecha and Yañez transferred their loyalties to the pretender, Enrique, Pedro's half-brother. Enrique supported the Jerónimos well, as did the subsequent monarch, Juan I, who handed over the Guadalupe monastery to them.

If the Jerónimos were indeed the monks of the king, then there had to be an intense identification between the group and the monarchy. What was it that the monarchy found so attractive? Was it the noble genealogy of the monk's families of origin? Was it the wealth that so often saved the monarchy from disaster? Was it the order's identification with the Virgin of Guadalupe who was known to bring prosperity and many miracles to her devotees? If conversos were a predominant population within the Jerónimos and the order "belonged to the king," was their relationship the same as the converso and *judaizante* administrators who were employed by the monarchs long after the Expulsion of 1492? Was there some type of emotional identification, or was it a bond of convenience?

Why were "the Jerónimos' growth and survival" so "dependent on the benevolence of the monarchs?"[1] Why did Américo Castro repeatedly say "knowing the Jerónimos is knowing Castilla?"[2] Could this be related to Castro's formulation regarding the Jerónimos representing the converso presence (and history) in Spanish society? Castro implies that the Jewish undercurrent was a mainstay of what was Spain. Considering that Castro's ideas regarding Spain are frequently questioned in the early twenty-first century, his specific insights on the Jerónimos continue to resonate with the work of later scholars who focus on the order. During the Jerónimos' Inquisition, when Diego de Marchena was burned at the stake, the proceedings of 1485–1490 showed that "between fifteen and twenty percent" of the monks at Guadalupe were accused of heresy.[3] Sophie Coussemacker proposes that the need to cleanse was related to a power struggle between two factions in the order—pro-converso and anti-converso—more than a need to purge the order of *judaizantes*. The conflict was not so much about heresy. By 1486 the Jerónimos had accumulated a large amount of debt. The relationship with the nobility, their traditional protector, was fragile; their continued support depended on the outcome of not only who would remain in power but also what would happen regarding conversos being allowed in the order. Coussemacker also questions whether the Inquisition proceedings against the Jerónimos were a direct attack "against the religious politics of the Catholic Kings."[4] It is quite possible, however, since the monarchs continued to have numerous collaborations and intimate ties with conversos in their administration and through ecclesiastic connections (even through the seventeenth century), that the attack was not because of their interest in having conversos in their midst; if this were the reason, more monks would have died or been banished. Coussemacker labels it more of a conflict of power. There was a lack of communication with the order's general about Marchena's burning; the burning of the monk was an extreme breach of protocol—and evidence of insubordination. It is true there had been ongoing tension for decades between those who were identified as conversos and those who saw themselves as Old Christians.

A decade before his death, Marchena's family was captured by Juan de Guzman, Lord of Tebaon, on their way to Malaga. Marchena "received permission from the prior to make at least two trips south to ransom" his relatives. During the same period, Marchena's brother-in-law was sentenced to death by the Inquisition in Cordoba. While the condemned man was awaiting death, Marchena brought food to his jail cell. This was not kept secret from his fellow monks and caused quite a stir. Marchena was able to travel throughout Spain gathering money for Jews that had been captured by Moors.[5] A number of monks admitted in their testimony to the Inquisition that they had been inside certain synagogues. A common saying was that the monks of Guadalupe were better off in the monastery than they would have been if they were counts or dukes. This may not have been correct, yet it can be said that some of them saw much more of Spain than even the average nobleman. As they traveled, monks from Guadalupe were allowed to accept donations from any location in the realm. In addition, it is logical to assume that a Jerónimo from Guadalupe enjoyed the special protection of the monarchy's representatives.

The Jerónimos and the Garden of Earthly Delights

It is no surprise that Hieronymus Bosch's painting *Garden of Earthly Delights* (1503–1504) landed in San Lorenzo de Escorial, the Jerónimos' monastery that Felipe II purposefully built to rival King Solomon's Temple.[6] In so many ways, the painting is an allegory that tells the story of the Jerónimos, the only contemplative order emanating solely from Spain. Its tumultuous images full of irreverent symbols of good and evil, paganism, and the Christian religion bespoke of the confusing image portrayed by the Jerónimos in early modern Spain. Although Bosch did not have in mind the Jerónimos while executing the painting, Felipe II must have felt some connection to the piece since it was purchased and hung inside Escorial, Felipe II's personal monastery.

The story of the order and Bosch's trajectory are parallel in their complexity. There is so much detail and surprise in *Garden* that the viewer can easily get lost within its landscape, as Michel de Certeau says in *The Mystic Fable*. As he states, the "secret of the *Garden* is to *make you believe* that it possesses some sayable secret."[7]

Amid the numerous nude bodies—mostly white, and a few black—are couples in erotic positions, animals dressed as clergy, and nude couples traveling in clear bubbles. Almost all are in groups of three, four, six, and occasionally two. The painting is a triptych with God and the creation of Man (and Woman) on the left, a cacophony of people and animals in all sorts of positions and combinations portraying mankind indulging in every sort of sinful behavior in the middle, and on the right damnation after man and woman have ruined themselves. The triptych is basically the three moments in one's moral life—God creates Man, Man sins, and Man is sent to damnation. Bosch does not show reality in his images; he displays what is imagined.

The narrative appears to overwhelmingly and simply focus on sinful behavior. However, upon closer examination, Bosch's message becomes intensely complex. The multitudinous scenes evoke excitement and confusion. Looking closely at the characters, you see many of them fiercely concentrating on their unimaginable task. They are inventing new ways of being. The panorama contains so much activity that the viewer can get lost and confused. To avoid disorientation, the viewer must look at each individual scene as a particular chapter. The painting's three panels can be "read" like three books, with many chapters containing wild and unimaginable vignettes. Upon quick glance, the viewer is left with the binary of good and evil. Yet, as always, there is much more.

It does not matter that Bosch did not paint *Garden* for the Jerónimos. Standing in front of the painting, the viewer begins to believe that the painting is whispering a secret through its narrative. It is a trick to seduce the observer into thinking "there has to be more" to this cacophony of interacting bodies. It is this idea that brings to mind the Jerónimos: their ascetic beginnings, their enormous wealth and influence, and their drive to create a different world for themselves.

Finally, the blending of bodies and outrageous nature of the representations evokes the image of the *alborayco*, described by Norman Roth as "the legendary beast of Muhammad which was neither horse nor mule (*al-burāq*)." As Bosch depicts in the center panel of *Garden*, the figures are not working and "promenade the streets" with a hybrid identity that cannot be specified. The *alborayco* is "part horse, part woman"—a "picture of a certain vacillating element among the conversos."[8] Taking in the complex story of the order can be as confusing as Bosch's trajectory.

Looking closely at *Garden*, I realize that there is no coherent story. It is madness. Standing in front of the painting where it is exhibited at the Prado, I begin to wonder if Bosch was insane or under the influence of a hallucinogen. De Certeau's descriptions of the sensation that emanates from viewing *Garden* come in phrases such as: "getting lost in it," producing "exquisite pleasures of the eye," and "blind enjoyment."[9] There is something about the painting that tells multitudinous stories but yet tells nothing. At times it pretends to have a hidden meaning, but the truth is that every Spanish historian knows the story of the Jerónimos. It is an imagined secret that shows itself in all the histories of the Jerónimos. In this imagining, it has seduced thousands into believing they know the truth. It plays with the mind.

Contemplative Men

Their name—los Jerónimos—comes from Saint Jerome (347–420 C.E.). After 374, Saint Jerome lived for a time as a hermit in a desert, during which time he developed close relationships with a number of rabbis and learned Hebrew.[10] He is best known for his translation of the Bible that led to what is now called the Latin Vulgate.

The beginning of the order has been documented repeatedly, often having the flavor of a legend. It could be said that it is a foundational narrative, since many historians link the Jerónimos with the identity of Castilla. As Charles F. Fraker writes that "the Hieronymites [Jerónimos] themselves had a special consciousness of their importance in history," notably sealed by their chief historian, José de Sigüenza, who "surrounds the earliest origins of the institute with an aura of the miraculous."[11]

The Jerónimos began as hermits. They left the nobility of Castilla and isolated themselves in the Castañar Mountains, located near Toledo. This separation was precipitated by Pedro el Cruel's disastrous reign. As José de Sigüenza described the new king, "King Pedro turned out to be so destructively inclined and with such a cruel personality, as everyone knows: he put the kingdom in chaos, made the most secure feel insecure: [for him] everything was suspect, full of insults, blood, vengefulness, and death, [he was] a lion in his customs and a tiger by character."[12]

The three founding members—Pedro Fernández Pecha, Alonso Fernández Pecha, and Fernando Yañez de Figueroa—were raised in the royal palace as companions to the young Prince Pedro. The Pechas were sons of the chief attendant of Alfonso XI. Yañez, whose mother was of the nobility, was left as a child at the court.[13] As young adults, the three showed impressive success. Favored by now King Pedro (his father, Alfonso XI, died in 1350), Fernando Yañez entered the clergy and was named a *capellán* of the Cathedral of Toledo. At the age of twenty-two, Pedro Fernández Pecha was already employed as the royal treasurer of King Alfonso. After Alfonso XI died, Pecha was named keeper of the Royal Seal and keeper of the keys (*canciller y tenedor de la llave*) for the queen mother.[14] Alonso Fernández Pecha was the bishop of Jean before he joined the hermits.[15]

Sometime after King Pedro took the throne, Yañez left his duties as a priest and went to live in a primitive compound with a number of hermits.[16] Pecha left court to join the hermits much later in 1366, when a combined army of Castilian nobles and French mercenaries overtook King Pedro's forces.[17] The king was murdered by his half-brother Enrique in 1369.

The goal of the pre-Jerónimos was to converse with God. They lived in primitive and isolated circumstances, without any type of religious structure so they could devote all their time and energy to divine contemplation. The group consisted of Italians, Portuguese, and a small number of recruits from Castilla. They had their own individual cells and came together for prayers. It is said that they initially lived in caves and slept on a dirt floor. They gathered together not as a cohesive group but as a number of men who singularly wanted to be separate from the outside world. It was after Pecha joined Yañez that the group began to develop a sense of cohesion.

Gente Peligrosa—Dangerous People

José de Sigüenza writes in his history of the Jerónimos "that suspicions and murmurs were heard from brothers of the Beghards or henchmen of Beghards from other regions. They would say that the Beghards were dangerous people who disguised themselves with their dedication to God."[18]

During the mid-fourteenth-century, there was significant controversy regarding other informal religious groups being established throughout Europe. These groups had no consistent rules; each community developed its own. They did not take religious vows and were called Beghards and Beguines. The name "Beghards" derives from the word "beggars." Beghards were generally male, and the Beguines were female. They were at times associated with the mendicant orders, subsisting from begging or donations. There were other groups from the same period that have similarities, such as the Fraticelli and Brothers of the Free Spirit, both of whom were often identified as Beghards. The Fraticelli were a group of what were called "minor" Franciscans who took the vow of poverty and were known be in serious conflict with the main body of the order. They were persecuted regularly during the Middle Ages, and a significant number were burned at the stake.[19]

Pedro Fernández Pecha and his group were compared to the Beghards and the Beguines because of their asceticism and lack of religious orders or structure.[20] Sigüenza explains that the followers of King Pedro el Cruel sought out the Jerónimos in their isolated location and attempted to kill them and discredit their reputation with "malicious rumors," and that the early Jerónimos had a strange way of acting and speaking and lived like Lutherans.[21] In a reference to the Beguines, Sigüenza wrote that the pre-Jerónimos lived "without vows, without obedience, without order, calling them Beguines and Beghards, an extremely dishonorable name, taken from an evil sect started by a group of women in Germany."[22] Author Castro supports Sigüenza's comments that there are a number of similarities between the spiritual attitude of the Jerónimos and the Beghards and Beguines. Castro continues: "The Beguines are a derivation of the Franciscans . . . they believe in three major tenets, the Old Testament, the Christian sacraments and the Holy Spirit."[23] There is, in fact, a similarity between the pre-Jerónimos and the Flemish Beguines, who are described in *The Mystic Fable* as "strongly independent and well-endowed republics . . . or monasteries, often of bourgeois origin."[24] One famous Beguine, Marguerite Porete, who burned at the stake for heresy in 1310, wrote *Mirror of Simple Souls* in which she speaks of the "union of the soul with God," a concept identified with the Brethren of the Free Spirit.[25]

The Beghards and Beguines as well as the Brethren of the Free Spirit were criticized and often treated violently. "The very word beguine was first a nickname for heretics, originating from an abbreviation for '*al-bigen*-sis.'"[26] The Beghards and Beguines were identified with sexual excess, which, not surprisingly, appears in Bosch's *Garden*. Bosch himself was a lay member of Illustrious Brotherhood of Our Blessed Lady, a quasi-religious-social network in the southern region of the Netherlands. His depictions in *Garden* ring true to the wild stories circulating about the Beghards and the Beguines. While Bosch may not have been thinking of the Jerónimos when he painted *Garden*, the acquisition of the painting by Felipe II for Escorial, a monastery of Jerónimos, is telling. The painting's middle panel depicts dozens of people behaving in the most erotic manner. With the accusations against the pre-Jerónimos about sexual impropriety and heresy, it is almost as if the painting was kept at Escorial as a reminder of the fantasized past of the Jerónimo's forebears. The painting was executed shortly after the order had a significant encounter with the Inquisition at the famous Guadalupe monastery. Sigüenza is so taken by the painting he spends more than two and a half pages on Bosch, much more than he does on the generals of the Hieronymite Order. Sigüenza explains that the importance he places on *Garden* is because many people judge Bosch as a heretic, yet he believes that Bosch's painting gives evidence to man's "desires, fears, furies, vain appetites, enjoyments, satisfaction, and discourse."[27]

The Jerónimos' impetus for the transition from informal organizing to an official Church-sanctioned religious order was mainly due to the criticism and threats they were receiving because of their similarity to the Beguines and Beghards. Yet Coussemacker adds that the order also entered a period of more stability when they received approval from the pope. With the approval came the establishment of the monastery San Bartolomé de Lupiana, located about sixty kilometers northwest of Madrid. The new monastery was a donation from Pecha's family. Although not mentioned by Sigüenza, according to Pedro de la Vega (an earlier historian of the order), there continued to be problems. After the founders received permission to organize, they proceeded to construct three monasteries. One of these was located in "a flat deserted area where only weeds grow." In August 1374 a group of young men destroyed the monastery, stole valuables, and took the prior and monks captive.[28]

The rules of the order were based on solitary prayer. As mentioned earlier, each monk had an individual cell. They gathered for public prayers but still had a significant amount of time for solitude. Separation from their previous opulent circumstances and powerful social positions made them extremely unusual. Their desire to leave their lives at court in order to live in primitive circumstances because of the "love of God" made them circumspect. They became a curiosity, and their former associates sought out their "hidden places," leading the monks to search for more solitary environments.

During the fourteenth century, the Church entered a brutal polemic between those orders that took a vow of poverty and those that did not. Pedro de la Vega situates the Jerónimos' founding narrative during a time of great strife for the Church, when the pope moved Church headquarters from the Vatican to Avignon. This period is known as the Babylonian Captivity of the Papacy. Seven years after Pecha left the court, he and another hermit traveled to see the pope to ask for permission to found an order.[29] Historians are divided about where Pecha went to see the pope. Some say it was Avignon; others say it was Rome.[30]

Whether in an organized form after papal approval or as isolated hermits in the mountains near Toledo, Pecha, Yañez, and their companions took on the role of mystics. As de Certeau explains, mysticism is not about theology; it is not a discourse about God. Mysticism is a "manner of speaking" about "spiritual things," and while the Spanish spirituals and *alumbrados* (the enlightened ones) were not as prevalent until the sixteenth century, the pre-Jerónimos and their hermit cohorts were the beginning phase of this type of contemplation. The disastrous reign of Pedro el Cruel and the long civil war with Enrique de Trastamara, along with the chaos in the Church related to the Avignon papacy, all promoted the separation of Pecha, Yañez, and the others from regular society. The source of God was not evident; therefore, the Jerónimos created their own source of God in the desert just as their patron, Saint Jerome, had done in the deserts of Syria. Their intimate awareness of the dissolving power structure made them *gente peligrosa* (dangerous people) as they rejected the trappings of the court for the primitive environment of their new hermitage.

Radical Change

In Lupiana and the subsequent monasteries established by the Jerónimos, the structure of their lives was filled with the "continuous chanting of the psalms and hymns, praise of the Lord; the constant meditation of the Holy Scripture; the hospitable character of the monasteries towards pilgrims; the silent and solitary environment."[31] It was considered a "peculiar way of life," adding numerous freedoms that other monastic orders did not incorporate.[32] For one, the society was somewhat democratic. Every monk had the right to vote, and each monastery was fairly independent from Lupiana, the motherhouse. The Jerónimos were overseen by a "general" who was elected every four years. Each monastery had a prior who handled local administrative duties. The idea of work was placed at the forefront from the beginning. This was contrary to Iberian custom for the upper class and is significant since the order was mostly composed of nobility. It is possible that the Beghard movement from the Low Countries influenced the Jerónimos into perceiving their own labor as valuable. This helped spur the construction of their monasteries and the development of their artistic abilities. In the monastery, monks became accomplished artisans, creating luxurious embroidered vestments and exquisite religious iconography in oversized opulent choir books. They were also shoemakers, bricklayers, farmers, and blacksmiths. This enthusiastic acceptance of the continuous production of things had a flavor of Lutheranism and was one of the main reasons they were later able to attain so much wealth.

The implementation of freedom was not just in how the monks voted. They were able to use their professions. Many entered the order already educated as physicians or lawyers. The order allowed them to practice their knowledge even to the point of allowing them to leave the monastery to conduct their assignments. In addition, as they had much privacy for oration in the pre-Hieronymite stage, they continued to do so in the monasteries. Although there was much organized prayer, the Jerónimos had fewer public obligations than other monks.[33] In the ultimate act of freedom, the monks had the choice to take priestly vows or to remain *legos* (laymen). Curiously, one of the founders, Pedro Fernández Pecha, never took vows even though he was general of the order for more than twenty years.[34] All of these anomalies in a monastic order contributed to the unusual and productive role the Jerónimos would ultimately take in Spanish society. While primarily known for their deadly encounter with the Inquisition (to be addressed at length later in this chapter), by the mid-fifteenth century they were known as the most prosperous and inventive order not only in Spain but in all of Europe.

From Spiritual to the Material

The contemplative Order of Jerónimos was well established by the time King Juan I of Castilla sent the bishop of Sigüenza to Lupiana to convince the Jerónimos to take charge of the Sanctuary of Guadalupe. At first Yañez, their general, was against the move. The ideal of the contemplative life would be lost at such a pilgrimage site where hundreds of people were constantly passing through. The king made an unusual offer: if the Jerónimos were given charge of Guadalupe, they would have ownership of all the territory in and around

Guadalupe and all the livestock. Historian Enrique Llopis Agelán details the transfer of livestock: "[In 1389], the Jerónimos were handed over 17 pastures or portions thereof . . . 773 head of cattle, 1,259 sheep, more than 23 vineyards, wheat fields and farms that employ 123 oxen."[35] Most surprisingly, permission was given to request donations from any territory belonging to the crown.[36] According to José Sánchez Herrero, the king proposed these gifts to provide financial security so the monks could focus on their monastic spirituality.[37] It is curious, however, that a monarch would be so willing to convey such exaggerated favors so his monks would be able to "dedicate themselves to the growth of the divine cult."[38] Going back to the reign of Alfonso X a century before, there was already a move by the monarchy to promote certain religious sites for the purpose of creating settlements as barriers to Muslim territory. There was also political interest. Alfonso X and later monarchs were able to make the Guadalupe sanctuary "their own" by giving it special donations and privileges.[39] Whatever the intent of the monarchs, the Jerónimos transposed their lives once they arrived at Guadalupe in October 1389. They were no longer isolated. As Llopis Agelán explains, they "sacrificed in part their contemplative vocation so they could consolidate their ties of privilege with the Castilian monarchy." They were the lords of a great "corporation, powerfully protected and privileged."[40]

It was this transformation, along with the unique characteristics of the order, that pushed the Jerónimos into early modernity and to what Jonathan Israel describes as "fundamental shifts in ideas."[41] The Jerónimos began something that had not been seen before in Europe. Although the impetus to transform the order appeared in many ways like a premodern version of capitalism, conducted outside of the desire to commune with God, the result was something different and phenomenal.[42]

The Jerónimos continued to be monks, but their interests diverted significantly from the solitary worship they were known for. They became entrepreneurs, landowners, supervisors, and in some ways the administrators of a circus (or a premodern capitalistic system). The pilgrims came because of their devotion but also for the theatrics of the miracles that often occurred at Guadalupe.[43] The money made from donations paid for the numerous enterprises developed by the order. They established a medical school and had clinics that were later considered to be the best hospitals in the peninsula.[44] The Jerónimos in Guadalupe were known for curing syphilis. This brought many patients from throughout Europe.[45] They had separate hospitals for men, women, and children. It is commonly said, incorrectly, that the monks were the first to receive permission from the papacy to perform autopsies, yet according to medical historian José María López Piñero, papal permission was given to practice medicine but not dissections.[46] They consorted with monarchs, providing lodging, advice, and financial support. The monastery became known as one of the first banking establishments of Europe. Early in the Jerónimos' residence at Guadalupe, the monastery loaned King Juan I of Castilla "one thousand *marcos de plata*" to assist him in his war with Portugal.[47] This economic practice continued well into the sixteenth century.

In retrospect, it should not be a surprise that an order that was founded by the treasurer of the king should ultimately become the richest group of monks in Europe.[48] While men from all social classes joined the Jerónimos, they were (and are still promoted as) the monks who came from the nobility. They were the order belonging to the kings. As the often-cited Américo Castro's *Aspectos* notes, the Jerónimos *were* Castilla; he states, "Fernando the Catholic king, author and observer of history, once said to the Queen 'if she wanted to get closer to Castilla, to learn more about the Jerónimos,' the richest Order at that time."[49]

Hebrew in the Monastery

Two years after the Jerónimos took over Guadalupe, the Iberian Peninsula experienced tragedy throughout from the pogroms directed at the Jews. The largest was in Sevilla, occurring in June 1391, where more than four thousand people were killed in one day. The violence spread all around, as nearby as Toledo on June 20, where two-thirds of the population of the Juderia (Jewish neighborhood) was killed and an unknown number converted to Christianity.[50] There is only speculation as to how many Jews might have gone to the monastery seeking refuge. One story tells of a Jew who arrived at the monastery requesting that a converso who was running from the Inquisition be allowed into its confines for one year in return for giving a donation of 100,000 *maravedis*.[51] It is unclear whether Jews entered the monastery to escape persecution or to practice their religion more freely; the presence of *judaizantes* or conversos in the Guadalupe monastery was more the rule than an anomaly. Yitzhak Baer explains one Jerónimo's impetus for entering a monastery: "so that he might live as a Jew without interference by his relatives."[52]

Albert Sicroff explains that, in addition to the opportunity to practice Jewish rituals in the private cells, the Jerónimos' emphasis on "religion of the spirit" while not neglecting "the material needs of the religious community" was attractive to new Christians, "just as they would be drawn, in the sixteenth century, to the religion of the *alumbrados*, the Erasmists and the mystics."[53] Castro elaborates in a footnote that the Jerónimos' spirituality coincided with that of the Jews, and the conversos' preference for the order centered on its encouragement toward more open contact with God while not having to be conscripted by religious vows.[54] As an aside, in a footnote, Sicroff muses on whether "the Monastery learned to use the economic and administrative energies of the Jews in managing and developing its enormous holdings."[55]

There are numerous writings on the Jerónimos by French, Spanish, and American authors. The details from the archives have been repeated continuously since Castro published *Aspectos* in 1949. The striking news that the wealthiest order in Spain was full of *judaizantes* seems to intrigue people to this day. Yet a general perusal of Iberian history along with a closer look at the monastery and the order brings to mind de Certeau's comment about the *Garden*—the observer is seduced into thinking there is a secret involved, when actually there is no secret.[56] The information has always been readily available. A cryptic commentary by Castro in *Aspectos* (in fact, more than once in the book) alludes to the secret that is no secret: "If you recall how Alfonso VII made his solemn entry into Toledo in 1139, amidst the hymns praising God and the Victor, in Castilian, Arab, and Hebrew. Menendez Pidal comments: 'because they . . . liked to call themselves kings of the three religions.'"[57] What Castro says next is noteworthy: "Perhaps these comments indicate something more than tolerance or intolerance on the part of the kings; I hope at least to suggest an additional explanation."[58]

There are numerous indications that *judaizantes* were numerous in the Jerónimos' order long before the Inquisition arrived in the mid-fifteenth century. Although the connection between the medical practices in Guadalupe and its *judaizante* population are never mentioned, it is common knowledge that medicine was a Jewish profession in fifteenth-century Iberia. One historian claims that there was already a hospital at the Guadalupe sanctuary sixty years before the Jerónimos arrived.[59] However, this information has been frequently contradicted by subsequent scholars.[60] Within a few years, there were three hospitals and, as Sigüenza proudly says, the "physicians and medicine here, are the best in the kingdom."[61] A medical school was added during the fifteenth century. It was known for producing the most renowned physicians, one being Fray Luis de Madrid, who was sent by Queen Isabel to treat her daughter, Queen Maria of Portugal. As Norman Roth attests, before the Expulsion, "every one of the kings, both in Castile-León and Aragón-Catalonia, had more than one Jewish physician and surgeon serving him personally." While there is no actual count of how many conversos became physicians after the expulsion of Jews in 1492, it is more likely than not that the profession continued to be one of Jewish descendants.[62]

The Inquisitors

With permission from Pope Sixtus IV in 1481, the Spanish crown authorized the organization of the Inquisition, whose officials arrived in Guadalupe in December 1484 seeking to indentify and adjudicate *judaizantes*. This was a unique situation because the village was "controlled exclusively by the Order of Saint Jerome," due to their special relationship with the monarchy. Since the monks were, for the most part, immune, the villagers were targeted first. In all, 226 living and dead people from the *puebla* were "sentenced by the court in Guadalupe." Of these, 80 were either "reconciled, exiled, imprisoned, given penance, or absolved"; 71 were executed. Another 45 who were deceased or no longer living in the *puebla* were "burned in effigy, or exhumed and their bones burned."[63] The money confiscated from the conversos was used for the construction of the Hospedería Real, a residence for the monarchs that adjoined the monastery. Isabel "magnanimously donated all proceeds from the Guadalupense [Inquisition] court to the friary."[64] In addition, she added another one million *maravedis* to the million gathered by the Inquisition for the construction. Fernando and Isabel joined together with the Inquisition to execute a group of people whose monies and goods were used to build a royal house at the Guadalupe monastery.[65]

The interrogations of the villagers led to accusations against the friars. By March 1484 inquisitor Francisco Sánchez de la Fuente requested permission to proceed with the inquisitorial process. While there had been some inquisitorial activity two decades earlier, the Inquisition's significant entrance into the Guadalupe monastery in 1484 left a mark on the order and, as previously mentioned, has been the subject of numerous studies.[66] The most attention is given to the monk named Diego de Marchena. He was executed in 1485, more than twenty years after he had taken orders.[67] He is known for his audacious behavior and candid commentary. His Inquisition testimony has been lost; however, there are statements from other friars about Marchena: "He is a very vindictive man, extremely annoying and never wants to recognize his faults a[s] *culpas*, he has the reputation of not being a good man, and I hear the majority of his brothers speak badly of him."[68] He took frequent forays outside of the monastery, traveling as far as Gibraltar. He was known for gathering donations for synagogues and Jewish captives. He was outspoken and argumentative. According to Inquisition archives, it became known during his trial that he was not even a baptized Catholic but was still conducting mass and giving communion as if he were an ordained priest. His fellow friars believed he had friends in high places. There was a report that he had a letter from Queen Isabel endorsing his attempt to rescue family members who had been abducted by Muslims in Andalucia.[69] It was said that these relatives were captured while attempting to go to an area where they could freely practice Judaism.

The Inquisitors at Guadalupe wanted Marchena dead. One of the main witnesses against him, with whom he had been arguing for over twenty years, was a longtime enemy. The Inquisitors seriously breached protocol when they did not notify the general of the Jerónimos (located in Lupiana, 300 kilometers away) that Marchena was to be executed. The story of Marchena is tragic, and a number of authors have focused on him as they describe the presence of *judaizantes* at the monastery. Yet the drama of his demise is more like Bosch's painting, full of vignettes that tantalize the observer and seduce her into thinking there is a secret behind the friars' bold adventures. But the truth is that Marchena held no secret. He was allowed and encouraged to rescue Jewish captives and gather money for synagogues. He lived in an environment that tolerated and at times encouraged the presence of *judaizantes*.

Coussemacker relates that the turning point for the "converso conflict" began in 1461 when the Franciscan Order in Spain publicized allegations of judaizing among the Jerónimos.[70] After this, there were scattered incidents of accusations that culminated in the 1485 *auto-da-fe* in which Marchena was burned at the stake. As Coussemacker indicates, it was not so much that more conversos (who were crypto-Jews) were entering the order; it was that outside forces were becoming more and more vocal about what had been common knowledge for almost a century, that many Jerónimos were crypto-Jews.[71]

The Monks, the Virgin, and the Americas

Américo Castro writes that the Jerónimos had a prodigious role in the conquest of the Americas. He views the Jerónimos "as prodigious masters of ceremonies [who] guided the conquistadors from Guadalupe Extremadura."[72]

The order's connection with Guadalupe was solidified when they were given control of the monastery in 1389. Since the shrine to the Virgin of Guadalupe was the second most important religious site in Spain (after Santiago de Compostela), the monks soon became almost as significant as the Virgin by association. They both became central to Spanish mythohistory. A number of foundational narratives emanated from the monastery.

The Virgin also became central to the exploration narrative. Historians within the order report that Columbus signed the contract with the Spanish monarchs while at Guadalupe.[73] They state that the Virgin saved Columbus as he was returning from one of his voyages to the Americas; the ship encountered a storm off the coast of Portugal and was saved when the sailors prayed to Guadalupe. Afterward, Columbus came to the monastery to give thanks.

The histories of the Jerónimos also tell of Hernán Córtes and how he was devoted to the Virgin. Córtes was also from Extremadura and, according to the histories, he also visited the monastery before he left for the Americas. He is said to have returned to the monastery with an infection caused by a scorpion bite that was cured by Guadalupe physicians. In return for this cure, he gave the Virgin a diamond-studded gold figurine in the shape of a scorpion.[74] During my visit to the monastery in 2006, I saw a painting, toward the back of the church that depicts a group of Native Americans being baptized. In the painting, Columbus is represented as the person who brought them to see the Virgin. The scene is said to have occurred in front of the monastery in the village square, at the water fountain—the same location where, less than a decade before, Diego de Marchena and scores of villagers were burned at the stake.[75]

An additional, and perhaps most significant, connection between the Jerónimos and the Americas is the statue commonly referred to as la Virgen del Coro (the Virgin of the the choir loft), installed in the monastery in approximately 1497. The Virgin of the choir loft, titled "Nuestra Señora de la Concepción" (Our Lady of the Conception), is generally accepted to be a work by a Flemish sculptor, Guillermín de Gante.[76] The sculpture presents a completely different representation as compared to the Black Madonna. The statue resembles Virgins of the Apocalypse seen throughout Europe. She has a child in her arms, she is standing on the clouds with a new moon and a *puti* (cherub) at her feet, and she is surrounded by the rays of the sun. There is a strong similarity to the Mexican Guadalupe, except the Mexican Guadalupe

FIG. 4 Virgen del Coro—Virgin of the Choir Loft, located in the Basilica of the Virgin of Guadalupe, Extremadura, Spain. Attributed to Guillermín de Gante, ca. 1497. Photo courtesy Archive of the Monastery of the Virgin of Guadalupe.

has no child; she is *enceinte* (pregnant). Staff members at the monastery believe la Virgen del Coro is the model for the Mexican Guadalupe.[77] However, there is no documentation available to indicate more than a coincidental connection between the two.[78] What is certain is that the fame of the Jerónimos and their monastery propelled transmigration of devotion toward the Virgin Mary to New Spain where her presentation was again transformed into what is now considered Guadalupe of Tepeyac.

One Eye Closed—One Eye Open

> Jerónimo, preacher and friend
> Bernado, Francisco in their monastery
> It is believed they live with much happiness
> without fear of flames or fire that would burn them.[79]

The Iberian monarchs are known for having Jews or conversos as their most trusted advisors.[80] A formalized statute of *limpieza de sangre* within the order did not appear to affect this pattern. As Américo Castro notes, during the Jerónimos' encounters with the Inquisition, los Reyes Católicos were against the order "tearing apart Christian unity" yet were simultaneously maintaining conversos in high positions at court.[81] During the reigns of a number of monarchs, ongoing movements within the order regarding the exclusion of conversos were simultaneous and antithetical. The internal private inquisition of April 1486 was established for Guadalupe at the same time as a *limpieza de sangre* statute for monks entering the order at the same monastery. While monks were burning in Guadalupe and La Sisla, conversos wanting to join the Jerónimos were allowed to do so at the order's other monasteries, including Lupiana.[82]

A Jerónimo from Toledo—1487

When Fernán Álvarez de Toledo was secretary to los Reyes Católicos, Fernando and Isabel, his family was faced with an embarrassing and horrendous tragedy. His brother, Fray García Zapata de Toledo, convicted of being a *judaizante*, was burned at the stake in 1488.[83] Fray García Zapata, a Jerónimo, was prior of Monasterio de la Sisla. It was a good place for him, since he was only twenty-seven kilometers from his family home in Toledo (most of the family, including Fray García, added "de Toledo" to their surname). His was considered a significant position, since being a member of the Jerónimos was like belonging to the Spanish nobility. When Coussemacker conducted her thorough search of the Spanish archives, she did not find anything on García's *proceso*.[84] It was removed, along with that of five other friars. What is known about the tribunal is from the sole remaining *proceso* of a friar named Alonso de Toledo (no relation to García).[85] There had been a problem in 1474 when Rodrigo de Orenes, the prior of the monastery, was transferred to another monastery. García is said to have provoked trouble with the prior's successor. This caused such a stir that the deputies of the chapter sent a letter requesting that Orenes remain as prior in order to reestablish calm.[86]

García Zapata de Toledo was promoted to prior of the Monasterio de la Sisla in August 1478, and soon after the monks rebelled against him. Coussemacker considers the revolt highly unusual. Within the order (and throughout the Iberian Peninsula) there had already been significant tension for several decades between old and new Christians. Rodrigo de Orenes, the general of the Hieronymite Order, had named García Zapata de Toledo prior of la Sisla with full knowledge that García was an actively practicing *judaizante*. They had known each other for a long time. García was in charge of purchasing for la Sisla while Orenes had been the prior there. Subsequent problems arose at la Sisla. There had been an altercation between two monks, yet García only punished one. The subsequent report implicated García, Orenes, and a number of other monks as secretly practicing *judaizantes*. It was a scandal of double intensity: the revolt in the monastery and the unfair practices of the prior. The news spread throughout the monarchy, creating severe disgrace for the order.[87] The events at la Sisla were so damaging that the deputies of both the clergy and the lay monks requested that General Orenes return to la Sisla, along with the priors of two other monasteries (Guisando and Madrid) so they could conduct a "diligent inquisition." Orenes and the priors attended to the investigation. Seven monks were disciplined and moved to other monasteries. The only one not reprimanded was García, who submitted a resignation that was not accepted by General Orenes on the premise that the deputies of the order examined García's competency as a prior. Six months after the revolt, García was still prior of la Sisla.[88]

García continued to be in favor. Orenes assigned him a special mission from 1480 to 1483.[89] Then he appointed García prior of the Prado Monastery in Madrid, a position he held until 1486. Then things began to change. In late 1484 Friar Alonso de Ulloa, canon of Salamanca, archdeacon of Avila, and inquisitor from Jaen, arrived at la Sisla ill with fever. He refused any herbs offered to him as remedies because he was very concerned that García wanted to have him poisoned. There had been significant tension between García and the other monks for some time. In addition, García had a reputation for being extremely difficult. That night Ulloa slept in the infirmary and was given a bowl of almond milk that was intended to soothe his symptoms. He was found dead in the morning.[90]

García left the monastery early that morning to get something to purge Ulloa, but it was too late. García became a suspect because of his "rejoiceful" tone upon hearing of the death. The inquisitor spoke with two physicians who said that Ulloa's ailments at the time he went to sleep were not so severe to have caused death. They also reported that Ulloa's tongue was thick and brown matter came out of his mouth just after he died. With this information, officials decided that the almond milk masked a poison given to the deceased, and the guilty party was García. About this time Orenes started distancing himself from his old friend.[91]

A monk seeking revenge against García for the incident at la Sisla in 1474 reported the Prado Monastery to the Inquisition,[92] where García was currently prior. García's situation began unraveling when a monk named Benito de Toledo was charged by the Inquisition. According to Coussemacker, Toledo was subjected to three depositions and was most probably tortured. The two had worked closely together, with García becoming known as Toledo's "confessor and accomplice."[93] Both formally observed the Christian faith yet were involved in numerous activities together; they observed *mitzvot* (what was written in the Torah) and they celebrated what was then called Cabanuelas (Sukkot) by building a secret cabin made of leaves inside García's cell, where they commemorated the Jews' escape from Egypt. During confession, García encouraged Toledo "to respect the law of Moses." They prepared for Yom Kippur by pretending they were ill, and thus not eating. They ate unleavened bread and lit candles on Friday.[94] Toledo describes their conversations beginning one day while at mass when García discussed the holy day of Cabanuelas. Toledo said "he [García] was circumcised and that he desired to live and die within the law of Moses." The conversations between the two clearly indicated that both García and Toledo were of Jewish origin.[95] García was denounced by a number of monks from Extremadura, who were sure he was a *judaizante*, but they did not have any specific details to offer. There was a story about how García's brother, "*su hermano judio*" (his Jewish brother) was going to be a rabbi. At García's father's house "they all ate together," which to a monk testifying, sounded like heresy. A story had been circulating around the order about a monk going to García's family's house for dinner; he observed that García's father gave money to send for a Jewish delicacy to eat.[96]

The only existing *proceso* from that period was from the trial of Alonso de Toledo, who although he admitted (and later denounced) that he was circumcised and was a practicing *judaizante*, was acquitted.[97] Alonso's trial ended in July 1488, so it is likely that García's *proceso* and execution occurred within a few months of that date. There were reports that the testimony against García was falsified, yet Rabadé Obradó, who has written extensively on the Álvarez Zapata family, recounts that a "number of witnesses affirmed that García's family, the Álvarez Zapatas, observed the Sabbath, dressing in fresh clothes and celebrating, using the time to visit their parents. Their mother regularly gave money to a certain Jew. Most importantly, all the members (except the patriarch) of the family participated in a meeting with a visitor, a 'Hebrew,' in which they closed themselves up in their sitting room for hours."[98] After García's death, his family petitioned the monarchs to clear his name, which they did. His brother Fernando requested those who perjured themselves by submitting false allegations toward García be condemned to death. Those arrested were tried and found guilty and executed in April 1489.

Fray García's success was outshone by that of his siblings. The influence of their father propelled them all. Juan Álvarez de Toledo had been a page to King Juan II and later a *regidor* (magistrate) of Toledo. García's brother Fernan Álvarez de Toledo was secretary to King Fernando and Queen Isabel. Fernán and García's other brothers, Luis Álvarez Zapata, Pedro Zapata, and Diego Lopez de Toledo, were also magistrates of Toledo during different periods. A sister, Catalina Álvarez de Toledo, married a secretary to the monarchs, Juan Álvarez Gato, who was also a famous poet. García's brother Francisco Álvarez de Toledo was the scholastic canon of the Cathedral of Toledo who founded the college of Santa Catalina that eventually became the University of Toledo.[99] There was an additional sibling who left Spain and at some point wrote a demanding letter to Francisco, ordering the canon of the cathedral to leave the country, join his brother, and practice Judaism.[100] It is not known whether the unknown brother who returned to Judaism outside of Spain and García Álvarez were the only ones in the family who still believed in the law of Moses. The rest of the family was firmly embedded in the highest echelons of the Church. Although there was antagonism toward Jews and conversos throughout Spain, the Álvarez de Toledo family continued to be strongly favored by the monarchs.[101]

Poetry and Historical Narrative

> Grand Jerónimo, in clothing
> Twice bloodied yet pure
>
> —Luis de Góngora y Argote,
> "Religion. Justicia"

The famous poet Luis de Góngora y Argote was pondering the relationship between the monarchs and the Jerónimos when he wrote the poem "Religion. Justicia." At the time, King Felipe III was returning from Portugal.[102] When the entourage arrived at the Guadalupe monastery, he was greeted by a "highly adorned triumphal arch, topped with a cloud that dropped down when his majesty approached." The cloud opened to the words "Justicia y Religion"—at which time Gongora's poem was read.[103] The poem begins with Felipe III's arrival is celebrated at Guadalupe, and praise is given to the Spanish Empire. The second section leads into satire. It is hard to imagine that this would have been read in front of the king as he entered Guadalupe. Perhaps the king was not listening.

> If you want to know what
>> Illustrious protections
>> This holy temple [Guadalupe] owes
>> To the Spanish kings,
> Detain mayor Talia,
>> Hear what I heard one night
>> That our king was waiting
>> Bathed in imagination
> In the temple of faith
>> Morality is composed
>> When money changes the outcome
>> My voice heard what was said:
> On the east side of the temple
>> The light from a fire mysteriously shines
>> The ardent mountains illuminate the countryside[104]

By 1612, when the poem was written, the Guadalupe monastery was no longer the light of Spain. It had been 243 years since the Jerónimos arrived and took over the monastery at the request of King Juan. The story continued at San Lorenzo de Escorial, the magnificent shrine constructed by Felipe III's father, with the Jerónimos following the king to the new monument.[105] Two and half centuries of narrative emanating from Guadalupe and the founding of the order were still fresh in the mind of Spain. Fernando, el Rey Católico, told Isabel that to know the Jerónimos is to know Castilla, yet his story does not have a linear explanation. Fernando's story was temporal and limited. The Jerónimos represented something unusual in their time, something that was tied to the heart of the monarchy. Yet their ideas did not integrate well in the tendentious society of Iberia. As Castro explains: "If this type of Hieronymite religiosity could have taken root in the Spanish community—thinking that the community is an idle utopia—maybe Spain would have attained the same industrial and technological capitalism of the rest of Europe, based on the sanctification of intelligent work with one's hands, that was primarily cultivated in the fifteenth century by those friars, who were Jews (conversos or not) and Moors."[106]

"Religion. Justicia" represents this precapitalist type of arrangement, and of the curious relationship between the monastery and the monarchy. The outstanding riches of the monastery were made possible by the exceedingly generous (and outlandish) privileges given by the kings. The kings may have honored Guadalupe for other reasons (as discussed in the previous chapter), but the existence of the monastery as a banking establishment in service of the kingdom created the need for a lucrative business arrangement that kept both parties satisfied. In other words, the money created the privileges, and the privileges created the money. For clarity, Góngora y Argote is suggesting that his reader ask Talia/Guadalupe about the many protections given to the temple (the monastery) and ask why the morality of those in the temple is established with the presence of money. The question of morality surrounds the ongoing presence of Judaism in the order, along with the probable reference to the early history of the Jerónimos when they were identified with the Beghards and Beguines.[107]

In *Aspectos*, Castro cryptically addresses a number of issues regarding *judaizantes* within the order. Yet, within the labyrinth of discourse he presents, he explains that the founding of the order, with all its oddities and antiestablishment traditions, was a "compromise between intentions (presently seen as utopic) and the people and circumstances they were creating."[108] The order developed a personality with numerous parts, one being an ascetic spirituality, originally dedicated to a type of *devotio moderna*, and the other being wealth and fame while living among the miracles of the Guadalupe monastery.[109] What came to be was a social architecture similar to that of the oddly constructed Guadalupe monastery "made of *pegadizos* (pieces put together) without much harmony." Yet within "these delicious occurrences (like the *templete mudéjar*...[110])," the structure of the order can be found.[111]

The impetus of *devotio moderna* is "a reformation of the soul and the rejuvenation of the spirit as the basis for renewal of the communal life" that incorporated the study of scripture and involvement in manual labor.[112] As Castro notes, many of the religious people at Guadalupe (especially) never went beyond being lay friars. They did not take Holy Orders, and they gave themselves to manual labor. An example of such asceticism is a cobbler named Friar Francisco, who constructed a corral out of *losas* (large stones) for his workshop.[113] According to Sigüenza, Francisco said, "to pray in any place is good, because God is everywhere."[114] Castro tellingly says, "We already know what this means."[115] In a footnote, he refers to a Judaic prayer in the *proceso* of a man from the Guadalupe *puebla* named Manuel González. "You hear and understand everything and are in all places, and I believe and am secure that you hear me."[116] Castro notes that "in more than one case, Jerónimo spirituality coincides with the Hebrew, showing why the *conversos* would solicit this Order."[117]

Returning to Góngora's poem, a mysterious fire is described as so bright it lights up the fields surrounding the *puebla*. Resonating with an *auto* attributed to Cervantes published two years earlier, the fire that Góngora describes brings to mind a passage from *Comedia de la Soberana Virgen de Guadalupe*, where Gil Cordero discovers the statue of the Virgin and exclaims "A bush,

Saint of Moses, fire that burns but does not incinerate." Eleven stanzas later, Góngora again writes of another light:

> José the tutor has left,[118]
> Seeing that the sun, is perplexed for what he sees,
> The light that fell at her divine feet
> You, that the rays of another sun are more clear
> For you is opening many paths . . .[119]

The first sun is perplexed at what he sees. It is the second sun whose rays open the path. Is the second sun the God of Moses? The author would be logically referencing el Gran Jerónimo, whose clothing is bloodied by the Inquisition but who in the end is officially labeled as pure. El Gran Jerónimo could have been any of several monks. He was a friar who either had blood on his hands or who was victim of such a man. Paradoxically, the prior from the monastery, el Prado, could be classified as a murderer or a victim, and with the help of his influential family, he is now "pure."

Inquisition records report that after García Zapata de Toledo was burned, a monk named Andres de Ledesma exclaimed, "Oh my body, they [Alonso de Toledo and others] barely were saved! How many more will be martyred!"[120]

3

Divine Splendor

———————————————————•

In numerous paintings from Spain's Golden Age, the Virgin Mary is surrounded by a blinding light in her role as the Woman of the Apocalypse. Going further back in time to the Middle Ages, the Virgin Mary was associated with a different type of blinding light, that of Moses's burning bush. The "radiant splendor" is the feminine aspect of God and is known as the Shekhinah. According to numerous Christian scholars, the blinding light is connected to the Virgin's conception "by the Holy Ghost" because she was not "consumed by the flames" of sexual desire.[1] In contrast, the Shekhinah is the wife, part of the consummated marriage.[2] I believe the idea of the Church being the spouse of Christ is related to this concept. A position somewhere in between the two is presented by Manuel Espinosa de los Monteros, a priest living in early nineteenth-century México. Richard Popkin would have described him as a Christian Jew. Monteros perceived the Virgin of Guadalupe who appeared in México in 1531 as a brown-skinned Woman of the Apocalypse. Monteros writes that she is "the sun as it rises . . . in the heavens with God."[3] To the probable surprise of those who have read his work, he explains that she is the wife of God, dressed in a manner that represents the Hebrew Nation restored to its past dignity.[4]

The Virgin as a Savior

While the famous descendant of conversos Luis de León was in the Inquisition prison, he wrote a short poem to the Virgin Mary titled "A Nuestra Señora" (To Our Lady).[5] It begins with praise about her purity:

Virgin of the sun and most pure,
glory of the mortals, light of the heavens,
whose piety is the highest[6]

Writing a poem about the purity of the Virgin was not unusual at the time. Yet as León continues, he changes his trajectory:

look at the ground
and see a miserable man in a harsh prison,
surrounded by darkness and grief.
At his lowest point.[7]

The desperate request from the poet asking the Virgin to save him does not adhere to León's regular style. He is generally seen as a highly intellectual writer who is "a thinker about the nature of language, an interpreter of literature in several languages, and an artist."[8] There were never any passionate moments in his writings, and, as William Nowak explains, he was redeemed in the eyes of a number of scholars for sounding more human as he wrote of his chains and incarceration.[9] León had a strong personality and rarely asked for help. Yet his situation was desperate. A colleague who was imprisoned along with him died while they waited for their trials. There are reports that the poet was tortured; at a point where he seriously believed he was going to die, he sent a "confessional letter" to the Holy Office telling them that he would live and die in the Catholic faith.[10]

"A Nuestra Señora" appears to follow the trajectory of León's mental state and optimism. At the end of the first stanza he asks the Virgin to use a "strong hand" to break the chains of the confinement:

with a strong hand
Queen of the heavens, break this chain.[11]

But "a strong hand" from the Virgin is an anomaly; especially by 1572, when the poet entered prison, the accepted representation of the Virgin was as a meek young woman, usually with her eyes downcast and her hands held together in prayer. The Majestic Virgins (to whom the Spanish Guadalupe belonged) were powerful, graced with a direct, uncompromising gaze and often with large hands. The women painted as the Virgin during León's time were not in this mode. Perhaps León, so erudite regarding the Old Testament, was thinking of those known as las Mujeres Fuertes (the strong women), related to the phrase from the Bible: "Who shall find a valiant woman?" (Prov. 31:10). León would have known quite well who this woman was and would have known that there was a lucid and impressive representation of all seven of the Bible's

Mujeres Fuertes standing near Extremadura's Black Virgin in the Guadalupe monastery. The day of the Majestic Virgins had passed. The Virgins of León's sixteenth century had their eyes lowered. They were younger, more delicate, and did not have strong hands.

Salamanca, 1572

On March 26, 1572, officials of the Holy Office of the Inquisition signed orders to imprison Luis de León. He was charged with preferring biblical translations of censored sources that favored Jewish texts.[12] At 6:00 P.M. the next day he entered the Inquisition compound. The repeatedly told story is that the University of Salamanca established a commission in 1569 to reevaluate the use of the Vulgate in the Bible of Vatable, and to assess the possibility of a reimpression.[13] After a number of bitter discussions between theology professor Luis de León and members of the commission on the question of Hebrew translations, León and two of his colleagues, Gaspar de Grajal and Martín Martinez de Cantalapiedra, were reported to the Inquisition.[14] They were arrested in 1572. Grajal died in prison, and León remained in solitary confinement until 1576.[15] All three were eventually exonerated.[16]

The arrest of Luis de León was of consequence. He is considered one of the greatest figures of Spain's sixteenth-century literature.[17] His encounter with the Inquisition, known as "the trial of the Salamanca Hebraists" is "one of the most significant crises of Spanish religious and intellectual history in the sixteenth century."[18] The initial charges were based on his accused "predilection towards the original [Hebrew] texts of the Old Testament and their partiality to Judaic interpretations."[19] Although León's trial and imprisonment were torturous, he was still able to write. It was during this time that he wrote most of his poetry and theological interpretations.[20] He was a prodigious writer, but of all his work, only the poem on the Virgin expresses intense emotion. His other writings done while incarcerated are much more rational and analytic. Considering this, could he have produced the poem for additional reasons other than expressing his pain at being incarcerated? In the third stanza, he writes:

> Virgin and mother
> From your maker you conceived,
> From your breasts flowed life,
> See the worsening
> And growth of my pain at every moment
> The hatred grows, the friendship is forgotten;
> It is not valid if not from you
> Justice and truth that you conceived,
> Where can refuge be found?

And mother you are, hasten
With you or abandonment.[21]

His tribulations continue as each stanza begins with the power of the Virgin
and how he desperately needs her help. In the ninth stanza, he writes:

Virgin who is not infected
Of the common stain and evil beginning
That which the human line is contaminated,
You well know that I have waited for you
Since I was very young; and the malicious
Power that defeated me, has vulgarized
Your divine protection
My sinful life, your clemency
Will demonstrate your great goodness
How much is my suffering,
And it is valid that I deserve less.[22]

He notes that she is special; she is not infected with the original sin pressed
upon all humans. Since a child, he has had hopes he would receive her grace
and is hoping for her intercession from the powerful force that has overtaken
him. In the last stanza, however, he shows that his hope is diminished. She has
not come to save him. He does not celebrate the powers of her intercession.
He ends the poem with a wail:

Virgin, the savage pain
Knots the tongue, does not allow
To speak the voice it desires
Only hear the one in pain
Encourage the voice to continue speaking to you.[23]

"A Nuestra Señora" is generally considered an expression of León's desperation
while in prison,[24] but it may have been his "playing the *picaro* (mischievous ras-
cal)" for the Inquisitors—sardonically mimicking religious beliefs that were
currently the mode, in order to avoid sounding like a heretic.[25] Even if this is so,
his mimic is complex. He is not just reciting about the Virgin's purity. Three
aspects of his approach are worth consideration.

First, in the ninth stanza he states the Virgin is free from the stains men are
born with. He immediately mentions his childhood devotion to her, saying he
has waited for her since that time. Is he saying that as a child he wanted her to
cleanse him of the stain of being a converso? A childhood thought such as this
would not be unusual. How many children have wished their problems to be

wiped away by some magical person? Looking past the perspective of a child, was León using his "double-voice to tell his reader something else?"[26] Was this a sardonic hint insinuating that only childlike thinkers expect miracles from the Virgin?

Second, his repeated mention of the Virgin as a shield, using the words "*escudo*," "*escudarme*," and "*guarda*" (shield, to shield me, guard, respectively[27]), and his use of the word "*amparo*" (to protect or succor) indicate his desire for her to protect him. But, for a poet who rarely focuses on the helpful powers of the Virgin, these are odd terms. His use of this metaphor disappears after release from prison.[28]

Third, even though León explains in the last lines of the poem that he cannot really say what he wants, perhaps actually he has. Because León is known for his knowledge of the Kabbalah, and "the Hebraic nature" of his spiritual writings, there has been continued argument among scholars about his position on Judaism and Christianity.[29] It is indisputable that his frequent use of light in "A Nuestra Señora" is related to his knowledge of the Kabbalah. As Catherine Swietlicki notes in the *Spanish Christian Cabala*, "Cabalistic references to light have more profound meaning as sacred mystery" than the usual symbology, representing light.[30] As Swietlicki describes, "every Cabalistic description of the upper world usually contains some aspect of light imagery." The upper world "reflect[s] light on the lower worlds," which receives it and sends it back. The two regions Swietlicki describes—the upper world that is divine and the lower world that is inhabited by humans—are part of the *sefirot*.[31] León's poem describes the Virgin as full of purity that lights the day. She is dressed by the sun, eternally crowned by lights, a beloved bright star, and a holy ray of light, which are also representations of the upper world full of divine light that beams down to man.[32] While León undoubtedly is praising the Virgin for her purity, as was normally done in his lifetime, he is also incorporating descriptions of light into a seemingly masked presentation of what in Jewish mysticism is known as the *sefirot*. In "A Nuestra Señora," the poet's lower world is inhabited by his imprisoned self, his *mayor bajeza* (his lowest point); he has fallen in an abyss, where there is darkness and he is frightened and fatigued.[33] He is not only stating that the Virgin did not save him, he is also telling his reader that the aspect of God that is a mediator and savior has not been present for him. He has not received any light from the upper world and at that moment believes he cannot be saved from the abyss. The Virgin is not his redeemer.

Limpia y Pura—Clean and Pure

The Spanish Inquisition's reason for arresting Luis de León was because his faith was not pure. León is praying to the Virgin through his poem; he is asking for her to save him. His request is for her purity to cleanse him and save him from the depths of his terror. While this is something he did not normally do, he was well aware that all around him, people were asking the Virgin for help or some type of intercession.

Requests were made to her for many reasons, yet the underlying reason for her popularity was that she contained what the Iberian world desired—that is, her immaculate state of purity. She represented what Spain wanted, not what Spain *was*. There existed an obsession to cleanse the makeup of the new nation. The result was an intense focus on *limpieza de sangre*, the cleansing of blood (in a genealogical sense), and the Virgin of the Immaculate Conception (la Inmaculada). The obsession grew as the nation came together and grew in strength, especially under los Reyes Católicos.

La Inmaculada has no *macula*. The *macula* is the stain, the impurity, the foul, the evil. While the Catholic Church fought and debated over whether she ever had a trace of *macula* in her, she was taken on as society's idealized self, as if she was able to push away all the impurities that were being erased from Spanish reality. The term "Immaculate Conception of the Virgin Mary" means that she was born without original sin.[34] The concept circulated extensively in the fifteenth century, most particularly, as many scholars have noted, on the Iberian Peninsula. Although the Church did not formally approve the dogma until the nineteenth century, it was taken very seriously. A number of religious orders required an oath of allegiance to the Immaculate Conception.[35] The populace was obsessed with her. The tension was so high at times that riots erupted when factions with opposing views toward the doctrine verbally and physically assaulted each other.[36]

The emotion focused on la Inmaculada was also exhibited in the literature and art of the period. Numerous paintings of the Immaculate Conception appeared throughout Spain and Portugal. There were a number with the rays of the sun, but most often she was presented standing on a crescent moon, with her feet surrounded by cherubs. She stands in the clouds, usually with eyes lowered. Rarely is she painted with the Christ child.

Inmaculada—The Immaculate Woman

A number of scholars have associated early modern Spain's intense focus on the Immaculate Conception with the nation's obsession with purity in its identity and demography.[37] The term "Immaculate Conception," or "Inmaculada," meaning conceived without sin, is a shortened description of the Virgin Mary, mother of Christ, known for having been conceived without original sin. Although she is rarely mentioned in the Bible, Christian society uses the scant information provided by the four Evangelists (Matthew, Mark, Luke, and John) to grow such a powerful object of devotion that in a number of cultures her popularity could be said to have overshadowed that of Christ.[38]

Adeline Rucquoi presents an interesting perspective on Spain's seeming obsession with *limpieza* as it developed a devotion to the Virgin Mary and la Inmaculada that in effect surpassed the importance of Christ in Spanish Christian theology. Related to the obsession "that progressively invaded all of a society in anguish about the idea of sin and stain" that was present in man from the time of Adam, fifteenth-century Spain desperately searched for a way to clean the stain. Rucquoi proposes that the requirement of *limpieza de sangre* was a response by academics, ecclesiastics, poets, and historians to the intolerable conviction that *la macula* (the stain or sin) was something men (especially Spanish men) were born with and that this condition ultimately condemned them to eternal damnation. Spanish honor and the compulsive preoccupation with nobility have been seen as the consequences of the fear of *la macula*.[39] At the end of her essay, she mentions that the devotion to la Inmaculada is a "corollary" to *la macula*.[40] Rucquoi notes that the source of the Immaculate Conception's extreme popularity in the Church developed as a remedy, a movement that demonized Arabs, Jews, and women.[41] Yet I believe it goes far beyond a strategic move by the Church. While the Church and especially its Holy Office of the Inquisition defined and propagated people's anxiety about their *limpieza de sangre*, it is clear that the fixation on the Virgin of the Immaculate Conception spread throughout society as a parallel to everyone's concern about how their own *limpieza de sangre* would be evaluated. La Inmaculada's popularity grew immensely about the same time the Spanish Inquisition began its work.

Two Virgins

Most Inmaculadas are portrayed standing in the heavens, but there are a number that are surrounded by *mandorlas*. In Spain and its dependencies, there are two that have an unusual relationship. As previously mentioned, in Spain it is la Virgen del Coro at the Guadalupe monastery, and in México it is the Virgin of Guadalupe (also known as la Virgen de Tepeyac).

The *mandorla* (or *vesica piscis*) is a sacred symbol produced by the intersection of two circles, creating the shape of an almond "or nimbus that surrounds the whole body of the subject" that "often surrounded objects of glory" and "symbolizes the point at which opposing forces simultaneously divide and meet." Aurelie A. Hagstrom explains that it was frequently associated with female deities from Greek and Roman mythology such as Juno, Ceres, Diana, and Venus and was known as "the female principle of nature." "*Vesica* literally means vulva and *piscis* means fish." "The *vesica piscis*, the birth canal, or gate of life, is a door from one whole world to another. The other world into which the *mandorla* opens is the world of the supernatural, the world of eternal life, the world of God." Taken in this context, the *mandorla* provides the believer a visual clue that the sainted image or mythological pre-Christian deity is from another dimension. An image surrounded by a *mandorla* is ethereal. It is not from the mortal world and, for Christianity, not from the world of the saints. Only Christ and his mother qualify for this marker of the divine. It is an opening to the realm of God, from which the seated Christ or the Woman of the Apocalypse can pass to and fro.[42]

The *mandorla* continued to be a common religious image during the Middle Ages because it was associated with significant events such as the moment Christ became full of light (known as his transfiguration) and his resurrection. Medieval images of Christ are frequently shown inside a *mandorla* and are known as "*majestas domini*: an image of Christ, that is either standing or seated."[43] The *majestas* Christ appears during the same period as the Majestic Virgins, as discussed in an earlier chapter, where the Virgin Mary is also seated as if on a throne. Yet during this period it is only Christ that is surrounded by the *mandorla*. The Majestic Virgins, such as the Virgin of Guadalupe of Extremadura, Spain, are generally not presented inside a *mandorla*. During the later Middle Ages, these seated virgins transform into standing virgins surrounded by the *mandorla* and are generally associated with the apocalypse. Oftentimes the *mandorla* is full of rays. She becomes the "Woman Clothed in the Sun," representing chapter 12 of the book of Revelations. In the late fifteenth century, artists began conflating the image from Revelations with la Inmaculada. The Virgen del Coro at the Guadalupe monastery is a representation of the Woman of the Apocalypse from the New Testament book of Revelations written by John of Patmos, yet at the monastery she is described as the Virgin of the Immaculate Conception.[44]

According to Bernard McGinn, the Immaculate Conception's popularity is attributed to an extraordinary hymn, possibly written by Pope Sixtus IV close to the beginning of his reign in 1470.[45] Without a doubt, this greatly intensified people's devotion to the Virgin Mary. Sixtus succeeded in transferring a highly coded image representing the divine from Christ to His mother, yet for the most part, Sixtus is not credited for la Inmaculada's popularity in Spain.[46] Sixtus had published an order in 1477 that "the feast of the Immaculate Conception be celebrated in all churches." It was strongly resisted by the Dominican Order (who are usually associated with the Inquisition), and they forced Sixtus to rescind it.

The increasing proliferation of images in the early part of the sixteenth century may have been a result of propaganda. The papacy was allowing artistic representation of the Virgin as the Spanish monarchs commissioned Spain's great artists to create numerous Inmaculadas.[47] There were repeated protests and confrontations among the clergy and the populace, with the Spanish archbishops constantly entreating Rome to legitimize the dogma. In the meantime, la Virgen del Coro appeared at the monastery looking like something in between the Woman of the Apocalypse and the Virgin of the Immaculate Conception. Although she was not at center stage in the monastery basilica, the monks saw her constantly since she stood in front of them as they sang several times per day.

The Inmaculada came to be in the Guadalupe Monastery at the end of a brutal century. The statue standing in the choir loft was created at a time when the monks and the villagers needed to be cleansed of their impurities. There needed to be a symbol of divine cleanliness that would stand at the top of the mountain (high up in the choir loft) and cleanse the population below with her immaculate spirit. As Spain was promoting its pure and unified character, the eternally popular Black Virgin of Guadalupe, while still the most important female (and Catholic), contained the unspoken blackness that was associated with the people, which Spain wanted to eliminate. Even though there is no mention of la Inmaculada's connection to the Muslims, the Virgin of Guadalupe of Extremadura is black. There has been much intense speculation about her skin color. A number of scholars believe her face and hands became black from the smoke of surrounding candles.[48] Yet her association with the Moors was cemented by her color. Darker peoples were generally referred to as Muslims. This included Turks, Arabs, Indians, and Ethiopians. Monique Scheer cites texts that identify dark-colored Virgins as being Jewish.[49] At the moment the Virgen del Coro appeared in the monastery, the Virgin Mary's identification whitened. Before that time, a clear labeling of the Virgin's "racial heritage was secondary."[50] The Black Virgin continued to be the most revered Virgin Mary in Spain, but the statue in the choir loft indicated that the Jerónimos were pursuing a "whiter" Mary—in line with late-fifteenth-century drives to cleanse Spain. Color was a constant issue of importance.[51]

The general popularity of la Inmaculada was significant throughout Europe, especially in Spain, Germany, and France. Yet there was no comparison to Spain's devotion to the woman without the stain.[52] Numerous Marian scholars note that Spain took this particular Virgin to heart, but there is little analysis as to why. During the thirteenth century, the preeminent Ramon Lull, a "Doctor Illuminatus," theologian, alchemist, courtier to King Jaime I of Aragón, and, later, a tertiary Franciscan, promoted the Immaculate Conception in a number of his writings. "Lull believed that Islam was the barrier to the conversion of mankind to Christianity." His promotion of "one language, one belief, one faith" blended well with the promotion of la Inmaculada because to remove the *macula* took away the stain or impurities of Islam, leaving a clean nation.[53] Two centuries later, los Reyes Católicos took on Lull's notion of joining the Immaculate Conception with their push to rid the nation of Islam. In her excellent work on early modern Spain, Barbara Fuchs explains that, once under Fernando and Isabel, the nation promoted a constructed identity that was not coherent with the realities of the population. There has never been one particular group that could be solely identified in the Iberian Peninsula. The Visigoth kings belonged to the Arians, an offshoot of Christianity that was deemed heretical. They converted in the seventh century, along with about ninety thousand Jews.[54] All of these converts were later considered "old Christians." The Moors ruled most of the territory for almost a millennium. Even though they were ultimately forced out, many of their cultural traditions remained embedded in Iberian life. The Jews had always been present, having migrated to Spain a millennia before, after the fall of the second temple in Jerusalem.[55]

As has been often noted, the joining of Castilla and Aragón with the marriage of Isabel and Fernando did the most to establish a sense of nation. La Inmaculada had a significant role in changing events in the late fifteenth century. The nation-building agenda initiated by los Reyes Católicos required a model for homogenizing the disparate histories, peoples, and cultures that came under their rule. The individual desires of Iberians were deeply overshadowed by the constant crisis that erupted when New Spain came to be. Much of the population found itself in the center of an unavoidable polemic regarding *limpieza de sangre.* Only a divinity whose striking importance was based on her uninfected blood could be of assistance. It is no coincidence that the popularity of la Inmaculada burgeoned just as the Spanish Inquisition was initiated in 1480.

In terms of policy, los Reyes Católicos were solidly in the court of the Immaculate Conception. The queen had three chapels built to la Inmaculada, and she said Vespers and a mass on the Virgin's feast day (December 8). She also donated forty thousand *maravedis* for these celebrations.[56] Isabel was instrumental in the establishment of the Orden de la Concepción Santísima (the Order of the Holiest Conception). Founded by Beatriz de Silva in 1484, the group settled in a palace donated by Queen Isabel.[57] The Spanish monarchy also contributed to the importance of la Inmaculada by their support of the Franciscan Order. The order accepted the doctrine by the end of the fourteenth century. At the Council of Basil in 1431, "Spaniards were the most fervent discussants," with the Franciscans favoring the doctrine and the Dominican Order fervently opposed. The doctrine was approved at the Council in 1439, officially ending any question of its validity in the kingdom of Aragón.[58] Ultimately, the *maculist* Dominicans ruled the Inquisition, believing that Mary was born with original sin.[59] If Mary was the mother of the nation, then the Dominicans would be saying that the nation was stained from its inception. The Franciscans, ultimately so well supported by Fernando and Isabel, pursued the doctrine of la Inmaculada and in a sense concluded that Spain was born free of stain even though her population was full of Muslims and Jews. This idea collaborated wholeheartedly with the idea of a pure and homogenous national identity.

Crossing Over

Barbara Fuchs begins *Passing for Spain* with a description of the difficulties early modern Spain encountered as it attempted to construct a national identity. In hopes of solidifying the nation by pursuing an obsessive Catholicism, Fernando and Isabel's monarchy "assumed the mantle of Defender of the Faith." Fuchs mentions a "triple landmark" in 1492, encompassing "the fall of Granada to the Catholic kings, the expulsion of the Jews," and the beginning of Columbus's exploration of the Indies, which necessitated "the elaboration of a national myth based on a 'pure' Christianity' and an unadulterated ethnic history."[60] The capture of Granada, the last stronghold of the Moors, left Isabel and Fernando in command of Spain. The seven hundred years in which the Muslims lived in Spain filled los Reyes Católicos with determination to erase a Moorish identification, if at least through the Muslim religion. Their kingdom was now complete. There would be no other groups dominating Catholic Spain.

The voyage of Columbus to the Indies further required Spain to exhibit a coherent self. A nation exploring beyond its borders in such a phenomenal fashion had to present a united front and a clear-cut identity. The expulsion of the Jews, while relieving the stress of containing what was seen as a questionably loyal minority within its borders required those that remained to be undoubtedly loyal citizens and good Christians. This was not identified by behavior but by a genealogical marker. The Spaniard with a pure Visigoth ancestry was what the country needed. La Inmaculada, as the mother of Spain, provided symbolic relief from the anxiety about an impure nation. Yet the implementation of a single ethnic foundational narrative was a confounding enterprise in a place where the official word promoted a solid Catholic (and Visigoth/Old Christian) identity, while everyday practices throughout Spanish society betrayed a deep ambivalence regarding who the new Spaniard was supposed to be.

Isabel, who continuously supported the Black Guadalupe of Extremadura during her reign as queen, provided significant financial support in the name of the Immaculate Conception. In 1497, the same year the Virgen del Coro was installed at Guadalupe, a book Isabel requested, titled *Vita Christi*, was published containing a detailed narrative about la Inmaculada.[61] There is no documented evidence that she specifically influenced the arrival of the statue, but the timing is significant. It is possible that the Jerónimos, knowing of her predilection to the doctrine, might have thought of this as they worked their agreement with the sculptor, Guillermín de Gante. It is noteworthy that although most Inmaculadas are represented alone, the Virgen del Coro has a child. The statue's conflation of the Woman of the Apocalypse and the Virgin of the Immaculate Conception has a close parallel to how Isabel is described.[62]

While the Woman of the Apocalypse, from Revelations 12, had already been conflated with the Immaculate Conception in certain images, the connection was reinforced by a popular narrative circulating during Isabel's reign as expressed by Elizabeth Lehfeldt: "In the religious culture of Spain at the time, it was a logical step to associate her with this figure as well. Like the Woman of the Apocalypse she was a redemptive figure who had brought forth a male child. Further, an association with the apocalyptic sentiments of this figure served to emphasize the eschatological significance of the rule of Isabel."[63]

Interestingly, according to Suzanne Stratton, an inventory of Isabel's art collection made after her death did not contain any representations of la Inmaculada, but a tapestry depicting Queen Esther was listed. "Esther was considered a type of the Virgin Immaculate because [her husband and king] exempted her from his law (Esther 15:12–15)" that all who entered his chambers would die, "as God exempted the Virgin from the law by which all are born in sin."[64]

Queen Esther and the Jesuit Felipe Godíñez

> Gabriel: Thus you should not fear
> The death of your people, Esther
> For you shall deliver them
> Since you are a figure of her
> From whom God will be born.

Felipe Godíñez (1585–1659) wrote the play *La Reina Ester* (Queen Esther), for which he was arrested by the Spanish Inquisition, incarcerated for two years, and ordered never to perform his priestly duties again. Godíñez conflated Esther's figure with that of the Virgin Mary. It could be said that in Godíñez's play, he established Esther as a transitional figure between Catholicism and Judaism. While the actual Jewish narrative about Esther does not state that she is more pure than the other women, it does state that she was allowed by her king to take revenge for her people. The Jewish feast of Purim is based on her story.

After the pogroms of 1391, the story of Esther took on a more intense meaning.[65] The narrative continued to be cited in the Americas three centuries later. She became a symbol of hope and freedom for conversos and *judaizantes* in Spain and its dependencies. Although Godíñez never said specifically that he was conflating Esther and la Inmaculada, he emphasized how Esther saved her people, making her a redeemer much like the Virgin Mary had become. Even more significant for *judaizantes*, Esther had kept her Jewish identity a secret from her husband, the king.[66] When she finally revealed herself, he accepted and honored her with a decree that the Jews could now take revenge against their enemies.

Less than a decade before the Godíñez work, Félix Arturo Lope de Vega y Carpio authored a *comedia* on Queen Esther. The theme itself was controversial at the time because of Spain's ongoing obsession with ridding itself of conversos. But he did not face punishment as did Godíñez. Lope de Vega also wrote *La limpieza no manchada*, which dealt specifically with the Immaculate Conception and purity of blood. The *comedia* does not focus on Jews or Muslims. Instead it implements the emotions and behaviors of nations as characters debating back and forth. Spain's representation, in contrast to a number of nations, as characters is quite revealing. France and Germany discuss Spain's unparalleled devotion to la Inmaculada. The author is giving these nations a voice that expresses the importance of purity and the Virgin of the Immaculate Conception. Two passages point to a concern over Spain's genealogy. In Act I, the character Spain becomes conflated with la Inmaculada, entering the scene wearing a crown of flowers. Germany and France are also present, and they announce that they support Spain dressed as the Virgin. Spain happily responds, saying that they should all embrace so they can all be of the same family.[67] This is significant because France and Germany were considered nations with a pure genealogy. Becoming one family with Germany and France would bring Spain into a group of nations that had unified national identity, one without stain.

Earlier in Act I the character Cuidado (preoccupation) tells one of the few voices that are actual people—Saint Brigida (who assisted in the founding of the Jerónimos)—that he is worried about the descendants of Adam who were born with a *macula*. Brigida makes a statement that resonates with concerns of conversos:

> like the child who was not
> aware and has no
> memory of seeing the tree
> of life and death
> and did not hear
> the first woman
> in Paradise
> who among the green branches
> spoke with the serpent,
> the child was conceived with the stain
> and his parents created him
> while in the state of sin[68]

Providing support for Spain, a nation full of the descendants of conversos, Lope de Vega provides an escape from the *macula*. He conflates the Virgin and the Jewish queen, Esther. During Act II, Esther faints; Saint Brigida removes

Esther's veil and exclaims, "Oh beautiful Queen! Oh Lady of Heaven! Oh Virgin, who today pretends to be Esther!"[69]

As Guadalupe of Extremadura cleansed the herdsman and made him a noble (mentioned in chapter 1), la Inmaculada cleanses the nation of Spain and its populace that has so many descendants of conversos who, as the author reminds his audience, were born while their parents were in the state of sin, not having been converted to Catholicism or, if they did convert, continuing to secretly practice their Jewish faith.

Lastly, and perhaps most important, *La limpieza no manchada* provided solace to a Spain that was not sure of the purity of its populace. La Inmaculada was the mother of all Spaniards (or at least successive monarchies proposed this was so); she was given the exception, as were all her people from the stain of impure blood. In the sixteenth century, as the Black Legend was born from the stories of the Spanish Conquest, la Inmaculada, especially Guadalupe in the Americas, aided in cleansing the colonial Spaniard of all the demonic spirits that came with the brutality of the Conquest.

The Shekhinah, the *Mandorla*, and the Space of the Divine

When Luis de Carvajal (el Mozo) wrote to his mother while he was in the Inquisition prison of México, he would at times begin his letters with the word "Sequina": "See the blessed God Sequina that is his highest presence, may he be with you and everyone amen."[70] His biographer, Seymour Liebman, questioned the meaning of the term. Not having found an exact definition of "Sequina," Liebman did not venture to say with certainty that Carvajal was talking about the Jewish Shekhinah.[71] Carvajal's letter, written in 1595, begins with "Oh mother of my soul, Sequina be with you."[72]

Carvajal's case has famously circulated throughout Mexican history. Narratives of his demise were published in *El Libro Rojo* (The Red Book) by Vicente Riva Palacio, and in the famous work on Carvajal's family by Alfonso Toro. Carvajal left his memoirs and letters, an extremely unusual testament to the life of *judaizantes* in colonial México.

The Divine Garment

It is my contention that la Inmaculada, in the form of the Virgin surrounded by rays of light, is a symbolic representation of the Shekhinah and the Space of the Divine. Arthur Green presents a convincing argument that the "unequivocal feminization of shekhina in the Kabbalah of the thirteenth century is a Jewish response to an adaptation of the revival of devotion to Mary."[73] Examples given by Green indicating the Shekhinah/Virgin Mary parallels are "intercessor," "great mother," "nourisher," "suffering mother," "divine female," "consort to the Holy One," and "conduit of Divine Grace."[74]

The doctrine of the Virgin and the circulation of the Jewish Kabbalah met at numerous moments, leaving the boundary between the two blurred and perhaps confusing. As Green mentions, "The Lady is thus the universal go-between, from above to below and from below to above. She is the emissary of all."[75] For Catholics, the preceding citation would certainly appear to emanate from some devotional prayer to the Virgin. Instead, the passage is actually from the Zohar, a section of the Jewish Kabbalah, attributed to a Rabbi Shim'on, who lived during the second century C.E.

It is likely that Jewish Kabbalists were influenced by the growing significance of the Virgin Mary. Christians also appropriated aspects of Jewish (or Kabbalistic) doctrine in their representation of the divine, especially within the role of the mother of Christ. This is exceedingly evident in the images of "Nuestra Señora de la Concepción" (Our Lady of the Conception), also known as la Virgen del Coro of the Guadalupe Monastery in Extremadura, and as Guadalupe of Tepeyac, in México. This positioning is demonstrated in the frontispiece of a book on the Spanish Empire's devotion to the Virgin Mary. Within the many aspects of this 1682 engraving by Augustin Bouttate is a *pendon* (banner) carried by Spain with the image of la Inmaculada surrounded by a *mandorla* full of rays.[76] The engraving has no evidence of any type of Jewish religious motif. It shows Spain dominating the world with the Virgin as its patron. The Virgin is the driving force behind Spain's success, as seen in the carriage taking her toward the sun.

The sun surrounding the Virgin is the centerpiece to this story. In Revelations 12, the Woman of the Apocalypse is clothed in the sun (*mulier amicta sole*)—an expression describing the *mandorla* that surrounds her. The sun fills the *mandorla* with its rays. In Catholic doctrine, *mandorlas* generally indicate what is commonly termed a halo. The rays of light surrounding the Virgin are like a giant halo that envelope her. The sun or light associated with the Virgin is also sometimes described as the Sun of Justice, another name for Jesus Christ. At the least, the brilliant rays indicate a divine presence, whether God himself (herself), Christ, or simply heavenly grace.

In Arthur Green's analysis, where he describes the Shekhinah in detail and concludes that there are inextricable links between this aspect of the Jewish God and the Christian Virgin Mary, there remains the possibility of an even further joining of the two. Returning to a Jewish narrative, the spectacular vision of an overwhelming light, where the rays could also be flames of a fire that does not consume bring to mind Moses's encounter of the burning bush in Exodus 3:2–3. Moses sees the fire and is puzzled that it does not consume the bush. As he approaches, God speaks to him. Several verses later (verse 14), when Moses asks, who shall he say sent him, God tells him, "He who is has sent me to you." There are a number of opinions regarding this passage, including that God is speaking from the bush. It is also said that the Archangel Michael, who often accompanies the Shekhinah, first speaks to Moses announcing her presence. This aspect of the story becomes particularly significant in 1648 when Miguel Sánchez publishes *Imagen de la virgen Maria Madre de Dios de Guadalupe*, which focuses on the role of Michael the Archangel in the rescue of the Woman of the Apocalypse.[77]

The Shekhinah and the *mandorla* resonate with the space of the divine. The *mandorla* full of the sun's rays is akin to Moses' burning bush. Is it the location of God. The significance of la Inmaculada as she stands in front of the blazing *mandorlas* is that she is the intermediary between man and God, which resonates with Gershom Scholem's explanation that the Shekhinah is "never being separated from God himself." She is standing next to God, yet we can see her material form. She stands in the intermediary position. Her role is to be between God and man/woman. She is also the messenger for man, taking his wishes and requests and passing them through the *mandorla*, which is where God dwells.[78]

She is a protector. Catholic dogma has generally espoused the idea that she exists with the sun behind her because of her own magnificent grace, but it is quite possible that at some moment in time her devoted may have thought of her as standing before God so that she can shield man from the blinding divinity of the Holy One. In this context, she protects man from seeing God—a significant tenet of the Jewish faith. The punishment for this transgression (seeing God) is death.[79] Elliot Wolfson translated a section of the *Hekhalot Rabbati*:

> . . . the Lord of hosts
> . . . is wrapped when He comes to sit upon the throne of His glory . . .
> The eyes of no creature can behold it,
> Neither the eyes of any being of flesh and blood nor the eyes of His servants.
> The one who looks upon it, or glimpses or sees it,
> His eyeballs are seized by pulsations,
> And they kindle him and burn him up.[80]

In Catholic iconography, the Shekhinah is standing in front of the brilliant light that could burn the eyes. Yet, she also wears the "cosmic garment," that contains all the stars of the sky, as does the Mexican Woman of the Apocalypse.[81] Manuel Espinosa de los Monteros's Kabbalistic explanation of the Virgin of Guadalupe describes her stole as having forty-six stars that represent a grand multitude of holy Israelites who are wise prophets that will appear after the apocalypse.[82] This Catholic priest who lived at the center of Mexican Catholicism in the early nineteenth century incorporated the Jewish and Catholic aspects of the Virgin/Shekhinah.[83] The blending of the image of the pregnant woman wearing a cloak of stars while standing in front of the brilliant illumination of God would be the ideal representation of a syncretic religious thought of a *judaizante*, of which I believe there were an untold number in colonial México. The lack of a Christ child in the image would be less offensive to a converso who still retained loyalty to the Jewish faith.

Those espousing devotion to her would also have some protection from the Inquisition. William Nowak tells of the poetry that Luis de León wrote to the Virgin Mary while imprisoned by the Spanish Inquisition, even though he had previously not shown any significant interest in her. Nowak explains that the "poem's appeal to the holy name of the Virgin may have been meant to provide just such a politically savvy shield for a prisoner of the Inquisition," proposing that de León wrote about his devotion as a way to appear more Christian to the Inquisitors.[84] This is likely in 1648, when Miguel Sánchez wrote *Imagen*, timed to appear just after the most brutal Inquisition trials in the history of New Spain.

The End of Days

The Virgin of the Immaculate Conception portrayed at the center of a *mandorla* is a response to the conflation between la Inmaculada and *mulier amicta sole* (woman clothed in the sun). It is no coincidence that the Virgen del Coro was installed in the Guadalupe Monastery in 1497. She was the personification of Spain's identity at the time. As the Woman of the Apocalypse, holding the already-born male child, she symbolized the crucial events of the decade, the voyages of Columbus, the fall of Granada, and the expulsion of the Jews. The Virgen del Coro looks directly at the world. She and her child have survived the attack of the dragon. She is an indication that Spain will survive into the sixteenth century. Although she appears to be the Woman of the Apocalypse, she is called la Inmaculada, perhaps from the need to have a cleansing agent in the monastery that only a decade before was known for an intimate infiltration of *judaizantes* among its clergy.

The discovery of the Americas brings a new narrative. It is said that the Virgin of Guadalupe of México appears on a cloak worn by an indigenous man named Juan Diego. The Mexican Guadalupe is also surrounded by a *mandorla*. There are similarities between her and the one in the choir loft at the monastery. The basic differences are that the Mexican Guadalupe is looking toward the ground and does not present an authoritative stance, as does the Spanish Virgin. There is also no child, only a narrative of a pregnancy and a sash indicating such.[85] Guadalupe of México was also heralded as an apocalyptic Virgin in the work of Miguel Sánchez (discussed in detail in a later chapter). She is portrayed as the Woman of the Apocalypse who is about to give birth to a male child. She is attacked by a seven-headed dragon but is swept away to safety by Michael the Archangel. Just as the Virgen del Coro is created during a period of drastic change, Sánchez's book appears during a cataclysmic time in New Spain–when the Inquisition has brought chaos to México City. Both are associated with the presence of *judaizantes*. They have been saved from the dragon, which at times is identified as the Antichrist. Perhaps it could be said that the two Virgins, in their role as the Woman of the Apocalypse, were being attacked by the dragon/Inquisition. Adela Yarbro Collins, in her writing on Revelations, notes the relationship between the Antichrist and Rome, the geographic center of the Church. While the Antichrist in Revelations is from the first century C.E., Guillermín de Gante and Miguel Sánchez were thinking of a more eminent apocalypse. The Inquisition was bearing down on the Jerónimos during the time that de Gante was sculpting the Virgen del Coro; two centuries later, Miguel Sánchez published *Imagen*. Almost two centuries more passed and the image of the dragon/Church remained when Monteros recalled the dragon and likened it to the Church (and monarchs): "The kings and highest pontiff and perverse priests will form an extremely grotesque Dragon, the tale of which is made of the clergy themselves."[86] In contrast, the Virgin of Guadalupe takes the role of "representative of the Hebrew Nation, she is the first Wife re-established to her earliest dignity where she is supported by her consort [YWH] [the Jewish god]."[87]

4

Hebrew Truth

Hebraica veritas

There are unpublishable (and perhaps incorrect) narratives circulating among Italian scholars that attest to the Jewish ancestry of the powerful Florentine Medici family. *Hebraica veritas*—the Hebrew truth—a term used when a scholar seeks to study the Old Testament in its original Hebrew language, was the focus of learning in the Renaissance Florence of the Medicis in the late fifteenth century, where the Neo-Platonists held ongoing discussions regarding ancient knowledge that included the study of Greek and Hebrew texts. At the same moment, a nascent movement of Hebrew studies appeared in Spain with the rise to power of Archbishop Francisco Jiménez de Cisneros, confessor to Queen Isabel.[1] Works of translation from Hebrew to Latin commissioned by Cisneros in conjunction with the frequent travel of clergy between the peninsula and Italy ensured that the movement seeking *Hebraica veritas* remained alive long after the Florentine Medici salons no longer existed. Those scholars who learned of *Hebraica veritas* in the home of Lorenzo de' Medici initiated a line of Hebraists in Spain and in Italy whose works kept Jewish writing alive after many thousands of Jews went underground.

Shortly after the Expulsion of the Jews from Spain in 1492, Archbishop Cisneros, close advisor to los Reyes Católicos, embarked on a project to produce a Bible in Latin, Hebrew, Greek, and Aramaic. This expansion of knowledge was a remarkable event, considering that the sixteenth century also saw a closing of Spain's religious and intellectual boundaries. This Bible came to be known as the "most monumental publishing venture in the history of printing."[2] At the time, it was considered to be significantly out of the norm for a "Latin text of the Bible to reflect with the best possible accuracy, the Hebrew or Greek originals."[3] Cisneros used all the resources available to produce what came to be known as the *Complutense Polyglot Bible*. The scheme was so enormous that its final cost came to be fifty thousand ducats, most of which was funded out of Archbishop Cisneros's own revenues.[4] The Bible's production was so labor intensive that it was not published until 1517, shortly before Cisneros's death. The *Complutense Polyglot Bible* was groundbreaking, presenting the scriptures in four languages—Hebrew, Latin, Greek, and Aramaic—alongside each other. "An entire folio tome was devoted exclusively to a Hebrew grammar, a Hebrew and Aramaic lexicon . . . dictionaries, including pronunciation aids and instructions."[5]

Cisneros's objective is stated in his preface to the Polyglot Bible:

> Every Theologian should . . . be able to drink of the Water which springeth up to eternal life. . . . This is the reason, therefore, why we have ordered the Bible to be printed in the original language with different translations. . . . To accomplish this task we have been obliged to have recourse to the knowledge of the most able Philologists, and to make researches in every direction for the best and most ancient Hebrew and Greek manuscripts. Our object is to revive the hitherto dormant study of the sacred Scriptures.[6]

Cisneros did not document his deeper desires about the Polyglot Bible. Richard Popkin surmises that the cardinal's motivation was actually "to prepare for the Second coming." There can be other explanations: one is that Cisneros was significantly influenced by contact with the Florentine Neo-Platonists—such as Giovanni Pico della Mirandola and Marsilio Ficino—who were studying Hebrew and the Kabbalah at the end of the fifteenth century.[7] In addition to possible contact with the Italians, Cisneros had other unspoken interests in Hebrew studies related to a significant interest in the well-being of conversos, an issue discussed later in this chapter.

Cisneros (and other Christian-Hebraists) presented what Jerome Friedman calls a "new approach to Scripture." The translations went beyond dogma; they included "a consistent application" of a "historical-philological method," avoiding typology, with its "Christocentric interpretation."[8] Each prophet's narrative from the Old Testament was studied and explained "according to the letter, their history" and the context of their history.[9] This method, because it was incorporated by high ecclesiastical rank, was short-lived. It ended a century later when the Church, responding to the Reformation, closed in on such radical thinking. While it was alive, however, it spawned two major Polyglot Bibles (the *Complutense Bible* and the *Antwerp Bible*); a number of deeply learned Hebraists in Spain, France, Germany, and Italy; scores of translations of extremely important Hebrew documents; and, most surprisingly, the design of the Sistine Chapel as painted by Michelangelo.[10]

Zapatero y Tornadizo—Changeable Identities

Sergio Fernández Lopez's in-depth study of the early humanists cites documents indicating the precarious position of one of Cisneros's translators. "Alonso de Arcos [Zamora], zapatero, podia enseñar major la lengua (hebrea), siendo nombrado profesor de forma interina" (Alonso of Arcos [Zamora], shoemaker, could better teach the (Hebrew) language if named interim professor).[11] In 1511, when a professor of Hebrew was needed at the University of Salamanca, the university chose an Italian who did not know the language.[12] It was also decided that the new professor would share his salary with Alonso de Zamora, who would then teach Hebrew to the Italian. Zamora was not considered for a formal position because he was a converso. He was called a *zapatero* (shoemaker) because it was either his or his father's occupation, and a *tornadizo*, which is a perjorative term for conversos, indicating that their attitudes or commitments were subject to fluctuation. The term notes ambiguity—the *tornadizo*'s conversion represents an abandonment of his heritage (even if it was to avoid the Inquisition pyre) while simultaneously creating a new, potentially insincere persona.[13]

Zamora's life depicted what Julio Caro Baroja writes about *tornadizos*. Caro Baroja describes several generations of a converso family as they leave Judaism and incorporate themselves into Spanish society. The story begins with the patriarch who is a *tornadizo*; in the next generation the son is a shopkeeper (dyer); the grandson is a banker; and the great-grandchildren, a nun and a Jesuit priest.[14] Although there is little documentation available on Zamora's life, a number of scholars believe he was twenty-six years old in 1500 when he began working for Cisneros, the second most powerful man in Spain.[15] Zamora's work was to assist in preparing translations for the *Complutense Polyglot Bible.* In addition to Zamora, Cisneros hired two recent converts, Pablo Nuñez Coronel and physician Alfonso de Alcalá.

Alonso de Zamora was from a village named Arcos, near the Portuguese border. The community was close to Zamora, a city "renowned for Jewish learning, and for resistance to Christian proselytizing."[16] He was the son of Rabbi Juan de Zamora, known as Bibel.[17] He most probably attended the Hebrew school, as did Coronel and Alcalá, even though Zamora's Hebrew indicates more substantial learning than what he would have received at a small Hebrew school.[18] Fernández López states that Zamora converted on or before 1492, as did Coronel and Alcalá.[19]

There is no doubt that Cisneros greatly protected Zamora as well as other conversos. When the former confessor to Queen Isabel, the bishop of

Granada, Fray Hernando de Talavera, was arrested by the Inquisition in 1506, Cisneros sent a letter to Rome requesting that the pope favor Talavera.[20] The bishop was accused of involvement in the "coming of the Messiah" scandal.[21] It was reported that Talavera, along with a number of other conversos, organized a movement to send preachers throughout the entire kingdom so they could spread knowledge about the law of Moses and announce the coming of the messiah, along with that of the Prophet Elias.[22] Among the group associated with Talavera was Francisco Álvarez de Toledo, the *maestre-escuela* (scholastic canon) of the Cathedral of Toledo who was also supported by Cisneros when charged by the Inquisition.[23] The Álvarez de Toledo family had a long history with the Holy Office. As discussed in a previous chapter, the brother of Álvarez de Toledo, Jerónimo Friar García Zapata de Toledo, was executed by the Inquisition in 1469. Álvarez and Cisneros had a close relationship. Four years later the *maestre-escuela* accompanied the cardinal on a journey to Cartagena.[24]

There is little information available on Cisneros's early life. As an exhibition of his preferences, Cisneros supported a confraternity of conversos named La Virgen y Madre de Dios (The Virgin and Mother of God). In 1505 he gave the group a chapel in the archbishop's palace.[25] It is reported that his father was a tax collector—a popular Jewish occupation in early modern Spain. Even so, there is no mention by anyone that Cisneros could have been a converso.[26]

Cisneros was not merely an important Spanish figure. He was a powerful man in many realms and one of the few who actually spent several years in a cloister before taking a role in public life.[27] He was the "leader of the reformed spiritual Franciscans" before he was named confessor to Queen Isabel in 1492. He was the man behind the throne after the death of Isabel until her grandson, Spain's King Carlos (Charles) I, was anointed Holy Roman Emperor Carlos V in 1518.[28]

Returning to Alonso de Zamora: a university document from Salamanca identified Zamora as a *tornadizo*.[29] In a document dated 1518 that describes life in the court of Carlos V, Zamora writes about how the emperor's administration is bankrupting the kingdom, and that Spain is experiencing poverty because of the huge amounts of money spent by the crown on frivolity and festivals. He calls the king's tutor, Chièvres, a perfidious traitor and ends the piece by calling on Jesus Christ to liberate the government from Chièvres so that all the crown's money will not be spent before the sun sets on Spain.[30] In light of his later writings, Zamora's sincerity is suspect in his reference to Christ.

While Zamora was supported during Cisneros's lifetime, with the death of the prelate and the arrival of Carlos V (with his presumed traitorous advisor, Chièvres), Zamora was left with the vivid isolation of a *judaizante* in a post-Expulsion Spain. He was placed in an emotionally impossible role of keeping alive the precious writings of the sages who were forced to leave their religion and their country. As Popkin explains, Zamora "was just left with sadness and sympathy for the Jews of the Diaspora."[31] This despondency is illustrated in a document written by Zamora (using a pseudonym). It is titled "Letter sent by Professor Zornoza, judge and Rector of the University of Alcalá de Henares, to the Holy Father in the City of Rome, Our Lord Paul III, prince of the saintly and Catholic Roman Church."

> Now Your Holiness . . . Solomon said with great knowledge that God gave him, he did much to glorify knowledge and said 'Happy is the man who found knowledge and the gentleman that has acquired intelligence because obtaining knowledge is worth more than the acquisition of silver and more than pure gold' (Proverbs 3, 13–14). And, Your Holiness knows that the man who sees and does not comprehend is similar to the beasts and the science that is true and correct is that which is used to understand the Holy Scripture. . . . Saint Jerome tells us if we have a question about the twenty-four books [of the Old Testament], turn to the Hebrew language. . . .
>
> We entreat and request you, Your Holiness to assist us for your love of God to save us from our enemy, the Bishop of Toledo, Don Juan Talavera, who every day, continuously causes us numerous and disagreeable afflictions, and transgresses your orders and the holy writings that you gave us, in addition to the writings of the Holy Fathers [Old Testament Prophets]. . . . The judge that oversees us destroys your holy writings; the one who resides in this city and is named Quiroga. He also infringes on the orders left by the Emperor Don Carlos. They are not content with tearing up your writings, but have also interfered with all the messages we have sent the Emperor. We certainly find ourselves in great anguish, and he sees us like beasts standing in front of the slaughterhouse. In addition, we do not know what precipitates these perversities, if for envy, or hatred of science, or love of money, or to diminish the reputation of the previous Bishop of Toledo. . . . Fray Francisco Ximenez 'an honorable and correct man, fearful of God and distant from evil' (Job 1, 8). . . . We have tolerated until today all these unpleasant afflictions. We mention these with the hope that we will receive your assistance, since you are located in God's place and are his representative (Dios Santo). If Your Holiness responds to our plea "Yahweh will be your security and keep you safe from capture" (Proverbs 3, 24).
>
> This letter was written and finished in the service of God on Monday, March 31, 1544 . . . in the University of Alcalá of Henares, by the hand of Alfonso [sic] de Zamora, who teaches the Hebrew languages in this university to all those who desire to learn; and even though I have seventy years, I do not remember even to this day a single day where I was happy. And I write this letter . . . so that all people with some culture will understand, even though they may not be sages. . . . That I am the only [Hebrew] that remained after the expulsion from the Kingdom of Castilla that occurred in the year 5252 [1492] during the era of

the creation of the world of the heretics, because today the Jews are scattered throughout the world for their sin.[32]

Between the years 1500 and 1544, Zamora produced several translations of the Old Testament from Hebrew to Latin, in addition to the *Targum* (the Jewish Bible in Aramaic). His work on several medieval Jewish philosophers is notable. Zamora translated into Spanish the "prologue and commentary of David Qinhi" on the books of Isaiah, Jeremiah, and Daniel, in addition to a copying and restoring a manuscript of commentaries by Mosé bar Nahmán on the book of Job, and sections of the Kabbalah.[33] His is well known for writing a book on Hebrew grammar, among other works.[34] Most notably, his translations were not only literal but also "interlineal."[35]

Considered "one of the greatest Hebraists of Spain's Golden Age," Zamora stood at a pivotal moment in the history of Judaism in Spain. In a broad sense, his work was the "point of union between medieval Judaism and Christian humanism."[36] Fernández López writes that Zamora "was clearly the veritable motor of [H]ebrew humanism in Spain. No one besides Alonso de Zamora knew how to put in service . . . the complete legacy of Jewish culture, directly inherited from the most prodigious exegesis that was practiced in *al-Andalus*." Because of Zamora's translations, "the reading rooms of the most brilliant university libraries of that moment were filled with the biblical and philological works of Rashi, 'Ezra or Qimhi."[37] While later Hebraists would produce significant material in this area, there was no comparison to the work of a man who had studied in a Hebrew school before the Expulsion. Zamora's writing kept Jewish thought alive and provided a solid foundation for later scholars. It was a significant resource for those who produced the *Antwerp Bible* fifty years later.[38]

Dionisio Vázquez

In October 1506, while Zamora was working on the *Complutense*, an Augustinian from Toledo named Dionisio Vázquez (1479–1539) accompanied Fernándo of Aragón, el Rey Católico, on a trip to Naples, in the priest's role as preacher to the king.[39] Ordained in 1500 and quickly rising through the clerical ranks of Spanish prelates, Vázquez was to change the course of events regarding the survival of Jewish thought in Spain. It is in Naples that Vázquez first met the famous Neo-Platonist cardinal Egidio da Viterbo (1465–1532),[40] who was sent by Pope Julius II to greet Fernándo and discuss political issues with him. Spanish historian Morocho Gayo believes it was here that Vázquez collaborated with Viterbo on one of the cardinal's manuscripts. Most importantly, the two established a close relationship that continued for the next eleven years and would deeply influence the future of Hebraic studies in the sixteenth century.[41]

Vázquez returned to Spain in July 1507 and was soon charged by the Inquisition for preaching a heretical sermon. He was reported by a certain Fernándo de Prejamo. Morocho Gayo believes this was related to his work regarding "theological problems related to the Kabbalah."[42] Historian Fernández López notes that for decades, scholars believed that Vázquez was an Old Christian. However, in 1970 a book on conversos from Toledo announced that Vázquez's mother was from a converso family, and most probably his father was as well.[43] The *proceso* (case with the Inquisition) started in Valladolid and ended in Rome. The case was delayed by Diego de Deza, the Spanish Inquisitor.[44] It was eventually dismissed, perhaps because of Viterbo's influence. In the meantime, Cisneros took over Deza's position, at which time Vázquez traveled to Rome and remained there for eleven years.[45] Questions about Vázquez's potential heresy continued, as noted in a letter written by Pope Adrian VI in 1522, where he states that "some want to slander him"; however, Vázquez, showing himself to be well-versed and enthusiastic to the service of God and his majesties, gave no sermons that indicated any scandal.[46] Vázquez's association with the highest levels of power continued.

Questions about his orthodoxy did not impede his appointment in 1510 as regent of the Agustiniana, the prestigious *studium* of the Convent of Saint Augustine in Rome.[47] Viterbo also appointed him orator to the pope, where he served Julius II (1443–1513) and Leo X (1475–1521). In January 1518 Viterbo named Vázquez his *vicario* (deputy in ecclesiastic affairs) and *visitadór* of Castilla and the colonies.[48] In the role of *visitadór*, Vázquez was given the authority not only to inspect Church administration in his assigned geographic area but also to appoint clergy to Church positions. Clearly, Viterbo was his friend and protector.[49] Once in Spain, Vázquez was named orator to the king, who was said to be dazzled by Vázquez's sermons. Carlos V "was delighted in his [Vázquez's] erudite and penetrating language and would stand up when listening to him to avoid becoming sleepy or distracted. He [Carlos V] would expand the discussion . . . He would become amazingly affected . . . he would become so impassioned that he would speak in a torrent of words that everyone else would also get excited, without even wanting to . . . . In his [Vázquez's] time there was no other orator born who was as exceptional as Dionisio Vázquez."[50]

While Carlos V was thrilled with his orator, there were also problems. Vázquez was named professor of Hebrew at Cisneros's University of Alcalá at Henares in 1530. The scholar was not so well received among his peers for "wasting time with explications of Greek and Hebrew."[51] Historian Morocho Gayo notes that after significant searching, he has not been able to find much of Vázquez's writings. Most of what he has located appears to have been altered and cannot be certifiably from Vázquez's hand.[52] Fernández López reports that Vázquez's manuscripts scattered throughout Spain, with one particularly important manuscript being found in the library of a scholar who died in the Inquisition prison.[53] The Portuguese Inquisition censured several of Vázquez's works in 1581.[54]

The ten years he lived among the Neo-Platonists of Italy greatly influenced Vázquez's thinking. As Morocho Gayo explains, Vázquez's fortune of living in this decidedly "overcharged" Neo-Platonic environment created a path for numerous religious thinkers. Vázquez initiated a line of Hebraic scholars who had a deep interest in the Kabbalah. Among them were the famed Cipriano de la Huerga (teacher of Benito Arias Montano, who will be discussed in the following chapter), Luis de León, and Teresa of Avila. His own maestro, Egidio da Viterbo, had already cleared the path for him.

Egidio da Viterbo

Cardinal Viterbo and Dionisio Vázquez met again in Spain soon after Carlos V became king. On November 14, 1517, Pope Leo X proclaimed a crusade against the Turks. The following year, Leo X sent envoys to Emperor Maximilian and the kings of England, France, and Spain, seeking support for the crusade.[55] Viterbo was sent to Spain, arriving June 10, 1518. He was also there to discuss what was termed the "Turkish menace," hoping Spain would assist in protecting the Kingdoms of Naples and Sicily.[56] The trip was considered extremely successful. He was also exceedingly popular. A commentary on his presence in the court noted that "all of Spain ran to hear him."[57]

Carlos V agreed to Viterbo's request, committing to send an official envoy—Juan García Loaysa—to the Turkish court. García Loaysa, who was well received, told that the Turks wanted peace and that Christian pilgrims would be guaranteed safe passage to the Holy Land.[58] Even with these signs of peace, Carlos V agreed to send nineteen thousand troops on the crusade, including himself, if the pope so requested.[59]

Viterbo was present in Spain when Carlos V's grandfather, Emperor Maximilian, died. The death of the emperor created the opening for the Spanish king to succeed. The pope was against Carlos V's taking the crown, concerned that the Hapsburg would be too powerful for the Vatican to contain.[60] Even so, Viterbo wrote to Leo X from Barcelona in support of Carlos V's election to emperor.[61] In the end, the pope supported the king of France, yet this appears not to have diminished Viterbo's influence with the papacy. Most importantly, Viterbo's endorsement of Carlos V sealed the future of their relationship, which provided a moment of safety for the Hebraists of Spain to continue their work.[62]

Viterbo was in Spain for at least eight months. His presence at the time of the previous emperor's death was significant. There is no specific information available as to Viterbo's conversations with Carlos V. Yet there are two documents that indicate an intense desire to form an alliance with the new emperor. One of these is *Dialogo en Honor de César Carlos* (Barcelona, 1518), now lost.[63] It is documented that Spanish scholars reacted with suspicion to Viterbo's new way of thinking that took seriously Greek and Hebrew philosophy.[64] Ultimately, however, it was the emperor's opinion that mattered. Carlos V was thrilled with the cardinal's dynamic view.

The Philo-Semitic Cardinal

Philip Beitchman states in *The Alchemy of the Word* that "in pre-Counter Reformation Renaissance" the pope was surrounded by individuals who believed, studied, and wrote about religion in its most "unorthodox, pagan, and magical" form.[65]

Egidio da Viterbo related in a letter dated January 6, 1515, that Pope Leo X "made him a gift of a *Targum*" and certain documents on the Kabbalah.[66] Viterbo had already been studying Aramaic and Hebrew for several years. Fifteen years later a different pope, Clement VII, commissioned Viterbo to write a treatise on the Shekhinah (Viterbo spells it Scechina), requesting that it be directed to Emperor Carlos V.[67] The book, *Scechina e Libellus de litteris hebraicis* (Scechina, the Little Book of Hebrew Letters) is "a veritable *summa* of Egidio's [Kabbalistic] learning acquired over many years of study and meditation."[68]

It could be said that the Renaissance radiated in Egidio da Viterbo. The cardinal personified the openness of the era. He was a man of religion, yet he looked upon all forms of knowledge available to him, quoting Plato and Aristotle as easily as he quoted the Kabbalah. Under the protection of the Medicis (for which he was often criticized), he was named general of the Augustinian Order in 1506, and cardinal in 1517. A complex and enigmatic man, he took on numerous challenging roles in his lifetime. Described as "mercurial,"[69] he was an outstanding orator, having been made famous by a sermon he gave at the opening of the Fifth Lateran Council in 1511, where he reportedly said "Men should be changed by religion, not religion by men."[70] He even took on the role of soldier during the Sack of Rome in 1527, when he gathered an army together of several thousand men in an attempt to rescue Pope Clement VII from captivity in the Castle of Saint Angelo.[71] Viterbo "was among the most distinguished of Renaissance Platonists."[72] He was a great "humanist, poet, philosopher and historian, . . . ambassador and reformer" and "was instrumental in bringing about a resurgence in Hebraic Studies."[73] Viterbo's thinking was "symbolic and synthetic"—significantly different from the "scholastic dogmatic formulations" of this time.[74] He worked toward the reformation of his order and of the Church in Rome, frequently displaying signs of dissatisfaction regarding the chaotic immorality rampant in Rome during his lifetime.[75]

Viterbo is considered one of the greatest Hebraists of the early sixteenth century.[76] "There is scarcely a classic of Jewish medieval mysticism that he has not translated, annotated, or commented upon."[77] He was not only fluent in Hebrew but also in Aramaic and Arabic. Most significant is that he was involved with all the Italian Hebraists of his time, and in fact took into his home a Jew named Eliyahu ben Asher Ha-Levi, also known as Elye Levita.[78]

Viterbo began his Hebrew studies two decades before Levita became his teacher. It is likely that the cardinal started to learn Hebrew while in Florence in 1494–1495.[79] His first Hebrew master was Neo-Platonist Marsilio Ficino, known for his enduring influence on Renaissance thought.[80] There was a paucity of Hebrew teachers at the time as a result of the numerous expulsions the Jews were experiencing in the different regions. His watershed moment occurred when he encountered Levita. It is the breadth of knowledge Levita presented that most likely excited Viterbo. François Secret defines Levita as the "premier Jewish grammarian of the Renaissance." In the words of Zelda Newman, "Levita had so great a familiarity with Jewish texts that he was able to compose a concordance of terms in the (Jewish) Bible as well as all the Aramaic in the Talmud."[81] The collaboration they developed was a unique relationship for the time. During the more than ten years Levita was in residence in the cardinal's palace, Viterbo taught him Latin and Greek, and Levita taught Viterbo Hebrew and Aramaic.[82] They both had much to offer each other. "No other Jew had" Levita's "breadth of knowledge," but only Viterbo had access to a plethora of available ancient Hebrew manuscripts.[83]

Their relationship went beyond the teaching and the translations Levita provided for Viterbo. In the prologue of Levita's *Massoreth Ha-Massoreth*, he explains that he was penniless after having lost everything in sack of Padua that occurred in 1509. He had heard of Viterbo's interest in Hebrew and visited his home. Levita told Viterbo "Know, Sire,/ that I, an ordinary man from Germany,/ . . . . . and all my life I've studied this,/ so it happens/ there is no man in reality/ who can beat me in textual familiarity . . . / [Viterbo responded] Are you Eliyahu,/ the man whose words have spread and whose books have reached all corners?/ Blessed is God, the God of the world,/ who brought you here and placed you near me./ Now stay here with me;/ you'll be a teacher to me,/ and I a father to you."[84]

The cardinal had in his service numerous Jews and conversos. They served as teachers, copiers, and translators.[85] With his assistants, Viterbo produced an immense body of work, including translations of passages from "the *Zohar*, the *Comentario* of *Raziel*, the *Sefer ha temunah*, the *Ginnat Egoz*, the *Bahir*, and the *Ma'arecth haelohut*."[86] Even though one of Viterbo's early works, dated 1517, is written against the Jews, it appears to be an anomaly.[87] The text, based on the writings of the Spaniard Pablo de Heredia, may possibly have been written for political reasons. By 1517 Viterbo was already heavily involved with a number of Jews and conversos; in fact, he had already taken in Levita (and family) by this time.[88] He has been noted by numerous scholars for supporting conversos in 1531 against the impending establishment of a Portuguese Inquisition. Even though his voice was overruled, his support was noticed and is often cited in Jewish scholarly texts. Viterbo was even able to convince Pope Leo X to allow a Hebrew printing press to be constructed.[89] He is also known for having supported the famous Hebraist Johann Reuchlin, after the German was charged with heresy by the Inquisition.[90] Viterbo's reputation as a supporter of the Jews was solidified when a comment he made in a letter he wrote to Reuchlin proposed that he was supporting Reuchlin "for the salvation of the Talmud."[91] He also is said to have written criticisms of Pope Clement V for having decreed the Expulsion of the Jews in France in the early fourteenth century. He never used his considerable power to propose "any politically restrictive or vindictive measures against the Jews."[92] By the end of his life, Egidio da Viterbo, a cardinal of the Roman Catholic Church who had been known to promote the works of Aristotle and Pliny, came so far that he "converted into one of those . . . Jewish writers that teach against the Christian religion."[93] In his last major work, *Scechina*, he writes "everything is not expressed in the New Testament," and that "our exegetes, says the *Scechina*, ignoring the mysteries, have preferred the eloquence of the sacred letters, the little adornment of the arcane, the infantile trifles of the truth."[94] François Secret, summarizing the text, continues "it is not Pliny, Dioscórides . . . or Aristotle, in science or philosophy where we find the key to this revelation . . . [human or earthly] dialectics has nothing to do with this, it is the divine dialectic that presents the seventy-two aspects of the law"; in other words, it is in the *Zohar*, the principal text of the Jewish Kabbalah.[95]

While Viterbo's friend Reuchlin was threatened with censure, the cardinal never encountered such problems. This is particularly interesting because as both Viterbo and Reuchlin grew older, their interest in Judaism only intensified. It may have been Viterbo's power that allowed him to remain unscathed as he translated Jewish works. It may also have been the support of three popes who undoubtedly had some interest in Jewish studies. However, the most significant difference between the two men is that Reuchlin published, and his texts traveled throughout Europe. Viterbo did not publish his manuscripts, so his work on the Kabbalah was unknown to scholars until several centuries after his death.[96] François Secret published Viterbo's now famous *Scechina* in 1959. Unfortunately, Secret's Italian translation was not included in the publication. The text remains in Latin, making it unavailable to a wide range of readers.[97] *Scechina* was written at the end of Viterbo's life. As previously mentioned, it was commissioned by Pope Clement VII and dedicated to Carlos V. A compendium of Viterbo's knowledge on the Kabbalah, *Scechina* is an extremely detailed exegesis on (what had come to be almost an obsession) on the Shekhinah.

Sol de Los Espíritus—Sun of the Spirits

As a prefix to his discussion on Egidio da Viterbo, religious historian Morocho Gayo reminds his readers that "according to St. Augustine, 'Sun of the spirits' assists man in obtaining the light of the truth."[98] Morocho Gayo knows well that the phrase describes the center trajectory of Viterbo's writings. Viterbo was continuously searching for the Divine Light that would illuminate his search for knowledge. He did so for three and a half decades, while taking an active role in the administration of the Church. The power that resulted from his close association with three popes allowed him a profound influence on the history of ideas that emanates from the early sixteenth century.[99]

Viterbo was involved in numerous history-making projects. His fame comes mostly from his political involvements, his relationship with the Vatican, and his sermons. Three projects provide a comprehensive narrative of his thought, all three of which were unknown to most scholars until the twentieth century. As mentioned previously, he was keenly aware of his unorthodox views and was wise enough to minimize his risk. Yet there was an additional aspect to his trajectory that influenced how knowledge about his endeavors circulated. For Viterbo, the secret was necessary. To this end, he used a mute dove to represent his own esoteric thought, which could have been for protection, but it also related to the concept that one of Viterbo's biographers terms "the poetic veil" that camouflages the narrative.[100] Viterbo rather crudely explains this by saying that "the concept of a higher truth is not meant for all by the Gospel prohibition of giving holy things to dogs."[101] Whether he perceived his fellow cardinals as dogs is not clear. But in consideration of his position at the "progressive fringe of Catholic thought," it is probable that most of Viterbo's fellow prelates in Rome were not interested or knowledgeable about the Kabbalah.[102]

Divine Archana

A few years after Viterbo began studying Hebrew, he wrote a story about a bishop visited by Michael the Archangel.[103] Michael appears while the bishop is performing a sacred rite and asks that "temples and altars" be erected in his honor atop a mountain. A second visit comes at night while the bishop is sleeping. This time the prelate "asks to be enlightened about divine matters so that he can answer the many questions that will be put to him." The story continues for several chapters, telling of the corruption of Rome by relating an altered version of the Europa myth. The original story is that Zeus fell in love with a princess and, in order to woo her, changed himself into a handsome bull, convincing her to ride on his back to Crete, where she ultimately gives birth to two of his sons. In Viterbo's version, the princess is an adulterous woman, and the beautiful beast is a false image like the "fine words" used by theologians to hide wantonness. In fact, the story continues that "all Italy is the bull of the fable," with the Apennine mountains as the spine of the bull, the Alps as the horns, and the Italian ports as the "mouth seeking and absorbing every sort of wantonness and wickedness." The story is prophetic. Devastation is coming.[104] The Sack of Rome of 1527 is predicted. The open mouth is bringing people and beliefs from all over the known world. The Church and its theology have no filter for the coming evil.

There is no resolution to the story, but it is clear that the bishop in the story is Viterbo. The presence of Michael is significant. The ultimate purpose of the apparitions is for Michael to reveal the divine secrets, which is a constant theme in Viterbo's writings throughout his life.[105] In addition, considering Viterbo's lifelong passion for the Kabbalah, including his later writing on the Shekhinah, it is no surprise that he chose Michael the Archangel to be God's messenger because "wherever Michael appears the Shekhinah also is to be found."[106]

There are two other brief notations of interest in the story of Michael and the bishop. As Michael is about to tell the story of Europa to guardian angels of other regions, he mentions that only the Jews had been preached "the truth concerning God." When the angel of Italy heard this, he began running "on about consuls, tribunes and emperors," diverting from what Michael said about the Jews.[107] The second instance is in an earlier chapter titled "That Divine Things Cannot Be Naturally Learned," and Michael proposes that mortals "should not strive to know what is beyond the capacity of the human sense to perceive." He warns of the fate of Icarius and Lucifer, and recalls Virgil, who "shrouded all his teachings in elegant but obscure verses." Ultimately Michael reminds the bishop that "unable to endure the light of day, the bat accepts dusk and night. . . . We need to seek higher things without insolence and superstition." Christ said "he who will have found me, will find life. What we seek is the wisdom which radiates into our minds from the Father and enlightens our thoughts. But [if the light is too bright, recall that] when the Jewish people could not look upon the unveiled visage of Moses, they observed it veiled."[108]

The Secret of the Chapel

It appears that by 1489 Marsilio Ficino foresaw the design of the Sistine Chapel ceiling twenty years later when he wrote, "In the very depth of his house, he [the practitioner of magic] should construct a chamber, vaulted and marked with these [celestial] figures and colors, and he should spend most of his waking hours there and also sleep. And when he has emerged from his house, he will not note with so much attention the spectacle of colors."[109]

Michelangelo began his project on the Sistine Chapel ceiling one year after Dionisio Vázquez arrived in Italy.[110] Vázquez must have undoubtedly been informed of the ceiling's trajectory because of his close association with Viterbo, who by all accounts was the "likely developer of the content of the Sistine Ceiling frescoes."[111] The collaboration between Michelangelo and Viterbo was natural. Michelangelo was also a student of Marsilio Ficino and had at least minimal contact with the famous Neo-Platonist Pico della Mirandola.[112] Ficino was employed by the Medici family in Florence. Michelangelo was taken in by Lorenzo de' Medici at the age of fourteen, where the boy studied under Ficino along with the Medici children.

While contemporary focus on the ceiling often notes the spectacular image of God creating Adam, the entire ceiling is, using Ficino's words, a "spectacle of individual things as the figure of the universe and its colors."[113] Even though it is located in the Vatican, the heart of the Catholic world, it is clearly not a Christian project. Within the ceiling itself, there is not one image of Christ.[114] Art historian Robert Sagerman has published two significant studies on the ceiling and the influence of Viterbo on its execution, where he proposes that "embedded in the program and imagery of the Sistine Ceiling is a detailed and systematic elaboration of . . . Jewish Kabbalistic mysticism."[115] According to Gershom Scholem, considered the master of Kabbalistic studies, the "Kabbalah is the traditional and most commonly used term for the esoteric teachings of Judaism and for Jewish mysticism, especially the forms which it assumed in the Middle Ages from the twelfth century onward. In its wider sense, it signifies all the successive esoteric movements in Judaism that evolved from the end of the period of the Second Temple [70 A.D.] and became active factors in Jewish history."[116] The Kabbalah focuses on what is called the *sefirot*, which can be explained as the "stages in the creation of the world."[117] These are "the theosophical and cosmological core of the Kabbalah," and are comprised of ten different levels and mean a "great deal more than the physical world."[118] It is Sagerman's contention that the Sistine Chapel ceiling is a representation of the *sefirot*, with the first nine stages represented in the main upper section and with the tenth "the real stage upon which the flesh and blood drama of human conduct is played out."[119] The complete picture that Viterbo hoped to present was a global representation of the "Shekhinah—the 'Divine Presence'" that "streams down from the" first level down to the tenth, "sustaining and remaking God's work of Creation from moment to moment," and is a "type of partnership, or covenant, [that] emerges between God and man."[120] It is here that the Viterbo's trajectory and the Sistine Chapel ceiling project intersect with the concept of the Shekhinah who has manifested herself in the material world. Viterbo writes: "And because no man can see You face to face and live . . . we would contemplate You through these formulas as befits our mortal condition."[121] The formula painted by Michelangelo on the Sistine ceiling represents the Divine, a juxtaposition of mystical meaning that represents a story that cannot be told. The production of the ceiling is a concrete marker in the development of Viterbo's esoteric thinking. His later association with Levita and other Jewish and converso scholars in Rome projected him deeper and deeper into the world of the Kabbalah and of the Jews. Although Viterbo does not reference the Virgin, it is my contention that the "formula as befits our mortal conditions" is actually the Virgin of the Apocalypse.

The Ontology of Light

In *Scechina*, Viterbo tells Carlos V to read aloud the verses of scripture; "Given by the light," learn Cesar, scrutinize, not just the exterior but penetrate the profound sense of the verse.[122]

The Shekhinah is the "feminine axis of the divine." She is the female aspect of God. She is many things. She is the image that manifests itself in "prophetic visions" in the likeness of a human. She lives in the imaginary of human beings.[123] She is associated with a burning light that does not burn. She is also knowledge from God that penetrates all of humankind existence. It was this knowledge that Viterbo sought with a passion. While the pope requested *Scechina* be written for the emperor, Viterbo wrote it for himself. *Scechina* is the culmination of more than three decades of study. It contains all that Viterbo knew about the Divine Presence.

The famous cardinal, also known as a politician, prelate soldier, and friend of the Medici, was not made famous by his writings. His choice not to publish most of his work kept his scholarly thoughts secret, just as the message he embedded in the ceiling of the Sistine Chapel. For centuries, he was known for having been the leader of the Augustinians when Luther "revolted" from the Church, receiving criticism in the form of a story publicized by the biographer Paolo Giovio in the mid-sixteenth century that depicted Viterbo as playing the lyre, according to Francis Martin, which implied that Viterbo was like Nero, who fiddled while Rome burned.[124] Martin also notes that until the mid-twentieth century Viterbo was considered one of the "frivolous" men surrounding the "hollow world of [Pope] Leo X."[125] In a section titled "Distorted Image," Martin notes that "during post-Reformation days" Viterbo might have been see as a "cultured" and "virtuous Renaissance prelate," yet he was also considered a "pioneer biblical scholar astray in cabalistic literature."[126]

No mention of his magnum opus, *Scechina*, is made until the twentieth century. In the 1950s Secret translated the folios into Italian, and published the work in its original Latin in 1959. *Scechina*'s dedication to Carlos V was perhaps associated with the pope's continued awareness of the emperor's tremendous power.[127] The date for *Scechina* is 1530, but considering its length of 240 folios, it is highly probable that Viterbo began writing the book soon after the Sack of Rome of May 1527.

In *Scechina*, Viterbo encourages Carlos V to take seriously the illumination he is to receive from God and the Shekhinah, to, essentially, study the narrative and allow the light—or divine knowledge—to enter his way of thinking. The divine knowledge in the *Scechina* indicates that he is the new Ulysses who will triumph over the Sirenes.[128] "Shekhinah offers him multiple aspects of what awaits him if he partakes of the Kabbalah's gifts."[129] He is encouraged to be silent in his thoughts and think of the "moon among the clouds" which is actually an invocation of the Shekhinah. Viterbo gives the emperor instructions on how to make his way through the *sefirot*—God's explanation of the creation—and promises numerous victories once he believes in the God of Abraham and Isaac.[130] In consideration of the lethal attack the army of Carlos V made upon Rome, it is remarkable to see Viterbo tell the emperor that he is "*pinceps missus a celo* (the prince who releases the secret), the new David, Solomon, and the new Cyrus."[131]

It is not likely that Viterbo's pronouncement that Carlos V was the new King of Israel actually influenced the emperor's later identification with David. Yet the coincidence is striking in that Viterbo's passion for Israel manifesting itself so strongly in the Sistine Chapel and in the *Scechina* again became visible when Carlos V's son, Felipe II, constructed his magnificent palace, Escorial, where all visitors were greeted with the six towering Kings of Israel.[132]

Viterbo's influence on *Hebraica veritas* in Spain is profound. If the history of ideas is explained generationally, the line begins at the home of the Medicis where Marsilio Ficino conversed with Pico della Mirandola and taught Michelangelo. Ficino later became Viterbo's teacher. Viterbo was the protector and mentor of Dionisio Vázquez, both in Spain and Italy. Dionisio Vázquez was the teacher of the great Hebraist Cirpriano de la Huerga, who was the teacher of two men known to be the greatest Hebraists (and great intellects) of Spain's Golden Age—Luis de León and Benito Arias Montano.

François Secret does not write of Dionisio Vázquez or Benito Arias Montano. But in his article on Viterbo's *Scechina* he explains, "The ouvre of the cardinal is situated precisely in the Gnostic tradition that is seen later in the century in . . . *The Names of Christ*, a Kabbalistic work by Augustinian Friar Luis de León, and the writings of de León's student, John of the Cross."[133]

5

The Sphinx

Carlos V, Escorial, and Benito Arias Montano

For Your Name to receive glory
order us to know your Torah

—Benito Arias Montano

The mythological sphinx brings to mind intellectual uncertainty and the quest for knowledge. Felipe II elected his *capellán* Benito Arias Montano to take on the role of the sphinx for the monarchy.[1] Montano's life was a constant riddle. Although Montano was one of the most prolific writers of the sixteenth century, even with all his words, no one quite knows who he was.

Benito Arias Montano, author of the verse opening this chapter and chaplain to the king, was in his early thirties when he became a priest in the prestigious Order of Santiago. Montano was the arm of intellect for the Spanish throne during the last decades of the sixteenth century. It was through Montano that Felipe II sought to achieve intellectual mastery over Europe through a mass of books that came from all parts of the Western world. Yet it is the mere existence of Montano, so deep within the royal enclave, that belies the grand design of Catholicism with his words "order us to know your Torah."

The father of the king, Emperor Carlos V, precipitated this theological ambiguity with his far-reaching religious ideas and associations. Felipe II was the inheritor of his father's ideals; nevertheless, the son created the grandest paradox. While Felipe II personally espoused the Christian-Jewish beliefs of his father, he forced the growing Spanish Empire to bend to his own type of Counter-Reformation that formed an intensely Catholic dominion. But, as did his agent Montano, Felipe II had his own Torah. It stood at the forefront of his sphinx-like palace, Escorial, in the form of six ancient Hebrew kings who held court over what used to be called Sepharad (the Iberian peninsula).

The Edifice

José de Sigüenza writes in his history of the Jerónimos that "some ask if there is another edifice in the world as grand [as Escorial]; and then they recall the Temple of Solomon."[2] San Lorenzo de Escorial sits like a gray sphinx on Mount Abantos in the Sierra de Guadarrama mountain range, forty-five kilometers northwest of Madrid, standing tribute to the Felipe II, king of Spain.[3] It was built during the Counter-Reformation period and is said to be a symbol of religious strength during Rome's intense battle with Protestantism.[4] Its construction came soon after the historic meetings of the Council of Trent, and its rigid outside design and solemn appearance speak of religious orthodoxy.[5] The somber presence of Felipe II's great project (with its ambiguously Catholic interiors) masked an altered trajectory that spoke of an intellectual, cultural, and religious mission that turned the conservative directives of Trent upside down.

There is common agreement that it is not an attractive place, yet its size and its history are noteworthy. The exterior is spartan, with nothing of note except its long blank walls. The original entrance has a front façade with the lone statue of San Lorenzo over the entry gate.[6] The structure is exceedingly grand—massive, gray, solemn, imposing.[7] For centuries, it was the grandest building in all of Europe. Its library's grandeur was said to surpass that of the Vatican's.[8] Escorial was said to contain the best art, the widest range of books, and the largest collection of holy relics in all of Christendom.

The builder of the Royal Monastery of Escorial was lord over a kingdom so large that it was said the sun was always shining over one of his territories. He was the son of the Holy Roman Emperor, Carlos V. Although his father had been elected and the glorious empire emanating from Italy no longer existed, the son of Caesar carried with him the weight of ruling most of the world. While it is hard to say whether Felipe II bore this responsibility any differently than other monarchs of his time, the most striking aspect of his reign is the product of his imperial dream—the building of Escorial, the palace-monastery that came to be titled the Eighth Wonder of the World.

From its inception, the palace/monastery/college named San Lorenzo de Escorial, located a day's ride west of Madrid, was a paean to knowledge. Creating his mark regarding the Church, Felipe II ordered his chief librarian, noted

Hebraist Benito Arias Montano, to assemble a new Polyglot Bible that would include side-by-side translations of Latin, Aramaic, Greek, and Hebrew. Conceived of as a new edition of Cisneros's *Complutense Polyglot Bible*, Montano's version would also include broadly extended sections on the Old Testament. *La Biblia Políglota* (also known as the *Antwerp Polyglot Bible*) came to be a succinct representation of Felipe II—the monarch with multiple allegiances, contradictory ideas on religion (for his time), and an insatiable thirst for creating things the world had never seen before.

The House of David

In a country where Jewish things were seen as despicable, the great-grandson of los Reyes Católicos chose to create with his monument for posterity an edifice that gave praise to the kings of Israel. Felipe's father, Carlos V, was the grandson of los Reyes Católicos. Born in the Low Countries, Carlos became king of Spain in 1516 even though he did not live on the Iberian Peninsula until he was seventeen.[9] His mother was Juana of Castilla (daughter of Isabel and Fernando) and his father was Felipe el Hermoso (Philip the beautiful), son of the Holy Roman Emperor Maximilian. Carlos V remained in the Low Countries when his parents moved to the Iberian Peninsula after his mother inherited the Spanish crown upon her brother's death in 1502. He never lived with either parent and only saw them a handful of times during his lifetime.[10]

Carlos V's education and training were his guides that assisted him in creating a "cosmopolitan" monarchy that exemplified a "universal temper" and that was "open to Italians, Flemings, and Burgundians" who, through the course of his reign, had ongoing contact with Spaniards. It was through this type of "Universal Monarchy" that conversos found a voice within the Christian religion, whether they believed in the tenets of Christianity or not.[11] A testament to this is a letter written to Carlos V by his agent (and former confessor) in Rome, which states that Carlos V should permit certain heretics their ceremonies so that they would remain loyal to the emperor.[12]

With the reign of Carlos V, Spain entered an era in which the monarchy took on a different position. Carlos V is described as highly spiritual but not Catholic. He was not known as el Católico (the Catholic) even though numerous texts have demonstrated his support of Catholicism. His was a monarch-controlled Catholicism. Américo Castro explains that Carlos V's "imperial movement aspired to draw a national profile that would stand in front of Carlos V's rivals and opponents, Luther and Rome."[13] A number of astonishing events placed these leaders in strategically powerful roles vis-à-vis the papacy. While the effect on Spain, at least on the surface, did not appear greatly changed, the effect on the colonies was significant. The struggle for power between Spain and the Vatican created an opening for multiple variations, producing a more heterogeneous development of religiosity as Spanish dominions spread throughout the world. Although the official pronouncements remained that Spain was the most Catholic country, with an intense devotion to the Holy Virgin, the reality of religious thought and belief was far from what los Reyes Católicos, Fernando and Isabel, had publicly proposed.

Identifying himself as Catholic, Carlos V placed himself among theologians who were consistently on the edge of tradition, at least in relation to the Spanish Church. Carlos V enthusiastically supported Erasmus's "cult of the spirit," which was seen as an affront to the rituals and dogma of the Church.[14] Erasmus of Rotterdam was Carlos V's counselor during the monarch's early adult years. Erasmus is known for his heterodox ideas that criticized many of the Church's rituals, including devotion to the Virgin Mary and other saints. Carlos V was so devoted to Erasmus that for a number of years he unsuccessfully tried to bring Erasmus to Spain, and he pressed the Spanish prelates to accept Erasmus' writings. Carlos V was also deeply involved in biblical hermetism and the Christian Cabala, as was the norm for European monarchs at the time.[15] A number of Hebraists, hermetists, and Kabbalists were closely allied with Carlos V, notably dedicating their major works to him.[16] As for Erasmus, it is well known that most of his following consisted of conversos.

Carlos V and the followers of Erasmus promoted, more than Catholicism itself, a unique Spanish Catholicism, emanating from a freedom created by an emperor who wanted to "throw the Pope out of Rome" and a significant and ambivalent population of recent Catholic converts.[17] A large number were eventually jailed and burned by the Inquisition after Felipe II took the throne. Even so, his popularity made it possible for later theological and spiritual movements, such as Florentine Neo-Platonism and humanism (vis-à-vis Erasmus), to enter the Spanish belief system.[18]

Solomon

After poor health forced Carlos V to abdicate the throne in 1556, Felipe traveled through Europe as the new king, Felipe II, and was greeted by large-scale celebrations. A banner placed on a triumphal arch in Antwerp read "In times past, the people of Israel were glad that King Solomon would rule the kingdoms that his father had granted him . . . . Just as Israel rejoiced, seeing Solomon triumph, even while the father put him in the royal throne, at which Israel rejoiced and gladly accepted him, as ordained by David."[19] There were similar displays in Ghent, Bruges, and Tournay.[20]

The association between Carlos V, Felipe II, and the kings of Israel was noted frequently in both their lifetimes. Historian Juan Rafael de la Cuadra Blanco writes that these associations arose from writers living in the Low Countries, appearing as early as 1515, the year before he was crowned king of

Spain, and three years before he was elected Holy Roman emperor.[21] The narrative begins with the fifteen-year-old Carlos V being named governor of the Low Countries by his grandfather, Emperor Maximilian. A celebration was given when the young governor arrived in Bruges. The event was documented in a "manuscript with magnificent miniatures and a text by Remy du Pues.... In one miniature . . . Carlos V sits on the throne of Solomon between four pillars of gold, surrounded by his counselors and subjects," with a script stating "in this day God sent the son of David to reign over his subjects."[22] This correlation continued throughout his life, especially in 1530, when Egidio da Viterbo dedicated *Scechina* to Carlos V—because he could be the new David, noting that he was the great monarch who would bring the world into the tenth century (or era):

> while it is the century of tribulations such that have never before appeared . . .
> there will also be the discovery of new lands . . . the rebirth of the holy language
> [Hebrew], and will be the century in which God has sent the new Messiah, or
> at least his minister, Carlos V to bring . . . the world that is slave to avarice, to a
> new jubilee, a new liberation . . . . The door that Ezekiel said was closed will open
> on the day of the Sabbath, and the key to the Kabbalah will be opened when the
> book *Scechina* is read.[23]

Although it is likely that Carlos V never read *Scechina*, his perspective on the religion of his subjects was (at least at times) the most open-minded that had been seen in early modern Europe. The same year that Viterbo was encouraging Carlos V to consider (for Christians) the nontraditional teachings of the Kabbalah, the emperor was working through a policy with his advisors that would permit Protestants to continue their traditions in case their services would be needed later. Viterbo writes: "Close your eyes Majesty, because you do not have the power to castigate the heretics, nor any way to change them nor their descendants. Be content that they serve you and are loyal, even though God may see them worse than devils."[24]

The election of Carlos V as emperor of the Holy Roman Empire came in 1519, when he was an unimaginable nineteen years of age. Over time his military and political power firmly established his independence from the Vatican, making him more of a Jewish/Hebrew (David/Solomon) figure than a Christian. Although his grandparents, Fernando and Isabel, never "bowed in unquestioning obedience before the Pope," they never imposed their will upon the Vatican as would their grandson Carlos V.[25] He came upon the throne of Spain with particular strength, having become by inheritance the ruler of a large percentage of the world known by Europeans at that time.[26]

There was constant sentiment that the reign of Carlos V was propitious and significant for the world, for the bad or for the good. As it was, his century is termed "'*inquieto siglo* (turbulent century)' . . . because of the ongoing and profound tension between the new and old, between the medieval and the modern."[27] As José Maravall describes, "a spiritual crisis such as this consistently brings enormous calamities."[28] The concern regarding the election of Carlos V was borne out in 1527, when the worst of all catastrophes befell Rome.

The Omen—Rome 1527

The "omens and divination" emanating from "the Sack of Rome . . . terrorized the common people" and weighed "heavily on Felipe II since his birth." The tragedy was announced during Felipe's baptism celebration, which "gave the diviners" an opportunity to announce great calamities that would occur in the future monarchy.[29]

Two major events were occurring at the time of Felipe II's birth. The first was the advancement of the Spanish army toward Rome, and the second was the gathering of a group of prominent Spanish clergy to discuss the Catholic Counter-Reformation.

In the city of Valladolid in mid-June, a group of clergymen gathered to discuss the Roman Catholic Counter-Reformation. The discussion centered on whether the innovative ideas of the humanist theologian Erasmus of Rotterdam (1466–1536) could be published and distributed in Spain.[30] Erasmus had been an advisor to Carlos V, Holy Roman emperor and king of Spain in 1517, while the young emperor was still living in the Low Countries.[31] The emperor was so enamored of Erasmus's work, he is quoted as saying he would build a bridge of gold if Erasmus came to Spain and taught at the University of Alcalá.[32] Although the Inquisition ordered the meeting, it was greatly supported and encouraged by Carlos V. The event was extremely significant. The attendees consisted of thirty-three of Iberia's most prominent theologians.[33] Approving Erasmus's new ideas would have brought reformation to the Spanish Church without the sense of revolt brought on by an entrance of Protestantism into the country. But the Spanish theologians were not ready for a change.

Months before the Asemblea de Valladolid there was already significant tension in the air. Pope Clement VII and the emperor were at odds. There had been conflict between Spain and France, and France's king had been captured. It was reported in early September 1526 that Carlos V "had submitted to his confessor the question, if he could withdraw from obedience to the Pope."[34] This particular request is of consequence because of the supreme symbolic authority carried by the pope; it was very likely meant as a warning of an upcoming confrontation. The continued tension and intrigue led to violence.

In a meeting previous to the Asemblea de Valladolid, Carlos V tried to gather all the important prelates and nobles in Spain in hopes of getting financial support from them so his armies could advance to Rome.[35] He was humiliated from the minimal response, yet he still sent his general (the Duke of Borbón) and troops to Italy. The emperor's secretary wrote at the time, "Cesar . . . did not know from where the money would come to maintain the troops; the Viceroy and Cardinal of Naples, our allies, do not support us; the Spanish soldiers murmur mutiny against Borbón and provoke everyone."[36] It was expected that blood would soon run in Italy.[37]

Back at the Asemblea, by the time most were in Valladolid, the news of the assault on Rome had already arrived. Borbón entered the city and destroyed everything, capturing the pope. The meetings were postponed for two weeks. The court was celebrating the christening of Prince Felipe (the future Felipe II) when the news arrived that the imperial army had sacked Rome and imprisoned the pope.[38] "Orders were instantly issued to abandon the intended festivities." More importantly, the announcement produced an "uncomfortable augury that the reign of the young prince boded no good to the Catholic religion.[39]

Although Carlos V was in Spain when the violence occurred in Italy, he was responsible for the disaster. His troops, Spanish and *Lansknechts* (German) mercenaries, who were advancing to Italy were poorly clothed and had not been paid. The generals in charge had told them that a pillage of Florence or Rome would satisfy the men's need for money. Yet the violence was attributed more to the general antagonism the army had for the papacy than for their general state of deprivation.

The news that arrived the day of Felipe II's christening was astounding. The city of Rome had not only been attacked; it was destroyed beyond recognition. Cardinals and bishops were herded half-naked through the city, sacred objects carried away from churches, and untold numbers of "people were hacked to pieces, their bodies lying about the streets and plazas."[40] One prelate wearing a diamond ring was taken prisoner. Not having the patience to remove the ring, a group of German soldiers simply cut off his finger. "Mothers, wives, sisters, daughters, and virgins" were taken from their houses or from churches and were raped. One priest was killed because he refused to give the Sacrament to a donkey dressed in human's clothing.[41] An unsigned letter found in the national archives of Spain related that "when the sack started, none were excluded, that meant all types of persons, all the churches, monasteries of monks and nuns, and the lodgings of the Pope at St. Peters. There was no chalice, Eucharistic dish, no gold, no silver left in any church . . . the vestments and other ornaments were taken without leaving a single thing, all was stolen without any respect. No house of friend or enemy was left that was not sacked or robbed."[42] The order for the attack came specifically from the Court of the emperor. There are a number of accounts that many Jews and conversos among the soldiers had "the palm for ingenuity in unearthing treasure and contriving tortures."[43]

The pope was imprisoned in the Castello San Angelo in a small dark area guarded by Spanish soldiers. One historian reports that the directive from the Spanish was to starve the pope and other inmates of the castle.[44] The army continued its stay in Rome until Felipe II was nine months old, while the pope was incarcerated for seven months. Opinion was exceedingly negative regarding the emperor's decision to imprison the pope. An advisor informed Carlos V that if the pope was not released, Carlos V "could no longer claim to be styled '*Emperor*,' but '*Luther's Captain*,' as the Lutherans, in his name, and under his flag perpetrated all their atrocities."[45] The emperor's court was able to suppress news that the prelates in Spain were threatening to suspend liturgical services throughout the entire kingdom "as long as the Pope's captivity lasted."[46]

Alonso de Santa Cruz wrote in *Crónica del Emperador Carlos V* what appears to be an attempt to reduce negative opinion, that the emperor had not encouraged the violence.[47] Yet letters written to and from Carlos V in that period indicate that the emperor was fully aware of what was happening long before his troops attacked the city.[48] Two months after the sack, in a letter written by Carlos V to the Roman Senate, the emperor disclaimed "all responsibility for the Sack of Rome, to which he was not accessory," blaming the pope for the travesty.[49] That same year, Alfonso de Valdés, secretary of Carlos V, published a literary work explaining that "the Emperor is not guilty of any malfeasance . . . and how God permits all that occurs for the good of Christianity."[50] Stating that God had ordained the destruction of Rome, Carlos V spoke of the event as designed by Providence. This extreme act of defiance against the Church placed the Spanish monarch in a position of power against the policies of an antiquated system that was plagued with corruption. The coincidental christening of his son the day Spain received the news added weight to the position Felipe II later took regarding the Church. At the same time, this did not diminish either monarch's reverence to God. It allowed each to create his own vision of what he believed the Catholic religion should be, with its rules and its possibilities. This position of creativity allowed for a unique type of mission for not only the monks that lived in Felipe II's magnificent Escorial but also the *curas* (priests) who traveled to Spain's dependencies and created a new Catholicism that incorporated the old religion of the Israelites.

Interestingly, the Sack of Rome is not mentioned in many contemporary Spanish histories. Yet the timing of the violence as it occurs shortly after the birth of Felipe II and the excessive nature of the destruction in, of all places, the home of the pope and the center of the Catholic religion demonstrates the actual nature of the relationship between the Church, Felipe II's father, and Spain.

The Portuguese Felipe

Henry Kamen describes Felipe II as an individual who was "as Portuguese as he was Castilian."[51] This is related to circumstances that came into place before Felipe II's birth, strongly affecting the development of his religious and cultural perspectives. When his parents married, his mother, Isabel of Portugal (1503–1539), brought with her to Spain an entourage of Portuguese women. Among them was Leonor Mascareñas, who was born in Almada in 1503. According to Olwen Hufton, Mascareñas was orphaned as a child and sent to live in the Portuguese court. Born the same year as the empress, Mascareñas remained a constant companion to Isabel until Isabel's death. Carlos V thought so highly of her competency that he named Leonor Mascareñas governess for his three children after their mother died.[52] In the next generation, Mascareñas was also appointed the *aya* (nurse) of Prince Carlos (1545–1568), Felipe II's oldest son. The influence of the royal governess's role in the history of the early modern court cannot be underestimated. As Hufton explains, "this personage could leave an indelible print on the formation of her charges, the next generation of king and consorts."[53] As an attendant to the empress, she was among "the offspring of the most notable families of the Portuguese nobility."[54] Her father is said to have been a member of the third expedition to the Indies. Other Mascareñases were involved in the "discovery and conquests" of Africa and Asia.[55]

Ultimately, the court became Portuguese. With Carlos V constantly away and Felipe II's mother left in charge of the administration of the monarchy, Leonor Mascareñas was the most important person for the young prince. As it is constantly noted about the Jews of the Diaspora, in the early modern period, the term "Portuguese" was synonymous with Jew. Mascareñas's Portuguese background, while obviously Catholic (she gave freely to the Church), may still be questioned regarding her religious preferences.[56] During her life, Mascareñas was a chief benefactor of the Jesuit Order.[57] It is known that public Christians who were private Jews often gave to religious charities in order to avoid suspicion.[58] Having a conversa living within the royal house was not unusual. For instance, the mother of the famous convert Abraham Senior was an attendant to the queen of Portugal and *aya* to Prince Sebastian, Felipe II's cousin. Her husband belonged to the Royal House of Portugal and died with Sebastian in battle in 1578.[59]

Felipe II's choices in the building of his monument, San Lorenzo de Escorial, reflect the travel, education, and influence of his Erasmus-believing father, Carlos V. The emperor arranged for his son to be well educated in the ways of "illustrious humanists and scholars," such as Juan Cristóbal Calvet de Estrella and Juan Ginés de Sepúlveda.[60] Felipe traveled extensively in his younger years.

In fact, next to his father, he was the most traveled of all the European monarchs. During his reign, he lived a total of six years outside of Spain. Most significant for his views on religion, he spent one year in Germany, living among a number of Lutherans.[61] As Prince Felipe in 1548, he even attended sessions of the Council of Trent.[62]

The King's Identity

The stage was set for Felipe II when he was born. His father, the emperor, demonstrated to the world that he could overtake and destroy Rome. Although risking the ire of every other nation in Europe, Carlos V displayed his power, indicating that the Church was no longer interminable. and indicating that the pope was indeed a mortal man who could be captured and imprisoned. Simultaneous to his attack on Rome, Carlos V also attempted to reform Catholicism in Spain by his support of Erasmus at the Conference of Valladolid in the summer of 1527.

Felipe II's early caretakers, the influence of his father, his education, his travels, the people he consorted with while away from Spain: all these things helped develop a perspective toward the world that had not been seen before in any European monarch. As Marcel Bataillon explains, "Felipe took the vitality and power of the irradiation of the illuminist impulse that came from the Spain of Cisneros, through the assistance of Carlos V."[63] Even though Felipe did not come to the throne until half way through the sixteenth century, the influence of his policies on the Jews and conversos of Spain, Portugal, and the Americas is unquestioned. His approach to the rules of religion and heresy were another matter. While the reign of Carlos V was known for its openness, where Erasmus and the *alumbrados* were freely able to write their spiritual treatises, under Felipe II, nontraditional religious thinking again became a crime.[64] Felipe II's personal views on theology were secondary to the necessity of curbing Martin Luther's encroachment.

The Temple

The construction of Felipe II's monument was met with criticism about its proposed location, its grandeur, and its relationship to power. San Lorenzo de Escorial stands over the small village of Escorial, far from the nearest city. When it was built in the last half of the sixteenth century, it was considered far from civilization, inconvenient, and unattractive. The Corte (Royal Court) complained about Escorial's distance to any large city. The project has been described as hubristic, ungainly, ugly, dour, depressing, and wasteful. Others have identified it as the greatest edifice built in Spain, a tribute to the Renaissance.

Previous to the construction of Escorial, the Spanish kings maintained a nomadic court. Toledo had been the symbolic center of the kingdom because of its association with the most powerful prelate in the nation, the archbishop of Toledo. At the time, the decision was made for Escorial (and Madrid) to become the seat of the monarchy. The archbishop of Toledo objected strongly because the geographic change would mean diminished power for his position. There were also complaints because the village was barely inhabited, with very little commerce. Yet Felipe II proceeded. The construction took twenty-one years. He was almost at the end of his life when it was completed. What he produced was a monument to what was seen as Spain's greatness, in addition to the broad knowledge and sophistication of its king.

Existing like a riddle in the history and development of the Spanish Empire and the colonies that paid for its construction, Escorial, within its fortress-like walls, seemingly holds the explanation to the real ideology and history of the empire. In the present day, the entrance to the monastery is located on the south wall of the complex. A tourist enters and pays the fee. A group of employees, mostly men, are waiting for those who request a tour. If it is wintertime, they wear heavy dark blue overcoats with the royal insignia. They keep these on during the entire tour because the rooms are exceedingly cold. The visitor is led up what seem like thousands of stairs, through dark rooms full of furniture and paintings (many needing restoration). The available light comes from windows that give spectacular views of the countryside.

Felipe II's personal rooms are in an area strategically placed behind the altar of the basilica. Near the end of his life, when he was incapacitated, he was able to lie in bed and look through a plate of glass between his room and the church to witness the Mass being held. Although it has been more than four centuries since his reign, a visitor to that room is assured that those books and personal objects next to his bed are exactly the ones present during his lifetime. The books include *Libro de la oración* (1566) by Luis de Granada and the writings of Saint Teresa of Avila. Both were popular during his lifetime, and both indicate his interest in Erasmian theology, which encouraged a more personal and intimate form of religiosity. Both authors were popular yet controversial, having been investigated by the Inquisition. Granada was considered the more controversial; his works were banned by the Spanish Inquisition in 1559.

After the visitor walks through the maze of rooms and halls, she arrives at the Patio of the Kings. Ahead is a large empty open space. At the other end are columns and a gate to the outside. Tucked away between the columns and the gate, toward the right, is an anteroom with a stairwell that leads to the remarkable *biblioteca* (library). Once leaving the other buildings, if facing ahead, a visitor would see nothing of interest until coming upon the dark staircase that leads to the library—which, thanks to Montano, rivals that of the Vatican's. Felipe II's idea of a superior project became clear with his decision to make his monarchy an "active promoter of science and learning." He chose Gonzalo Perez, "a renown humanist," as his "chief secretary," and ordered survey to "be made of all the known world."[65]

Spain's King Felipe II has long been associated with Solomon. Although disputed by some scholars, it is commonly believed that his beloved project, the Real Monasterio de Escorial, was modeled on Solomon's temple and that Felipe II's aim was to create a New Jerusalem. Sigüenza explains: "Here, similar to the tabernacle of Moses, God places himself in the true ark of the testament, carried by the wings of the Cherubins. Here the divine law is instructed, it is guarded, executed, disputed, defended." As he describes in minute detail the never-ending list of magnificent aspects of Felipe II's palace-monastery, San Lorenzo de Escorial, he notes that men who produce these types of new inventions at times commit the "sins of hubris, arrogance, and vanity."[66]

Benito Arias Montano—*Capellán* and Advisor to the King

As enigmatic as Escorial, Arias Montano (ca. 1527–1598) continues to confound historians four hundred years after his death. Scores of publications on his life, his writings, and his influence keep appearing, including a significant number within the past ten years. Considered by many to be the greatest Spanish scholar of the sixteenth century, his name is closely associated with Felipe II. The two (supposedly) were born and died the same year. Although they did not cross paths until their thirty-ninth year, when the priest was named *capellán* to the king, they maintained a significant association regarding monarchial politics, religiosity, and the construction of Escorial during the remainder of their lives.

The "Catholic King" did not consider Montano as intimate a friend as Juan de Herrera, the architect of the palace, yet Montano was involved in the most significant political intrigues of Felipe II's monarchy.[67] The revolt of the Low Countries occurred while Montano was in Antwerp. The violent response of the Duke of Alba was tempered by Montano's presence, although Montano was continuously sending secret correspondence to the king. Years later Montano was sent on a mission to Portugal in anticipation of Felipe II's taking the Portuguese crown. His mission was to "explore and seek out opinions from Portuguese intellectuals regarding the impending succession of Felipe II to the throne of Portugal."[68]

Montano represented the heterodox, semi-heretical aspect of Felipe II's monarchy. This became clear when Felipe II commissioned Montano to be in charge of production for the Antwerp Bible. This assignment, appearing to be a celebration of Felipe II's lack of orthodoxy, is claimed by some scholars to be the crowning achievement of the king's reign. Montano's project included additional languages and extensive explications, many of which were written by the Montano.[69] Felipe II's choice was an excellent one. Montano was

FIG. 5 Benito Arias Montano, from Aubrey Bell, *Benito Arias Montano* (London, 1922). Courtesy of Hathi Trust Digital Library.

a polymath, the most erudite Hebraist in Spain, perhaps only outdone by his professor at the University of Alcalá, Cipriano de la Huerga (ca. 1510–1560). He describes Montano's perfect Hebrew as comparable to that of *el judio* Alonso de Zamora (the Jew Alonso de Zamora) who had worked on the Cisneros Bible sixty years previous.[70]

The Court Converso

Arias Montano was of the court. While deeply embedded into the world of the monarchy, Montano also exhibited an extraordinary interest in and knowledge of Judaism at a time when his friends were being incarcerated for being "too Jewish." This makes his description as a "court converso" quite a possibility.[71] He moved within the highest and most powerful circles. For most of his adult life, he had significant influence on the workings of the monarchy,[72] especially regarding the politics of the Indies. What made his influence particularly impactful was that he stood on the ground of the court and the Atlantic trading market. Montano was purportedly raised by the Alcocer family, members of the Portuguese merchant network. The Alcocer family, along with the Tovar family, were closely associated with the court in previous generations, later gravitating more toward trade. Both families were descendants of conversos. They were similar to what Jonathan Israel would call "Port Jews"—those who maintained trading links from Curacao to Lima, to the Philippines to the East Indies to México—thus making, for several decades, Arias Montano the true link between the court and the worldwide Portuguese merchant network.

The Center of Power

Within the circle of the king, what ultimately had the most impact on the dissemination of Montano's writings and ideas was his relationship with Juan de Ovando, who was simultaneously president of the Council of Finance and the Council of the Indies, making him, next to the king, the most powerful man in the Spanish Empire.[73] In his appointment to the presidency of the Council of Indies (1571), "he emerged as the dominating figure in formulation of all policies of colonial government."[74]

Fernando Navarro Antolín speculates that Juan de Ovando could have met Montano while the latter was a student at Salamanca, or a few years later in 1556 when Ovando was appointed ecclesiastical judge to the archbishop of Sevilla. Ovando's circle of friends included a priest named Diego Vásquez de Alderete, who had been one of Montano's teachers in Sevilla.[75] It is not clear how their relationship developed. However, when Montano was arrested by the Inquisition in 1569, a number of scholars project that it was Ovando who arranged Montano's quick release, although there is nothing documenting Ovando's intervention.[76] Until a few months before, Ovando had been Sevilla's chief inquisitor and continued to have an association with the Holy Office until 1573.[77] By the time Montano and Christopher Plantin were in the Low Countries producing the Antwerp Bible, Ovando was regularly writing Montano solicitous letters and requesting shipments of books from Plantin's press. The main aspect of their correspondence was regarding Montano's shipments of books, scientific instruments, and maps.[78]

Ovando's appointment as president of Council of the Indies in 1571 was crucial to the movement of Montano's beliefs and ideas to the colonies.[79] Although there had been others in this position, Felipe II gave Ovando unprecedented freedom in how the office was managed.[80] This was not repeated with anyone succeeding Ovando. In this role, Ovando had control over the continuous shipment to the Indies of slaves and goods, including numerous books that had been censored.[81]

The Statues

In August 1584 six immense statues were installed at the front entrance of the palace in what came to be called Escorial's "Patio of the Kings." Five meters in height, made of marble, granite, and brass, they stand alongside facing each other, as if in conversation. They represent the kings of Israel who assisted in the construction of the First Temple in Jerusalem.[82] While Felipe II's *capellán*, Benito Arias Montano, reportedly suggested the acquisition of the

FIG. 6 Statues of the Kings of Israel, from the Courtyard of the Kings, San Lorenzo de Escorial, Spain. Photo by author.

statues, they ultimately had to be approved by Felipe II, Spain's "truly Catholic King."[83]

Felipe II was involved in every detail of the construction of Escorial, including the placement of the statues; he was aware that any visitor would see them immediately upon entering the monastery. Symbolically, the statues present a confounding situation. Felipe II, "the Catholic King," maintained an active Inquisition, incarcerating clerics for their overtly Jewish writings. These known facts raise the question: why choose to locate the greatest figures of power from the Hebraic tradition at the most accessible location within his extraordinary

FIG. 7 Domus Israel from *The Plantin Polyglot Bible* (Antwerp, 1569). This is identified by some scholars as Solomon's Temple, which is what Escorial was often compared to. Courtesy Repositorio Documental de la Universidad de Salamanca.

palace? Scholars have generally supported the opinion that the statues form a trajectory that places Felipe II above all else as an early modern King Solomon, with his father, Carlos V, representing King David. In this role, Felipe II is the mediator between the ancient world and the new modern world. His role as Solomon provides an analogy to Christ in his wisdom and significance to the monarchy. Felipe II continuously overlooks Montano's possible *judaizing*, the arrests by the Inquisition, and the poetry praising the Torah. Yet the relationship between Montano and Felipe II is crucial because Montano's knowledge of the ancient Hebrew world is essential for Felipe II to become Solomon.

Felipe II constructed a symbolic church that demonstrated his unwavering requirements of true fealty and Christian right. While his obvious Catholicism stood firm against the encroachment of Protestantism, he developed his own creative religious structure for the monarchy.[84] Felipe II was capable of overreaching protection, should one of his ministers be accused of heresy, as in the case of Montano. Yet a misstep could also be lethal, as Toledo archbishop Bartolomé Carranza and the famous Luis de León came to know. Luis de León's arrest by the Inquisition is discussed in chapter 3. Carranza, arrested on charges of heresy, was at one point a favorite of the king, having been appointed archbishop of Toledo, the highest clerical position in Spain.[85]

Montano was of constant necessity to Felipe II. The king knew that Montano's talents were immense. The scholar not only spoke ten languages but was an invaluable consultant on political issues as wide ranging as the conflicts in the Low Countries, Portugal, and England.[86] In addition, Montano was careful never to criticize the king in any way, contrary to what Carranza and de León had done. Montano's religious beliefs and writings were not a threat to the monarch. Felipe II seemed to celebrate Montano's lack of orthodoxy and provided an immense amount of money to the Antwerp Bible project that emphasized Montano's highly erudite and unusually deep knowledge of Hebrew and the Old Testament.

Montano was an enigmatic scholar who became one of the most influential men in sixteenth-century Spain. Aside from Miguel de Cervantes, Benito Arias Montano is the most well-regarded author of Spain's Golden Age. Numerous Spanish historians and philologists have noted the difficulty in studying his work. Historian Pedro Urbano González de la Calle has been repeatedly cited for having said that he experienced "terror" while conducting a scholarly analysis of Montano, that a solid knowledge of "linguistics, philology, history, philosophy, and theology" would be needed to even approach Montano's writing.[87] González de la Calle notably neglects to mention Judaism.

In 1570 Montano was completing his work on the Hebrew section of the Antwerp Bible when he was taken with a serious illness. After his recovery, he authored a poem thanking God for his returned health:

To you King, God Save you
    and to your subjects who fear you
    and that your works are successful
    and complete your book in his days
Not for us Lord, not for us
    only for Your Name to receive glory
    order us to know your Torah
    so that we can serve you so much, so much
What should I give in exchange to my God
    what should I express in my praise
    now that he has listened to the voice of my troubles
    and he granted me salvation
And he cured me from my illness
    he made me rise over my feet
    for my works he rewarded me
    when I was in the middle of my sorrow
I have confidence that my eyes will see
    to complete the sacred books
    and before my kin they will marvel
    in my presence, the great men
And the entire earth will praise
    to listen to his great kindness
    I urge in the language of Father
    so that his *Torah* will be good.[88]

While the Antwerp Bible has since become known as one of the great treasures of late-sixteenth-century Spain, at the time it was decidedly a great failure for Felipe II. The Vatican initially approved the publication but eventually banned it for reasons of heresy. Felipe II had been seduced by the idea that he would outdo los Reyes Católicos.[89] Montano wrote to Felipe II predicting the polyglot would "provide much glory to the name of the king and bring great enhancement to his esteem and reputation, that would extend to all Christians."[90] Yet there was much controversy. It was circulated that "collaborators were on the borderline between orthodoxy and heresy," with a number of theologians actually giving the Bible the name "flag of the synagogue."[91]

The project was fully supported by Felipe II even though it was continuously criticized or at least warily critiqued by Montano's friends and enemies. In a letter from his friend Fray Luis de Estrada to the influential secretary of the king, Gabriel de Zayas, Estrada writes that speaking to people who do not understand Hebrew will cause those listening to arrive at the wrong conclusion and make them think that to believe these ideas would mean being a heretic (a Judaiser).[92]

A Reconfigured Infancy

The mythical quality of Montano's life begins with the dates of his birth and death being conflated with those of Felipe II.[93] The details of Montano's life are continuously contested due to the paucity of (and contradictions in) existing records. Historians venture to say that he was born in Fregenal de la Sierra, near Bajadoz, in Extremadura, an area close to the Portuguese border, but there are no records that document his birth or the names of his parents. An early biographer of Montano, Tomás González Carvajal, notes that even though the *capellán* "was born in Fregenal de la Sierra, diocese of Badajoz," his close colleages Cipriano de Valera and Fr. José de Sigüenza "could not verify this information."[94]

Most sources ascertain that the name of his father was Benito Arias (although in one document regarding Montano's birth, his father is listed as Juan Arias), but his mother's name is not known. As Montano himself writes, the elder Arias was a literate man who was known to the Inquisition of Llerena, and he was an expert at calligraphy and sketching in addition to being an expert at astronomy, astrology, and music. The son also notes that his father authored for Montano a book regarding the movement of the stars and orbits.[95] There is no mention of how long the father lived, whether he lived outside of Llerena, or any information regarding his death. Montano explains that his father was "*bastante anciano* (exceedingly old)" when the astronomy book was authored.[96] Writings about younger Montano's life indicate that he left home at the approximate age of six and that he no longer lived with his parents after that time, yet there is no mention of what happened to his father and why they were separated. While Montano moved from place to place and lived with different families (and at times with different clergy), there is no notice of where his father was at the time, which would have been noteworthy if he were still alive.

Montano's mother is only mentioned once, in Montano's *limpieza de sangre* investigation. Her name was reported as either Isabel Gómez or Francisca Martín Boça or Boca.[97] The veracity of this information is highly questionable as many *limpieza de sangre* investigations contained numerous falsified documents, and especially because Montano was later found to have submitted an inaccurate baptismal certificate for this same investigation.[98] The person who Montano repeatedly said was his mother was Isabel Vélez, daughter of Álvaro de Alcocer and Isabel Vélez of Toledo (later Sevilla). Álvaro de Alcocer was a secretary to Carlos V and a known converso of some importance in Toledo.[99] According to Linda Martz, Álvaro de Alcocer committed suicide in 1556. According to a number of Spanish scholars, Montano was raised by the Alcocer family.

Here Arias Montano's life fits closely with that of the converso merchant families. Daviken Studnicki-Gizbert describes a practice "of sending young boys to be educated by their uncles or grandparents—a form of interfamilial adoption . . . . Raised in this manner, young men had two or more 'fathers.'"[100] In this case, Montano often referred to Isabel Velez as his mother, leading scholars to develop varying conclusions about his life, questioning if this was possibly true.

To confuse matters further, according to Montano biographers, the Alcocers lived in Sevilla. Yet, while Montano was still a child, the family home was Toledo. The Alcocers did not move to Andalucia until Montano would have been in his late fifties. Scholar Gaspar Morocho Gayo cites letters written by Montano indicating that he lived on Isla de la Palma in the Canary Islands as a child, and returned a number of times to Extremadura to study with a particular scholar.[101] If Montano was providing the correct information, this history, in combination with his deep relations with the Alcocers and the Tovars, places him in the center of the Sephardic merchant class (and slave traders), well established in Sevilla and Portugal's islands (las Canarias and Cabo Verde) off the west coast of Africa.[102]

In what appears to be a politically motivated comment, Morocho Gayo assures his reader that Montano is not a descendant of conversos because there is no evidence. In addition, he provides the example of a number of famous Hebraists, "including Pico della Mirandola, Reuchlin, Marsilio Ficino, and Egidio da Viterbo, who were considered the greatest thinkers of medieval Sephardic Jewry, yet they were not Jews."[103] In what appears to be a nod to those who demand that the Christianity of Montano be unquestioned, Morocho Gayo mentions famous conversos Pablo de Santa Maria, Alonso de Cartagena, and Gaspar de Grajal—either converts or descendants of converts—who were unquestionably the most pious Christians. Finally, he even cites the Virgin Mary and Jesus Christ, who were Jews yet became sincere Christians, "something the Church has not always taken into account."[104]

Perhaps the answer to Montano's lineage lies in the narrative describing how, in the mid-seventeenth century, the poet Francisco de Quevedo y Villegas is said to have written a (now lost and probably inaccurate) account providing information on Montano's mother and sisters. Quevedo wrote the text while in prison, having been incarcerated by Felipe IV and the king's minister, the Conde Duque (Count Duke) of Olivares. According to Morocho Gayo, Quevedo may have intentionally falsified the text to "salvage the good memory of Arias."[105] If there is any truth to the statement by Quevedo, the multitude of stories regarding the life of Montano are, for the most part, incorrect. It appears that the polymath himself encouraged (with reason) many types of misrepresentation. His concern about being identified as a converso does not appear to have been significant to him, considering the nature of his subject. Perhaps it was more about the significance of his parentage; he might have been the illegitimate son of a highly placed individual, perhaps a priest, and was forced to occlude his genealogy for that reason. In terms of his fantastic ability as a Hebraist, he did not seem concerned about the risk involved regarding the Inquisition.

A popular verse during Montano's lifetime alluded to his converso background:

> Pork assumed from a Spanish crypto-Jew
> The famous mountains of Aracena
> Where Arias escaped from the world[106]

As has been noted in the lives of numerous conversos after the Expulsion, there is much ambiguity regarding birth and family information. It was common knowledge that many or most of the resulting *limpieza* certificates, Montano's included, were based on falsified data.[107] Montano stated in his work on *Abdias 20* that after the Expulsion, Jews remaining in Spain maintained their language and traditions. The Jews made their practices obvious so they could easily recognize each other.[108]

In an excellent study of Montano's writing, Sergio Fernández López surmises that Montano must have had extensive exposure to the Hebrew language and Hebrew texts long before his university education, perhaps since infancy.[109] A converso placed at the highest levels of society and power was simultaneously privileged and vulnerable. As mentioned previously, Montano was a converso form of a court Jew. His unexpected entry into Spain's most prestigious Order of Santiago is attributed to his fear of facing a *proceso* (Inquisition trial). It is noteworthy that he only needed to complete three months of the novitiate to receive his full orders, which was unheard of at that time.[110] Montano's appointment of *capellán* to the king occurred seven years after his arrest by the Inquisition.[111] Montano's confrontation with the Inquisition did not keep Felipe II from making him as an intimate advisor for political and religious issues.[112] Yet even with the protection of the king, the Inquisition continued to hound the scholar for years, although he never suffered the consequences that his colleagues did.

At the time, scholars and theologians could cite freely from the Greek philosophers, but they ran afoul of the Inquisition if they cited any Jewish sources.[113] This was not the case for Montano. Attributed to his support from the king, Montano maintained a literary freedom not otherwise experienced in sixteenth-century Spain. He was able to use Hebrew sources openly and frequently.[114] As explained by Fernández López, "el amparo regio le permitió disfrutar de ciertas licencias que algunos de sus amigos no podían ni imaginar (the King's protection allowed him license that some of his friends could not even imagine)."[115]

Once Montano completed his mission regarding the Antwerp Bible, the king assigned him to assist in the design and development of the library at Escorial. The Hebraist considered this assignment to be tedious, but it proved to be his most significant contribution: to preserve scores of Hebrew texts from being burned by the Inquisition. Montano's protected position as librarian of Escorial promoted him into the unusual (considering his murky *limpieza de sangre* status) role of an Inquisition censor, allowing him to store censored material.[116] The Inquisition was heavily against the production and circulation of Bibles in Spanish.[117] Books were sent to the Escorial library and were evaluated for their orthodoxy.[118] Montano developed a method where he only extracted the "offending" pages instead of disposing of the entire book.[119] It is not clear how many books were saved in this manner, but, as Fernández López proposes, Montano's actions "changed the destiny of the few Jewish bibles published in Romance (Spanish) that still existed."[120] Using the power of a king who was dictatorial and (at least outwardly) profoundly Catholic, Montano forced the Inquisition to send disapproved Bibles to the care of the monks at Escorial.[121] The Escorial library, therefore, ultimately became a safe repository for heterodox writing either placed on the Index of Censures by the Inquisition or considered inappropriate because of its Arabic or Hebrew content.

The Indies through Sevilla

"The fabulous riches that arrived from the Indies attracted to her [Seville's] banks individuals from all parts of Spain and from the rest of Europe, and she soon became a 'new Babylonia.'"[122] Sevilla was the environment that suited an unorthodox thinker such as Montano. Stafford Poole describes the city as "a place not only of great commercial achievement but also of cultural and religious ferment, a rich breeding ground for every kind of heterodox belief and teaching." Poole adds "many saw in Seville a hotbed of crypto-Protestantism from which not even the clergy were exempt."[123]

Although Montano never traveled to the Americas, his presence in Sevilla, in addition to his connections with individuals deep in the colonial power structure, provided him a perfect view toward the West. His significant status among the power elite of Spain included relationships to those who established colonial policy and those who traveled to the colonies, and his choice to live in Sevilla after his retirement from service to the king placed him in a position of being intimately aware of the transatlantic relationship between Spain and the Americas. All these factors contributed to the safe passage of his writings (and ideas) to the Indies. High-ranking clergy had access to the Antwerp Bible and many publications that were considered unsavory by the Spanish Inquisition.[124] Montano's political and intellectual status in addition to previously existing familial relationships led his ideas to the precipice of the Iberian world. Montano's move to Sevilla as a boy was more likely connected to unknown familial relationships that were already part of the elite infrastructure of the city. Sevilla itself is known to have become the door to the Americas. It was an environment populated by merchants who, with their wares, changed the European perception of the marvelous and created a space for a new type of knowledge.[125]

The relationship between Montano and the Alcocers came to be of paramount importance to the future trajectory of Montano's religious beliefs and his writings to the colonies. The son-in-law of Álvaro de Alcocer, Diego Díaz de Becerril, was the treasurer of the Consejo de Cruzada, an entity that regulated orders from the pope regarding the privileges, favors, and pardons given to Spain as it sought to convert nonbelievers. There was a significant economic benefit to this as Montano most likely assisted the Alcocers while the Hebraist was in Rome in 1569.[126] In 1571 Montano intervened for Becerril's son, Gaspar Vélez de Alcocer, by writing to the scholar's close friend Juan de Ovando, president of the Council of the Indies, requesting a license to trade in the Americas.[127]

Montano's friends the Tovar family were also known as a powerful Portuguese merchant family. This relationship evolved from Montano's friendship with Simon de Tovar's father in-law, a physician named Acosta. Tovar's second wife was Acosta's daughter. At some point Montano made a commitment to Acosta about looking after his daughter upon the physician's death. Over time, Montano became so close to Tovar that the merchant dictated his last will and testament to Montano and left the scholar in charge of his estate after his death. It is also documented that Montano spent his last days and actually died in the Tovar home.

Tovar was a pivotal player in the trade between Iberia and the Indies. He was born in Faro, in the Algarve region of Portugal, and studied at Salamanca and later at the School of Medicine in Guadalupe.[128] By age forty-two he was established as a merchant in Sevilla in addition to being a well-respected and published botanist.[129] He is known for making the avocado popular in Europe and for bringing the tulip to Spain from the Low Countries. His goods traveled between Sevilla, Lisbon, Antwerp, Cartagena de Indias, and Lima.[130] He was known for importing gold, silver, and precious stones from the Indies and in 1595 contracted to export slaves to the colonies.[131] One of his collaborators was Jorge de Almeida, whose wife was the niece of Nuevo León's first governor, Luis Carvajal y de la Cueva.

It is at this point that the link between Arias Montano's world and the *judaizante* and converso world of Nueva España becomes clear. In 1595, Portuguese-born Luis Carvajal y de la Cueva (mentioned in a previous chapter) died in México City's Inquisition prison. His sister, nephew (Luis de Carvajal, "el Mozo"), and nieces were burned alive at the stake. That same year, Simon de Tovar contracted with Jorge de Almeida and two other men for the export of 250 slaves to the Indies.[132] Almeida was part of the Portuguese network of converso merchants working between México, Sevilla, and the Canary Islands.

The transatlantic aspect of the Portuguese merchant network has become a frequent topic of discussion in numerous academic texts. It was a tightly knit group of merchants of converso origin, working a seafaring network between Sevilla and the Canary Islands.[133] Tovar would not have contracted Almeida if they had not been part of the same trade group, termed the Portuguese Nation:

> Its members were to be found in all the major ports and cities of the Atlantic world . . . . All told, the Portuguese Nation numbered twenty-thousand souls and would have constituted a sizable city if they had ever been gathered in a single location . . . . [There were] . . . large, well-established quarters of Seville and México City, reaching close to three thousand individuals . . . . The foundation and rapid growth of the community of Portuguese *conversos* and Sephardim . . . flourished in the small market towns throughout the Americas and the Iberian Peninsula, as the traders of the Nation involved themselves in small-scale regional trading or were drawn to emerging centers of economic activity such as Guanajuato, Zacatecas, and San Luis Potosi in northern New Spain.[134]

Jonathan Israel describes the Portuguese trading merchants as epitomizing the restlessly fluid, border-crossing, and culture-bridging qualities that characterized life in the Atlantic basin.[135] Most importantly they were "extraordinarily diverse": among them were "practicing Jews who adhered closely to the traditions, crypto-Jews and Christians descended from Jews known as New Christians, *cristaos novos* [conversos] . . . who maintained, however imperfectly, some form of Judaic religious observance and identity."[136]

The Circulation of Books

Through the legitimate trade network leaving out of Sevilla and through the Portuguese Nation of Atlantic traders, Montano's books were frequently shipped to the Indies. The publisher of the Antwerp Bible, Christopher Plantin, printed seven hundred copies of the five-volume set. Other works by Montano also sold well through the legitimate market. *Comentarios a los doce profetas* (Comments on the Twelve Prophets) sold for the "high price" of forty-two *reales* and was later reshipped where the price dropped to only five *reales*.[137]

Legal trade was only a fraction of what was traveling to the Americas. There was significantly more sent to the Americas as contraband. It is believed that "permissive attitude" of Juan de Ovando, president of the Indian territories allowed "many books [to enter] America that were at the time prohibited in Spain."[138] The transatlantic nature of the merchant network also contributed to the movement of books. As Studnicki-Gizbert describes in his excellent book on the Atlantic trade of the Portuguese merchants, "This transnational trading system rested, perforce, on contraband trade, smuggling, and close relations with other merchants based in states that were, at one time or another, at war with the Spanish empire."[139] One shipment confiscated in 1585 indicates the possibility of what could have been traveling to the colonies "without license." A 1914 publication by the Mexican government on the circulation of books to colonial Mexico explains: "The book was, and has always been, the central medium of propaganda, for this reason the entrance of prohibited books was strictly controlled, so that heretical [Lutheran and Jewish] doctrines would not contaminate those who were not strong believers."[140]

Transatlantic Tradition and Religiosity

Arias Montano was central to the distribution and circulation of Jewish tradition and religiosity through his associations with Ovando and the Alcocer and Tovar families. The limitations normally placed on the movement of published texts were eliminated—providing the same type of freedom that Montano was able to exercise in his theological writings. During his life, it is said that he sent hundreds of books to the Americas.[141]

Merchants with the required licenses generally engaged in contraband trade that included books *afuera de registro* (not registered) with the Casa de Contratación (Spain's Custom House). For example, on December 11, 1585, a book vendor named Diego Navarro Maldonado was tried for bringing prohibited books to the Indies without a license on the ships *Que Dios Salve* (God That Saves) and *Santa Maria de Arratia* (Holy Mary of Arratia). The books were confiscated at the port of Vera Cruz.[142] The cache was significantly controversial, especially because 197 copies of censored *Biblia de Vatable* (Vatable Bible), published in Latin and Hebrew, was included in the shipment. Among the group were eight copies of the Antwerp Bible, two copies of *Libros de Prophetas*, and four of *Libro de José, o sobre el lenguaje Aracano* (Book of Joseph, or regarding the secret language). In addition to Montano's works, numerous other censored books were in the group. These included seven books by Fray Juan Luis Vives, thirteen copies of *Flos Sanctorum* (Lives of the Saints), twenty books by Luis de Granada,[143] and six copies of Luis de León's *Nombres de Dios* (Names of God).[144]

The books were loaded on the ship in Sevilla and, according to the bookseller, Benito Boyer, were examined by the Inquisition before leaving Spain. A bookseller named José Treviño, who had already paid for the shipment in México City, sued Boyer because the shipment was confiscated. Treviño lost the case, and even though the Mexican Inquisition ordered the Bibles to be burned, the rest of the books were ordered to be sold.[145] As with other Spanish colonial regulations, the prohibition of books was only enforced sporadically.[146]

By the seventeenth century, book lists by the most prosperous bookseller in México City list Luis de Granada's works. Due to the prohibition against Bibles written in Spanish (or Hebrew) the Antwerp Bible (or any other Bible) is not mentioned. Yet by this time it is difficult to find a book list with Montano's works. It is known that the Antwerp Bible existed in México, having been cited by Manuel Espinosa de los Monteros in México City in 1825.[147]

In 1600 the famous library of Santiago de Tlatelolco in México City did not contain any text by Montano. Listed, however, were the works of Luis de León and Oleastro's commentary on Maimonides, Luis de Granada, and Pico della Mirandola.[148] As the following chapters will indicate, although the writings of Benito Arias Montano were banned by the Roman Inquisition in 1602, censorship and lack of visibility did not mean Montano's Jewish ideas had disappeared.[149] They were hidden for reasons of safety, and they resurfaced in a surprising and vibrant form. Although Montano's work was subject to "extensive expurgation," there were a small number of his texts located in México City's libraries.[150]

6

Miguel Sánchez, Guadalupe, and the Inquisition

─────────────────────●

Half a century after the death of Benito Arias Montano, Miguel Sánchez, a priest in México City, wrote of a Woman Clothed in the Sun—surrounded by brilliant light—and about to give birth to a child whose destiny is to save the world. In the story an evil dragon seeks to destroy the unborn child. The story does not end tragically. The child and his mother are saved by the Archangel Michael and an eagle that flies with them far away from the claws of the dragon. Michael is said to be the constant companion of another brilliant light—named the Shekhinah.

Numerous scholars on the history of the Mexican colonial Church consider a 1648 book by Miguel Sánchez to be the most influential text written in seventeenth-century New Spain. Sánchez's book is about the Virgin of Guadalupe, identified as the mother of Christ, who appeared near México City in 1531. He may have used his devotion to the Virgin in an attempt to reach the persecuted Jewish community of México, or at least to address his own thoughts and beliefs regarding Judaism. As Leo Strauss aptly notes, "The real opinion of an author is not necessarily identical with that which he expresses in the largest number of passages."[1]

El Santo Oficio—The Holy Office of the Inquisition

What was termed the "great conspiracy" of the Jews in New Spain reached its end at an *auto-da-fé* on March 30, 1648.[2] For the previous six years, México had been in chaos because of the overarching activities of the Holy Inquisition.

FIG. 8 Michael the Archangel, from *Novenas de la virgen Maria madre de Dios, parasus dos devotisimos santvarios de los Remedios y Gvadalvpe* by Miguel Sánchez (México City, 1665). Photo courtesy D. R. Biblioteca "Lorenzo Boturini," Basilica de Santa Maria Guadalupe.

Most of the *judaizantes* thought to be living in and around México City had already been arrested. A few weeks before the auto-da-fe, Father Miguel Sánchez received ecclesiastic approval for a manuscript he had just completed titled *Imagen de la Virgen Maria Madre de Dios de Guadalupe* (Image of the Virgin Mary Mother of God of Guadalupe). The book circulated among high-ranking Church officials for the next few months. The third and final approval came on July 2. *Imagen de la Virgen* appeared for distribution by the end of the year.

Sánchez was an eccentric secular priest who received much acclaim in his lifetime. He was born in Puebla near the end of the sixteenth century and educated at the Royal Pontifical University in México City. After having been rejected for a teaching position at the university, he gave up worldly comforts and lived in a bare room at the sanctuary of Guadalupe. He was famous for his

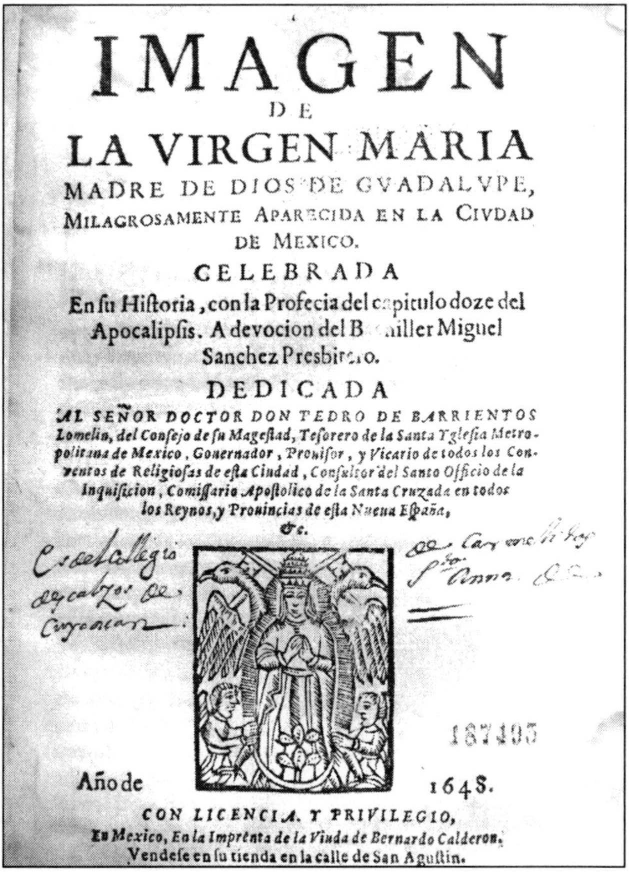
IMAGEN
DE
LA VIRGEN MARIA
MADRE DE DIOS DE GVADALVPE,
MILAGROSAMENTE APARECIDA EN LA CIVDAD
DE MEXICO.
CELEBRADA
En ſu Hiſtoria, con la Profecia del capitulo doze del
Apocalipſis. A devocion del Bachiller Miguel
Sanchez Presbitero.
DEDICADA
AL SEÑOR DOCTOR DON PEDRO DE BARRIENTOS
Lomelin, del Conſejo de ſu Mageſtad, Teſorero de la Santa Yglesia Metro-
politana de Mexico, Gouernador, Prouiſor, y Vicario de todos los Con-
uentos de Religioſas de eſta Ciudad, Conſultor del Santo Officio de la
Inquiſicion, Comiſſario Apoſtolico de la Santa Cruzada en todos
los Reynos, y Prouincias de eſta Nueua Eſpaña,
&c.
Año de 1648.
CON LICENCIA, Y PRIVILEGIO,
En Mexico, En la Imprenta de la Viuda de Bernardo Calderon.
Vendeſe en ſu tienda en la calle de San Aguſtin.

FIG. 9 Cover from *Imagen de la virgen Maria Madre de Dios de Guadalupe, milagrosamente aparecida en la ciudad de México* by Miguel Sánchez (México City, 1648). Courtesy of Benson Latin American Collection, University of Texas Libraries, the University of Texas at Austin.

sermons and was a friend of the most powerful of the colony, including the viceroy. Erudite to the extreme, it is said that he could recite all of Saint Augustine's writings from memory.[3]

The year that Sánchez published *Imagen de la Virgen*, 1648, was a watershed year for global events. The Treaty of Westphalia was signed, ending the Thirty Years' War. Sabbatai Zevi proclaimed himself the Messiah in Smyrna (what is now Turkey). The Dutch and the Spanish signed the Treaty of Munster ending the Eighty Years' War. The Spanish dependencies continued to pour money and resources into the crown's coffers. In New Spain, new viceroys kept replacing the old (with four in one decade). The colony moved further toward thinking it should be a separate entity with an economy, perspective, and identity distinct from Spain's.[4] Yet the *criollos'* frequent complaints did not quite yet amount to sedition. They continued to be loyal to the king but hated the Peninsulares (Spaniards born in Iberia).[5]

Of the public events affecting the life of Sánchez in 1648, the most notable was the "termination" of *la complicidád grande* (the great conspiracy), the Inquisition's supposed dissolution of the "main network of crypto-Jewish groups in México."[6] Sánchez was already working on *Imagen de la Virgen* when the Inquisition staged a series of arrests in México City in July of 1642 that were described as the "beginning of the destruction of the crypto-Jewish community in México."[7]

The Provocation of Evil

While a number of factors provoked the resurgence of the Mexican Inquisition, the arrival of the Spanish *visitadór* (visitor-general), Juan de Palafox y Mendoza, signaled the beginning of changes that a number of scholars believe brought the Inquisition to life again. Problems in the colony at the time required the presence of an authorized representative (investigator) of the crown. México was falling apart. In February 1639 news reached Madrid that "most members of the *audiencia* [congress] had openly defied Viceroy Cadereita," and the viceroy himself entered into "a bitter feud with the new archbishop." The viceroy's "control over the territory" was "at risk." Palafox arrived in New Spain in June 1640, sent to México as visitor-general by the king's minister, the Count Duke of Olivares, "to restore order and see that the crown's interests were secured."[8] The move was significant in that a visitor-general was "the foremost instrument of surveillance at the crown's disposal, designed to reduce corruption and increase efficiency in the administration."[9] Unfortunately for Palafox, the history of visitations in New Spain was problematic. He was sent to restore order to a place where the local officials strongly resisted any oversight. One viceroy, Montesclaros, wrote in 1607 that a visitation was "dangerous medicine" like "those whirlwinds that frequently arise in squares and streets, whose only merit is to stir the dust and filth that may be found in them and fling it all to the face."[10]

Palafox's intentions were ambitious. During his tenure, he sought reform in the ecclesiastic and secular areas of New Spain's administration. He intended to restructure indigenous parishes and compel the ever-powerful "Jesuits to pay tithes to the diocesan church."[11] He also "intended to reform the *audiencia*, curb the transgressions perpetrated by royal officials, reduce fraud in mines and ports, and grant the American *cabildos* [government administrators] the political responsibility and degree of autonomy enjoyed by their peninsular [Spanish-born] counterparts."[12]

What would ultimately have the most profound consequences for Palafox and for the people of the colony was his purposeful exaggeration of "the Portuguese menace" after Portugal revolted against Spain in late 1640. In an excellent analysis of these events, Cayetana Alvarez de Toledo explains that Palafox proceeded, thinking that any changes would assist in "effecting his reforms."[13] Palafox sent a letter to the viceroy asking for intervention by the Inquisition in order to maintain the security of the colony, noting that the Portuguese could easily take over New Spain. The Holy Office wasted no time in responding.[14] On July 9, 1642, the Inquisition ordered that Portuguese who did not have special permission from the Holy Office were no longer authorized to depart from México's primary port, Vera Cruz. The arrests began, and within two years the jail was overflowing.[15] The Inquisition trials of the prisoners continued in the background of Mexican public life through the 1640s. They were followed by the series of autos-da-fe staged in México City from the years 1646 to 1649.[16]

The tension, fear, and terror continued indefinitely. Vicente Riva Palacio, a Mexican historian and novelist, notes in the prologue of his 1908 novel *Memoria de un Impostor*,"while writing of the Mexican colonial period an author or historian cannot go more than one step in his research without encountering the Holy Office, which invades and monopolizes everything." Riva Palacio explains:

> "Why are most of my novels about the Inquisition? I answer you that in each period of the Spanish domination in México, a novelist or historian cannot go more than one step in his research without encountering the Holy Office, that invaded and monopolized everything, and if you are displeased when you find it in a novel, consider what it caused those who lived in those times, they encountered the Holy Office every minute of their lives, from the cradle to the grave, from the memory of their ancestors to the future of their most remote generation."[17]

It was in this context that the most prominent publisher in México, la Imprenta Viuda de Bernardo Calderon, released the Sánchez book, *Imagen de la Virgen Maria Madre de Dios*.[18]

Sánchez Imagining the Virgin

The Sánchez text brought notice to an almost forgotten century-old religious figure.[19] Through his passionate narrative on Guadalupe, he assisted in strengthening the *criollo* identity in New Spain and became known as a patriot for the colony. He also established a more solid base for Catholicism among the indigenous people.

Until 1648, the only written accounts regarding Guadalupe were minor notations about her apparitions. In what seems to be a reverie of enjoyment, Sánchez wrote the book *Imagen de la Virgen*, detailing her entrance into the material world and expounding on his considerable knowledge of the Old Testament, the theology of Saint Augustine, and the philosophy of Aristotle (among others). David Brading states in his monumental *Mexican Phoenix*, "The story . . . [of *Imagen de la Virgen*] enthralled the *criollo* elite of the capital [México City]."[20] Timothy Matovina, author of "Guadalupe at Calvary," describes Sánchez's book as having an "extensive influence" on the Mexican Guadalupan tradition.[21] Ernesto de la Torre Villar and Ramiro Navarro de Anda comment on the value of Sánchez's work: "the author as a vibrant *criollo*, placed his roots in the values of the indigenous past and crystallized this into the knowledge of *criollo* saints like Rosa of Lima and San Felipe de Jesus."[22] A noted historian of the Mexican colonial period, Jonathan Israel, plainly states that *Imagen de la Virgen* is "arguably the most important single publication of colonial México."[23]

The book, an elaborately written hagiography on the Virgin of Guadalupe of México, tells the story of how Guadalupe appeared to an indigenous man and of the miracles associated with her devotion and the importance of her presence for the *criollos* of New Spain. Sánchez is noted for bringing focus to her so many years after her initial appearance.[24] He is also well known for characterizing her as the Woman of the Apocalypse by John of Patmos, as seen in chapter twelve from the book of Revelations in the New Testament.

In *Imagen de la Virgen*, Sánchez portrays the Virgin as a woman about to give birth who is running from a seven-headed dragon: "At that moment another signal appeared in the heavens, it was a monstrous Dragon, very deformed, with the colors of blood, a horrible figure, it had seven heads, that carried seven crowns, he was diligent and attentive, directly in front of her showing his opposition to her, seeking to contain her so that the child would not be born to his proper destiny."[25]

Previous explanations have described the Woman of the Apocalypse as Christianity and the Dragon as the Devil. A close reading of Sánchez's text indicates that these interpretations have been misguided. As will be discussed later in this chapter, it is rather that the Woman of the Apocalypse represents the *judaizantes* and the Dragon is the Roman Church or the Inquisition. While Sánchez uses *Imagen de la Virgen* to cover numerous issues, the book has been noted over the past four centuries because it recounts the Guadalupe story. The inclusion of Revelations has always placed *Imagen de la Virgen* as a Christian or Catholic book. There has never been any question as to the author's theological trajectory. Yet Sánchez's occasional placement of one or two words, when taken in complete context, creates an entirely different meaning.[26]

My previous book, *Delirio*, centered on northern México, a region in which the first European settlers were Portuguese *judaizantes*.[27] The surprising location of converso narratives in so many places of Nuevo León often made me wonder just how many *judaizantes* migrated to northern México during the colonial period. While historical texts repeatedly denied this presence after the demise of the family of Luis Carvajal y de la Cueva, the first governor of Nuevo León, narratives kept surfacing about traces of Jewish traditions, albeit somewhat convoluted with Christianity.[28] It was this research that ultimately led me to the idea that the Mexican Guadalupe was somehow connected to the *judaizantes*. Conversations with Miguel Angel Muñoz Borrego, archivist at the State Archives of Coahuila in northern México, were encouraging. He had read about a Jewish–Guadalupe connection and was convinced of the possibility.[29] A close reading of *Imagen de la Virgen* surprised me with its frequent Old Testament references. David Brading identified the author's approach as Neo-Platonism, yet did not provide further explanations as to Sánchez's theoretical preferences.[30] Investigations into other writings by Sánchez are intriguing. In one text, deemed "unfortunate" by Brading, Sánchez wrote that "God called the Patriarch Moses to the lofty summit of Mount Sinai in order to graduate him as Doctor, to constitute chairs, and to give him the books of the law written in his own hands on the two tablets of stone."[31] Sánchez's mention of the Inquisition in *Imagen de la Virgen*, in addition to his reference to Guadalupe as a menorah, provided sufficient impetus to proceed with the investigation. With this information in mind, a close analysis of the premier text on the Virgin of Guadalupe in search of references to *judaizantes* does not appear so peculiar, especially in consideration of events occurring in New Spain as *Imagen de la Virgen* was written and published.

The Inquisition in a Hagiography?

Imagen de la Virgen is the only religious publication from mid-seventeenth-century México that mentions the Inquisition. Sánchez writes: "I do not believe there is a street, a corner, a plaza, or neighborhood that does not have many Holy Crosses exhibited with sacred veneration. In these years with a singular aim (I have noted this pattern) . . . as is publicly known, the never waning, notorious vigilance, the Apostolic Solicitude, the irrefutable zeal of the Very Holy Tribunal for the Inquisition has discovered, sentenced with its accustomed mercy, so many enemies of our Holy Faith."[32]

Sánchez references the Inquisition as he is saying that God has given the Virgin of the Apocalypse (Guadalupe) wings of an eagle. He notes that this image has a strong semblance to the Holy Cross. It is at this point that he notes the proliferation of crosses everywhere, "in these years with singular diligence," explaining that this is due to the intensified activity and "vigilance" of the Holy Office that occurred in New Spain between 1642 and 1649.[33] Solange Alberro, a historian of the Mexican Inquisition, is the only scholar that has referred to Sánchez's mention of the Inquisition in *Imagen de la Virgen*. She explains: "Since the patriotism of Miguel Sánchez is tied to religious faith, it is significant and logical that the enemies of the *criollo* nation are also those enemies of Catholicism, namely, converts who continue to practice Jewish rites." She emphasizes his mention of a "bad seed" and "enemies of our Holy Faith" and concludes that he is endorsing the work of the Inquisition, writing "obviously about the crypto Jews and México's '*Gran Complicidad*' that was discovered in 1642."[34]

Yet it appears that Alberro is mistaken—that the subtext of *Imagen de la Virgen* is not about *judaizantes* as enemies but about the Inquisition as the enemy of the *judaizantes*, and of God. As I show later in this chapter, Alberro is very clear in her condemnation of the Inquisition and its actors. She describes them as voracious and incompetent.[35] She is well aware of Sánchez's erudition. It is difficult to understand that she did not guess that Sánchez's praise for Inquisitor Juan de Mañozca and the others was a ruse.

Sánchez provides a clue when he brings up the subject of persecution (and the secret) describing Apocalypse 12. Sánchez writes of the dragon who has been thwarted in his pursuit of the woman and has decided to take vengeance on her descendants.[36] In response to the dragon's violence, Sánchez says the persecuted *hijos* (sons and daughters) can secretly apply all the verses of David's Psalm 16. The author's use of the term "secret" as he discusses how the dragon is looking for the woman's children brings to mind the *judaizantes*. An image arises of a woman about to give birth to a Messiah, plainly stated in the interpretation of the book of Revelation. The dragon cannot destroy her; therefore, he seeks out her children and their children. Here, the Inquisition comes to mind; while it has not been able to rid New Spain of *judaizantes*, it seeks to eradicate their descendants.

Sánchez was completely devoted to the work of Saint Augustine. His use of the Psalms from the Old Testament was surely influenced by Augustine's analysis in *Exposition of the Psalms*. As Sánchez explains, "each one of the sons of México can secretly ponder his intentions and feelings with all the verses of Psalm 16: Oration of David, and in secret apply all of his verses."[37] Augustine's explanation of Psalm 16 is telling. Those persecuting David are God's greedy and prideful enemies, "ungodly" people who do not understand him, and "are stuffed with pork." They are the ones who cried out before Christ's death, "Hail, King of the Jews."[38]

The question remains, why would Sánchez mention the Inquisition and shortly after use the word "secret"? Is there any other reason possible besides a connection to the Inquisition or crypto-Judaism? The word "secret" very strongly suggests a connection to *judaizantes* in hiding—as Saint Augustine states, "as if I am a small animal that inhabits hidden places." The idea of greedy and prideful persecutors brings to mind the men of the Holy Office. The practice of confiscating goods from the reconciled was a norm for the Inquisition; in New Spain, this more often than not meant that the monies were not handed over to the crown. Solange Alberro explains: "When the money and goods were confiscated by the handful from the rich *judaizantes* the Inquisitors' wealth became obvious; the money filled the chests of the Inquisition, it seems like they forgot the gold was supposed to be handed over to the Supreme Office of the Inquisition [in Spain] and they proceeded to divide up what they had put in their boots: their salaries were suddenly inflated, the number of assistants increased greatly, they filled their hands with the money they took."[39]

Augustine's interpretation of Psalm 16 refers to gentiles who eat pork, which could be easily interpreted by Sánchez as the officials of the Inquisition. They were not *judaizantes* (or at least those who denied this) and they ate pork. They literally condemned the "King of the Jews" in New Spain: they incarcerated (for years) the richest Jew in México, Simon Váez Sevilla, who was arrested by the Holy Office in 1642.[40]

Duplicity

Shortly after Sánchez mentions the Inquisition, he cites Psalm 8:3, "The children are witnesses, to confuse [confound] our enemies, when ordered, they openly demonstrate warm affection and amorous applause to our Holy Cross."[41] Psalm 8:3 is central to the implementation of Sánchez's alternate message concerning the Inquisition. Here he tells of children praising the Holy Cross to show their loyalty to the Inquisition, yet in using the words "confound" and "when ordered," he questions the honesty and loyalty on the part of the children—and their parents. Sánchez adapts his interpretation to the presence of the Inquisition and its ubiquitous representative, the Holy Cross. He uses the word to confound in the psalm. Instead of the children praising God, as the psalm states, Sánchez has the children praising the Holy Cross.

In the other versions, the psalm states that the children are praising God so that their enemies can be overcome. Using the word "*confundira*" changes the context of the act. To confuse is to present a situation that has a hidden or double meaning. It is a representation of something that is not easily decoded. It is especially conspicuous when the children are ordered to perform the act "on demand." Normally the psalm is interpreted as the children being more honest—and saying what is really going on—in contrast to the duplicity often shown by adults. Yet the children are reciting on demand—the issue of innocence is no longer valid. Could this not be an action that would keep the Inquisition at bay, just as Sánchez insinuates that the placement of crosses everywhere is a way for people to make the Holy Office believe they are good Christians? Yet there had to be another text of the psalm somewhere that contained the word "confound" or "confuse"; otherwise, where did Sánchez get his interpretation? The French Bible *Louis Segond* contained these words within the psalm.[42]

Most significantly, the book *Memorias de Luis de Carvajal* contains the same psalm cited by Sánchez: "God brings praise from the mouths of babes that suckle to confound the enemy and avenger."[43] Although it is not known if Sánchez knew of Carvajal's mention of Psalm 8:3, the importance of the message for Mexican *judaizantes* would have been significant for both men. During his torture and imprisonment in 1595, Carvajal mentions Psalm 8:3 in his letters to his family, which prompts the Inquisitors to interrogate him regarding why his sister remained silent about her family's judaizing.[44] In *Memorias*, Carvajal speaks about his younger sister Anica, who was placed in a secret house of the Inquisition and was threatened with torture but never divulged damaging information about the rest of her family.[45] Her siblings taught her so well that even after two years among Christians, she had not forgotten the Jewish traditions she had learned. Here Anica provided evidence that she was well taught and loyal to her family. She presented a strong constitution, at least at that time, which very likely surprised and confounded the Inquisitors. Anica later had a mental breakdown, delaying her execution a number of years. She was burned at the stake shortly after the Sánchez book was published in 1649.[46]

A third example of Psalm 8:3 gives further evidence that the phrase "*confundira*" was probably used in connection to *judaizantes*. Andrés Bernáldez alludes to this link in his *Cronica de los reyes católicos*, originally published in 1515.[47] In the book Bernáldez includes occasional personal commentary about his life. It is in one of these commentaries that he brings in Psalm 8:3: "Lord, you produced honored praise through the mouths of children and those who suckled, because of your enemies, so that you can destroy the enemy and the avenger."[48] Bernáldez cites the psalm after telling a story of his childhood: "After the wars began in Castilla between King Enrique and the nobles of his kingdom, the new people of Castilla would sing a song: The flowers of Aragón are inside of Castilla. And the children would make small banners; pretend to be nobles with riding horses, using sticks of cane; they would say: Banner of Aragón, banner of Aragón. And I would say it and would say it more than five times; well we can very well say here, according to the experience that followed."[49]

Bernáldez's locating the song "Pendón de Aragón" "after the wars began in Castilla between King Enrique and the nobles of his kingdom" is notable. Bernáldez reports that Fernando and Isabel were able to conquer Spain for God, and that the song "Pendón de Aragón" was an omen of what was to come. Yet a few paragraphs later he writes: "It is commonly known that when they [Fernando and Isabel] began their reign, most of the people of these kingdoms were against them." Considering this last comment, Bernáldez was singing "Pendón de Aragón" with the other children while most of Spain was against Aragón. What was he implying? While he does not use the words "confuse" or "confound," his later mention of the song is just that. He does not explain the inconsistency. He only details how Spain was full of thieves, heretics, and violent people, and that the Catholic Kings, as Fernando and Isabel came to be known, were able to bring order to the land. In the same paragraph he tells his reader that "they broke the arrogance of the evil ones, and placed their kingdoms in much justice, they started the fire against the heretics, with just reason, and constitutional approval the heretics have burned, and burn, and will burn in flames until there is none left; and even more, bring the mosaic heresy to its end."[50]

In consideration of the limitations he had on what he could say openly, it would be reasonable to expect that Bernáldez would counter a controversial statement with something more politically acceptable. As Leo Strauss discussed in *Persecution and the Art of Writing*, one incongruent word or sentence in a text is a strong indicator of a relevant subtext present in the work.[51] Américo Castro provides further evidence of Bernáldez's obscure trajectory in *Aspectos de Vivir Hispanico*: "Bernáldez's motive in citing this psalm is very clear, but his meaning is dark and those commenting on the original Hebrew text give various interpretations on which I cannot elaborate at this moment."[52] Castro provides this commentary immediately after he mentions an incident concerning the archbishop of Toledo, Alfonso Carrillo de Acuña, who was disloyal to Fernando and Isabel. Castro provides his own riddle when he notes how Carrillo betrayed the Catholic Kings. His subsequent mention of the Bernáldez's story of Enrique and his rebellious nobles is part of a trajectory Castro implements regarding the concept of falsehood and misrepresentation.

The Bernáldez narrative relating to the "Pendón de Aragón" concerns la Farsa de Ávila (The Farse of Avila), when on June 5, 1465, the nobles of Castilla made a wood effigy of King Enrique and systematically disrobed him of his crown, lance, and scepter. They were symbolically taking away his position as king so that his younger half-brother Alfonso could take over the throne. Archbishop Carrillo was a principal actor in the Farsa de Ávila.[53] Just as Castro notes Bernáldez's ambiguous trajectory with the story of the "Pendón de Aragón," he does not refer to it as outright duplicity. Yet this event is about treason and falsehood; even the name of the event, *farsa* (farce), is about falsehood, something empty without meaning. It is important to note that while Bernáldez castigated Jews, he himself was also a converso.[54]

Returning to Sánchez, the issue of duplicity expressed in his interpretation of Psalm 8:3 lies in Saint Augustine's *Expositions*. "I praise you, Father, Lord of heaven and earth, because you have hidden these matters from the wise and knowing, and have revealed them to the little ones (Mt. 11:25)." In saying, "from the wise," he meant not those who are truly wise but people who think they are. "In order that you may destroy the enemy and the defender. Who is this, except the heretic? The person who gives the impression of defending the Christian faith, when in fact he is attacking it, is an enemy-cum-defender."[55] It is this passage that brings to mind Alberro's description of the Mexican

Inquisitors during the mid-seventeenth century who "regressed many times over, in New Spain at least, sharing with the bureaucrats and the adventurers that came before them, the thirst for riches."[56] "It can be concluded that the inquisitors named to New Spain did not have the capacity or quality to direct the Tribunal. . . . The lack of solid formation and experience . . . assisted them in accepting the assignment in the Indies as a way to forge a rapid fortune."[57] Instead of defending the faith, the Inquisitors came to defend their own fortunes. It is this duplicity that Sánchez was addressing. This situation was also inclusive of the community, who came to form its own duplicity, with children being ordered to praise the Holy Cross so that their families would not be arrested. Falsehood was necessary for survival.

Mañozca, the Prophecy of Isaiah, and the Empty House

Solange Alberro analyzes the position of Sánchez among the Inquisitors as a person working within the interior of their society. As shown in *Imagen de la Virgen*, Sánchez's condemnation of "heretics" and his listing of supporters within the highest echelons of the Mexican Church, especially his glowing praise of Inquisitor Juan de Mañozca, undeniably indicate Sánchez's position.

But if further analysis is made of Sánchez's interpretive reference, the entire context of the story appears to change. Sánchez provides a clue when he lauds Mañozca the Inquisitor with six words taken from the book of Isaiah: "Thou has clothing, be thou our ruler." Upon reading the phrase, it can be assumed that Mañozca has the clothing (the position and trappings of power), so he should be the ruler. Yet Sánchez takes the phrase out of context. Isaiah predicts the fall of a rich Jerusalem. The man who has "clothing" and is told to be the "ruler" actually responds by saying that his house is empty, "I am no healer . . . make me not ruler of the people. For Jerusalem is ruined, and Juda is fallen: because their tongue, and their devices are against the Lord, to provoke the eyes of his majesty" (Isa. 3:5).

When the entire chapter is read, it is clear that Mañozca would become the ruler of an empty house. There is nothing for him to accept because the land is destitute. In *Imagen de la Virgen*, Sánchez avoids mentioning this destitution. Sánchez says the Inquisitor has the cloth of the Guadalupe, and adds a citation from Psalm 30, in which David beseeches God to protect him: "Deliver me out of the hands of my enemies; and from them that persecute me" (Ps. 31:15). Sánchez, in effect, is asking God for protection from Mañozca.

The "empty house" references the problems encountered within the Mexican Holy Office. Alberro explains that during "the most active decade [of the Inquisition], 1640–1650, stimulated by the persecution of converted Jews, the ministers basically ignored their responsibilities."[58] Alberro notes that even ten years after the "great conspiracy," Visitor-General Pedro de Medina Rico "brought about twenty-four charges against the Inquisitors for not respecting norms regarding the selection of positions for the Holy Office and all other types of irregularities concerning this."[59] The Tribunal was in chaos. Alberro writes that during the 1640s, "documents were left on the floor of the Tribunal, the folios of old *procesos* were completely disorganized and thrown about."[60] The house built by Mañozca in the 1640s was destroyed by the end of the decade. He had nothing to preside over. The chaos and disorganization saved people from the Inquisition. The consequences of disarray erupted centuries later because the Holy Office did not in fact annihilate the *judaizantes* in México.[61] Sánchez's writing attests to the presence of many more believers in Santo Moisén (Saint Moses) who remained undercover while the Inquisition fires were burning.[62]

Typology

The Virgin Mary, mother of Christ, is often compared to various aspects of the Old Testament. This comparison has been a common theme, and Sánchez partakes in it through his designation of the Virgin Mary of Guadalupe as the Ark of the Covenant. Guadalupan scholar David Brading makes serious note of the Virgin as the Ark. He dates this analogy to the inclusion of the book of Revelations in the New Testament, where "the intellectual reach of typological reasoning was projected into the Christian future."[63] Brading explains this synchronicity as Christian theologians seeking (and finding) prophetic statements that show the coming of Christ and his mother, adding later that, "all the scriptural figures generally applied to the Virgin Mary were transferred to the image of Guadalupe."[64] There is no denying that Brading is correct in his assessment of the typology used in Sánchez's presentation of Guadalupe.

It was common to see *judaizantes* (during the first two centuries after the Expulsion) use the idea of the Virgin Mary in various creative ways. While Seymour Liebman does not cite his source, he states that some Jewish traditions "were observed openly" as Christian, "by stating that they were in honor of the Virgin of Carmen."[65] In Liebman's translation of Matias de Bocanegra's narrative of the Mexican Inquisition, one penitent, Isabel de Silva, tells the Inquisitors that she taught other Jews scripture and traditions. She told them "that it was not proper for Jews to mention Jesus Christ or his holy Mother; that in order to invoke the holy Prophet Elias so that Catholics would not understand, they should say 'Virgin of Carmen.'"[66] Bocanegra also reports that another *judaizante*, Beatriz Texoso, held a rosary in her hand so that people would think she was praying to the Virgin Mary.[67] Other references to the Virgin are documented in the Spanish Inquisition's trial of Elvira Gonzalez, wife of the king's accountant. Gonzalez would intentionally refrain from weaving on Saturdays (the Shabbat) and tell those around her that she did this in devotion to the Virgin Mary.[68]

SVSPICE COELVM,ET NVMERA STELL

FIG. 10 Virgin of Guadalupe from *Imagen de la virgen Maria Madre de Dios de Guadalupe, milagrosamente aparecida en la ciudad de México* by Miguel Sánchez (México City, 1648). Courtesy of Benson Latin American Collection, University of Texas Libraries, the University of Texas at Austin.

Janet Liebman Jacobs, in her book *Hidden Heritage: The Legacy of the Crypto-Jews*, analyzes the role of the Virgin of Guadalupe in the lives of the descendants of Sephardic *judaizantes*. She sees Guadalupe as the intercessor, the Jewish mother, the provider of "nurturance, understanding, and wisdom, and the mother of the Jewish messiah."[69] More convincing is a work discussed in chapter 3, that of Arthur Green, "Shekhinah, the Virgin Mary, and the Song of Songs."[70] He proposes that "the unequivocal feminization of shekhinah in the Kabbalah of the thirteenth century is a Jewish response to and adaptation of the revival of devotion to Mary in the twelfth century Western church," which may seem heretical to some, yet the natural interaction between cultures and tradition would make this transformation very possible. "During the early Middle Ages, the majority (Christian) culture was awash with romantic ballads and troubadour romances." The link identified by Green is the Song of Songs, one of the last books of the Jewish Bible to be accepted, and one that Christian theologians use extensively when writing of the Black Virgin of Guadalupe in Extremadura Spain.[71]

Brading does not mention the Virgin's being associated with a menorah, yet a century before Sánchez, an image of the Virgin Mary "symbolized by the seven-branched candlestick of Zacharias 4:2" was published in a French Book of Hours.[72] When Sánchez discusses the apparitions of the Virgin, he states that the "House of Guadalupe is to contain and guard the true Ark, who is MARIA." Although he does not use the specific term "menorah," he explains that Zacharias dreams that an angel shows him "a candlestick all of gold, and its lamp upon the top of it: and the seven lights thereof upon it."[73] Sánchez later mentions the candelabrum with seven lamps with regard to a miracle that occurred when a lamp above the painting of Guadalupe fell on the head of devotee without injuring the man.

Sánchez references a narrative from the Middle Ages. He tells the reader that András II (ca. 1177–1235), king of Hungary gave the Virgin Mary the title of "Candelabrum aureum totum feptem gratiæ lucernis ornatim" (candelabra with seven lamps)—a menorah.[74] The notation of András II is significant. While this could generally be seen as simply another example of how the Virgin Mary was linked to the Old Testament, what makes this particular statement most interesting is that András II is known best for incorporating Jews and Muslims into his monarchy, and for being reprimanded by the pope for these activities. The standoff between the pope and András II became an early medieval international incident. Throughout his life, András II never changed his policy toward non-Christians. Pope Gregory IX excommunicated András the year before the king died.[75] When Sánchez cites András II, the author appears to be presenting an inverted message within his narrative. András II was devoted to the Virgin and wrote a text where he states his veneration to her, yet the story is really about how András II defied the pope and continued with his Jewish counselors. It is likely that Sánchez was one of the very few in New Spain who knew the history of the obscure battle between András II and Pope Gregory IX. Nora Berend describes the tactic András II used with the pope: "King András died in 1235 without obeying papal wishes concerning non-Christians. He never resisted openly; he promised to obey and took several oaths to that effect. But his promises and vows were never fulfilled."[76] Sánchez's use of András II's description of the Virgin as menorah accomplishes several objectives. Mary is again paired with the *judaizantes*, as she was when Sánchez called her the new Eve and the Ark of the Covenant. More importantly, Sánchez is referencing a monarch who believed so strongly in the inclusion of non-Christians in his court that he defied the pope, which is no small matter. András II's method of resistance is also significant. It is possible that, like András II, Sanchéz was also "not resisting openly." He promised to be a true Christian, yet he supported the *judaizantes* through writing *Imagen de la Virgen*.

The Presence of Death among the Living

In the afterword to *Imagen de la Virgen*, Francisco de Siles writes of Sánchez's passion and daring: "in poetry, the force of a consonant obligates one to say what cannot be thought."[77] Sánchez writes a paean to the Virgin of Guadalupe while scores of *judaizantes* are dying in the Inquisition's cells and hundreds of others are leaving the city for remote areas of New Spain where no one can find them.[78] He describes Guadalupe as the light of humankind, where prophecies as far back as Moses and the book of Genesis have told of her apparitions. He is ecstatic in his devotion to her. Yet there is death among his passionate phrases.[79]

Ethnologist Serge Gruzinski is the only scholar to note the timing of *Imagen de la Virgen*'s appearance and the Inquisition's intense activity. In his book *Images at War*, Gruzinski states that the publication of *Imagen de la Virgen* "coincided with the culmination of the persecutions against the Marranos. . . . The great *auto-da-fé* of 1649 sounded the death knell for . . . [the] Jewish community in México. . . . The simultaneity of the two projects—the annihilation of Mexican Judaism and the launching of the Guadalupan cult—was perhaps more than a chronological coincidence."[80] Gruzinski focuses on the nation-building actions of *Imagen de la Virgen*, not any type of empathy or warning to the *judaizantes* implied in the text. Even so, Gruzinski's observation is supported by two commentaries at the end of *Imagen de la Virgen* written by Sánchez's close friends and colleagues.[81]

Francisco de Bárcenas writes cryptically in the afterword of *Imagen de la Virgen* about his concern that the author is risking a confrontation with the Inquisition. "I want to distance myself and from afar admire the energy that you sir have wanted, for your nation, to expose yourself to various censors by certain people."[82] The emotion demonstrated by Francisco de Siles in the afterword of *Imagen de la Virgen* is quite striking. Siles is more direct in his concern for Sánchez and the well-being of México City's people (i.e., whites—there was little concern for the indigenous peoples or African slaves at this time). He also directly connects the present tragedy of México City's *judaizantes* with the redemption offered by Guadalupe:

> I have to emphasize in this occasion, of the gravity, of the serious nature in his [Sánchez's] prose, even though the cost may be that I will be censored for doing this . . . and he [Sánchez] is at fault for not having stopped before he wrote this history. . . .

The envy that came from Aman grew toward those of Queen Esther's nation: he condemned many to death, thousands of innocents, without guilt, without having committed a crime. Mardocheo, friend of Esther, companion, and of the same [Hebrew] nation and lineage; declared himself the guardian of her people, and with public demonstrations of sentiment, words, and tears, he was able to solicit the redemption, the lives, and consolation of so many who were envied . . . giving Esther notice of what he did and happily reunited with her defending and protecting those of her nation, prudently informing the king and interceding as Mother. . . . The king . . . conceded his favor, giving them permission to obtain letters with his seal that announce their favor, liberty, life, and respect for all of her nation.[83]

Francisco de Siles's narrative about Queen Esther is a story of a woman saving her people. He likens Esther to Guadalupe. His use of this book from the Old Testament is surprising: any discussion of Esther at that particular time would have probably sent a person to the Inquisition jails. Esther was a significant figure for *judaizantes* in México and in Spain. The phrase "innocent dying" is strongly analogous to those dying in the jails and on the pyres. He explains that in *Imagen de la Virgen*, Guadalupe is Esther, that *judaizantes* are an integral part of the Mexican Church and the México City community. He worries that he should have stopped Sánchez before the book was written and admits that *Imagen de la Virgen* contains words that cannot be thought.

Sánchez apparently proceeded regardless of any risk involved. It is as de Siles describes in his commentary. *Imagen de la Virgen* was meant to promote the Virgin of Guadalupe as a redeemer of the *judaizantes* who were under attack at the time by the Holy Inquisition. In sum, *Imagen de la Virgen* is a presentation of a syncretic converso theology frequently seen in Spain and its dependencies after the Expulsion.

A Postscript of Censors

The Mexican Inquisition was not always efficient with its authority. A certain ambivalence permeated its movements. This ambivalence extends to the ways the Inquisition censored books. Donald Castanien writes in *A Seventeenth-Century Mexican Library and the Inquisition*: "It was a practice in México, as in Spain, to permit the circulation of a book which contained objectionable statements . . . if the unacceptable sections were removed either in a new edition or by erasure."[84]

Two of Sánchez's commentators mention the possibility of censure. The book states it was approved by representatives of the Inquisition. It is dedicated to Pedro de Barrientos Lomelin, *consultor* to the Inquisition who at times had influence over the final sentencing of prosecuted penitents, and at other times was not informed of significant issues within the Holy Office, such as the establishment of additional jails. Alberro cites Inquisition documents that indicate a concern that the *consultores* were biased toward some of the incarcerated, after it became known that there was open communication between the two groups.[85]

Perhaps an intervention from either Barrientos Lomelin or de Siles (who was quite prominent in the community) assisted Sánchez in getting through the censors. It had only been twenty-four years since Jesuit Felipe Godíñez was sentenced by the Spanish Inquisition for writing theatrical works focusing too heavily on Old Testament narratives. Yet even Godíñez benefited from assistance in high places. The Jesuit had a number of influential supporters, including Ramiro Felipe Nuñez de Guzman, son-in-law of the Count Duke of Olivares, the king's powerful minister who could have easily assisted Godíñez in studying for a doctorate, in addition to resuming his priestly duties and writing career after he was sentenced by the Inquisition and held under house arrest for two years.[86]

Sánchez was not persecuted by the Holy Office. In fact, he continued to be treated with respect and awe for the rest of his life. Even so, twelve years after the publication of *Imagen de la Virgen*, a significantly edited, condensed version of Sánchez's book was released. Curiously titled *Original profético de la Santa Imagen: Relacion de la milagrosa aparicion de la Santa Imagen de la Virgen de Guadalupe de Mexico, sacada de la historia que compuso el Br. Miguel Sanchez* (Original Prophecy of the Holy Image: Narrative from the Miraculous Apparition of the Holy Image of the Virgin of Guadalupe of México, From a History Written by Bachiller Miguel Sánchez) by Mateo de la Cruz, the subtitle indicates that it was taken from *Imagen de la Virgen*, yet the text barely resembles the original. The apparitions are still present, yet most of the book is gone. There is no mention of the candelabra with seven lamps, the numerous Holy Crosses spread throughout the city, the children who upon command sang praises of the cross, or those inhabitants of México City who secretly prayed Psalm 16 requesting God's assistance. The citation from the book of Revelations is limited to a few words. There are no Old Testament prophets Abraham and Moses that conversos turned into Catholic saints, Santo Abraham and Santo Patriarca Moysen. All the psalms are taken out, as are references to the books of Genesis, Deuteronomy, Job, Isaiah, Ezekiel, and Esther.[87]

Imagen de la Virgen was republished in 1982 in *Testimonios historicos Guadalupanos*. It is accompanied by the version written by Mateo de la Cruz. The editors of *Testimonios*, Torre Villar and Navarro de Anda, explain the problems with *Imagen de la Virgen*: "The historical narration is blended with baroque theological digressions, his [Sánchez's] text is difficult for those who only want to gain information about the historical narration, this is why Father Mateo de la Cruz, motivated by Bishop Juan García de Palacio, cleansed it of all digressions."[88] Perhaps the changes were made because of the dense character of Sánchez's text. However, the removal of so much information, including all references to the Old Testament, lead me to conclude that the second edition was more likely an edit by Church censors. In an edition of Guadalupan writings published in 1785, the original text of *Imagen de la Virgen* was notably absent while the edited volume by Cruz was included. David Brading mentions in *Mexican Phoenix*: "The omission in this collection of Sánchez' *Image of the Virgin Mary* demonstrated the degree to which this work was now seen as a baroque embarrassment, alien to the 'good taste' of the late eighteenth century."[89]

The Mexican Church was well aware of its secret *judaizantes*, even in 1785. As I found in the documents written by Guadalupe archivist Manuel Espinosa de los Monteros in 1825, the Jewish reference to the Virgin was still present. The writings of Monteros were hidden in an American archive. In contrast, the text of *Imagen de la Virgen* has been available to the public since it was first published in 1648. Sánchez's words expressed what cannot be thought, yet the rest of the world has kept silent or has been blind to the author's trajectory.

7

Madre Sion

———————————————•

Manuel Espinosa de los Monteros states that the Virgin of Guadalupe speaks to Juan Diego (the indigenous man she appeared to) as "representative of Madre Sion, Madre Jerusalem." He further positions himself as a Christian Jew in the following description of the Virgin Mary, "first as mother of Christ and in second place as representative of Mother Sion that is hiding in (*un latibulo*) a secret location."[1] Richard Popkin writes that he "was fascinated by the Marrano experience, by the fact that the forced converts and their descendants in Spain were forced to live a double life, outwardly conforming to the culture around them, but internally guarding the true faith."[2] It is very possible that Monteros was one of these individuals.

Writing with frescoes of Sybils peering over his shoulder at the Monastery of Acolman near México City, Monteros wrote for days and nights, expressing every possible thought he had in his mind about the unlikely association between Judaism and the Virgin of Guadalupe of México. In long sentences that betray his detailed knowledge of Jewish history, he formulated a story that very few could conceptualize.

It is known that Monteros was a Catholic, yet from his writings it is difficult to discern whether he was a sincere Catholic, a secret Jew, or what Richard Popkin terms "a Christian Jew"—a Christian grounded in the Jewish faith.[3] Monteros descended from sixteenth-century colonists who traveled to New Spain. He was a secular priest in México City during the early part of the nineteenth century and was devoted to the Virgin of Guadalupe. He was well aware of her significance. Also known as the Virgin Mary, mother of Christ (yet in New World form), she was all-important for Catholics. Later in the century,

Guadalupe became the patroness of México and all the Americas. During the last six years of his life, Monteros was the archivist at her central sanctuary, the Basilica of the Virgin of Guadalupe in México City. A collection of his writings that came to be known as *Monumentos Guadalupanos* arrived in New York six decades after Monteros laboriously wrote about the importance and symbolism of Guadalupe. In the hundreds of handwritten pages that he produced, he took on the uncanny position of historical reporter and quasi-heretic, devotee of Christ and Philo-Semite who incessantly thought of the Virgin of Guadalupe and how she represented the Jewish nation.

Monteros's obsession with the past and future of Judaism could be identified with a new type of Christianity—Jewish theology that perpetually sought a millennial solution.[4] Two Jesuits—the Portuguese Antonio Vieira and Chilean

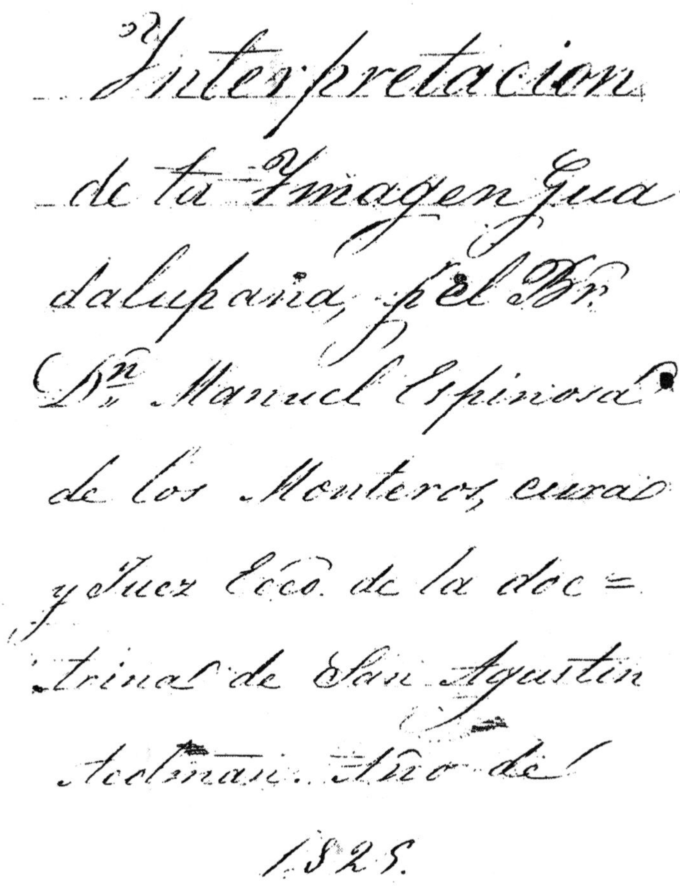
Interpretacion
de la Ymagen Gua
dalupana, p.r el Br.
D.n Manuel Espinosa
de los Monteros, cura
y Juez Ecco. de la doc=
trinal de San Agustin
Acolman. Año de
1825.

FIG. 11 Cover from *Interpretacion de la Imagen Guadalupana* by Manuel Espinosa de los Monteros. Unpublished manuscript. Acolman, México, 1825. Courtesy New York Public Library.

Manuel Lacunza—greatly influenced Monteros. Vieira sought the answer through the mystical return of the lost King Sebastián of Portugal (1554–1578), who disappeared during battle in Morocco.[5] Vieira, author of *Esperanças de Portugal, quinto império de mundo* (The Hope of Portugal, the fifth empire of the world) and *Em defesa dos Judeos* (In defense of the Jews), was known for defending Portuguese conversos, in addition to establishing a relationship with Menassah ben Israel, author of *La Esperanza de Israel* (The Hope of Israel).[6] Lacunza's writings were also messianic, indicating that all the Jews would convert at the second coming of the Messiah. His most celebrated writing is *La venida del Mesías en gloria y majestad* (The coming of the Messiah in glory and majesty), for which he used the pseudonym, Juan Josephat ben Ezra.

For Monteros, Guadalupe is the Messiah. He is not the first to write of this possibility. Jacob Alting wrote in the late seventeenth century that the Messiah "is the mother of all that lives."[7] Geneviève Javary noted this in her analysis of the Shekhinah.[8] As Javary describes it, the role of the Messiah is one who supports, sympathizes, empathizes, and mediates: "We see that the Messiah is essentially the mediator, or Shekhinah, as the mother very attuned to the world, an excellent mediator between God and our world. It is easy to pass from the notion [of this type of mother] to the Messiah."[9]

While Monteros does not explicitly say that Guadalupe is the Messiah, he offers long, intricate explanations for her importance to the second coming. For Monteros, she was a representative and savior of the Jews. There were others in México that published such controversial ideas regarding Guadalupe. It had not been so long before Monteros's intimation that Servando Teresa de Mier was banished from México for writing that Guadalupe was brought from the Old World by Saint Thomas the Apostle during the time of Christ. This narrative was particularly controversial because it meant that the Virgin did not first appear to an indigenous man in 1531.[10] Mier later returned to México and was instrumental in the country's independence from Spain. It is certain that Monteros knew every detail of Mier's experience.[11]

Monteros was not a revolutionary like Mier. He came into adulthood during a tumultuous period of Mexican history. He was priest at Chiautla, Texcoco, in 1811 when insurgent troops attacked the city and executed the royalist commandant. Four months later, in March 1812, royalists returned to the area in an attempt to retake Chiautla but were defeated.[12] His name does not appear in relation to these events. Even though his writings that date after the war for independence indicate that he supported the insurgents, before that time he was a confirmed royalist.[13] Between 1814 and 1818, while stationed at the parish of Ixtapaluca, he convinced "more than thirty insurgents to surrender."[14] In an addendum titled "Otro Tabernaculo en el Apocalipsis," he indicates his intense animosity toward Spaniards: "the most painful are the Europeans, the most terrible of the terrible flying now to our America like foul-smelling birds and bringing a bad smell with their insolent faces."[15]

Further indicating his sympathies toward the crown, shortly before México won its independence, Monteros was elected as a deputy to the Spanish Corte, yet he was not able to carry out the role because the war ended.[16]

In his introduction to *Interpretacion de la Imagen Guadalupana y confirmacion del systema milenario* (Interpretation of the Guadalupe Image and Confirmation of the Millennial System), he explains that he is concerned that he will "estampar un desatino contra la Escritura (write something foolish against the Holy Scripture)." His ideas were guided by his predecessor, Manuel Lacunza, in *La venida del Mesías*, a book Monteros would have been reading about the time he wrote *Interpretacion*. Monteros writes that he would be traveling through a dangerous and unknown path that was paved by Lacunza. He adds that the manuscript would be evaluated by "the most Illustrious Governor and Counselor," and if his work is not approved, he would acquiesce without reluctance.[17] The manuscripts were never published, they are not listed in any known archive besides the New York Public Library, and they may have never been evaluated by Church authorities. Forty-one years after the death of Monteros, his papers were sold at auction in London to the New York Public Library.[18] In consideration of the contents, *Interpretacion* would have caused an even greater stir in 1825 than Mier's pronouncements did in 1794.

Monteros was ordained a secular priest in 1800. His knowledge of indigenous languages placed him at a number of Indian parishes near México City during the early nineteenth century.[19] He produced numerous texts during the last thirteen years of his life that focused mostly on Guadalupe yet included a number of other themes regarding the Old Testament, the Catholic religion, indigenous culture, and what he believed to be the Messiah's second coming.

Known primarily for his work as an archivist at the Sanctuary of the Virgin of Guadalupe in México City, Monteros is not acknowledged by many historians as an extraordinarily prolific writer. The basilica has published a brief biography of Monteros on its website. It is clear the basilica's officials hold him in high esteem. The sanctuary's website states that Monteros was "an ecclesiastic that during the early time of independence collaborated like no other with this archive." Monteros was archivist at Coyoacán two decades earlier and had written numerous texts before he arrived at the basilica in 1832. The director of the basilica archive notes on the web page that his "analysis and aggregation of the archive transcend the simple organization of the documents."[20]

Monteros wrote hundreds of pages of text, mostly about Guadalupe, much of which are only being published (or cited) in the early twenty-first century.[21] In his lifetime, Monteros was surely influenced by that changing tide of opinion toward the Virgin of Tepeyac. The last decades of the eighteenth century brought scandal and controversy to the devotion toward the Virgin. Published eighteenth-century authors questioned the foundations of the Guadalupan narrative. Writings of the well-known Juan Bautista Muñoz and Servando Teresa de Mier circulated widely.[22] The new century and Mexican independence from Spain brought a change of trajectory. Guadalupan apologists, such as José Miguel Guridi y Alcocer and José Joaquín Fernández de Lizardi, praised the Virgin and lauded what she had done for the new Mexican nation.

While Monteros had already written a great deal about Guadalupe before 1831, the events of that year would have influenced how he distributed his work. During preparation for "the third centenary anniversary of the Virgin's apparition to Juan Diego," a *convenio* (conference) titled "Guadalupan Junta" was held in México City. It is very likely that Monteros was in attendance. Conducted by a "committee of prominent citizens of México City appointed by the city government,"[23] the coordinators set about to organize "an impressive round of celebrations that lasted for four days . . . beginning in the [national] cathedral and ending in the [Guadalupe] sanctuary at Tepeyac. A procession from the cathedral to sanctuary was completed with a sermon by a priest who was noted for his insurgent activities. The celebration was concluded with a spectacular fireworks display."[24] Guadalupe had become a nationalist icon of religious devotion. Stafford Poole explains: "The first half of the nineteenth century was the formative period for the identification of *guadalupanismo* (devotion to the Virgin of Guadalupe) and *mexicanidad* (Mexican Identity). This identity became so fixed that from the time to the present any criticism of the former was viewed as an attack on the latter. Even the scholarly critic of the apparitions ran the risk of being considered a traitor to his nation and people."[25]

Although Monteros was not criticizing Guadalupe, the Jewish trajectory of his role for her placed him far outside the acceptable norm of Guadalupan discourse. With a superb education, time, and the instruments to write, Monteros produced a number of manuscripts that discuss the Virgin.[26] He delved into the question of the apparitions, conducting a dense theological analysis of her image. He wrote on the importance of her cult to the people of México and produced a series of discussions regarding her relationship to the Jews and how she will bring their nation to its previous glory. As he states in *La interpretacion del misterio*, "Maria was the representative of the Jewish nation, at the foot of the Cross already in the form of the Guadalupana."[27] This idea was not quite so unusual in that a number of authors, including the Santa Marias, a powerful converso family in fourteenth- and fifteenth-century Spain, publicized that they were descended from the House of David and therefore were descendants of the Virgin Mary.[28] The Santa Marias used this proclamation to show themselves as the original Christians by blood. This did not assist them in denying their Jewish ancestry, but it did propose that their lineage was the most pure since it could be traced to Mary, known for her immaculate state. In addition, Manuel Lacunza, a theologian closely followed by Monteros, incorporated into his work *La venida del Mesías* the belief that "my own brothers [are] the Jews, whose parents and Christ had the same ancestors."[29] This citation, taken from the introduction of *La venida del Mesías*, is signed in Lacunza's Jewish pseudonym, Juan Josephat ben Ezra.

Lacunza and Monteros are connected by their marked interest in the fate of the Jewish nation. Monteros never identifies himself as a Jew. He does not say "I am a Jew, or I am a Christian Jew," but he continuously writes of the Jews in a voice that carries an internal identification. Monteros describes the dispersion, the devaluing, and the violence against the Jews in a heartfelt manner. Lacunza, however, is more forthright about his identification with the Jews in his text. Early in the second volume of *La venida del Mesías*, Lacunza comments on his identity:

> I explain myself with more liberty, do not admire me, in case I utter an uncivil word.... I am a Christian, it is true, and I accept with the most gratitude I am capable of, the great benefit I have received from the kindness of God; even more so because I am a Jew, and I am not embarrassed to be one. As a Christian, I am a debtor to any tribe, town, people, or nation. More so, as a Christian Jew, I am also a debtor with a particular obligation to those unfortunate men.[30]

Monteros's religious alliances are confusing. His text (for the most part) exhibits a firm belief in Christ. At one point, he reassures his reader that he is proud to be part of the Roman Church. Yet, while he firmly states his loyalty and respect for the Church in one statement, throughout his writing he continuously criticizes the Church and the clergy for their corruption. He also tells his reader that the "Dragon . . . is none other than an evil Pontiff."[31] There are numerous pages where he proposes that the Jews will convert to Christianity. Yet it is a Christianity that is more Jewish than Christian, where the Jewish high priest will rule the world along the Virgin of Guadalupe. He defends European Jews, saying they are identical to non-Jews in every way, except religion.[32] He refers to an extremely detailed exposition on Moses' Holy of Holies (what he calls Santa Sanctorum).[33]

In a text written in 1831, he notes that his ancestors prayed or sang the psalms of Saint Michael during funerals, which were related to the ritual practice of reciting a psalm at burial.[34] Yet, from what he actually admits, there is no other firm indication that he is descended from Jews. For scholars looking for absolute proof, there is none at this time. Nevertheless, a sweep through his writings leaves the reader with strong feelings that Monteros's positioning is slippery or variegated in some way that does not fit with his pronouncements about his religion and the importance of Christ in the world.

The Mysterious Veil of Guadalupe

Monteros uses the pseudonym "Pio Saens" when writing *El observador Guadalupano*. The text is an attempt to promote devotion to Guadalupe, to diminish doubts regarding her existence and to explain various aspects of her narrative. The author proposes that the painting of Guadalupe is prophetic. He reminds his reader that Miguel Sánchez had also thought there were hidden signs in her presentation that alluded to the story of Apocalypse 12. As he states, "there is something occulted in all aspects of the Guadalupan devotion. This is formalized through its design, composition, and how its different aspects intersect."[35] Surprisingly, he does not discuss any particular secret in his writing. In *Interpretacion del misterio Guadalupano*—he begins a section titled "Sumaria interpretacion del misterio (Summary interpretation of the mystery)," yet he does not use the word "mystery" again throughout the section.

In 1825, while at San Agustin de Acolman, a former monastery just north of México City with a decidedly esoteric environment, Monteros wrote a number of his monographs, including *Interpretacion de la Imagen Guadalupana*. Acolman is an unusual colonial monastery whose walls are full of striking murals, making it the most notable in México.[36] At the time Monteros was in residence at Acolman, the nave of the church displayed spectacular "frescoes of Church fathers and the Sibyls" that indicated a relationship between where Monteros lived and the writing he produced. The frescos of Acolman (along with many of the convents of New Spain) carried a millennial tone. The Sibyls personified in the paintings and were "prophetesses who gave obscure messages with double meanings; they 'foretold' *post factum* the history of the world."[37] This came to be the dominant theme in most of Monteros's writing. In 1831 he was at the Basilica of Guadalupe as canon of native languages.[38] Five years later, he was appointed archivist of the basilica. He continued writing during those years and is well respected for having organized and analyzed the archives of the Basilica of Guadalupe. He remained there until his death in 1838.

Monteros collected a number of documents during his career. He would obtain the originals (or copies of the originals) and make his own copies. He read copiously and had a broad range of knowledge of Old Testament sources as well as contemporary writers who focused on what they believed to be the impending millennium. His writings at times worked through the typology of the Old Testament and the foretelling of Christianity, such as when he explains that "when Adam was honored with the power of the universe, he was also representing the future Christ."[39] Presenting himself as a true Christian in the first paragraph of his text, Monteros begins by telling his reader "Here we all agree that in the year 1531 Our Lady appeared to a Mexican Indian named Juan Diego."[40] He speaks of the blessings brought upon México because of Guadalupe: "Mexicans, there is much to be thankful for." "She is a great mystery that we barely know" and provides "much comfort to all the Christians, especially Indians."[41]

Jesuits Vieira and Lacunza as Models for the Jewish-Christian Perspective

Antonio Vieira (1608–1697) was a brilliant writer, orator, and consultant to kings. He was born in Portugal and emigrated with his family to Bahia, Brazil, at the age of six. He lived almost the entire span of the seventeenth century. As previously mentioned, his most noted work is *Esperanças de Portugal* (The Hope of Portugal) published in 1659. Vieira, similar to Monteros, linked his own "ideas about Christianity and the conversion of the Jews to the larger problem of the conversion of non-Christian peoples throughout the New World."[42] Yet as Monteros noted in *Interpretacion*, Vieira focused less on Christ than on the prophecies of Gonçalo Bandara regarding the resurrection of the disappeared King Sebastian of Portugal. Even so, Monteros was greatly influenced by Vieira's "Lusocentric millenarianism," a term used by Vieira scholar José van den Besselaar. From 1646 to 1648, Vieira had regular conversations with millennialist Menasseh ben Israel,[43] during which time Vieira's idea was formed regarding "the pivotal role of the Jews in the missionary enterprise."[44]

Monteros was even more influenced by Manuel Lacunza's *La venida del Mesías*, which became available in México as Monteros was writing his various versions of *Interpretacion*. He used the writing of Manuel Lacunza (1731–1801) to base his discovery of Guadalupe's mystery as related to the millennium. In Monteros's words, Lacunza had "planted a tree with his writings about the millennium, yet in the years since Lacunza's death, the tree had been pulled out by its roots and abandoned."[45] It was Monteros's intent to reestablish the trajectory of Lacunza's writing.

Lacunza was among the Jesuits who were removed from the Americas in 1767 by edict of the Spanish king. He was born in Chile to a merchant family and entered the Jesuit seminary at age sixteen, reaching ordination at age thirty-one.[46] The expulsion of the Jesuits was a great tragedy for Lacunza, which occurred only six years after his ordination. He spent the rest of his life in exile in Imola, Italy, thirty-five kilometers southwest of Bologna, and was never to see his family again. He was even unfortunate in death; having lived a long life in Imola, his body was found in a well in June 1801. He was seventy years of age at the time.

The controversial *La venida del Mesías* was written between 1775 and 1790.[47] Lacunza writes that Christ is expected to return a second time and the Jews will regain the glory they experienced during the time of Solomon. Lacunza's book was published in a number of countries, including England. However, the Spanish Inquisition censored *La venida del Mesías*. Anyone found to be reading the book in Spain or its dependencies would be excommunicated and fined 200 ducats. Edict IX of 1819 from the Mexican Holy Office noted that "the reading of this work can and may produce scandals and divisions, with a tendency to create a war of religious opinions."[48] In a later work, Monteros mentions that Lacunza's ideas were not well received in México.[49] By the time Monteros was writing at Acolman, the Republic of México was already in existence and the Holy Office had been disbanded. Monteros did not indicate any concern regarding the negative reception of *La venida del Mesías*, perhaps because the era of significant danger regarding the prohibition of censured books had passed.

Monteros's Intention

By pairing Guadalupe with the Jews, Monteros did not seek to devalue her role as national symbol of México. He believed her desire was to save México. The México he imagined was one that was populated and governed by *judaizantes* presently in hiding. However, based on the history of national (and Church) attitudes toward Guadalupan devotion, the publication of his writings would have surely labeled him a heretic. Yet the timing of his work was in his favor. México's recent independence from Spain created an opening because the Inquisition was abolished and the new order had not yet formalized.

To Monteros, the lost tribes were not so much the indigenous peoples, as Lacunza and Menasseh ben Israel claimed. For him the lost tribes were really those *judaizantes* and conversos who left Europe for the Americas and found themselves without an anchor for their religious beliefs. A different manuscript, *Interpretacion de la pintura Guadalupana y confirmacion del systema milenario*, is his vehicle for probing the ramifications of what he sees as choices made at the time of Jesus's death. His phrase "unknown and dangerous paths" concerns the open secret behind Mexican colonial identity, the history of thousands of *judaizantes* and conversos who migrated to México in the guise of true Christians who lived two lives.[50] While Monteros's only direct mention of this lies in his passing comment that his ancestors used to pray psalms at burials, his passionate focus on Jewish history and its redeemable future is more striking than any direct commentary regarding his second identity.

He explains the trajectory of his book as being in three parts, with the third being the "most promising."[51] This section, titled "First Preliminary Instruction," begins with a focus on Adam, Jacob, David, Solomon, and Jesus, son of Toredec. Using typology, Monteros tells the story, relating how each prophet resembles Christ. He tells of Adam having temporal and spiritual power, a similar figure to that of Christ. The story of Jacob is about civil and spiritual power. He tells of Jacob and Esau and how Jacob obtained the favor given to the eldest son. Significantly, in this section he mentions the danger of ecclesiastic and civil power coming together to further purely human desires. The apocalyptic beast (or Antichrist) with seven heads and ten horns appears, which is announced in the Scriptures. Monteros does not dwell on this scene; he quickly reverts to the millennium, where there will be peace and prosperity in the world.[52] In his brief description of the potential disaster, the Antichrist is the Inquisition. Two centuries earlier, Miguel Sánchez, who was also a secular priest of high rank in México City, wrote of the beast in the Apocalypse that strongly resembled the Inquisition pursuing Jews in mid-seventeenth-century México. In Sánchez's narratives, it is the corrupt Roman Church and its clergy who are oppressing the Jews and the indigenous people.

Monteros's essay on Aaron (Moses's brother) leaves Christianity behind and provides minute detail on the sumptuous robes that he wore as the Jewish high priest. Aaron's diadem, as described in the book of Wisdom (*el libro de la Sabiduria*) is the focus of a long explication. The diadem contains twelve precious stones signifying the twelve tribes of Israel. It is termed *El racional del juicio* (The Reasoning of Justice) because the high priest, a mediator between God and his people, wears the diadem on his chest when consulting with God.[53] The *racional* assists the priest in understanding God's judgments and directives.[54] Monteros notes that God orders Moses to place the *racional* in the Urim and Thummin, which in Hebrew signify "doctrine" and "truth."[55] Urim and Thumin are often defined as part of the *racional* and are "related to a method of divine communication,"[56] worn when the high priest "needed to inquire of Yahweh . . . to seek an oracle."[57] It is a tradition that ended with the destruction of the first Temple. However, in the sixteenth century, Benito Arias Montano (librarian at the famous Escorial) wrote of God's giving two brilliant stones to Moses so they would be placed in the *racional*.[58] The brilliant light is the Shekhinah, as described in *Antiquities of the Jews* by Josephus Flavius: "But as to those stones, which we told you before, the high priest bare on his shoulders . . . the one of them shined out when God was present at their sacrifices . . . bright rays darting out thence; and being seen even by those that were most remote; which splendor yet was not before natural to the stone."[59]

While Monteros does not mention the Shekhinah, he explains that "Rabbi Solomon and the Jews say that the Urim and Thummin was the name of God, made of four letters from the Greek Tetragrammaton: signifying the Trinity of persons and the incarnation of The Verb, but this has been lost."[60] The result is that the twelve tribes will gather together to pay homage to the "highest Pontiff and Monarch," and all the kings of the world will obey and serve him. Christ is almost always involved in Monteros's discussions, yet he continuously includes the future actions of the *judaizantes*. "The diadem of the high priest announces the power of the Hebrew Nation, with diverse territories and settlements divided into provinces, cities and villages; an independent and sovereign nation."[61] He reaffirms the future of Israel: "This Glory will not be halted or repressed in the Lord, instead it will overflow in the Jewish nation, who like the Queen Consort will consult regarding the governing of the world."[62] The Queen Consort is the Virgin of Guadalupe.

Guadalupe of the Ten Tribes

Monteros begins the section "Discurso 2" with the title "A treatment of the ancient opinion that the Indians are descended from the tribes of Israel."[63] Curiously, he starts with "the Jews in Europe are so physically similar to the other people; in color, language, clothing, and other common styles, no one knows the difference unless they become aware of the Jew's religion." In a more personal manner, Monteros reports, "I want to say that in substance, even though their sect is seen with contempt, the [Jewish] persons are not degraded in other ways [besides their religion]."[64] In his discussion of the proposition by Antonio Vieira and Menasseh ben Israel that the indigenous peoples of the Americas are the Lost Tribes of Israel, he writes of the improbability of this statement. Representing the disgust of a *criollo* toward the natives, he writes, "Well, it would be a major surprise if I said that the Indians were those Jews . . . the Indian who is so stupid, a brute not worthy of baptism, the Indian who naturally judged himself a slave, or born to servitude."[65] Paradoxically, Monteros questions: "If the Indians are not Israelites, why does the Virgin wear clothing only of the Hebrew Nation?"[66]

However, after he affirms his doubt regarding the theory of indigenous Jews, he returns to information from previous authors who consistently insist on its veracity. In a sudden twist, as if he believes the indigenous-Jewish narrative, he continues, explaining different aspects of the story. Then he realizes another possibility. "I do not find it repugnant that many Benjaminites were mixed with the ten tribes when they were captured and because of this were able to accompany them in their pilgrimage until they reached America."[67] He gives as proof a reading from Psalm 79, which he recommends to his reader. Later he notes that God discovered and gave redemption to the tribes of Benjamin and Juda who were in America. They were found in what Monteros calls *el latibulo*—a place of hiding. The subject of hidden Jews is mentioned numerous times in *Interpretacion de la pintura*. Are those who were hiding in the *latibulo* (the secret place) the crypto Jews who have been in México since the conquest?

La Virgen, La Mujer Fuerte y Ester—The Virgin, the Strong Woman, and Esther

According to Monteros, while Jesus was dying on the cross, he called out to His Father "Why do you forsake me?" Mary, who is at his feet, responds to Jesus's cry by trying to do what she can to save her people. Monteros explains that her actions prove that the Virgin Mary (Guadalupe) is "la Mujer Fuerte" who is needed desperately by the Jewish nation.[68] Here he focuses on the preference for la Mujer Fuerte, who was originally the first wife of God. When the Jews rejected Jesus and the Gentiles converted, there entered a second wife. God did not favor her, and she proved to be corrupted. In the end, the first wife will return and present herself to be the favorite again. He expresses a phrase often used, "Strong woman. Who will find her? Far and in the last confines of the Earth."[69] She will be found and will help form the new kingdom of Christ in the second coming. She will be seated at the right of the King. Her companions will be brought to her. These virgins, her own relatives, represent the ten tribes obedient to the queen, who is also the Virgin Mary (la Señora).

This community forms la Mujer Fuerte. He quotes the book of Wisdom. "Oh how beautiful is the chaste generation with clarity! Its memory is immortal. This generation is the beautiful Rachel, the perfect moon, Ana in distress, and the woman surrounded by brilliance."[70]

At the end of this section, Monteros tells his reader that he has recently read the book of Esther and found that it was "full of mysteries related to the Jewish people that are hidden in an enclosed place." He retells the story of how Esther saved her people by interceding with King Asuero.[71] Monteros sees Esther's actions as resonating with those of the Virgin Mary when the latter was at the foot of the cross of the dying Jesus. He reports that this event is known as Phurim.[72]

It is at this moment that Monteros begins the specific introduction to the relationship between Guadalupe and the Jewish people. He indicates how he began to see the connection. He gives a detailed history from the Old Testament (which would not be readily available to many people outside the Church). On the day of the Second Coming, the Virgin Mary is resuscitated (along with Moses and other prophets). He writes that it is easily proven that Mary "is the tabernacle of Christ" because she carried him in her womb for nine months. She was present during her son's death and "was penetrated with the sword of pain to see her son's anguish and his abandonment by the Jewish people." It is here, in her moment of honor when her son's head is comforted on her lap, that she shows she is the mother of Christ and simultaneously a representative of Madre Sion that is hidden in the *latibulo*.[73]

For Monteros, she is already the "reestablished Wife," presented in her dignity as she would have been when the Hebrew nation was at its zenith. She is "adorned with the sun, moon, stars, and crown as representative of the Hebrew monarchy or the Israelite Nation, that is also queen or princess of all the nations, and mother mediatrix of Christ, converted to Catholicism."[74] "There is no person in the Heavens nor the earth that has all the qualities necessary to represent that holy, chaste, and illustrious generation of Israelites that will be arriving. The Virgin is among all the family or house of Israel, ... [She] is the sun at birth in the holiest place of God."[75]

Interpreting the Image

The brilliance of the gold on Guadalupe's tunic is important to Monteros. The gold's purity and "excellent virtues" are part of the Jewish nation. The Jews have experienced fire and many tribulations, and the brilliant gold publicly and "gloriously" announces their heroism. They are the mark of the "Nation that is so perfect."[76] Monteros compares the Virgin to Jacob, who is father of the Jewish nation.[77] In the author's numerous references to how she will represent the nation and how she will have the leadership and the power, he presents her more as a messiah than a mediatrix. The idea of the *la mujer fuerte* is more of a woman with agency, a woman who is not specifically identified as the Messiah yet is certainly described as such. Monteros also sees certain images on the fabric of Guadalupe's clothing. He sees a cross and an oval with an angel that to him resemble the two precious stones previously mentioned—the Urim and Thummin; to him, her outer tunic signifies the spiritual and earthly power of "the holy people."

In the last section of his *Interpretacion*, he includes a subheading, "Sumaria interpretacion del misterio." In this section, he repeats what he has said in each section of the book, finally indicating the specific mystery of the Virgin:

> ... adorned with the sun, moon, stars, and crown, she is the Representative of the Hebrew Monarchy or Israelite Nation, which is also the queen, or princess of all the nations. The Virgin is also the mother mediator of Christ converted to Catholicism, gathered from the four winds of the earth and located in her nation Palestine. Her clothing indicates that she is a Spouse reestablished to her ancient dignity, or decorated with spiritual and temporal power that from her court in Jerusalem she exercises over all the nations as Teacher, Mother, and Mistress of all those nations, from the end of corrupted present century to the end of the millennial century.[78]

The Persona of the Author

In a curious comment, Monteros notes: "We are not interested in the piece of the globe, only the scant bit of land where the High Priest resides, with equal land for our brothers the Catholics."[79] In stating "our brothers the Catholics" is he not saying that he belongs to the group that is subject to the "High Priest"?

Previous generations of his family had been among the elite of México. He was part of the Espinosa de los Monteros family who had an illustrious history in Spain and colonial México. The town of Espinosa de los Monteros is near Burgos in northern Spain. It is associated with a special group who in the eleventh century was designated the private protectors of the king. On his mother's side he is descended from the Velascos and the Ferrers. He was born in México City in 1773. The church ledger states that he is the son of Mariano Espinosa de los Monteros and Maria Gertrudis Ferrer Velasco.[80] He matriculated at Santiago Tlatelolco and later spent a year studying the work of the Dominican Spaniard San Vicente Ferrer (1350–1419) in Tepozotlán at the Colegio de Novicios of the Jesuits.[81] Ferrer is famous for his millennial beliefs and his mass conversion of Spanish Jews.[82] Although Ferrer was canonized a saint in the Catholic Church, he is seen as a dangerous provocateur who set off numerous riots in which thousands of Jews were killed.[83] The relationship between Monteros's study of Ferrer and the author's intense interest in the Jews vis-à-vis "Jewish conversion" indicate that Monteros found some type of answer, albeit imperfect, in the work of the amazingly popular saint. Known for his erudite oratory, Ferrer "knew how to penetrate into the soul of his listeners."[84] He is said to have converted more than twenty-five thousand Jews. While Jewish scholars have rightly located Ferrer as the central provocateur behind much of the Iberian violence of the early fourteenth century, the texts that Monteros was reading on the saint were focused on how Ferrer was well educated in the Old Testament and very aware of Jewish history, and they often stated that he abhorred the violence toward the Jews. During Monteros's time there was no critique of Ferrer's violence against the Jews and conversos. Monteros saw that Ferrer understood the Jews and did not want any violence against them, believing that once they converted they would find peace in God's kingdom.

Monteros writes of a coin that was minted in Rome during the reign of Titus. It shows a melancholy woman sitting with her legs stretched out in front of her. She is beneath a palm tree and is facing to the right. Behind the tree is a Roman soldier with his right arm raised and his left hand holding his sword that appears to be sheathed. His position is powerful. His foot is on a stone and his left leg bent and slightly elevated. He shows control over the woman, who is facing down as she sits on the ground. The coin reads "Judea Capta."[85] Monteros writes:

> Two symbols confront each other. A coin was minted in Rome with a woman sitting under a palm looking despondent. The inscription was Captive Judea. . . . Guadalupe is the symbol of this same nation, not below the palm tree, but on the palm, and the coin would be minted with the inscription Free Judea. The theme of the coin would be a triumphant carriage. There could be another carriage that would be the glory of God as seen by Ezekiel. It would have the inscription "destroy the chariot out of Ephraim." In Rome, she is represented as a slave: in Tepeyac, as a Queen. In the old world she is a captive, poor, and scorned, she is told in the new world "Arise, arise, put on thy strength, O Sion, put on the garments of thy glory, O Jerusalem . . . Shake thyself from the dust, arise, sit up, O Jerusalem: loose the bonds from off thy neck, O captive daughter of Sion."[86]

After he notes the passage from Isaiah 52:1–2, he continues with an additional ten citations from the Old Testament, all written in Latin. Nine are from Isaiah and one is from Baruch.[87] The aggregate of their message is that the Jewish nation will arise and be strong and will be favored by God. What presses Monteros to place citation after citation from Isaiah? The later chapters of the book of Isaiah are for the most part about restoration. The nine citations from Isaiah written on half of a handwritten page of manuscripts indicates the intensity of his feelings and desires of such a restoration.

FIG. 12 *Judea Capta*, Titus Sestertius coin 80–81 C.E., from *Jewish Coins* by Theodore Reinach (London, 1903).

Why would the restoration be so important to a Catholic priest who has indicated repeatedly that he has a strong belief in Christ? Even having the knowledge regarding an ancient coin minted in Rome, telling the story of a lost Judea is unusual for a priest in early nineteenth-century México City. The most compelling reason would be that Monteros had an association or history with what was left of the *judaizante* community in México. As he noted in his text written in Iztacalco about his family reciting psalms during burials, he provides minimal information. Perhaps more revealing is his notice of the book *Cartas de unos Judios* (Letters of some Jews) in the text by Pio Saens/Monteros.[88] He writes of how Voltaire has been an enemy of the Church: "Voltaire is among those destroyers who has worked laboriously against the Roman Church for fifty years. He has worked harder than even Luther and Calvin. With his writings that had inundated the Americas, he continues even after his death to harm the Church." He also notes that "Voltaire infers that the enemies of the Catholic Church, now like animals, now like the winds, now finally like bricklayers that destroy; they are deep in corruption and contemplate the Church as a mystic body of Christ." Monteros reports that a P. Ceballos, bishop of Puebla, wrote about Voltaire's insults in the "prologue . . . of the translation" of the book.[89]

Surprisingly, a perusal of *Cartas de unos Judios* indicates an extremely thorough treatise on the condition of the Jews in Europe, with letters from Voltaire intensely criticizing their community as well as letters from a number of European Jews. The text of the book begins the title *Cartas de unos Judios Portugueses, con reflexiones criticas* (Letters by some Portuguese Jews, with critical reflections). An M. Guasco, a Portuguese Jew from London, writes to a canon from Winchester: "About eight or ten years ago, a disagreement arose among the Portuguese Jews established in Burdeos and some Jews of other nations."[90] *Cartas* continues in this format. The theme of every chapter is about the Jews. There is no mention of Voltaire attacking the Catholic Church. With chapter titles such as "Was It Impossible for Moses to Write the Pentateuch?" and "Considering the Ritual Laws of the Jews," Saens's/Monteros's reader would wonder what the author of *Observador Guadalupano* was thinking. Was he trying to hide something within his communication?

In consideration of Monteros's deep interest in the Jews as shown within his *Interpretacion*, the numerous hours he labored writing or copying the manuscript indicates a significant correlation between the real (Jewish) theme of the book and Monteros's own Philo-Semitism. An additional consideration: if Monteros misrepresented the focus of *Cartas*, what else was he manipulating in his writings?

An Estimation of Identity

The combination of the notation of Monteros's family reading psalms at burials and the incorrectly described book *Cartas de unos judíos* transforms a scholarly observation into a statement of fact. At the least, Monteros very likely came from a family that had once been conversos or even *judaizantes*. His continuous musings on how the Jews abandoned Christ yet would be forgiven, on good Jews that had become Christian, and on Jewish children that were circumcised and would all be saved when Christ returned a second time indicate that he had indeed become a Catholic, yet the converso aspect of his history continued to hold a significant portion of his identity. He believed in Christ, yet he also believed in the redemption of the Jews. He sought to remediate what he believed to be the history of the Jews engaging in deicide. He acknowledged the pain of the Jewish Diaspora and found something (the mystery?) in the Virgin of Guadalupe that would bring the Jews back into favor in the eyes of God.

Monteros's far-reaching knowledge of Judaism is paradoxical for a priest specializing in indigenous languages stationed at the Basilica of Guadalupe in México City in the 1830s. His desire to document details from the Old Testament, such as Moses's Tabernacle; the histories of Adam, Jacob, Solomon, David; and the lesser-known Jesus, son of Toredec, is indicative of an affected emotion. His intent was not to erase or diminish the Jew within him. He strove to integrate this aspect with what he was as a sixty-year-old man living in recently independent México. As *Cartas* so clearly exhibits, Monteros sought to purge the negative discourse about the Jews while seeking a way for them to integrate the message of Christ.

Reyna de los Judíos—Queen of the Jews

Monteros was born into a community that was, at that time, formalizing its dedication to the Virgin of Guadalupe. A number of movements promoted by the Mexican colonial Church impressed upon the people that Guadalupe was a necessary devotion. The war of independence from Spain emphasized the tradition and cemented Guadalupe's position among the people of the new nation of México.[91] He, as most Mexicans did and still do in the present day, saw Guadalupe as a representation of their national identity.

But the pairing of Guadalupe and Judaism was not an idea original to Monteros. Guadalupe was the center of Miguel Sánchez's famous book that focused on the Old Testament, even though *Imagen* was publicly acknowledged as a solidly Catholic text that brought the importance of Guadalupe to new heights in the eyes of the seventeenth-century Mexican Church. What is curious is that Sánchez's book was well received once the Jewish themes were purged, but Monteros's books were never published. As noted previously, after four hundred years, the original version of *Imagen* continues to be a book of prominence.

While Sánchez remains the hero of Guadalupe, Monteros's endless manuscripts left México and remained in what almost appears to be a secret hiding place for the last 120 years, never to be cited or even mentioned by anyone. The fate of *Interpretacion* and the *judaizing* heritage of México that is so well represented by Monteros's work are strikingly parallel, having become a subterranean fault line that jostles and unsettles all foundations. Monteros's writings were never published and were left hiding in an unmarked archival section of a foreign library. The *judaizing* background of so many Mexican citizens has rarely been discussed, and the foregoing conclusion is that, after the Mexican Inquisition's *auto-da-fé* of 1649, those who were not executed or permanently imprisoned "left for other parts of Spain."[92]

Monteros's thousands of words on the history of the Jewish people and the eminent return of the powerful Hebrew nation, and his surety that Guadalupe is their representative, presents a man who identifies with Judaism. His words are echoed in Lacunza's *Venida del Mesías*: "In the end I am a Jew and I am not far from practicing Judiasm."[93] Monteros's double discourse of Christianity and a triumphant Judaism indicate that he was, as Richard Popkin describes, "outwardly conforming to the culture around [him], but internally guarding the true faith."[94]

Sion

At the end of *Interpretacion del Imagen Guadalupano*, Monteros signs and dates his manuscript October 2, 1825.[95] Just under his signature, he adds a section cryptically titled "Regarding the Opinion of the Israelites and the Indians." Monteros makes note of a newspaper article that appeared in a México City newspaper. The title is "Reestablishment of the Hebrew Nation." After giving specific details about where he found the information, he writes that a Mayor Noah purchased property on Grand Island on the Niagara River for the establishment of a Jewish territory that is planned to be a refuge for Jews.[96]

Mordecai Manuel Noah is considered by many to be "most prominent and influential Jew in the United States during the first half of the nineteenth century.[97] He was a playwright, journalist, and a diplomat, having been ambassador to Tunisia. He has been called an "American-style Messiah."[98] Monteros would have found that pleasing. Noah's language regarding the Jews would have been familiar to Monteros. During the inauguration of a New York City synagogue in 1818, Noah told his audience that the Jews would only be protected from "tyranny and oppression" when "the Jews can recover their ancient rights and dominions, and take their ranks among the governments of the earth."[99]

Monteros frequently repeated two aspects of the Jewish story. Their being in hiding is mentioned constantly in his texts. In page after page, he writes statements such as "Jews that are hiding," "Jews hiding in an occulted space," "those that are hiding in the occulted space of Mount Sion."[100] He connects the need to hide with the need to return and reestablish their nation, with the assistance of Guadalupe.

While Monteros is focused on the millennium, Guadalupe, and the return of the Hebrew nation, it is clear that the need to hide and the desire to return is prominent on his mind. His note of Mordecai Noah's Zionist project provides the most valuable evidence that his interests were focused on the Jews, and that he very likely carries the internal identity of a *criollo* Jew that continues to be in hiding.

As Monteros completes his notation of the famed Mordecai Noah's Zionist project, the priest ends the manuscript of *Interpretaciones del la Imagen Guadalapana* with a citation from Micah 4:13 that is a reference to Guadalupe: "Rise and show your brilliance, [Guadalupe] daughter of Sion, because you will be made of iron and your fingernails of bronze and you will destroy many cities and sacrifice to the Lord of their people."[101]

Conclusion

━━━━━━━━━━━━━━━━━━━━━━━━━━●

Lost Narratives

In the summer of 1932 Jac Nachbin, a professor from Northwestern University, was arrested in México City on the charge of having stolen documents from the national archives (Archivo General de la Nación).[1] He was accused of taking the Inquisition *proceso*, the memoir, and the personal letters of Luis de Carvajal, "el Mozo," who was burned at the stake by the Mexican Inquisition on December 8, 1596. The professor was released three months later due to lack of evidence.[2] However, there remained a great deal of suspicion. When the papers were eventually published by the Archivo General, a footnote from the introduction contained a narrative of the paper's travels: They were mailed from Las Vegas to New Mexico to New York City, where they were then routed to México City, destined for a recipient named Mr. Lang, who never retrieved them. Subsequently, the package was opened and the contents were forwarded to the Archivo General. Nachbin was listed as the person responsible for the disappearence of the documents.[3]

An ensuing conflict, later known as the *Memorias* controversy, began between the administrators of the archive and Alfonso Toro, a historian (and former staff member) writing a book on the Carvajal family. Toro stated that he had transcribed the memoir before it disappeared. He reported that the administration requested that it be used for their 1935 publication of the Carvajal *proceso*. He agreed, but the Archivo General did not list his name in the credits;[4] the archive administrators stated he had only transcribed a few pages from the manuscript, which they believed was not enough for Toro to be credited.[5] Letters between Toro and the archive administration grew tense. Copies were soon released to the newspapers, with insults flying from both sides.[6]

There might have been a number of reasons behind the escalating tension between Toro and the Archivo General administration. The object of the strife—a memoir written by a *judaizante* living in México at the end of the sixteenth century—should not be overlooked or underestimated. Although Toro was also requesting acknowledgment regarding his discovery of the manuscripts, the polemic centered on who held the right of citation. Charges of incompetence and lack of professionalism between the two parties traveled all over México, even crossing into the United States in a vitriolic essay written by the famed historian Vito Alessio Robles and published in a San Antonio newspaper. Toro accused the Archivo General's lead historian, Luis González Obregón, of "adorning himself with other people's work . . . a man who orchestrates a morning gathering of those who yearn for the useless tinsel of the Porfirian dictatorship."[7] Robles, who clearly was on the side of the Archivo General, returned the insult by calling Toro "fugaz, tornadizo pseudocomunista" (volatile, vacillating pseudo-communist).[8] Robles's choice of words is telling. As mentioned in chapter 5, the term "tornadizo" was used during the early modern period to describe a Jew converted to Christianity—who could or might have already returned to Judaism. Although Robles used the term in association with communism, it is curious that he retrieved a term from the era of the Inquisition to describe Toro. From what I found conducting research in northern México in the 1990s, it appeared that scholars would often decry Jewish associations publicly, yet in private cherished the possibility of a secret genealogy.[9] The history of *judaizantes* in México was (and is) secretly cherished, yet publicly derided. The interest and attachment to this past periodically erupts in squabbles over questionable histories or lost texts.

Robles himself had the same type of problem. The year *Memorias* controversy erupted, he wrote an essay titled "La Judería de Monterrey" in which he surmised that the Carvajal family had been part of a larger group of *judaizantes* who intended to establish a community in northern México.[10] Robles also became embroiled in a public controversy regarding the story of *judaizantes* in Nuevo León, when fellow historian Santiago Roel accused Robles of exaggerating the presence of *judaizantes* in Monterrey.[11] Robles backtracked on his initial claims in a subsequent reprinting of the work, saying "none of Carvajal's Jews were among the later settlers."[12]

The problem between Alfonso Toro and the Archivo General administration relates to the symbolic issue of identity, or rather the ownership of identity. Each group is fighting for its stake in the *Memorias*, which symbolizes early Jewish history in México. While the fight might have been about egos and professional strategizing, it was also about who could be associated with the *judaizantes*. This was significant because even in the twenty-first century it is impossible for México to own its Jewishness.[13] If Toro or any of the archivists knew of Jewish genealogy in their families, they were not able to publicly address this knowledge. Yet, identification through association (with Judaism) became possible with the study and publication of Carvajal's *Memorias*, where the author's text leaves no doubt of who he is: "Librado José Lumbroso [Luis de Carvajal], of the Hebrew Nation."[14] In other words, it was the historian's way of acknowledging México's history of *judaizantes*. Since it was Carvajal's personal story, it was possible to keep a proper distance.

A Foundational Narrative

On June 14, 1579, Felipe II of Spain issued twenty-one *cédulas* (royal orders) granting Luis Carvajal y de la Cueva special privileges, rights, and assistance from the king's officers regarding Carvajal's acquisition, and Felipe made him governor of "a vast territorial entity in New Spain, called Nuevo Reino de León (New Kingdom of León)."[15]

The story of Gov. Luis Carvajal y la Cueva and his family has not been identified as a foundational narrative to the Mexican nation. I propose that it should be. The narrative of Carvajal and the *judaizantes* he brought to the Indies is continuously repeated in the colonial history of México. There are few books on *judaizantes* in New Spain that do not include some aspect of the Carvajal narrative. The case is significant in that the governor's nephew, Luis de Carvajal, left what is considered the only known document of any *judaizante* in the colony that clearly states his identity.[16] The conjectures and questions posed by numerous texts when discussing those who might or might not be *judaizantes* or conversos shows itself at every turn.[17]

What the king gave Carvajal is almost beyond comprehension: the gift "encompassed 702,244 square kilometers, equal to one third of the present Mexican nation."[18] Equally extraordinary was that the king had only issued fourteen of these awards in the forty years of his reign.[19]

While Carvajal's role in colonial history is significant because of the size of the territory he was given, he is often noted because the families he brought to New Spain were not required to present proof of *limpieza de sangre*. Instead the king wrote, "We charge said captain Luis de Carvajal to be careful that all of them be clean, and not of the forbidden."[20] This was not a deliberate nullification of the *limpieza de sangre* requirement, yet it placed the responsibility in the hands of Carvajal. When Carvajal was arrested and interrogated in 1589 by the Mexican Inquisition, he was asked "whether they had presented proof of not being 'of the forbidden.'" He said that they did not have to because the king had issued a *cédula* ordering that they could pass into New Spain without it.[21]

Most of the governor's extended family was entangled in this morass. His nephew, Luis de Carvajal, was released but arrested again a few years later and was eventually burned at the stake in México City in 1596.[22] While incarcerated, he took the name José Lumbroso. He ardently defended his faith until the end, when it is said he converted to Catholicism. His conversion is still disputed by scholars.[23]

Carvajal (or Lumbroso) left behind a manuscript—the same manuscript that Toro claims to have transcribed—of his memoirs and letters he wrote to his sisters and mother. Carvajal's *Memorias* are the only known writings of anyone willing to admit to being Jewish during México's colonial period—that is, anyone who stated so outside of the Inquisition courts.[24] He begins his memoirs: "From México in New Spain. From the most serious dangers, by Sr. Librado Jose Lumbroso, of the Hebrew nation, of the pilgrims of the India of the occident and the captives in recognition of the mercy and gifts received by the hand of the most high."[25]

Carvajal's memoir provides a foundation regarding the Jewish presence in the colony that cannot be disputed. On numerous occasions, authors from later periods that do not clearly identify themselves as Jews use the same phrases and explanations as Carvajal. This could be said to be mere coincidence, yet the repetitive nature of these similarities requires analysis that will likely lean toward a meaningful foundational narrative.

Carvajal was born in Benavente, Castilla, Spain, in 1566. His parents were Catholic, and he was baptized soon after birth. He was educated at home until age eleven in reading, writing, and mathematics. The family then moved to Medina del Campo where he attended a Jesuit school for the next two years.[26] In 1579 he and his family left Spain for the Indies on a ship named *Nuestra Señora de la Luz* (Our Lady of the Light). The ship was commanded by his uncle, Luis Carvajal y de la Cueva.[27] There were approximately two hundred persons on board.[28]

According to Martin Cohen, Luis "el Mozo" learned from his brother that the Carvajals were *judaizantes* shortly before they left Spain. The Holy Office (the Inquisition) arrested the Carvajals ten years later. Governor Carvajal died in the Inquisition prison, and the rest of the family was released. Carvajal, his mother, and sisters were arrested again in 1595, and he was executed a year later. During his confinement, he wrote memoirs that detailed his life and his introduction and commitment to Judaism.

Carvajal's formal religious training in Judaism was scant, based primarily on what his father had taught him after he turned twelve. He augmented his knowledge significantly with readings from the Old Testament he accessed while working at the Colegio de Santiago Tlatelolco. He came to be extremely well versed. The movement of books that traversed the Atlantic provided the religious education Carvajal was lacking. The efforts of Benito Arias Montano and the Portuguese merchants preserved Jewish knowledge in the Americas.

As a result of his first trial, the Inquisition placed Carvajal in a Catholic convent, perhaps hoping that living among the clergy would inspire him to become more Christian. Interestingly, this inadvertently created a situation for him to deepen his knowledge of Judaism in ways he never dreamed. The priest at the college befriended his family and invited Luis to assist him in copying certain manuscripts. In a type of irony frequently repeated among the crypto-Jews of Iberia and New Spain, Luis found himself preparing "a collection of illustrative material from a commentary on the Pentateuch . . . based on post-biblical Jewish sources." Luis was not aware that this commentary "included Moses Maimonides' Thirteen Articles of Faith."[29] His supervisor, Friar Pedro de Oroz, also brought in Nicholas de Lyra's "Glosses," another "commentary with rabbinic sources."[30] In a curious turn of events, Oroz gave Luis the key to the library. Eventually, the college became a gathering place for México City's Jews, with Luis at the center. There is no documentation regarding the private religious preferences of Friar Oroz, yet his open acceptance of Carvajal, with full knowledge of his *judaizante* background, his intense interest in commentaries regarding the Old Testament, and his enthusiasm at providing them for Luis to read are worth noting. Cohen notes his surprise while explaining that Carvajal ultimately transformed the college into an "underground headquarters of the secret Jews of New Spain."[31] As it happens, Santiago Tlatelolco was not the only Catholic site that became a home to the *judaizantes*.

Unlike All Other Nations

There are a number of links between the writing of Carvajal and later authors who composed similar messages. *Memorias* tells of one incident that echoes four centuries later. Shortly before his second incarceration, as Carvajal was preparing to leave New Spain for Italy, he had second thoughts about leaving behind his brother Gaspar, who was a Dominican friar. Luis and his brother Baltasar visited their oldest brother, Gaspar, and tried to convince the monk to believe in Jewish law. Gaspar became furious, who responded, "aunque aquella avia sido ley de D. que ya era acabada (even though it had been the law of God, it was now finished)."[32] The disagreement continued, and as Luis was leaving, he repeated a verse from Psalm 147: "Non fecit talliter omni nationi (He hath not done in like manner to every nation)." He writes in his memoir that Gaspar "could not deny nor contradict the statement and remained speechless."[33]

Luis de Carvajal was attempting to convince his brother the friar that the law of Moses was still vibrant and relevant, that God had continued to bless "his nation" in a very special way. Gaspar's silence could have meant that the friar continued to maintain some belief or allegiance to his family's religion. Yet only Luis was willing to say he still believed. Gaspar might have been avoiding agreement with his brother because of the serious dangers involved in openly pronouncing that one is Jewish. Interestingly, it was Luis's citation of Psalm 147:20 that over time was to be repeated throughout México's history.

Luis read the psalm as an indication that the nation of Israel received special attention from God.

As it turned out, Psalm 147:20 became associated with the Virgin of Guadalupe, and México. In 1678 a Jesuit priest born in Spanish Florida named Francisco de Florencia, known as a fervent devotee of Guadalupe, commissioned a medallion of the Virgin along with the verse from Psalm 147:20. Designed by Cornelis Galle in Antwerp, the medal presented an image of Guadalupe along with a banner stating "Non fecti taliter omni nacione" (Not done so with any nation). Florencia had seen the inscription at the sanctuary of the Virgin of Loreto, considered one of the most important sanctuaries to the Virgin Mary in Europe. While visiting Loreto, he thought of Tepeyac and later described the emotive power of Guadalupe, "by that natural affection which includes so powerfully . . . and moves us with even more vehemence on everything that is of the *patria* (nation)."[34] A century and a half later, Manuel Espinosa de los Monteros explains that the Mexican Guadalupe's sanctuary is more significant than that of the Virgins located in Spain.[35] He bases this conclusion on an edict by Pope Benedict XIV.

Benedict is also cited by Torre and Villar in the footnotes of their encyclopedic anthology of writings on Guadalupe. According to *La Virgin de Tepeyac*, published in 1884, Benedict XIV spoke the words from Psalm 147 upon seeing an image of Guadalupe.[36] Eleven years before Benedict saw the image, the phrase "Non fecit taliter omni nationi" is found on pamphlet titled "La Octava Maravilla" by Jesuit Juan Carnero. Yet the most significant is that "Omni nacioni" is found in a text published in Alcalá de Henares in 1539, *Historia del divino misterio del Santísimo Sacramento* (History of the divine mystery of the Holiest Sacrament). The psalm had a history of being used for other Catholic cults, not just of the Virgin's. Torre and Villar question if Father Florencia was reporting with irony that only México and the Virgin were conveyed the blessings of Psalm 147.[37]

Pio Saens/Monteros, in *El oberservador Guadalupano*, discusses Psalm 147: "It was written during a time that the Lord was very pleased with the Hebrew nation, and detested the nations whose people used idols and did not know Him. . . . He himself spoke with the fathers of this nation, Abran, Isaac, and Jacob, and did the same with Moses, with the Prophets, and many other Hebrews, and the whole nation when the Lord gave them his Law from the summit of Sinai."[38]

A Paradoxical Position

Miguel Sánchez and Manuel Espinosa de los Monteros saw the messiah through the Virgin of Guadalupe. A deep analysis of their writing provides a strong indication that they had some type of special relationship with Judaism, which during their lifetimes would have surely meant an awareness of Jewish ancestors accompanied by some degree of risk. Matt Goldish describes three circumstances that are often found surrounding conversos who are deeply interested in Messianism: "upbringing in a Catholic environment tinctured with a collective memory of Jewish ancestry; their *relative* disconnection from authoritative messianic traditions of either Judaism or Christianity; and their untenable situation as pariahs in two faiths and cultures."[39] It is likely that Sánchez and Monteros had significant knowledge of Judaism through their families or friends. Their position as priests in the Catholic Church at a time and place where Judaism was outlawed placed them in a paradoxical position. Their status as clergy allowed them access to libraries that contained the polyglot Bibles and other censored material. Yet they could not speak or write publicly about their knowledge of Judaism unless their texts were veiled with distracting titles. From their position in society, Sánchez and Monteros do not appear to have been outsiders. Sánchez had numerous supporters, including the viceroys of New Spain. Monteros was securely inside a close-knit social circle within his family and social network among the *criollos* of México City.

Yet, along with this security, they both were aware of the dilemmas experienced by others who had Jewish or converso identifications. Sánchez sees the Woman of the Apocalypse (representing the people who he says should pray psalms to God "secretly") as instrumental to the arrival of the messiah (the unborn child) that the seven-headed dragon (the Roman Church and/or the Inquisition) is seeking to destroy. The dragon will not be deterred and also seeks the descendants of the Woman. Sánchez does not appear to be afraid of the Inquisition, but the mere fact that it is mentioned in *Imagen*, something so unusual in this type of writing, indicates he is well aware of the current dangers to others in his society. Who does he believe will read *Imagen*? Considering that a very limited number of individuals would be interested or want to read his erudite production, who was he really writing for? Was it the other priests in México who, like him, might also be descended from conversos? There could be a significant number, especially considering that there were no *limpieza de sangre* requirements for the university until dictated in 1648 by the archbishop of Puebla (and later acting viceroy), Juan de Palafox y Mendoza.[40] It is no coincidence that these regulations were instituted during a time of heightened Inquisitorial activity. As previously noted, this is the same year that *Imagen* was published.

Sánchez was in a unique position for his time. He had a significant amount of ambition and had sought a prestigious university position at one point. When he did not get that position, he reacted by removing himself (at least partially) from most material conveniences and lived in a room at the Basilica that had the bare minimum of convenience.[41] Paradoxically, while he lived in such simplicity, he often conversed with the powerful of the colony. *Imagen* was commissioned by Marcos Torres y Rueda, interim viceroy of New Spain from April 1648 to May 1649. The year 1648 was a watershed for events affecting not only the colony but also the Jews of both Europe and the Americas. The tenure of the previous viceroy, Salvatierra, is considered "among the most disturbed in the history of the viceroyalty [of New Spain]."[42] The visitor-general and emissary of the king, Palafox, had been battling with the viceroys, the Jesuits, and the Holy Office since he arrived in 1640. The publication of *Imagen* came shortly before Palafox finally left Mexico. Yet it occurred at a telling juncture in the political history of the colony.

Sánchez worked on *Imagen* for a number of years, throughout the period that the Mexican Inquisition had begun its tirade against the Portuguese Jews in the colony. The book was published sometime between July and December 1648. In November 1647, the new viceroy, Torres, the former bishop of Merida, arrived preemptively in México City. The outgoing viceroy (who did not want to leave México City), Salvatierra, would not move out of the viceregal palace. With this complication and the additional political intrigue connected with the feud between Palafox and the Jesuits, Torres was left waiting another five months for Salvatierra to leave.[43] Since *Imagen* was published sometime between July and December 1648, Torres did not have much time to have commissioned the work. Considering the timing, it is more likely that Torres became involved when the book was very close to publication.

The question remains, why did Torres pay the costs for a book that would have been considered heretical? *Imagen*'s constant mention of Old Testament figures, Sánchez's stating that Guadalupe was a candelabra with seven lamps (a menorah), and even Francisco de Siles's long exposition of Queen Esther as an afterword in the book would have stirred up the Inquisition to no end. Yet Torres arrived with the intention of showing support for Palafox and the visitor-general's followers.[44] Although Palafox had earlier provoked the Inquisition against the Jews, by 1648 he was against the Inquisition's activities. The tension was significantly high at the time, and Torres immediately changed out numerous positions that had been filled by Salvatierra. The anti-Palafox camp of the previous viceroy; the archbishop of México City, Mañozca; and the Holy Office would not have been pleased with such a book being printed. It is also possible that Torres sought some type of alliance with Sánchez because of the priest's popularity. As Robles states in *Diario de Sucesos Notables*, Sánchez was "highly esteemed by viceroys, archbishops, dignitaries, judges, prelates, and everyone else."[45]

Monteros repeatedly mentions the conditions that "old world" Jews and conversos were experiencing in Europe. He compares them to other Europeans and notes they are extremely similar and cannot be distinguished except when they are publicly identified as being Jewish. He lists the reasons they are respected: for their education, their accomplishments, their civilized behavior.[46] He mentions that Spain has done everything in its power to annihilate the Jews, and that the Inquisitorial system in México is not as barbarous. Yet it is clear he is not living in Europe. He is a Catholic priest functioning within a religious society that he detests. His continuous statements regarding the corruption of the clergy, the bishops, and the popes evoke humble arrogance.[47] He says he agrees with his religious contemporaries who believe that the Jews committed deicide. Yet he believes unconverted "good Jews" were forgiven by God for having abandoned Christ.[48] He speaks of Jews turned good Christians, good Jews, and innocent Jewish children who will be taken into God's fold because they have been circumcised.[49]

When he speaks of non-Jews, he uses the term "gentiles"; he believes that they are God's second choice, as in the case of the *segunda esposa* (second wife) who is gentile and eventually becomes corrupted. The incorruptible Jewish Esposa is the woman God wanted all along, yet he had to let her go when her people refused to accept Christ. The first Esposa is Guadalupe. According to Monteros, she will reign as monarch over all the nations. She will bring the Hebrew nation back to its summit of power.

The question is, if Monteros is so secure in his life and so easily able to criticize the Church and the Mother Nation of Spain (I realize this was after México's independence), then why is it so important for him to bring Israel back to its grandeur? He is not necessarily leaving Christ aside, yet the role of Christ is not quite as significant because of the presence of the all-powerful Guadalupe. This positioning taken by Monteros resonates with what Matt Goldish describes as "an outlook with elements unique or original in this community." Included in this are two characteristics: "a particular willingness to entertain a wide variety of messianic scenarios, and the reservation of a special place for the *conversos* in the messianic process, even at times including a *converso* messiah."[50]

The choice of Monteros and Sánchez is truly original; they have found a converso messiah that is a woman. She is the Virgin of Guadalupe.

Postscript

While conducting research on the Jews and the two Guadalupes, a number of other related issues have come into view. Several individuals contacted me regarding the Jewish history of their families. I have located what appears to be a long-ago Jewish community in Del Rio, Texas, that left behind a cemetery with many Jewish symbols intertwined with Christian crosses.[51] I also met a family named Olivares originally from northern México; they still have in their possession a ring of unknown age that has the word "Adonay" engraved on the inside. A great-grandmother (named Mendez) spoke Hebrew. Among their ancestors were Carvajals, yet neither the family nor I are sure there is a connection to Luis Carvajal, "el Mozo." Everyone, however, wishes there were.

The most striking surprise is an object I found at a museum in San Antonio, Texas. In a 2005 visit to the Alamo, I saw a brass candelabrum that appeared to have been damaged. I asked an attendant about its history and was told that it came from the home of the governor of Coahuila y Tejas, Juan Martin de Veramendi. The Veramendi family was from Saltillo, Coahuila. They were part of an extended group of Europeans who settled northern México in the mid-eighteenth century. As I stood in front of the candelabrum, I initially saw six candleholders. After a few moments, I realized there was one more holder, but it was turned down. The bent candleholder disguised the object's actual identity. It was a menorah. Several years later, in 2011, I returned to the Alamo and asked for more information regarding the candelabrum. A helpful docent told me that everyone on staff knew it was a menorah. Yet it had never been described as such in any of the museum's publications.

Appendix A

From *La interpretacion del Misterio Guadalupano* by Manuel Espinosa de los Monteros, Part II, no. 6, fol. 2b

. . . the painting characterizes the Guadalupe miracle, it contemplates a grave circumstance that shows itself to be singularly rare, and says more than it materially represents, or, as is the same, with this image that is extraordinarily exquisite and precious, hides secrets of importance to the favored nation with this extraordinarily exquisite precious object. So much as these words from the psalm [147] want to express: He did not manifest his Judgments. The painting has these writings. Are these remembrances of past successes? Even more, why are they hidden when their description can be seen in History, a book open to all the nations?

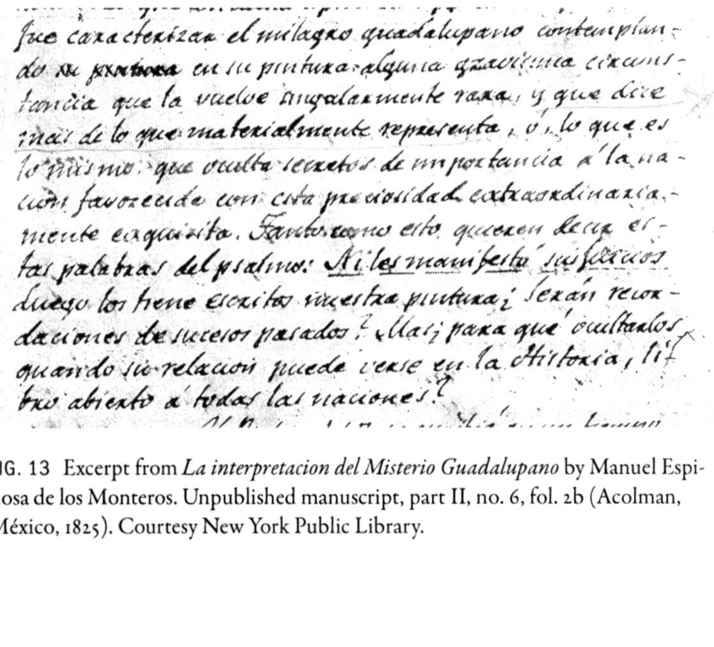
que caracteriza el milagro guadalupano contemplan-
do en su pintura alguna gravísima circuns-
tancia que la vuelve singularmente rara, y que dice
mas de lo que materialmente representa, ó, lo que es
lo mismo: que oculta secretos de importancia á la nacion favorecida con esta preciosidad extraordinaria-
mente exquisita. Tanto como esto quieren decir es-
tas palabras del psalmo: Ni les manifestó sus juicios
luego los tiene escritos nuestra pintura; serán recor-
daciones de sucesos pasados? Mas ¿para qué ocultarlos
quando su relacion puede verse en la Historia, libro abierto á todas las naciones?

FIG. 13 Excerpt from *La interpretacion del Misterio Guadalupano* by Manuel Espinosa de los Monteros. Unpublished manuscript, part II, no. 6, fol. 2b (Acolman, México, 1825). Courtesy New York Public Library.

Appendix B

From *El observador Guadalupano* by Pio Saens (Manuel Espinosa de los Monteros?), n.p.

The Holiest Virgin in the role of representative of the Hebrew Nation is the first Wife reestablished to her ancient dignity and is protected by her Beloved: the Judaic Church that is not founded on only one rock of limited size, but over the same rock as Christ that was separated without the hands of humans, and occupies the entire world as a wilderness. The Virgin will not protect the zeal or vigilance of a Vicar of Christ, but only Christ himself who establishes his court in Jerusalem. All of this will be clarified in two interpretations.

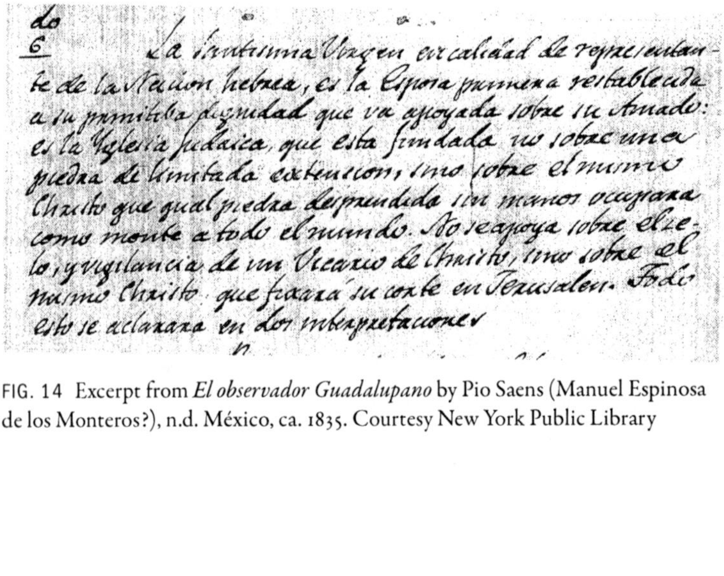

do
6 La Santisima Virgen en calidad de representante de la Nacion hebrea, es la Esposa primera restablecida a su primitiva dignidad que va apoyada sobre su Amado: es la Yglesia Judaica, que esta fundada no sobre una piedra de limitada extension, sino sobre el mismo Christo que qual piedra desprendida sin manos ocupara como monte a todo el mundo. No se apoya sobre el zelo, y vigilancia de un Vicario de Christo, sino sobre el mismo Christo que fixará su corte en Jerusalen. Todo esto se aclarara en las interpretaciones

FIG. 14 Excerpt from *El observador Guadalupano* by Pio Saens (Manuel Espinosa de los Monteros?), n.d. México, ca. 1835. Courtesy New York Public Library

Appendix C

Personages

Hieronymus Bosch (1450–1516). Netherlands. A lay member of the highly conservative Brotherhood of Our Lady. Painted religious allegories with frequent apocalyptic references. His painting *Garden of Earthly Delight* was purchased by Spanish king Felipe II for his art collection at San Lorenzo de Escorial.

Carlos V (1500–1558), also known as King Carlos I (Charles I) of Spain. Elected Holy Roman emperor in 1519. Born in the Burgundian Low Countries, he inherited the Spanish crown through his mother Juana, daughter of Isabel and Fernando of Spain, los Reyes Católicos (the Catholic Kings). He oversaw one of the largest empires in Western history, encompassing most of Europe and the East and West Indies (Spanish colonies in the Americas and Asia).

Luis de Carvajal, el Mozo (1566–1589). México. Born in Benavente, Spain. He migrated to New Spain with his parents in 1580. He was the nephew and namesake of Luis de Carvajal y de la Cueva, first governor of el Nuevo Reino de León (the New Kingdom of León). The governor and most of the Carvajal family were arrested and tried as *judaizantes* by the Mexican Inquisition by the end of the century. The younger Carvajal was burned at the stake after his second arrest. His *Memorias* are said to be the only extant writings showing the existence of *judaizantes* in colonial México.

Miguel de Cervantes (1547–1616). Spain. Greatest of writer of the Spanish Golden Age. Author of the first modern novel. Considered by numerous scholars to be of converso descent. The *Comedia de la Soberana Virgen de Guadalupe, y sus milagros, y grandezas de España* is attributed to Cervantes.

Manuel Espinosa de los Monteros (1773–1838). México. Priest educated at the famous Santiago Tlatelolco. Known for his mastery of numerous indigenous languages. His last eight years were served at the most important Catholic shrine in México, the Basilica of the Virgin of Guadalupe. He left a significant body of work regarding his unorthodox views about the Virgin of Guadalupe and her relationship with the Jews and the Old Testament.

Felipe II (1527–1598). Spain. Son of Carlos V. Also known as King Philip II of Spain. He was king of Portugal from 1581 to 1598, and king of Naples from 1554 to 1598. While the territories he controlled were much smaller than those of his father, he was still sovereign of much of the known world. His reign brought severe control to the practice of Catholicism, resulting from the encroachment of Protestantism.

Pedro Fernández Pecha (1326–1402). Spain. Lay brother and founder of the Hieronymite Order of Monks. He as born to a family of nobility, his father being the chief attendant to King Alfonso XI. He was brought to court to be a companion to Prince Pedro (later Pedro I). Before founding the order, at the age of twenty-two, Pecha was the royal treasurer to King Alfonso. After the king's death, Pecha became keeper of the Royal Seal and keeper of the keys for the queen mother for the successor, Pedro I.

Fernando V (1452–1516). Spain. King of Aragón and consort to Isabel I. Known as el Rey Católico. During his and his wife's reign, Spain defeated the Muslims in Granada, their stronghold on the peninsula. The same year, 1492, he and Isabel published the Edict of Expulsion of the Jews.

Felipe Godíñez (1588–1637). Spain. Jesuit, dramatist. Wrote "Auto Sacramental de la Virgen," which discusses the Black Virgin of Extremadura and miracles attributed to her. He was arrested, tried, and convicted as a *judaizante* by the Spanish Inquisition in 1624 for writing *La Reina Esther* (Queen Esther), which conflated the figure of the Virgin Mary and the Jewish Queen Esther.

Isabel I (1451–1504). Spain. Known as one of los Reyes Católicos. Queen of Castilla (Castille) and Aragón. Along with her consort, Fernando V, she ordered the Edict of Expulsion of the Jews from Spain in 1492. She also authorized the voyage of Columbus to the Indies, which occurred the same year.

Luis de León (1527–1591). Spain. Priest in the Order of Saint Augustine. Considered one of the greatest poets of Spain's Golden Age. Professor of Hebrew at the University of Salamanca. Descendent of *judaizantes* tried and convicted by the Spanish Inquisition. He was arrested in 1572 for his work on Hebrew biblical texts. He was released in 1576 after four years in solitary confinement. During this time he authored his greatest work, *De los nombres de Christo* (The Names of Christ), which has been noted for its Kabbalistic elements.

Benito Arias Montano (1527–1598). Spain. Priest, polymath, Hebraist, theological scholar, diplomat. *Capellán* to King Felipe II of Spain. Directed the production of the *Antwerp Polyglot Bible*, commissioned by Felipe II and the establishment of the Royal Library at Felipe II's palace, San Lorenzo de Escorial.

Pedro I (1334–1369). Spain. Known as Pedro el Cruel (the Cruel). His reign brought chaos and terror to the kingdom. He was known for easily murdering family members as well as close associates.

José Fernando Ramirez (1804–1871). México. Member of the Mexican Congress, director of the Academy of Fine Arts. Bibliophile and collector. During the reign of Emperor Maximilian, Ramirez was president of the cabinet and minister of exterior relations. He went into exile in Europe after the execution of Maximilian in 1866. His vast collection of Mexican colonial manuscripts was sold at auction in London in 1880.

Miguel Sánchez (ca. 1606–1674). México. Priest. Authored *Imagen de la Virgen Maria Madre de Dios de Guadalupe* (Image of the Virgin Mary Mother of God of Guadalupe), considered to be the most important book published in colonial México. During the last decades of his life he lived in at Basilica of the Virgin of Guadalupe in México City. Even though he lived as an aesthete, he is known to have been a favorite of viceroys and other elite of the city.

Dionisio Vázquez (1479–1539). Spain. Augustinian priest. Student of Alonso de Zamora. Mentored by Egidio da Viterbo. Director of the Augustinian school in Rome. Orator to Popes Julius II and Leo X. *Vicario* (deputy in ecclesiastic affairs) and *visitador* for Spain and its colonies in the Low Countries. Orator for Carlos V. Professor of Hebrew at the University of Alcalá. Arrested by the Spanish Inquisition in 1508 on charges of giving a heretical sermon. He traveled to Rome soon after the arrest, where he was eventually exonerated. Several of his works were censured by the Portuguese Inquisition in 1581.

Egidio da Viterbo (1469–1532). Italy. Cardinal. Also known as Aegiduis Antonini or Giles of Viterbo. Viterbo was closely associated with the Medici, having studied in their home as a young man with Florentine Neo-Platonist Marsilio Ficino. He developed relationships with Fernando el Rey Católico and Carlos V, and mentored noted Spanish Hebraist Dionisio Vazquez. He is known for his wide support of Jewish and converso scholars and was the force behind the translations and publications of numerous Hebrew texts. He was a prolific author, yet never published his work. He authored *Scechina e Libellus de litteris hebraicis*, a work on the Shekhinah from the Jewish Kabbalah, dedicated to Carlos V.

Fernando Yañez de Figueroa (ca. 1332–1412). Spain. Priest. Founder of the Hieronymite Order of Monks. Before founding the order, he was *capellán* at the Cathedral of Toledo. His mother was of the nobility. Left at court as companion to Prince Pedro, along with Pedro Fernández Pecha.

García Zapata de Toledo (d. 1488). Spain. Prior of Hieronymite monastery La Sisla. Brother of Fernan Álvarez de Toledo, secretary to King Fernando and Isabel and Francisco Álvarez de Toledo, canon of the Cathedral of Toledo. Burned at the stake on charges of being a *judaizante*.

Alonso de Zamora (1474?–1544). Spain. Hebraist at the University of Salamanca. Translator of the *Cisneros Polyglot Bible*. Translated numerous Hebrew documents, including the prologue and commentary of David Qinhi and the *Targum*—the Aramaic version of the Hebrew Bible. Teacher of Dionisio Vázquez. In 1544 he wrote that he was the last knowledgeable Jew living in Spain after the Expulsion.

Chronology

Europe

1st century C.E.—Black Virgin (later known as the Virgin of Guadalupe of Extremadura) said to have been sculpted by Saint Luke.

587—Pope Gregory the Great said to have given the statue of the Black Virgin to San Leandro, who takes her to Spain.

8th century—Guadalupe buried in a cave located in the mountains west of Toledo.

13th century—Cowherd named Gil Cordero discovers the statue of Guadalupe near the River Guadalupe in Extremadura.

1217—Sanctuary to the Black Virgin assigned to the Diocese of Toledo.

1326—Letter signed at Avignon by nine high-ranking Church officials promotes the importance of the sanctuary as a pilgrimage site.

1350—Pedro el Cruel crowned monarch of Castilla. Soon after, Fernando Yañez leaves post of Keeper of the Royal Seal and Keys to become a hermit.

1366—Pedro Fernández Pecha joins Fernando Yañez and a number of other hermits. They gather together with a group of Portuguese, Italians, and Spaniards in the forests of Castilla and live in primitive circumstances.

1369—Pedro el Cruel murdered by his half brother Enrique.

1370—Establishment of first Hieronymite monastery, San Bartolome de Lupiana, in Guadalajara.

1389—King Juan I of Castilla bestows Monastery of Guadalupe to the Hieronymites. Pedro Fernández Pecha is named prior.

1391—Pogrom against the Jews of Seville, with four thousand killed in one day.

1474—Fernando and Isabel ascend throne of Castilla and Aragón.

1481—Fernando and Isabel ordered the establishment of the Holy Inquisition.

1484—The Inquisition begins investigations of residents in the *puebla* of Guadalupe.

1485—The Inquisition begins investigating the presence of Judaizers among the monks of the Guadalupe Monastery.

1487—The Inquisition investigates the Monastery of La Sisla. Fray García Zapata de Toledo is accused of being a Judaizer. He is burned at the stake.

1492—Fall of Granada; Christopher Columbus's discovery of the Americas; expulsion of the Jews from Spain. Archbishop Francisco Jiménez de Cisneros initiates the production of a polyglot Bible.

1497 (approximate year)—A statue of Nuestra Señora de la Concepción (Our Lady of the Conception), also known as "la Virgen del Coro," or "la Inmaculada," is sculpted by Guillermín de Gante and placed in the choir loft. The Jews of Portugal are forced to convert.

1517—The *Cisneros Polyglot Bible* is published and distributed.

1518—Carlos V is anointed Holy Roman Emperor.

1527—Spanish soldiers and German mercenaries sack Rome and capture the pope for seven months. Birth of Felipe II and Benito Arias Montano.

1556—Felipe II takes the throne.

1563—Construction begins on the palace-monastery of Escorial.

1566—Benito Arias Montano goes into the service of Felipe II.

1568—Felipe II commissions the production of the *Antwerp Bible* (also known as *la Biblia Regia* and the *Plantin Polyglot*) with Benito Arias Montano directing the project.

1572—Luis de León is arrested on charges of Judaizing. He is imprisoned for seven years.

1573—Production of the Antwerp Bible is completed.

1581—Felipe II takes the crown of Portugal, which is now joined with Spain.

1584—Construction of Escorial is completed. Six statues of the kings of Israel are installed in Escorial's "Patio of the Kings."

1613—Felipe Godíñez writes *La Reina Ester.*

1616—Miguel de Cervantes writes *Los trabajos de Persiles y Sigismunda*.

1618—Lope de Vega y Carpio publishes *La limpieza no manchada*.

1619—Luis de Góngora y Argote publishes the poem "Justicia."

1624—Felipe Godíñez is sentenced by the Inquisition for Judaizing.

1640—Portugal revolts from Spain.

1659—Antonio Vieira publishes *Esperanças de Portugal*.

México

1531—Virgin of Guadalupe appears at Tepeyac, near México City.

1579—Felipe II give Luis Carvajal y de la Cueva permission to establish the Nuevo Reino de León in what is now northern México. He is named governor of the new territory and brings his immediate family to New Spain.

1589—Luis Carvajal y de la Cueva arrested by the Mexican Inquisition on charges of harboring Judaizers.

1596—The Inquisition charges Luis Carvajal, el Mozo (nephew of Governer Carvajal) with being a Judaizer. He is burned at the stake.

1606 (**approximate year**)—Miguel Sánchez born in Puebla.

1642—"La Gran Complicidad," a network of Portuguese Judaizers, is discovered in México City. The Mexican Inquisition arrests scores of Portuguese.

1648—Miguel Sánchez publishes *Imagen de la Virgen Maria de Guadalupe* while living in the *colegiata* of the Basilica. In a large *auto-da-fe* twenty-two Portuguese Judaizers are reconciled by the Inquisition.

1649—109 Judaizers reconciled in the largest *auto-da-fe* in the history of New Spain. Thirteen are burned alive.

1660—Significantly edited (and reduced) version of *Imagen de la Virgen Maria* is published.

1674—Death of Miguel Sánchez.

1773—Manuel Espinosa de los Monteros is born in México City.

1778—Juan de Veramendi born in San Fernando de Bexar in the province of Coahuila y Tejas—at the time part of México, in what is now San Antonio, Texas.

1800—Monteros is ordained a priest.

1804—José Fernando Ramírez is born in Durango.

1820—Mexican Inquisition abolished.

1825—Monteros writes *Interpretacion de la Pintura Guadalupana* while at the Monastery of Acolman.

1826—Manuel Lacunza publishes *La venida del Mesías en gloria y majestad* in London.

1831—Monteros appointed canon of native languages at the Basilica of Guadalupe in México City.

1831—Monteros promoted to archivist of the Basilica of Guadalupe.

1832—Veramendi appointed governor of the Coahuila y Tejas province.

1833—Veramendi dies in Saltillo, Coahuila.

1836—Veramendi's home sacked before or during the battle of the Alamo. Two menorahs from his home are taken by Texas soldiers.

1838—Death of Monteros.

1847—Beginning of the U.S.-Mexican War. José Fernando Ramírez appointed Mexican secretary of exterior relations.

1856—José Fernando Ramírez appointed director of the National Museum of México and president of the executive board of the Academy of Fine Arts.

1864—Maximilian proclaimed emperor of México. José Fernando Ramírez named minister of relations and president of Maximilian's cabinet.

1867—Maximilian executed. Ramírez leaves México for Europe.

1871—Ramírez dies in Bonn, Germany.

1880—Ramírez archive sold by Puttick and Simpson in London. Among the papers are the Monteros manuscripts. They are purchased by the New York Public Library.

1932—Memoirs and *proceso* of Luis Carvajal, el Mozo, are stolen from the Archivo General de la Nación (Mexican national archives).

Notes

Introduction

1. Ann Laura Stoler, *Along the Archival Grain: Epistemic Anxieties and Colonial Common Sense* (Princeton, NJ: Princeton University Press, 2009), 181. Cited in Roland Barthes, *Camera Lucida: Reflections on Photography* (New York: Hill and Wang, 1981), 53.

2. Richard H. Popkin, "Jewish Christians and Christian Jews in Spain, 1492 and After," *Judaism* 41, no. 3 (1992): 256. Popkin describes Jewish Christianity as being "grounded in direct contact with the Jewish world of the time of Jesus through the study of Hebrew and Aramaic texts." This description changes according to the field of study. While Popkin is considered an eminent scholar, a number of historians of Jewish history question the possibility of Jewish Christians and Christian Jews.

3. Brian Francis Connaughton Hanley, "Introduction," in *Manuel Espinosa de los Monteros: Miscelánea (1831–1832): Tomos I y II de varias doctrinas morales, costumbres, observaciones y otras noticias pertinentes al curato de Iztacalco* (México City: Universidad Autónoma Metropolitana, 2012), 48, 55.

4. A *colegiata* is a church that is not designated a cathedral, yet it has a rector and a dean.

5. I met with Monsignor Schulenburg in March 2008. He was the abbot of the Basilica of the Virgin of Guadalupe for twenty-five years, resigning abruptly in 1996 under pressure after he stated publicly that he doubted the validity of the canonization of Juan Diego, the indigenous man to whom Guadalupe appeared.

6. Monteros exhibits the typical racism of his day against indigenous people. Unfortunately, this issue will not be addressed in this book. A closer analysis of his life and writings will be the subject of a future project.

7. Miriam Bodian describes the "Hebrew nation" as "the population of conversos and ex-conversos with roots in post-Expulsion Spain and Portugal." See *Hebrews of the Portuguese Nation: Conversos and Community in Early Modern Amsterdam* (Bloomington: University of Indiana, 1999), ix.

8. Manuel Espinosa de los Monteros, *La Interpretacion del misterio Guadalupano: Obervaciones preparatorias contrahidas preciamente a los material de la Imagen.* Unpublished manuscript, 1830, part 2, no. 11, fol. 4b. *Monumentos Guadalupanos,*

Obadiah Rich Collection, New York Public Library (hereafter cited as Guadalupe manuscript).

9. Ibid., part 2, no. 12, fol. 4b. All translations are by the author unless otherwise noted.

10. Luis de la Rosa was the plenipotentiary for the Mexican government in 1848, while the Treaty of Guadalupe-Hidalgo was being negotiated. Mariano Cuevas, *Historia de la Iglesia en Mexico* (El Paso, TX: Editorial "Revista Catolica," 1923), 1:278n8.

11. *Bibliotheca Mexicana, or a Catalogue of the Library of Rare Books and Important Manuscripts relating to Mexico and other parts of Spanish America formed by the Late Señor Don José Fernando Ramirez* (London: G. Norman and son, printers, 1880), 53.

12. José Fernando Ramírez, *Obras del Lic: Don José Fernando Ramirez* (México City: Imp. de V. Agüeros, Editor, 1898), 1:viii.

13. Ibid., 1:xi.

14. Ibid.

15. Hubert Bancroft, *History of Mexico: 1824–1661* (San Francisco: A. L. Bancroft, 1885), 5:806.

16. Ramírez, *Obras del Lic. Don José Fernando Ramirez*, 1:xiv.

17. Ibid., 1:xxiv.

18. Ibid., 1:xviii.

19. Ibid., 1:xxiv.

20. *Bibliotheca Mexicana*, 53, no. 380.

21. Manuel Espinosa de los Monteros, *Interpretacion de la Pintura Guadalupana*. Acolman, México: unpublished manuscript, 1825, part III, no. 21, fol. 6b. *Monumentos Guadalupanos*, Obadiah Rich Collection, New York Public Library (hereafter cited as Guadalupe manuscript).

22. Espinosa de los Monteros, *Interpretacion del misterio*, part II, explicacion 33, no. 108, fol. 38a. Guadalupe manuscript.

23. Linda Martz discusses a Jerónimo executed by the Inquisition named Fray Garcia Zapata, a member of Spain's prominent converso families, in *A Network of Converso Families in Early Modern Toledo: Assimilating a Minority* (Ann Arbor: University of Michigan Press, 2003).

24. A secular priest does not belong to a religious order.

25. Manuel Espinosa de los Monteros, *Interpretacion de la Imagen Guadalupana y Confirmacion del Systema Milenario*. Acolman, México: unpublished manuscript, 1825, fol. 2b. Guadalupe manuscript.

26. Monsignor Guillermo Schulenberg, interviewed by the author, March 2008.

27. Marie-Theresa Hernández, *Delirio—The Fantastic, the Demonic, and the Réel: The Buried History of Nuevo León* (Austin: University of Texas Press, 2002), 244.

28. Stoler, *Along the Archival Grain*, 59.

29. Internet genealogical forums regarding Spanish surnamed families from Latin America and the U.S. Southwest are replete with stories of families reporting Jewish ancestry.

30. Michel de Certeau, *The Writing of History*, trans. Tom Conley (New York: Columbia University Press, 1988), 10.

31. Marilyn Ivy, *Discourses of the Vanishing: Modernity, Phantasm, Japan* (Chicago: University of Chicago Press, 1999), 24.

32. Miguel Sánchez, *Imagen de la virgen Maria Madre de Dios de Guadalupe, milagrosamente aparecida en la civdad de Mexico* (México City: Imprenta Biuda de Bernardo Calderon, 1648). Those approving the publication of *Imagen* (as noted in the book)

were Pedro Barrientos Lomelin, treasurer of the Cathedral of México City and official of the Mexican Holy Office (Inquisition); Francisco de Siles, prebend of the same cathedral; and Luis Lazo de la Vega, rector of the Church of Guadalupe.

33. David A. Brading, *Mexican Phoenix: Our Lady of Guadalupe: Image and Tradition across Five Centuries* (Cambridge: Cambridge University Press, 2001), 128.

34. Solange Alberro, "Crypto-Jews and the Mexican Holy Office in the Seventeenth Century," in *The Jews and the Expansion of Europe to the West, 1400–1800*, ed. Paolo Bernardini and Norman Fiering (New York: Berghahn Books, 2001), 183.

35. Schulamith Halevy, "Descendents of the Anusim (Crypto-Jews) in Contemporary Mexico" (PhD diss., Hebrew University, 2009), 27–28.

36. Monsignor Guillermo Schulenberg, interviewed by the author, March 2008.

37. De Certeau, *Writing of History*, 19. Emphasis original.

38. Brading, *Mexican Phoenix*, 74–75.

39. Ibid., 74, 75.

40. Alberro, "Crypto-Jews and the Mexican Holy Office," 183.

41. De Certeau, *Writing of History*, 140.

42. Jacques Lafaye, *Quetzalcóatl y Guadalupe: La formación de la conciencia nacional*, 2nd ed. (México City: Fondo de Cultura Economica, 2002), 41.

43. An unofficial inquisition burned Hernando Alonso at the stake in 1528. Alonso was an associate of the Conquistador of México, Hernán Cortés. See Seymour B. Liebman, "Hernando Alonso: The First Jew on the North-American Continent," *Journal of Inter-American Studies* 5, no. 2 (1963): 291–293.

44. Lafaye, *Quetzalcóatl y Guadalupe*, 300. The Hieronymite Order of monks is alternately known by the name Jerónimos or Gerónimos.

45. Ibid., 299–300.

46. Haim Beinart, "The Spanish Inquisition and a Converso Community in Extremadura," *Mediaeval Studies* 43 (1981): 445–471; Albert Sicroff, "Clandestine Judaism in the Hieronymite Monastery of Nuestra Señora de Guadalupe," in *Studies in Honor of M. J. Bernadete* (Essays in Hispanic and Sephardic Culture) (New York: Las Americas, 1965), 89–125; and Gretchen Starr-Lebeau, *In the Shadow of the Virgin: Inquisitors, Friars, and Conversos in Guadalupe, Spain* (Princeton, NJ: Princeton University Press, 2003).

47. Solange Alberro, *Inquisición y Sociedad en Mexico 1571–1700* (México City: Fondo de Cultura Economica, 1988); Seymour B. Liebman, *The Jews in New Spain: Faith, Flame, and the Inquisition* (Coral Gables, FL: University of Miami Press, 1970); and Nathan Wachtel, *La fe del recuerdo: Laberintos marranos*, trans. Sandra Garzonio (México City: Fondo de Cultura Economica, 2007).

48. Wachtel, *La fe del recuerdo*, 299–322. Wachtel goes beyond the Inquisition records in the epilogue, interviewing a number of Portuguese families.

49. Jules Michelet, "L'Hèroïsme de l'esprit," unpublished project from the preface to *L'Histoire de France*, 1869, *L'Arc* (1973), no. 52, 5, 7, 8. Quoted in De Certeau, *The Writing of History*, 1.

50. Francisco de Siles writes in an afterword to Miguel Sánchez's *Imagen de la virgen* "the force of a consonant obligates one to say what cannot be thought," referring to the impossible nature of Sánchez's subject. In Sánchez, *Imagen de la virgen*, n.p.

51. The book begins with the discovery of the statue of the Virgin of Guadalupe of Extremadura, Spain, and ends with the tenure at the Sanctuary of the Virgin of Guadalupe in México City of a secular priest named Manuel Espinoza de los Monteros. The eighteenth century is not part of this study.

52. Sophie Coussemacker, "L'Ordre of Saint Jerome en Espagne, 1373–1516" (PhD diss., Université de Paris X–Nanterre, 1994). Coussemacker studied the archives of nineteen Hieronymite monasteries. Her dissertation was never published in book form.

53. For an excellent treatment of this history, see the work of María del Pilar Rábade Obradó: *Un elite de poder en la corte de los Reyes Catolicos: Los Judeoconversos* (Madrid: Sigilo, 1993); and "Judeoconversos y monarquía: un problema de opinión pública," in *La monarquía como conflicto en la Corona castellano-leonesa (c. 1230–1504)*, ed. José Manuel Nieto Soria (Madrid: Silex Ediciones, 2006).

54. "*Limpieza de sangre*" was the term used to signify that an individual is free of Jewish or Moorish blood. Documents certifying purity of blood were common in Spain and its colonies.

55. In the twenty-first century, the term "*macula*" is associated with criminals.

56. The burning bush is also known as "the *seneh*," which is connected with God's revelation to Moses and of which it is stated that "the bush burned with fire, and the bush was not consumed" (Ex. 3:1–4). Jehuda Feliks. "Burning Bush," in *Encyclopaedia Judaica*, 2nd ed., ed. Michael Berenbaum and Fred Skolnick. *Gale Reference Library, Gale Virtual Reference Library.*

57. Arthur Green provides a solid argument for this theory in "Shekhinah, the Virgin Mary, and the Song of Songs: Reflections on a Kabbalistic Symbol in Its Historical Context," *AJS Review* 26, no. 1 (April 2002): 1–52. Various spellings are used for the term "Shekhinah"—Shekinah, Shechina, and Sequina.

58. Gaspar Morocho Gayo reports that de la Huerga had works by the Florentine Neo-Platonists in his library. See Morocho Gayo, "Hermetismo y cábala cristiana en la corte de Carlos V: Egidio de Viterbo, Dionisio Vázquez, Cipriano de la Huerga," *La Ciudad de Dios* 213 (December 2000): 852. I wish to thank Ismael Palacios Acero from the Biblioteca de la Real Academia de Extremadura for kindly sending me copies of Morocho Gayo's essays.

59. Ibid.

60. David M. Gitlitz, *Secrecy and Deceit: The Religion of the Crypto-Jews* (Albuquerque: University of New Mexico Press, 2002), 85; and Stafford Poole, "The Politics of Limpieza de Sangre: Juan de Ovando and His Circle in the Reign of Philip II," *Americas* 55, no. 3 (January 1999): 389.

61. Fernández López studied under Morocho Gayo. See Sergio Fernández López, *El Cantar de los Cantares en el humanismo español: La tradición judía* (Huelva: Universidad de Huelva, 2009), 115.

62. Francisco Rodriguez Marín, "Nuevos datos para las biografías de algunos escritores españoles de los siglos XVI y XVII: Benito Arias Montano," *Boletín de la Real Academia Española* 5 (1918): 452.

63. In the early twenty-first century the main entrance has been moved to the opposite side. Visitors walking through the palace do not actually see the statues unless they face backward as they leave.

64. Wachtel, *La fe del recuerdo*, 22–23.

65. Daviken Studnicki-Gizbert, *A Nation upon the Ocean Sea: Portugal's Atlantic Diaspora and the Crisis of the Spanish Empire, 1492–1640* (Oxford: Oxford University Press, 2007), 25.

66. Ibid., 26, citing *Prohibition of Portuguese ships in the Darian, 1513*, AGI Ind., leg. 419, r.1, lib. 4, fols. 113r–113v; *Proceeds from the seizure of a Portuguese vessel, August 15th, 1513: Accounts of Puerto Rico*, AGI Ctda., leg. 1071, no., 1, r. 2; *Royal missive regarding contraband in Santo Domingo, September 4th, 1536*, AGI Ind., leg. 1962, no. 1, lib. 4,

fols. 171r–172r; *Royal missive to the council and magistrates of the Canary Islands, 18th of June, 1540*, AGI Ind., leg. 423, lib. 19, fols. 358v–359v.

67. Ibid., 26–27, citing *Officials of the Casa de la Contratacion: Testimony against Diego de Ordaz, 1523*, AGI Pat., leg. 251, r. 16; *Royal missive relating to contraband in the Indies, April 9th, 1536, AGI Ind., leg. 1962, lib. 4, fols. 171r–172r;* Wachtel, *La fe del recuerdo*, 104; and Studnicki-Gizbert, *Nation upon the Ocean Sea*, 110, citing Alonso W. Quiroz, "The Expropriation of Portuguese New Christians in Spanish America, 1635–1649," *Ibero-Amerikanisches Archiv* 11, no. 1 (1985): 407–465.

68. Liebman, *Jews in New Spain*, 57. Liebman also states that there were additional synagogues throughout México before the mid-seventeenth century. There were three in Puebla, two each in Guadalajara and Vera Cruz, and one each in Zacatecas and Campeche. Narratives have circulated regarding the possibility of a synagogue in Monterrey during this time period, yet no evidence has resulted to support this.

69. Jonathan I. Israel, *Race, Class, and Politics in Colonial Mexico: 1610–1670* (Oxford: Oxford University Press, 1975), 54.

70. Sánchez, *Imagen de la virgen Maria*, fol. 17a.

71. Michel Foucault, *The Order of Things: An Archaeology of the Human Sciences* (New York: Vintage Books, 1970), 118.

72. While generally there was little division between Church and state in the late middle ages and early modern period, the blurring of boundaries intensified with Felipe II's decision in the late sixteenth century that he would appoint all bishops to their positions.

73. Americo Castro, *España en su historia; cristianos, moros y judíos* (Buenos Aires: Editorial Losada, 1948), 475.

74. Persons were not authorized to immigrate to the Indies without proof of *limpieza de sangre*. However, this regulation was not enforced if they traveled as someone's servant.

75. Semuel Temkin, "Luis de Carvajal and His People," *AJS Review* 32, no. 1 (2008): 86.

76. Wachtel, *La fe del recuerdo*, 15.

77. Ibid.

Chapter 1   Virgin of the Secret River

1. Arturo Álvarez Álvarez, *La Virgen de Guadalupe en el Mundo: Culto e Imágenes Antiguas* (Madrid: Viña Extremeña, S.A., 2000), 13.

2. Arturo Álvarez, interviewed by the author, December 2007.

3. Elisa Rovira, interviewed by the author, January 2013. Rovira, previously an archivist at the monastery, published a number of scholarly articles on the Virgin. She was also for some years the city librarian.

4. Julia Kristeva and Arthur Goldhammer, "Stabat Mater," *Poetics Today* 6, no. 1–2 (1985): 144.

5. Majestic virgins or enthroned virgins—also known as "majesties," date from the eleventh and twelfth centuries. They are generally made of wood and are sitting upright on a chair or throne.

6. E. Saillens, *Nos Vierges Noires: Leurs origines* (Paris: Les Editions Universelles, 1945), 28. Jacques Huynen notes that when the statues were repainted, the original colors were rarely replicated. See Huynen, *El Enigma de las Virgenes Negras*, trans. R. M. Bassols (Barcelona: Plaza y Janes Editorial, 1972), 33.

7. Huynen, *El enigma de las Virgenes Negras*, 8.

8. The translation for "Morena" is dark woman. "Morenita" is a diminutive form of "Morena"—the small dark one. Adding the "-ita" on the end is also an endearment.

9. Álvarez, *La Virgen de Guadalupe en el Mundo*, 17.

10. Sebastián García, interviewed by the author, 2006.

11. Sebastián García, *Guadalupe de Extremadura en America* (Guadalupe Extremadura, Spain: Comunidad Franciscana de Guadalupe, 1990), 78.

12. She is mentioned very briefly by Brading and by Lafaye. See David A. Brading, *Mexican Phoenix: Our Lady of Guadalupe: Image and Tradition across Five Centuries* (Cambridge: Cambridge University Press, 2001), 180; and Jacques Lafaye, *Quetzalcóatl y Guadalupe: La formación de la conciencia nacional*, 2nd ed. (México City: Fondo de Cultura Economica, 2002), 293–301.

13. Sebastian García, *Guadalupe: Siete siglos de fe y cultura* (Guadalupe Extremadura, Spain: Ediciones Guadalupe, 1993), 14.

14. Diego de Ecija and Arcángel Barrado Manzano, *Libro de la invención de esta Santa Imagen de Guadalupe; y de la erección y fundación de este monasterio; y de algunas cosas particulares y vidas de algunos religiosos de él* (Cacares, Spain: Departamento Provincial de Seminarios de F.E.T. y de las J.O.N.S., 1953), 37; and Joseph Pérez, *Los judíos en España* (Madrid: Marcial Pons, 2005), 23.

15. Maria Isabel Perez de Tudela y Velasco, "Alfonso XI y el Santuario de Santa Maria de Guadalupe," in *Estudios en memoria del Profesor D. Salvador de Moxó*, ed. Miguel Angel Ladero Quesada (Madrid: Universidad Complutense de Madrid, 1982), 2:272.

16. Ecija and Manzano, *Libro de la invención*, 38, 39. This particular statue of the Black Virgin was eventually known as la Morenita de las Villuercas or la Virgen de Guadalupe de Extremadura.

17. Huynen, *El enigma de las Virgenes Negras*, 23. There are numerous legends throughout southern Europe that attribute statues of the Virgin Mary to Saint Luke.

18. García, *Guadalupe*, 14.

19. Arturo Álvarez Álvarez, "Cuatro Hermanos, Sabios y Santos," *Historia* 16, no. 371 (2007): 51.

20. Wilfrid Bonser, "The Cult of Relics in the Middle Ages," *Folklore* 73, no. 4 (Winter 1962): 245.

21. Ibid., 245.

22. Lafaye, *Quetzalcóatl y Guadalupe*, 276. Lafaye notes that "many very popular devotions with obscure origins developed at the Monastery of Guadalupe in Extremadura."

23. Monique Scheer, "From Majesty to Mystery: Change in the Meanings of Black Madonnas from the: Sixteenth to Nineteenth Centuries," *American Historical Review* 105, no. 5 (December 2002): 1430.

24. José de Sigüenza, *Historia de la Orden de San Jerónimo* (Madrid: Bailly/Bailliére é Hijos Editores, 1909), 2:80; and Ecija and Manzano, *Libro de la invención*, 40.

25. Perez de Tudela y Velasco, "Alfonso XI y el Santuario de Santa Maria de Guadalupe," 272.

26. Ibid., citing the AHN (Archivo Nacional de España), Codice 48B, fol. 5v.

27. The surname of Gil Cordero varies in different historical and dramatic texts. He is also known as Gil Cacares and Gil the cowherd.

28. Brading, *Mexican Phoenix*, 77.

29. Sigüenza, *Historia de la Orden*, 2:77. Sigüenza explains the name as being of Moorish origin, "but not as some believe, it is not Rio de lobo . . . but interior river, or

river of milk, or as we say secret river . . . *Lub* (lupe) in Arabic and Hebrew signifies heart, or interior, and secret."

30. Álvarez Álvarez, "Cuatro Hermanos, Sabios y Santos," 53.
31. Arturo Álvarez, interviewed by the author, May 2010.
32. See Fernando Cervantes, *The Devil in the New World: The Impact of Diabolism in New Spain* (New Haven, CT: Yale University Press, 1994).
33. Peter Linehan, "The Beginnings of Santa Maria de Guadalupe and the Direction of the Fourteenth Century Castile," *Journal of Ecclesiastical History* 36, no. 1 (1985): 288.
34. Ibid., 289: "Barroso, *scolasticus* of Toledo, a coming man whose rapid rise to the heights of the ecclesiastical hierarchy began in September 1326 when John XXII created episcopal space for him at Cartagena and appointed him to that see."
35. Ibid., 389.
36. Linehan locates the time of the undated letter by matching the service dates during which the prelates signed the document; ibid., 288. See also ibid., 297; and José Maria Revuelta Somalo, *Los Jerónimos: Una orden religiosa nacida en Guadalajara* (Guadalajara, Spain: Institución Provincial de Cultura Marques de Santillana, 1982), 286.
37. Linehan, "Beginnings of Santa Maria de Guadalupe," 294.
38. Ibid., 297; and Revuelta Somalo, *Los Jerónimos*, 179n559.
39. Linehan, "Beginnings of Santa Maria de Guadalupe," 296.
40. Fulcanelli, *El misterio de las catedrales: La obra maestra de la hermetica en el siglo XX* (México City: Random House Mondadori, 1926), 67–68.
41. New Orleans Museum of Art, "Description of The Black Virgin," Oil on canvas, ca. seventeenth century, copy of painting done by Diego de Ocana.
42. Kristeva and Goldhammer, "Stabat Mater," 43.
43. Ilene H. Forsyth, *The Throne of Wisdom: Wood Sculptures of the Madonna in Romanesque France* (Princeton, NJ: Princeton University Press, 1972), 2. While Forsyth's analysis and description is exceedingly thorough, she avoids a substantial discussion on the Black Virgins, reporting that the dark color of the virgin was "not common to the Romanesque world" even though some of the dark virgins were related to "religious customs of the communities" where "the Majesties were honored." She posits that the statues were of women with light skin that at some point were painted black or made dark by the smoke of candles (22).
44. Huynen, *El enigma de las Virgenes Negras*, 25.
45. Kristeva and Goldhammer, "Stabat Mater," 135. Kristeva believes that Beauvoir was "too quick" to react to the kneeling virgin, with Kristeva promoting the idea the humble virgin was closer to women's "real life" experience (142). Kristeva has a point, but the Majestic Virgin is also symbol of power, even if appropriated by the church and the monks of the monasteries.
46. Fulcanelli, *El misterio de las catedrales*, 68. I thank my colleague Alessandro Carrera for his guidance on a number of subjects, including the study of alchemy.
47. Ibid., 72.
48. Elisa Rovira, interviewed by the author, May 2006.
49. *Oxford English Dictionary Online*, s.v. "Philosopher's Stone."
50. "According to current tradition the druids of Chartres worshiped the Virgin for a long period before the cathedral was built"; see Saillens, *Nos Vierges Noires*, 195.
51. Umberto Eco describes the Black Virgin's relationship to alchemy in his novel, *Foucault's Pendulum* (New York: Harcourt Brace Jovanovich, 1988), 145; see also

Leonard W. Moss and Stephen C. Cappannari, "The Black Madonna: An Example of Culture Borrowing," *Scientific Monthly* 76, no. 6 (June 1953): 320.

52. Mircea Eliade, *Myths, Rites, Symbols: A Mircea Eliade Reader* (New York: Harper & Row, 1976), 428.

53. J. C. Long, "Botticelli's 'Birth of Venus' as Wedding Painting," *Aurora* 9 (2008): 13. I thank Nachum Dershowitz for his commentary associating the Virgin Mary with the painting *Birth of Venus*.

54. Mircea Eliade, *The Forge and the Crucible: The Origins and Structures of Alchemy*, 2nd ed. (Chicago: University of Chicago Press, 1978), 163; and Carl Jung, *Collected Works*, vol. 12, *Psychology and Alchemy*, 2nd ed. (Princeton, NJ: Princeton University Press, 1968), 314n23.

55. During numerous conversations with Arturo Álvarez, he consistently reported that the village had a significant Jewish population before the Inquisition arrived in the 1480s. He also stated that most of the monks were conversos and/or *judaizantes*. This was possible because the early requirements for admission allowed men to remain *legos* (laymen).

56. Gretchen Starr-Lebeau, *In the Shadow of the Virgin: Inquisitors, Friars, and Conversos in Guadalupe, Spain* (Princeton, NJ: Princeton University Press, 2003), 257.

57. "Los Reyes Católicos" is a term used for the Catholic monarchs, Queen Isabel and King Fernando, who reigned over Castile and Aragón from 1474 to 1504. Fernando was king of Aragón, Sicily, and Naples until his death in 1516. From 1508 to 1516 he was regent for his supposed mentally ill daughter, Queen Juana.

58. Starr-Lebeau, *In the Shadow of the Virgin*, 254; and Peggy K. Liss, *Isabel the Queen: Life and Times* (New York: Oxford University Press, 1992), 50–53.

59. Starr-Lebeau, *In the Shadow of the Virgin*, 106.

60. Julie A. Evans, "Heresy as an Agent of Change: Inquisition in the Monastery of Guadalupe" (PhD diss., Stanford University, 1998), 268.

61. Sophie Coussemacker, "L'Ordre of Saint Jerome en Espagne, 1373–1516" (PhD diss., Université de Paris X–Nanterre, 1994).

62. By 1571 Felipe II completed the monastery San Lorenzo de Escorial, whose riches greatly overshadowed that of the Guadalupe monastery. After this point, Guadalupe was no longer seen as the favored monastery of the monarchs. See Enrique Llopis Agelán, "Milagros, Demandas y Prosperidad: El Monasterio Jerónimo de Guadalupe, 1389–1571," *Revista de Historia Económica* 16, no. 2 (Spring–Summer 1998): 420.

63. Miguel Cervantes, *Persiles y Sigismunda* (Madrid: Imprenta Bernardo Rodriguez, 1914), 2:50.

64. Felipe Godínez, "Auto Sacramental de La Virgen de Guadalupe" [1675], in *Autos sacramentales, y al Nacimiento de Christo, con sus loas y entremeses*, edited by Antonio Francisco de Zasra (Madrid: Juan Fernández Mercader de Libros), 167. It is significantly notable that in the *auto*, Godínez names his female protagonist Isabel.

65. Cervantes, *Persiles y Sigismunda*, 2:48.

66. "*Godo*" means "Visigoth"—persons assumed not to be Jews or Muslims.

67. Godínez, "Auto Sacramental de La Virgen," 147.

68. Ibid., 150.

69. Perez de Tudela y Velasco, "Alfonso XI y el Santuario de Santa Maria de Guadalupe," 272.

70. Godínez, "Auto Sacramental de La Virgen," 169.

71. Ibid.

72. Cervantes, *Persiles y Sigismunda*, 2:56–57.

73. Both of these men were conquistadors from the region of Extremadura. Francisco Pizarro (1478–1541) was born in Trujillo. He led the conquest of the Inca Empire. Juan de Orellana (?–1625) was born in Talavera de la Reina. He was involved in the conquest of Brazil. Elisa Rovira told me that Pizarro's family were pig farmers. After the conquest Pizarro was made a marques in addition to being appointed governor of Nueva Castilla. Orellana died in a shipwreck off the west coast of Africa.

74. Aurora Egido, "Poesia y peregrinacion en el persiles el templo de la Virgen de Guadalupe," in *Actas del Tercer Congreso Internacional de la Asocación de Cervantistas*, ed. Antonio Bernat Vistarini (Palma, Spain: Servei de Publicacions i Intercanvi Científic, Universitat de les Illes Balears, 1998), 26; and Américo Castro, *España en su historia; cristianos, moros y judíos* (Buenos Aires: Editorial Losada, 1948), 182.

75. Seymour Liebman, *The Jews in New Spain: Faith, Flame, and the Inquisition* (Coral Gables, FL: University of Miami Press, 1970), 185. Liebman cites a Dominican named Hernando de Ojea, who believed that New Spain was full of Jews. Ojea's *La venida de Cristo y su vida y Milagros, en que se concerdan los dos Testamentos divinos Viejo y Nuevo* is cited by Robert Ricard in "Pour une étude de judaisme portugais au Mexique pendant période coloniale," *Revue d'Histoire Moderne*, August 14, 1939, 522.

76. Because this is not certain, the author is generally listed as anonymous. *Comedia de la Soberana Virgen de Guadalupe, y sus Milagros, y Grandezas de Espana* (Sevilla: Bartolome Gomez de Pastrana, 1617), 19. In the *comedia*, when the cowherd sees the Virgin, he exclaims "*¡Santa de Moysen!*" (Saint of Moses!).

77. Ibid., 6.

78. Ibid., 20.

79. Luis de Carvajal, el Mozo, who was burned by the Mexican Inquisition in 1596, twenty-one years before the *comedia* was published, used the term "*santo*" (saint) in describing a number of Jewish patriarchs, such as when he explains that God is like Saint David, who says that he accompanies those who are lost. See Luis González Obregón, ed., *Procesos de Luis de Carvajal (El Mozo)*, vol. 28, Publicaciones del Archivo General de la Nacion (Mexico City: Talleres Graficos de la Nacion, 1935), 467. On the blending of the two religious belief systems, see Richard H. Popkin, "Christian Jews and Jewish Christians in the 17th Century," in *Jewish Christians and Christian Jews: From the Renaissance to the Enlightenment*, ed. Richard Popkin and Gordon Weiner (Dordrecht: Kluwer Academic Publishers, 1994), 57. It is my belief that this type of "fusion" was not rare.

80. This will be discussed again in more detail in a later chapter. See Arthur Green, "Shekhina, the Virgin Mary, and the Song of Songs: Reflections on a Kabbalistic Symbol in Its Historical Context," *AJS Review* 26, no. 1 (April 2002): 50.

81. Ibid., 52.

82. For more information on the life of Godínez, see Alice Goldberg, "Una vida de santos extraña: O el fraile ha de ser ladron o el ladron ha de ser fraile, de Felipe Godínez," *AIH ACTAS* (1983): 624–629. Godínez will be discussed in a later chapter.

83. Godínez, "Auto Sacramental de La Virgen," 170.

84. Leo Strauss, *Persecution and the Art of Writing* (Chicago: University of Chicago Press, 1988), 73.

85. Those entering the Jerónimos were not required to take Holy Orders. Fray Pedro Fernandez Pecha, one of the founders of the Jerónimos, remained a *lego* (lay brother), all his life even though he came to be the prior of the Guadalupe monastery. Sigüenza, *Historia de la Orden de San Jerónimo*, 2:31.

86. Linehan, "Beginnings of Santa Maria de Guadalupe," 303.

Chapter 2   The Monks of the King

1. Américo Castro, *Aspectos del vivir Hispanico: Espiritualismo, mesianismo, actitude personal en los Siglos XIV al XVI* (Santiago de Chile: Editorial Cruz del Sur, 1949), 81.

2. Ibid., 114.

3. Sophie Coussemacker, "L'Ordre of Saint Jerome en Espagne, 1373–1516" (PhD diss., Université de Paris X–Nanterre, 1994), 1:104.

4. Ibid., 2:105.

5. Gretchen Starr-LeBeau published an excellent treatment of this phase of the order's history. See *In the Shadow of the Virgin: Inquisitors, Friars, and Conversos in Guadalupe, Spain* (Princeton, NJ: Princeton University Press, 2003), 198n39.

6. For a thorough analysis of the painting, see Lynn F. Jacobs, "The Triptychs of Hieronymus Bosch," *Sixteenth Century Journal* 31, no. 3 (Autumn 2000): 1009.

7. Michel de Certeau, *The Mystic Fable: The Sixteenth and Seventeenth Centuries*, trans. Michael B. Smith (Chicago: University of Chicago Press, 1992), 48, 53. Emphasis original.

8. Norman Roth, *Conversos, Inquisition, and the Expulsion of Jews from Spain* (Madison: University of Wisconsin Press, 1995), 69.

9. Ibid., 49.

10. José de Sigüenza, *Vida de San Gerónimo doctor máximo de la Yglesia* (Madrid: Imprenta de la Esperanza, 1853), 398.

11. Charles F. Fraker, "Gonçalo Martínez de Medina, the Jerónimos, and the Devotio Moderna," *Hispanic Review* 34, no. 4 (July 1966): 202.

12. José de Sigüenza, *Historia de la Orden de San Jerónimo* (Madrid: Bailly/Bailliére é Hijos Editores, 1909), 1:13. Sigüenza writes with an emotional flair that emphasizes the passion the pre-Jerónimos had for their quest. While his biography of the order is an outstanding piece of work, it is more of an interesting hagiography, presenting what the Jerónimos of the early sixteenth century wanted to portray.

13. Yañez's parents were Juan Hernández de Sotomayor and Maria Yañez de Figueroa. The family was from Caceres in Extremadura. The Figueroas were a noble family, and Sotomayor was a *"caballero,"* of the lesser nobility. Yañez may have been left at the court in a move to raise the family's social status. See Sophie Coussemacker, "L'Ordre of Saint Jerome en Espagne, 1373–1516" (PhD diss., Université de Paris X–Nanterre, 1994), 1:147. Coussemacker's study of the Jerónimos is the most comprehensive to date.

14. Ibid., 1:148.

15. While historians continuously report that Alonso was deeply involved with the founding of the Jerónimos, he actually left Spain almost immediately, going on a journey to the Holy Land with Saint Brigida and stopping on the way back to visit the pope in Rome. Ibid., 1:153.

16. Neither Coussemacker nor Sigüenza list a date for the departure of Yañez from his post at the Cathedral of Toledo.

17. Clara Estow, *Pedro the Cruel of Castile: 1350–1369* (Leiden, Neth.: Brill, 1995), 258–259.

18. Sigüenza, *Historia de la Orden de San Jerónimo*, 1:xlvii.

19. Robert E. Lerner, *The Heresy of the Free Spirit in the Later Middle Ages* (Berkeley: University of California Press, 1972), 61–84.

20. They are at times compared to the *alumbrados*—the enlightened ones, who proliferated in the early sixteenth century.

21. Sigüenza, *Historia de la Orden de San Jerónimo*, 1:21. Sigüenza is using the term "Lutherans" (he was writing at the end of the sixteenth century), yet Luther was not born when the Jerónimos were first organized.

22. Ibid.

23. Américo Castro, *Aspectos del Vivir Hispanico: Espiritualismo, Mesianismo, Actitude Personal en los Siglos XIV al XVI* (Santiago de Chile: Editorial Cruz del Sur, 1949), 76–77n73. The focus on the Holy Spirit is significant in its relationship to Judaism; a number of scholars have compared it to the Shekhinah. This will be discussed in chapter 3.

24. Sigüenza, *Historia de la Orden de San Jerónimo*, 1:21.

25. Lerner, *Heresy of the Free Spirit*, 71–72, 202.

26. The Albigensis were also known as Cathars. They were executed on charges of heresy by the anti-Cathar crusade and a resultant Inquisition in France during the early thirteenth century. Ibid., 37.

27. Sigüenza, *Historia de la Orden de San Jerónimo*, 2:635–639.

28. Pedro de la Vega, *Cronica de los frayles de la orden del bienaventurado Fant Hieronymo* (Alcala de Henares: Casa de Juan de Brocer, 1539), F. 16a. De la Vega reports the incident of 1374 with "*fegun fe dize* (according to what is said)." They were rescued by Alonso de Aragón, Conde de Deniay de Ribagorza, first cousin King Pedro IV of Aragón.

29. Coussemacker, "L'Ordre of Saint Jerome," 1:168.

30. Antonio de Lugo, "El monacato 'sui generis,' de lo Jerónimos. Desde los origenes hasta la desamortización," *Cistertium* 23 (1970): 230. An origin narrative involving Rome provides the order more legitimacy. While some scholars believe the visit occurred in Rome, Coussemacker believes the location was Avignon. Coussemacker, "L'Ordre of Saint Jerome," 1:167.

31. de Lugo, "El monacato 'sui generis,'" 232.

32. Ibid.

33. Ibid., 234.

34. Sigüenza, *Historia de la Orden de San Jerónimo*, 1:31.

35. Enrique Llopis Agelán, "Milagros, Demandas y Prosperidad: El Monasterio Jerónimo de Guadalupe, 1389–1571," *Revista de Historia Económica* 16, no. 2 (Spring–Summer 1998): 424.

36. Ibid., 425; and Jacques Lafaye, *Quetzalcóatl y Guadalupe: La formación de la conciencia nacional*, 2nd ed. (México City: Fondo de Cultura Economica, 2002), 300–301. Lafaye cites Fray German Rubio, *Historia de Ntra. Sra. de Guadalupe* (Barcelona: Thomas, 1926), 223–224.

37. José Sánchez Herrero, "Fundación y desarrollo de la Orden de los Jerónimos, 1360–1561," *Codex Aqvilarensis: Cuadernos de investigación del Monasterio de Santa María la Real* 10 (December 1994): 73.

38. Ibid.

39. Llopis Agelán, "Milagros, Demandas y Prosperidad," 31.

40. Ibid., 431, 444.

41. Jonathan Israel, *Enlightenment Contested: Philosophy, Modernity, and the Emancipation of Man 1670–1752* (Oxford: Oxford University Press, 2006), 4.

42. Llopis Agelán, "Milagros, Demandas y Prosperidad," 432.

43. Ibid., 433.

44. See Sebastián García, "Medicina y cirugía en los Reales Hospitales de Guadalupe," *Revista de estudios extremeños* 59, no. 1 (2003): 11–77.

45. The hospital for syphilis was called "*hospital de la pasion*." Pedro de la Vega notes that "the [medical] school or pharmacy of our physician[s], that is the Holy Scripture: and in the hospital we find a species of ulcers and medicines" related to the treatment of syphilis. The Hieronymites clearly saw their religious mission intertwined with their medical interests. De la Vega, *Cronica de los frayles*, f. 6b.

46. José María López Piñero notes that King Fernando (el Católico) gave permission to conduct autopsies to the medical school of Zaragoza. See López Piñero, "La disección y el saber anatómico en la España de la primera mitad del siglo xvi," *Cuadernos de Historia de la Medicina Española* 13 (1974): 54, 91.

47. Albert A. Sicroff, "The Jeronymite Monastery of Guadalupe in 14th and 15th Century Spain," in *Collected Studies in Honour of Americo Castro's Eightieth Year*, ed. M. P. Hornik (Oxford: Lincombe Lodge Research Library, 1965), 403. A *marco de plata* equals 230 grams of silver.

48. It is noteworthy that before the Expulsion, almost all the treasurers to the Kings of Castilla were Jews.

49. Castro, *Aspectos del Vivir Hispanico*, 114.

50. Toledo is approximately two hundred kilometers from Guadalupe.

51. Albert Sicroff, "Clandestine Judaism in the Hieronymite Monastery of Nuestra Senora de Guadalupe," in *Studies in Honor of M. J. Bernadete (Essays in Hispanic and Sephardic culture)*, 89–125 (New York: Las Americas, 1965), 114.

52. Yitzhak Baer, *The History of the Jews in Christian Spain*, trans. Louis Schoffman (Philadelphia: Jewish Publication Society, 1992).

53. Sicroff, "Clandestine Judaism," 91.

54. Castro, *Aspectos del Vivir Hispanico*, 77–78.

55. Sicroff, "Clandestine Judaism," 90.

56. De Certeau, *Mystic Fable*, 52.

57. Castro, *Aspectos del Vivir Hispanico*, 91. Castro cites Ramón Menéndez Pidal, *Estudios Literarios* (Buenos Aires: Espasa-Calpe Argentina, 1938), 234.

58. Castro, *Aspectos del Vivir Hispanico*, 91n84.

59. Antonio Hernández Morejón, *Historia bibliográfica de la medicina española* (Madrid: Impr. de la viuda de Jordan e hijos, 1842), 2:26.

60. López Piñero, "La disección y el saber anatómico," 91.

61. Sigüenza, *Historia de la Orden de San Jerónimo*, 1: 94.

62. See Joseph Shatzmiller, *Jews, Medicine, and Medieval Society* (Berkeley: University of California Press, 1994).

63. Starr-Lebeau, *In the Shadow of the Virgin*, 172.

64. Ibid., 227–228.

65. Ibid. Elisa Rovira tells me that local officials ordered the demolition of the residence ("lo mandaron derribar las autoridades provinciales y locales en el siglo XIX, más de treinta años después de la exclaustración de los monjes, argumentando su estado ruinoso y para facilitar la apertura de la calle de esa zona"), although during my conversations with various individuals in 2006, it was mentioned that the villagers themselves took apart the *residencia* in the nineteenth century.

66. Coussemacker, "L'Ordre of Saint Jerome," 1:103. Between 1466 and 1469, Ferrand Gonzalez, the scribe of the *puebla* who was closely associated with the convent, was imprisoned for heresy (cryptojudaism) by ecclesiastic judges, but it appears he was absolved because of pressure from the prior.

67. Starr-Lebeau, *In the Shadow of the Virgin*, 215.

68. Julie A. Evans, "Heresy as an Agent of Change: Inquisition in the Monastery of Guadalupe" (PhD diss., Stanford University, 1998), 80.
69. Ibid. Evans states that she doubts the authenticity of the letter.
70. Coussemacker, "L'Ordre of Saint Jerome," 2:41.
71. Ibid.
72. Castro, *Aspectos del Vivir Hispanico*, 112.
73. Sebastian García, *Guadalupe: Siete siglos de fe y cultura*, ed. Sebastian García (Guadalupe Extremadura, Spain: Ediciones Guadalupe, 1993), 506–507.
74. Ibid., 513.
75. Ibid., 510–511.
76. There is a problem with the documentation on de Gante. A number of authors have incorrect information on his name. In the most important contemporary history of the monastery, Salvador Ordax lists the sculptor's name as Guillemin Digante. Ana Ericson Persson lists him as Dante Guillermín. Vicente Mendez Hernán, "Una Nueva Orbra del Entallador y Escultor Placentino Alonso Hipólito: La Piedad de la Iglesia de el Salvador, de Plasencia (Cácares)," *Norba-Arte* 22–23 (2003 2002): 61–71; Salvador A. Ordax, "Las artes plasticas de Guadalupe," in *Guadalupe: Siete siglos de fe y cultura*, ed. Sebastian García (Guadalupe Extremadura, Spain: Ediciones Guadalupe, 1993), 287–325; and Ana Lorena Ericson Persson, *La crisis del guadalupanismo: Cerca de cien años de silencio a través de lost textos del arzobispo Montúfar* (México City: Ediciones Navarra, 2006). In addition, Arturo Álvarez believes it might have been an entirely different sculptor. Arturo Álvarez, interviewed by author, 2008.
77. Persson, *La crisis del guadalupanismo*, 104–105. This was told to me by Elisa Rovira. Ms. Rovira coauthored a number of articles with Sebastian García.
78. Jeanette Favrot Peterson, "Creating the Virgin of Guadalupe: The Cloth, the Artist, and Sources in Sixteenth-Century New Spain," *Americas* 61, no. 4 (April 2005): 571–610.
79. Ramón de Llavia, *Cancionero de Ramón de Llavia*, ed. Rafael Benitez Claros (Madrid: Sociedad de Bibliófilos Españoles, 1945).
80. María del Pilar Rábade Obradó, "El entorno judeoconverso de la Casa y Corte de Isabel la Católica," in *Las relaciones discretas entre las monarquías hispana y portuguesa orlas casas de las reinas (siglos XV–XIX)*, ed. José Martínez Millán and Maria Paula Marçal Lourenço (Madrid: Ediciones Polifemo, 2008), 890–894.
81. Castro, *Aspectos del Vivir Hispanico*, 104; and María del Pilar Rábade Obradó, *Un elite de poder en la corte de los Reyes Catolicos: Los Judeoconversos* (Madrid: Sigilo, 1993), 26.
82. Coussemacker, "L'Ordre of Saint Jerome," 2:106.
83. Ibid., 2:86–233.
84. A *proceso* is the written document detailing a civil or criminal case held before a court. The term is often used in reference to the Inquisition. While the noted Spanish historian Fidel Fita Colomé mentions Fray Alonso de Toledo (319), García Zapata de Toledo is not listed among those tried by the Inquisition. Fidel Fita Colomé, "La Inquisición Toledana: Relación Contemporánea de los Autos y Autillos Que Celebro Desde el Ano 1485 hasta el de 1501," *Boletín de la Real Academia de la Historia* 11 (1887): 289–322.
85. Coussemacker, "L'Ordre of Saint Jerome," 2:136. Besides García's, the other missing *procesos* were from the trials of Juan de Madrid, Gonzalo de Alcala, Pedro de Alcala,

Jerónimo de Villa García, and Benito de Toledo. The only one left belonged to Alonso de Toledo.

86. Ibid., 2:90–91.

87. Ibid., 2:91.

88. Ibid., 2:92–93.

89. Ibid., 2:95. García was ordered to estimate the value of the income from property owned by the Jerónimos in the village of Pinto. Interestingly, he was to be accompanied by a Juan de Corrales, the new prior of la La Sisla who was hostile to conversos.

90. Ibid., 2:100–101. Coussemacker reports that this information came from inquisitor Pedro de Bejar, who interrogated a Juan Borrar (or Borras), who was at la Sisla when Ulloa died.

91. Ibid., 2:101–102.

92. Ibid., 1:169–170. Fernando de León reported the Madrid monastery to the Inquisition. He was one of the monks who revolted against García at la Sisla in 1478. León was exiled from la Sisla as punishment and sent to the monastery in Madrid, el Prado.

93. Ibid., 1:223. The *proceso* of Toledo is missing; only the monk's sentence exists in the archives.

94. Ibid., 1:226–227.

95. Ibid., 1:226.

96. Ibid., 1:207, 221–222.

97. Ibid., 2:108; and Carlos Carrete Parrondo, "Los conversos Jerónimos ante el estatuto de limpieza de sangre," *Helmantica: Revista de filología clásica y hebrea* 26, no. 79–81 (1975): 97–116. Coussemacker notes in her 1994 dissertation that the *proceso* could not be found.

98. Rábade Obradó, *Un elite de poder*, 67.

99. Coussemacker, "L'Ordre of Saint Jerome," 2:218–219. Francisco was charged by the Inquisition in 1488 after testifying for a Jerónimo who was accused of Judaizing. The charges were dropped when he was appointed *contador mayor* (head treasurer) of the monarchy. In 1520 he joined the revolution of the *comuneros*, a revolt that occurred during the early reign of Carlos V, which led to Francisco's imprisonment. He died in prison in 1523.

100. Ibid. It is not known if this same sibling is the one said to be the Jewish brother who was going to be a rabbi.

101. Rábade Obradó, "El entorno judeoconverso," 902.

102. Portugal and Spain were joined from 1581 to 1640.

103. Luis Góngora y Argote, "Religion: Justicia," in *Obras de Luis de Góngora y Argote. [Varias poesias. Fabula de Polifemo y Galatea. Las Soledades. Panegiciro][Dadas a luz por Geronymo de Villegas]*, ed. Geronymo de Villegas (Brussels: Imprenta de Francisco Foppens, 1659), 417.

104. Ibid., lines 107–120.

105. Castro, *Aspectos del Vivir Hispanico*, 112.

106. Ibid., 82.

107. Beghards and Beguines (in thirteenth and fourteenth centuries) were labeled as heretics, and a number were executed. They were accused of heresy, sodomy, and sexual orgies.

108. Castro, *Aspectos del Vivir Hispanico*, 82.

109. *Devotio moderna* was a Catholic religious movement that focused on meditation and the spirituality.

110. The *templete mudejar* is a small pavilion whose early modern architecture indicates a Muslim influence. The monastery *templete* is located in a courtyard within the monastery compound.
111. Castro, *Aspectos del Vivir Hispanico*, 83. Numerous scholars reference the hodge-podge nature of the monastery's construction.
112. Heiko A. Oberman, Preface to *Devotio moderna: Basic Writings*, edited by John Van Engen (Paulist Press: New York, 1988), xiv.
113. Castro, *Aspectos del Vivir Hispanico*, 83.
114. Sigüenza, *Historia de la Orden de San Jerónimo*, 2:209.
115. Castro, *Aspectos del Vivir Hispanico*, 83.
116. Fita Colomé, "La Inquisición en Guadalupe," *Boletín de la Real Academia de la Historia* 23 (1893): 283–343.
117. Castro, *Aspectos del Vivir Hispanico*, 83n77.
118. Gongora probably was alluding to José de Sigüenza, a close advisor of Felipe II, who is considered one of the most respected Spanish writers of his time. *Historia de la Orden de San Gerónimo* is acknowledged as the most authoritative account of the order's history.
119. Góngora y Argote, "Religion: Justicia," lines 206–211.
120. Coussemacker, "L'Ordre of Saint Jerome," 2:198.

Chapter 3   Divine Splendor

1. E. Harris, "Mary in the Burning Bush: Nicolas Froment's Triptych at Aix-en-Provence," *Journal of the Warburg Institute* 1, no. 4 (April 1938): 281.
2. Regarding sexuality, the Shekhinah is the opposite of the Virgin of the Immaculate Conception, who remained a virgin even after the birth the Christ. Moshe Idel, *Kabbalah and Eros* (New Haven, CT: Yale University Press, 2005), 47.
3. Manuel Espinosa de los Monteros, "La interpretacion del misterio," pt. II, fol. 4b (unpublished manuscript, 1825) *Monumentos Guadalupanos*, Obadiah Rich Collection, New York Public Library (hereafter cited as Guadalupe manuscript). Espinosa de los Montero's Christian-Jewish writings will be explained further in chapter 7.
4. Ibid., pt. II, fol. 4b.
5. Luis de León, "A Nuestra Señora," in *Obras del Maestro Fray Luis de León*, ed. Gregorio Mayans y Siscar, Biblioteca de Autores Espanoles (Madrid: M. Rivadeneyra, 1855), 2:12, line 14. There are two versions of "A Nuestra Señora." The poem written in prison begins with "Virgen, que al sol más pura." The second poem begins with "Ni veremos el rostro del Padre Eterno." There is no date on the second poem, and it is rarely mentioned. On León as a converso, see Colin P. Thompson, *The Strife of Tongues: Fray Luis de León and the Golden Age of Spain* (Cambridge: Cambridge University Press, 1988), 147–150. Thompson doubts charges by previous scholars that de León was a *judaizante*. Even so, Thompson reports that de León's converso genealogy is well documented. The poet's ancestors faced the Inquisition repeatedly—in 1491, 1510–1512, and 1579.
6. León, "Nuestra Señora," 2:12, lines 1–3.
7. Ibid., lines 4–7.
8. Thompson, *Strife of Tongues*, 8.
9. William J. Nowak, "Virgin Rhetoric: Fray Luis de Leon and Marian Piety in Virgen, que el sol mas pura," *Hispanic Review* 73, no. 4 (Autumn 2005): 492n4.
10. Luis de León, "Protestacion de fe que hizo Fray Luis de León estando en la carcel del Santo Oficio de Valladolid, temiendo morir en la prision," in *Proceso del P.M. Fray*

Luis de León: Doctor Teologo del Claustro y Gremio de la Universidad de Salamanca, ed. Alejandro Arango y Escandon (México City: Imprenta de Andrade y Escalante, 1856), 113.

11. León, *"Nuestra Señora,"* 2:12, lines 10–11.
12. Thompson, *Strife of Tongues,* 36. Thompson cites the testimony of Dominican Bartolome de Medina against de León, and of Martinez de Cantalpiedra, "They prefer Vatable, Pagnini and their Jews to the Vulgate. . . ." From *Colección de documentos inéditos para la historia de España* (CDIHE) X, 6–7 (translation by Thompson).
13. The Vatable Bible was placed on the Spanish Index (censure). This Bible will be discussed further in chapter 4. See Magne Saebo, Michael Fishbane, and John Louis Ska, *Hebrew Bible/Old Testament: The History of Its Interpretation, from the Renaissance to the Enlightenment* (Göttingen, Ger.: Vandenhoeck & Ruprecht, 2008), 2:238.
14. There appears to have been an additional motive for León's arrest. This will be discussed in a later chapter.
15. Thompson, *Strife of Tongues,* 37.
16. Javier San José Lera, "Fray Luis de León—El autor—Apunte biográfico," *Biblioteca Virtual,* http://www.cervantesvirtual.com/bib_autor/frayluisdeleon/pcuartonivel .jsp?conten=autor. The three were professors at the University of Salamanca. León held a chair in theology, Grajal in the Holy Scripture, and Cantalapiedra in Hebrew.
17. Thompson, *Strife of Tongues,* 7; and Francisco Pacheco, *Libro de descripción de verdaderos retratos de ilustres y memorables varones,* ed. Pedro M. Piñero Ramírez and Rogelio Reyes Cano (Sevilla, Spain: Diputación Provincial de Sevilla, 1985), 69–70. Pacheco said of de León, "His was the greatest capacity of mind known in his time for all the arts and sciences. . . . The Greek, Latin, Hebrew, Chaldean and Syriac languages he knew like their masters" (translation by Thompson).
18. Thompson, *Strife of Tongues,* 83, 37.
19. Alejandro Arango y Escandon, ed., *Proceso del p.m. Fray Luis de Leon: Doctor Teologo del Claustro y Gremio de la Universidad de Salamanca* (México City: Imprenta de Andrade y Escalante, 1856), 15.
20. Thompson, *Strife of Tongues,* 70.
21. León, *"Nuestra Señora,"* 2:12, lines 23–33.
22. Ibid., lines 89–99.
23. Ibid., lines 100–104.
24. Aubrey F. G. Bell, "Notes on Luis de Leon's Lyrics," *Modern Language Review* 21, no. 2 (April 1926): 168–177.
25. Nowak explains that León "borrow[s] the lexicon of the picaresque-whatever his Inquisitors like, but by mimicking Petrarch he can turn those imposed words into an ironically double-voiced expression of his own." Nowak, "Virgin Rhetoric," 501. See also Estrella Ruiz-Gálvez Priego, "'Sine Labe.' El inmaculismo en la España de los siglos XV a XVII: la proyección social de un imaginario religioso," *Revista de dialectología y tradiciones populares* 63, no. 2 (2008): 218–219.
26. Nowak, "Virgin Rhetoric," 499.
27. León, "Nuestra Señora," 2:12, lines 58, 75, 95.
28. Nowak, "Virgin Rhetoric," 506.
29. Karl A. Kottman, *Law and Apocalypse: The Moral Thought of Luis de Leon (1527?–1591)* (The Hague: Martinus Nijhoff, 1972), 88. See also ibid., ix–xii; and Thompson, *Strife of Tongues,* 145–147, 150.
30. Catherine Swietlicki, *The Spanish Christian Cabala* (Columbia: University of Missouri Press, 1986), 146. While Swietlicki finds the Jewish and the Christian

Kabbalah extremely similar, she uses the spelling "Cabala" to distinguish the Christian version.

31. Gershom Scholem, "Sefirot," in *Encyclopedia Judaica*, edited by Michael Berenbaum and Fred Skolnik, 2nd ed., vol. 18. Macmillan Reference USA, 2007.

32. Luis de León, "Nuestra Señora," 2:12, lines 1, 2, 20, 34, 35, 78, 80.

33. Ibid., lines 6, 7, 49, 52, 53, 82.

34. An aspect of sin and evil is inherent in every human being at the time of their birth, resulting from the fall of Adam and Eve in Paradise.

35. For a description of the Immaculate Conception and the controversy surrounding its formal acceptance by the Roman Catholic Church, see Nancy Mayberry, "The Controversy over the Immaculate Conception in Medieval and Renaissance Art, Literature, and Society," *Journal of Medieval and Renaissance Studies* 21, no. 2 (Fall 1991): 214.

36. José Sánchez Herrero, *Historia de la Iglesia en España e Hispanoamérica: Desde sus inicios hasta el siglo XXI* (Madrid: Silex Ediciones, 2008), 249.

37. Elizabeth Lehfeldt, Adeline Rucquoi, and Estrella Ruiz-Gálvez Priego have analyzed the relationship between the Immaculate Conception, *limpieza de sangre*, and the formation of the Spanish nation-state. See Elizabeth A. Lehfeldt, "Ruling Sexuality: The Political Legitimacy of Isabel of Castile," *Renaissance Quarterly* 53, no. 1 (Spring 2000): 31–56; Adeline Rucquoi, "Mancilla y Limpieza: La Obsesión por el Pecado en Castilla a Fines del Siglo XV," *Os "Últimos Fins" Na Cultura Ibérica (XV–XVIII)*, Anexo VIII (1997): 113–135; and Ruiz-Gálvez Priego, "Sine Labe."

38. Marina Warner, *Alone of All Her Sex: The Myth and the Cult of the Virgin Mary* (New York: Vintage Books, 1983), 14.

39. Rucquoi, "Mancilla y Limpieza," 134.

40. Ibid., 135.

41. Ibid. Rucquoi credits this idea to Jean Delumeau. No specific publication is given.

42. Aurelie A. Hagstrom, "The Symbol of the Mandorla in Christian Art: Recovery of a Feminine Archetype," *Arts; The Arts in Religious and Theological Studies* 10, no. 2 (1998): 26, 25, 27.

43. Aurelie A. Hagstrom, "The Symbol of the Mandorla in Christian Art: Recovery of a Feminine Archetype," *Month-London*-Longman's *Magazine of Lite* 29, no. 5 (1996): 192. This article is a slightly altered version published in a popular magazine. Hagstrom's mention of the "majestas" Christ was edited out of the article in the *Arts* journal.

44. Toward the late fifteenth century, artists began conflating the image of the Virgin's Assumption (as she floats up to heaven) with la Inmaculada. One example is the *Virgin of the Immaculate Conception* (1608) by El Greco. See Richard K. Emmerson and Bernard McGinn, eds., *The Apocalypse in the Middle Ages* (Ithaca, NY: Cornell University Press, 1992), 251.

45. An indulgence is a Catholic ritual in which the petitioner would pay for prayers or particular blessing. The practice was popular during the medieval and early modern period.

46. In 1475 Sixtus approved a "special Office of the Immaculate Conception." See Ludwig Pastor, *The History of the Popes from the Close of the Middle Ages: Drawn from the Secret Archives of the Vatican and Other Original Sources* (London: Kegan Paul, Trench, Trübner & Co., 1906), 4:394.

47. Suzanne L. Stratton, *The Immaculate Conception in Spanish Art* (Cambridge: Cambridge University Press, 1994), 52.

48. Monique Scheer, "From Majesty to Mystery: Change in the Meanings of Black Madonnas from the Sixteenth to Nineteenth Centuries," *American Historical Review* 105, no. 5 (December 2002): 1418.

49. Ibid., 1437. Scheer cites Gabriel de Barletta, *Sermones celeberrimi*, I (Venice, 1571), 173, in Michael Baxandall, *Painting and Experience in Fifteenth Century Italy: A Primer in the Social History of Pictorial Style* (Oxford: Clarendon Press, 1972), 57.

50. Scheer, "From Majesty to Mystery," 1436–1437. Scheer notes that black skin on Marian images "was multiply encoded and that is symbolic value as a marker of ethnic or racial origin was not primary until the turn of the nineteenth century." Adding to this complexity the Jerónimos' choice of representing the Virgin with golden hair and white skin was an attempt by the order to deal with the current purging of non-Visigoth influences in Spain.

51. Ibid.

52. Stratton, *Immaculate Conception*, 4.

53. Ibid., 5, 6. Stratton cites Henry Charles Lea, *A History of the Inquisition of the Middle Ages* (New York, 1958), 1:597.

54. Stratton, *Immaculate Conception*, 6.

55. For a solid analysis of the development of Spain as a nation, see Barbara Fuchs, *Exotic Nation: Maurophilia and the Construction of Early Modern Spain* (Philadelphia: University of Pennsylvania Press, 2009).

56. Antonio Jesús Jiménez Sánchez, "Beatriz de Silva y la Inmaculada Concepción: Orígenes de una orden," in *La Inmaculada Concepción en España: Religiosidad, historia y arte: actas del simposium*, ed. Francisco Javier Campos y Fernández de Sevilla (San Lorenzo de El Escorial, 2005), 1:696. Ironically, Beatriz was a lady in waiting for Queen Isabel's mother, Isabel of Portugal. The Portuguese queen believed that Silva was having an affair with the king and had the young woman sealed in a casket for three days (this occurred between 1447 and 1451). Silva survived and decided to organize an order dedicated to the Virgin.

57. Ibid., 695–696.

58. Stratton, *Immaculate Conception*, 8.

59. Miguel de la Pinta Llorente, ed., *Procesos inquisitoriales contra los catedráticos hebraistas de Salamanca: Gaspar de Grajal, Martínez de Cantalapiedra y Fray Luis de León / estudio y transcripción paleográfica por Miguel de la Pinta Llorente* (Madrid: Monasterio de Escorial, 1935), iv. In the book's introduction, Pinta Llorente writes, "The Spanish Dominicans, kings of our theological culture in the fifteenth century, the most illustrious representatives of our university spirit, constituted in Spain a moral and mental richness."

60. Barbara Fuchs, *Passing for Spain: Cervantes and the Fiction of Identity* (Urbana: University of Illinois Press, 2003), 1.

61. Stratton, *Immaculate Conception*, 9.

62. Elizabeth A. Lehfeldt, "Ruling Sexuality: The Political Legitimacy of Isabel of Castile," *Renaissance Quarterly* 53, no. 1 (Spring 2000): 52.

63. Ibid., 53.

64. Stratton, *Immaculate Conception*, 9–10.

65. For an interesting analysis of the Book of Esther among the Jewish Diaspora, see Elsie R. Stern, "Esther and the Politics of Diaspora," *Jewish Quarterly Review* 100, no. 1 (Winter 2010): 25–53.

66. Sara Turel, "The Annunciation to Esther: Felipe Godíñez' Dramatic Vision," in *Jews, Christians, and Muslims in the Mediterranean World After 1492*, ed. Alisa Meyuhas Ginio (London: Taylor and Francis, 1992), 48.

67. Pedro de la Vega, *Cronica de los frayles de la orden del bienaventurado Fant Hieronymo* (Alcala de Henares: Casa de Juan de Brocer, 1539), line 237.

68. Félix Arturo Lope de Vega y Carpio, *La limpieza no manchada*, 1618, lines 136–147.

69. Ibid., line 446.

70. Luis de Carvajal, "Memorias de Luis de Carvajal," in *Procesos de Luis de Carvajal (El Mozo)*, ed. Luis González Obregón (México City: Publicaciones del Archivo General de la Nación, 1935), 28:526.

71. Luis de Carvajal, *The Enlightened: The Writings of Luis de Carvajal, El Mozo*, ed. Seymour B. Liebman (Coral Gables, FL: University of Miami Press, 1967), 64n7.

72. Carvajal, "Memorias de Luis de Carvajal," 28:510. Carvajal's spelling of "Sequina" is identical to how the term is spelled in a work by Abner de Burgos, Alfonso de Valladolid after his conversion to Christianity. See *Mostrador de justicia* (Opladen: Westdeutscher Verlag, 1994), 8.

73. Arthur Green, "Shekhina, the Virgin Mary, and the Song of Songs: Reflections on a Kabbalistic Symbol in Its Historical Context," *AJS Review* 26, no. 1 (April 2002): 1.

74. Ibid., 15, 21, 32–35, 50.

75. Ibid, 32.

76. Stratton, *Immaculate Conception*, 141; and Augustin Bouttats, engraving on frontispiece to *España triunfante y la iglesia laureada, en todo el globo del mundo por el patrocinio de María Santissima en España*, 1682, The Hispanic Society of America.

77. Miguel Sánchez, *Imagen de la virgen Maria Madre de Dios de Guadalupe, milagrosamente aparecida en la civdad de Mexico* (México City: Imprenta Biuda de Bernardo Calderon, 1648), fols. 69b–71a.

78. Gershom Scholem, *Origins of the Kabbalah*, ed. R. I. Zwi Werblowsky, trans. Allan Arkush (Princeton, NJ: Princeton University Press, 1987), 163. As Scholem notes, "The Shekhinah, in Talmudic literature, is always simply God himself, that is, God insofar as he is present. . . . This 'presence' or 'indwelling' of God is precisely rendered by the Hebrew term Shekhinah."

79. Exodus 33: 20.

80. Elliot R. Wolfson, *Through a Speculum That Shines: Vision and Imagination in Medieval Jewish Mysticism* (Princeton, NJ: Princeton University Press, 1994), 92. Wolfson cites the *Hekhalot Rabbati, Synopse*, §102.

81. Swietlicki, *Spanish Christian Cabala*, 149.

82. Espinosa de los Monteros, *Interpretacion del misterio*, pt. II, fol. 22a. Guadalupe manuscript.

83. Ibid., pt. II, fol. 32a.

84. Nowak, "Virgin Rhetoric," 493.

85. Available texts do not say if the one in Spain was altered after the Mexican Virgin became so famous, although while staying at the Spanish monastery, I overheard conversations about how cherubs were added in the eighteenth century to the feet of the monastery Virgin so she would appear more like Guadalupe of México. See Jeanette Favrot Peterson, "Creating the Virgin of Guadalupe: The Cloth, the Artist, and Sources in Sixteenth-Century New Spain," *Americas* 61, no. 4 (2005): 602.

86. Espinosa de los Monteros, *Interpretacion del misterio*, no. 93, fol. 34a. Guadalupe manuscript.

87. Ibid., pt. II, fol. 3. Monteros continues, "It is the Judaic Church that is founded not on a rock of limited size, but over the same Christ that pried this rock with his hands and will occupy the world as would a forest."

Chapter 4 Hebrew Truth

1. Richard H. Popkin, "Savonarola and Cardinal Ximines: Millenarian Thinkers and Actors at the Eve of the Reformation," in *Catholic Millenarianism: From Savonarola to Abbé Grégoire*, ed. Karl Kottman (Dordrecht, Neth.: Kluwer Academic Publishers, 2001), 21. Popkin spells the name of the cardinal "Ximines"—generally it is spelled "Jimenez."

2. Ibid.

3. Marcel Bataillon, *Erasmo y España: estudios sobre la historia espiritual del siglo xvi*, trans. Antonio Alatorre (México City: Fondo de Cultural Economica, 1950), 45.

4. James P. Lyell, *Cardinal Ximenes, Statesman, Ecclesiastic, Soldier and Man of Letters, with an Account of the Complutensian Polyglot Bible* (London: Grafton & Co., 1917), 34. Lyell states that 50,000 ducats in the early sixteenth century equaled 230,000 British pounds in 1917. In 2011, this amount would equal over $160 billion. Popkin, "Savonarola and Cardinal Ximines," 21.

5. Popkin, "Savonarola and Cardinal Ximines," 21.

6. Lyell, *Cardinal Ximenes*, 26–27.

7. "Kabbalah is the traditional and most commonly used term for the esoteric teachings of Judaism and for Jewish mysticism, especially the forms which it assumed in the Middle Ages from the twelfth century onward. In its wider sense it signifies all the successive esoteric movements in Judaism that evolved from the end of the period of the Second Temple and became active factors in the history of Israel." See Gershom Scholem and Melila Hellner-Eshed, "Kabbalah," in *Encyclopaedia Judaica*, 2nd ed., ed. Michael Berenbaum and Fred Skolnik, *Gale Virtual Reference Library*.

8. Jerome Friedman, "Sixteenth-Century Christian-Hebraica: Scripture and the Renaissance Myth of the Past," *Sixteenth Century Journal* 11, no. 4 (1980): 71. Friedman notes that most of the Christian-Hebraists translated thirteenth-century Rabbi David Kimhi's work on the prophets, which is particularly interesting since "Kimhi was . . . one of Judaism's most competent anti-Christian polemicists" (70).

9. Ibid. Friedman cites Michael Servetus, *Biblia Sacra ex Santis Pagnini Tralatione sed ad Hebraicae linguae* (Lyon, 1542), Introduction, n.p.

10. For a thorough and convincing treatment of this remarkable thesis, see Robert Sagerman, "A Kabbalistic Reading of the Sistine Chapel Ceiling," *Acta ad archaeologiam et artium historiam pertinentia* 16 (2002): 93–177; and Robert Sagerman, "The Syncretic Esotericism of Egidio da Viterbo and the Development of the Sistine Chapel Ceiling Program," *Acta ad archaeologiam et artium historiam pertinentia* 19 (2005): 37–76.

11. Sergio Fernández López, *El Cantar de los Cantares en el humanismo español: La tradición judía* (Huelva, Spain: Universidad de Huelva, 2009), 83n206. López cites the Archivo de la Universidad de Salamanca, 5, fol. 312r, February 10, 1511.

12. Fernández López, *El Cantar de los Cantares*, 83; and Frederico Pérez Castro, "Semblanza Bio-Bibliografico de Alfonso de Zamora," in *El manuscrito apologético de Alfonso de Zamora: Traduccion y Estudio del Séfer Hokmat Elohim* (Madrid: Instituto Benito Arias Montano, 1950), xv.

13. Fernández López, *El Cantar de los Cantares*, 83; and Kevin Ingram, *The Conversos and Moriscos in Late Medieval Spain and Beyond* (Leiden: Brill, 2009), 78.

14. Julio Caro Baroja, *Las formas complejas de la vida religiosa: Religión, sociedad y carácter en la España de los siglos XVI y XVII* (Madrid: SARPE, 1985), 395; and Catherine Swietlicki, *The Spanish Christian Cabala* (Columbia: University of Missouri Press, 1986), 155.

15. Popkin reports that Zamora was preparing manuscripts for Cisneros in 1500. Lyell states that the Bible project was not begun until 1502. See also Bataillon, *Erasmo y España*, 2:45.

16. Popkin, "Savonarola and Cardinal Ximines," 22.

17. Pérez Castro cites Zamora. See Alfonso de Zamora, *El manuscrito apologético de Alfonso de Zamora: Traduccion y Estudio del Séfer Hokmat Elohim*, trans. Federico Pérez Castro (Madrid: Instituto Benito Arias Montano, 1950), liv. See also Fernández López, *El Cantar de los Cantares*, 82n202. Fernández López cites *Introductiones artis grammatice hebraice nunc recenter edite* (Alcalá de Henares, Spain: Miguel de Equia, 1526). See Fernández López's *El Cantar de los Cantares* for a superb history and analysis of the work of Alfonso de Zamora and later Spanish Hebraists.

18. Zamora, *El manuscrito apologético*, 82n200. Fernández López cites Alvar Gómez de Castro, who, in a document written in 1569, states that Zamora and Cisneros's other translators taught in a Hebrew school before being employed by the archbishop. See Alvar Gómez de Castro, *De la Hazañas de Francisco Jiménez de Cisneros*, ed. José Oroz Reta (Madrid: FUE, 1984), 194.

19. Richard Popkin states that Zamora did not convert to Christianity until 1506. Popkin, "Savonarola and Cardinal Ximines," 22.

20. Tarsicio Herrero del Collado, "El proceso inquisitorial por delito de herejía contra Hernando de Talavera," *Anuario de historia del derecho español* 39:695.

21. Linda Martz, *A Network of Converso Families in Early Modern Toledo: Assimilating a Minority* (Ann Arbor: University of Michigan Press, 2003), 60.

22. Herrero del Collado, "El proceso inquisitorial," 695.

23. Martz, *A Network of Converso Families*, 87–88. This was Álvarez's first of two arrests by the Inquisition.

24. Ibid., 88n26. Martz also notes that Álvarez "was in charge of the accounts for repairs to the archbishop's palace in Toledo."

25. Ibid., 87.

26. Ibid.

27. Cisneros joined the Reformed Franciscans and spent a year isolated in the convent San Juan de los Reyes in Toledo. After he finished his novitiate with the Franciscans, he requested a transfer to the remote Nuestra Señora de Castañar (Our Lady of Castañar), where he remained for three years until he was transferred to oversee the Convent of Salzeda. The author gives no date, except that this occurred before 1492. See William H. Prescott, *History of the Reign of Ferdinand and Isabella the Catholic*, 4th ed. (Boston: Charles C. Little and James Brown, 1838), 2:377, 379.

28. Carlos became king of Spain because his mother's Juana's incapacity. Although Juana inherited the throne after Isabel's death, her father, King Fernando, who was named regent, incarcerated her, stating that she had gone insane. She lived into her seventies. See Thérèse de Hemptinne, "Jeanne de Castille, une reine entre folie et pouvoir (1479–1555)," in *Charles V in Context: The Making of a European Identity*, ed. Marc Boone and Marysa Demoor (Brussels: VUB Brussels University Press, 2003), 235–248.

29. In a document from the university, the professors of Hebrew are described as "one of the *tornadizos* that know Hebrew well: one, is the shoemaker (from Arcos), and the other, Diego López, the musician." Fernández López, *El Cantar de los Cantares*, 83.

30. Zamora also praises Cisneros, saying there will not be another man in Spain that will have so much in riches, knowledge, and glory. He adds that Carlos V entered Spain two months before the death of Cisneros. Upon the king's arrival, the

inhabitants of Spain were written off for gold and silver—and that the grandees of Spain were not clever enough to protest the travesty. Moshe Lazar, "Alfonso de Zamora, copiste," *Sefarad* 18, no. 2 (1958): 318–319.

31. Richard H. Popkin, "Jewish Christians and Christian Jews in Spain, 1492 and After," *Judaism* 41, no. 3 (1992): 265.

32. Federico Pérez Castro states that the document was found in Leiden, at the Academia Lugduno-Batava. Zamora, *El manuscrito apologético*, xxv–xxvi. Note the discrepancy regarding the author of the letter. It begins with the name Dr. Zornoza, yet is signed by Alfonso [*sic*] de Zamora.

33. The spelling of David Qimhi's name varies among scholars. Alternately it is spelled Kimhi, Qinhi, or Qimhi. See also Zamora, *El manuscrito apologético*, xxv–xxvi.

34. Zamora, *El manuscrito apologético*, xlviii; Popkin, "Savonarola and Cardinal Ximines," 22; and Fernández López, *El Cantar de los Cantares*, 94n241.

35. Fernández López, *El Cantar de los Cantares*, 165.

36. Ibid.

37. Ibid., 81. Rashi, Ezra, and Qimhi are known as the great Jewish philosopher commentators. Their formal names are Solomon Ben Isaac "Rashi" (1040–1105), northern France; Moses Ben Jacob Ha-Sallah "Ibn Ezra" (1070–circa 1138), Granada; and David Qimhi or Kimch (1160–1235), Provence.

38. Ibid., 86–87.

39. Quirino Fernández, "Fray Dionisio Vázquez de Toledo orador sagrado del Siglo de Oro," *Archivo Agustiniano* 60, no. 178 (1976): 114, 10. Fernández cites David Gutierrez in *Annalecta Augustiniana* (1970): xxxiii, 106, 94.

40. While he is widely known as Egidio da Viterbo or Giles of Viterbo, the cardinal's name is Egidio Antonini.

41. Gaspar Morocho Gayo, "Hermetismo y cábala cristiana en la corte de Carlos V: Egidio de Viterbo, Dionisio Vázquez, Cipriano de la Huerga," *La Ciudad de Dios* 213 (December 2000): 838. Historian Morocho Gayo proposes that is when Vázquez and Viterbo met, and that encounter influenced one of Vázquez's manuscripts, the *Neapolitanus gr. 14*. Morocho Gayo has identified Viterbo's handwriting in Vázquez's manuscript. Morocho Gayo cites the Archivio del Stato Italiano, Fondo conventi Soppresi, legao Sig. Q.21.22 (29). According to Francis Martin, Viterbo was sent by the pope to Naples "to conciliate Ferdinand of Aragon," and appeal "for a united effort against the infidel," the Turkish emperor Bayezid II. See Francis X. Martin, *Friar, Reformer, and Renaissance Scholar: Life and Work of Giles of Viterbo 1469–1532* (Villanova, PA: Augustinian Press, 1992), 66.

42. Morocho Gayo cites the Archivo Historico National, *Inquisición*, Lib. 244, Lib. 244, fol. 21; Lib. 317, fol, 299; Lib 572, fol. 121. He notes this information was published in *Miscellanea*, vol. 5, by Vincente Beltrán de Heredia, documents 2060, 2061, 270.

43. José Gómez Menor states that Vázquez's parents were Pedro Vázquez and María de San Pedro. He believes that the orator's uncle was *regidor* of Toledo, García Vázquez, who was married to a woman from the Cota family, well known for being conversos. See José Gómez Menor, *Cristianos Nuevos y Mercaderes de Toledo: Notas y documentos para el estudio de la sociedad castellana en el siglo XVI* (Toledo: Imprenta Gómez-Menor, 1970), lii.

44. Fernández, "Fray Dionisio Vázquez," 116.

45. Ibid.

46. Fernández López, *El Cantar de los Cantares*, 96.

47. Vázquez remained regent until 1513. See Fernández, "Fray Dionisio Vázquez," 117.

48. Ibid. The "colonies" consisted of Flanders and the Low Countries. A *visitadór* was authorized to inspect Church administration and appoint clergy in his assigned geographic area. Vázquez, however, soon left for Spain, where Carlos was formally crowned king.

49. Morocho Gayo, "Hermetismo y cábala cristiana," 413. Morocho Gayo cites Vicente Beltrán de Heredia, "La Teologia en la Universidad de Alcalá," *Revista Española de Teología* 5 (1945).

50. Ibid., 841. Morocho Gayo cites Alvar Gómez de Castro, *De las Hazañas de Francisco Jiménez de Cisneros*, ed. De José Oroz Reta (Madrid: Fundación Universidad Empresa, 1984), 544.

51. Ibid., 843.

52. Ibid., 842–843, 848–849.

53. Fernández López, *El Cantar de los Cantares*, 100. "*Commentarium super Joannem ad literam*, by R. P. Fr. Dionyisum, Ceasarerae Maiestatis Praedicatorem (Cesar's Master Orator)" was found in the library of Alonso Gudiel several years after he died. Fernández López cites Miguel de la Pinta Llorente, ed., *Causa criminal contra el biblista Alonso Gudiel, catedrático de la Universidad de Osuna* (Madrid: CSIC, 1942), 261.

54. Morocho Gayo, "Hermetismo y cábala cristiana," 850. Immediately after Felipe II took the crown of Portugal, the Inquisition banned two texts by Vázquez, among them *Exposición sobre Isaias*, proving that the works contained "neoplatonic hermetism, christian cabala, and other things." Morocho Gayo cites Jorge Dalmeida, *Roi dos livros que se prohibem nestes regno & senhorios*, ed. J. M. de Bujanda (Lisbon: Antonio Ribeiro, 1581), n133.

55. Ibid., 830.

56. Ibid., 832. Morocho Gayo cites Carlos Seco Serrano, ed., *Historia de la vida y hechos del emperador Carlos V* (Madrid: BAE, 80, 1955), 1:136.

57. François Secret, "Le symbolisme de la Kabbale Chretienne dans la 'Scechina' de Egidio da Viterbo," *Umanesimo e Machiavellismo: Archivio di Filosofia* 2–3 (1958): 146n44. Secret cites Guiseppe Signorelli, *Il Cardinale Egidio da Viterbo, agostiniano, umanista e riformatore (1469–1532)* (Florence, 1929), 72.

58. Morocho Gayo, "Hermetismo y cábala cristiana," 831.

59. Ibid., 832.

60. Mandell Creighton, *A History of the Papacy: From the Great Schism to the Sack of Rome* (London: Longmans, Green, 1903), 6:112.

61. Morocho Gayo, "Hermetismo y cábala cristiana," 833n73. Morocho cites Francis Martin, "The Writings of Giles of Viterbo," *Augustinana* 29 (1979): 159.

62. Fernández López, *El Cantar de los Cantares*, 101.

63. Morocho Gayo, "Hermetismo y cábala cristiana," 833n73. He cites Martin, "Writings of Giles of Viterbo," 159.

64. Morocho Gayo, "Hermetismo y cábala cristiana," 825–826.

65. Philip Beitchman, *Alchemy of the Word: Cabala of the Renaissance* (Albany: State University of New York Press, 1998), 119.

66. John W. O'Malley, *Giles of Viterbo on Church and Reform: A Study in Renaissance Thought* (Leiden: Brill, 1968), 99, no. 4.

67. The production of this work was exceedingly strategic. It was begun after what is known as the Sack of Rome of 1527. The attack was orchestrated by Carlos V, the grandson of los Reyes Católicos, Fernando and Isabel. Carlos V's imperial troops,

consisting of Spanish soldiers and German mercenaries, utterly destroyed Rome and imprisoned the Pope for seven months. Shortly after, the pope requested that Viterbo dedicate a Kabbalistic treatise to Carlos V. This had to have been a political move. Similarly, two months after the sack, a missive to Carlos directed by the pope states that the pope and the emperor "had never really been enemies, but rather had worked reciprocally for each other's interests." The Sack of Rome will be addressed in chapter 5. See Ludwig Pastor, *The History of the Popes, from the Close of the Middle Ages: Drawn from the Secret Archives of the Vatican and Other Original Sources*, ed. Ralph Francis Kerr (London: Kegan Paul, Trench, Trübner & Co., 1910) 9:434–435. Pastor cites Nunziatura de Francia I., fols. 14–19 (Secret Archives of the Vatican), http://www.archive.org/stream/historyofpopesf09past#page/2/mode/2up.

68. Robert J. Wilkinson, *Orientalism, Aramaic, and Kabbalah in the Catholic Reformation: The First Printing of the Syriac New Testament* (Leiden: Brill, 2007), 40.

69. Meredith J. Gill, *Augustine in the Italian Renaissance: Art and Philosophy from Petrarch to Michelangelo* (Cambridge: Cambridge University Press, 2005), 25.

70. F. X. Martin, "The Problem of Giles of Viterbo: A Historiographical Survey," *Augustiniana* 9 (1959): 367.

71. Ferdinand Gregorov, *History of the City of Rome in the Middle Ages*, trans. Annie Hamilton (London: George Bell and Sons, 1902), 8:606.

72. Gill, *Augustine in the Italian Renaissance*, 151.

73. Secret, "Le symbolisme de la Kabbale," 132.

74. Ibid., 32.

75. It was in this environment of "broken morals and norms" that most likely made it more possible for Viterbo's Jewish writings and ideas to develop.

76. François Secret, *La Kabbala Cristiana del Renacimiento*, trans. Ignacio Gómez de Liaño and Tomás Pollán (Madrid: Taurus, 1979), 127; and Secret, "Le symbolisme de la Kabbale," 129.

77. H. G. Enelow, "Ægidius of Viterbo," *Jewish Encyclopedia.com*, n.d., http://www.jewishencyclopedia.com/view.jsp?artid=870&letter=A&search=viterbo.

78. Levita was also known as Eliyahu ben Asher ha-Levi Ashkenazi, Eliyahu ha-Medaqdez, "Elijah the Grammarian," Eliya Bahur, Eliza Evita, or, in Yiddish, Elye Bokher. See Jonas C. Greenfield, "Book Review of Élie Lévita, Humaniste et Massoréte," *Journal of the American Oriental Society* 88, no. 3 (1968): 529; and Meir Medan, "Levita, Elijah," in *Encyclopaedia Judaica*, 2nd ed., edited by Michael Berenbaum and Fred Skolnick, vol. 12. *Gale Reference Library*.

79. Martin, *Friar, Reformer*, 14; and O'Malley, *Giles of Viterbo*, 70.

80. Michael J. B. Allen, "Introduction," in *Marsilio Ficino: His Theology, His Philosophy, His Legacy* (Leiden: Brill, 2002), xvi.

81. Zelda Kahan Newman, "Elye Levita: A Man on the Cusp of Modernity," *Shofar: An Interdisciplinary Journal of Jewish Studies* 24, no. 4 (2006): 91n2.

82. Ibid., 90–91.

83. Ibid., 91n2. Newman notes "Levita's phenomenal memory and encyclopedic knowledge of Jewish texts."

84. Ibid., 92.

85. Secret, *La Kabbala Cristiana*, 131. Names of conversos and Hebraists mentioned by Secret in relation to Viterbo are Felice da Prato (Augustinian, translated the *Sefer Temunah* and the *Imre Sefer* as well as compiled a Hebrew dictionary with rules of grammar); Daniel Bomberg (student of Prato, produced the first printed Rabbinic Bible in 1516–1517); Abraham de Balmes (was protected by Cardinal Grimani,

wrote *Libro de la creación del mundo* in 1523); Michael ben Sabthai, also named Zematus, Baruch de Bénévent (distributed the *Zohar* to Christians); Nicolaus Camerarius (archbishop of Bénévent who translated a book of the Kabbala for Viterbo); José Hagri (taught on the Book of *Ehalot*); and Isaac ben Abraham (Viterbo purchased an edition of the *Zohar* for Abraham to copy).

86. Ibid.

87. Ibid, 132. Secret cites Biblioteque National Manuscript, *Italy* 612, fols. 148–194.

88. Ibid., 128–130; and Newman, "Elye Levita," 90. There is conflicting information regarding how long Levita lived in the home of the cardinal. Secret says that he was there for thirteen years, having arrived by 1512. Newman states that it was ten years.

89. Secret, *La Kabbala Cristiana*, 129–130; and Newman, "Elye Levita," 90.

90. Sharon Ann Leftley, *Millenarian Thought in Renaissance Rome with Special Reference to Pietro Galatino (c. 1464–c. 1540) and Egidio da Viterbo (c. 1469–1532)* (Bristol: University of Bristol, 1995), 114. Leftley cites F. Giacone and G. Bedouelle, "Une lettre de Gilles de Viterbe (1469–1532) à Jacques Lefèvre de'Etaples (c1460–1536) au sujet de l'affaire Reuchlin," *Bibliotheque d'humanisme et renaissance* 35 (1974): 343. Leftly reports that Bedouelle and Giacone analyzed a letter written by Viterbo in 1504 regarding the Reuchlin affair, stating that Viterbo was "informing Lefèvre of the decision so far in favour of Reuchlin in Rome and thanking him [Lefèvre] for his support." The case actually began when a converso bishop, Johann Pfefferkorn, requested that Emperor Maximilian "confiscate and destroy Jewish books" because "they were insulting to the Christian religion and an obstacle to the conversion of the Jews." Reuchlin was the only person on a panel appointed by the emperor who was against the idea. The controversy surrounding the books ended with no ban being implemented, but the polemic led to a heresy charge against Reuchlin. See Erika Rummel, *The Case against Johann Reuchlin: Religious and Social Controversy in Sixteenth-Century Germany* (Toronto: University of Toronto Press, 2002), vii–viii.

91. Isidore Singer and Cyrus Adler, ed., *The Jewish Encyclopedia: A Descriptive Record of the History, Religion, Literature, and Customs of the Jewish People from the Earliest Times to the Present Day*, s.v. "Italy."

92. O'Malley, *Giles of Viterbo*, 83–84.

93. Secret, *La Kabbala Cristiana*, 144.

94. Ibid.

95. The *Zohar* is "'Illumination' or 'Brightness,' the classical work of the Kabbalah, containing the record of revelations regarding the divine mysteries," *A Concise Companion to the Jewish Religion Oxford Reference*, s.v. "Zohar."

96. Sagerman, "Kabbalistic Reading," 100; and Secret, *La Kabbala Cristiana*, 127.

97. See Egidio Antonini [Egidio da Viterbo], *Scechina e Libellus de litteris hebraicis. Inediti a cura di François Secret*, ed. François Secret (Rome: Centro Internazionale di Studi Umanistic, 1959). The manuscript was published by Secret in its incomplete form.

98. Morocho Gayo, "Hermetismo y cábala cristiana," 825.

99. Leo X and Clement VII were both Medicis.

100. Javary, "Recherches sur l'utilisation du theme de la sekina dans l'apologetique Chretienne du XV éme au XVIII éme siecle" (Paris: Universite de Paris, 1976), 413.

101. O'Malley, *Giles of Viterbo*, 38; O'Malley cites Biblioteca Angelica, Cod. Lat. 502, fol. 95v, "Historia XX saeculorum."

102. Sagerman, "Kabbalistic Reading," 100.

103. John Monfasani, "Hermes Trismegistus, Rome, and the Myth of Europa: An Unknown Text of Giles of Viterbo," *Viator* 22 (1991): 318.
104. Ibid., 321.
105. Ibid., 318.
106. Singer and Adler, "Michael," in *Jewish Encyclopedia*.
107. Monfasani, "Hermes Trismegistus," 321.
108. Ibid., 319.
109. Sagerman, "Syncretic Esotericism," 74; Sagerman cites Marsilio Ficino, "De vita coelitus comparanda," in *Three Books on* Life, trans. Carol V. Kaske and John Richard Clark (Binghamton, NY: Medieval and Renaissance Texts and Studies, 1989), 347.
110. Fernández, "Fray Dionisio Vázquez," 115.
111. Sagerman, "Kabbalistic Reading," 95; Sagerman, "Syncretic Esotericism," 37n1; and Gill, *Augustine in the Italian Renaissance*, 151, 243n18.
112. Sagerman, "Kabbalistic Reading," 101.
113. Marsilio Ficino, *Marsilio Ficino*, ed. Angela Voss (Berkeley, CA: North Atlantic Books, 2006), 147.
114. The ceiling contains a section titled "The Ancestors of Christ," which is located in an area that does not receive much attention. There are no images from the New Testament on the walls of the Sistine Chapel. The major work on the walls below is Michelangelo's *Last Judgment* featuring a young Christ, with no beard, at the center.
115. Sagerman, "Kabbalistic Reading," 91. Sagerman studied under noted Judaic scholar Elliot R. Wolfson.
116. Gershom Scholem, *Kabbalah* (New York: Dorset Press, 1974), 3.
117. Ibid., 23.
118. Ibid., 95–96.
119. Ibid., 96.
120. Ibid.
121. Ibid., 97; and O'Malley, *Giles of Viterbo*, 89, 91.
122. Javary, "Recherches," 28. In this passage Viterbo gives instructions to Carlos V on how to learn from the Divine Light given to him by the Shekhinah.
123. Elliot R. Wolfson, *Through a Speculum That Shines: Vision and Imagination in Medieval Jewish Mysticism* (Princeton, NJ: Princeton University Press, 1994), 315, 314.
124. Martin, *Friar, Reformer*, 126; and Paolo Giovio, *An Italian Portrait Gallery; Being Brief Biographies of Scholars Illustrious within the Memory of Our Grandfathers for the Published Monuments of Their Genius*, trans. Florence Alden Gragg (Boston: Chapman and Grimes, 1935), 122–123.
125. Martin, *Friar, Reformer*, 127.
126. Martin, similar to Viterbo's other twentieth-century biographer, John O'Malley, produced excellent work on the cardinal; however, their religious affiliation (they are both priests) appears to have influenced how they managed Viterbo's Jewish interests. Ibid., 123. The ambivalence toward the cardinal's work on the Kabbalah is indicated by O'Malley's and Martin's bibliographies. O'Malley mentions the original manuscript of the *Scechina* under its listing at the Bibliothèque National de France under Cod. Lat. 3363 (O'Malley, 194). Under this listing, he notes the pseudo-Joachimite "in Isaiam" first and halfway through the second line, he finally writes, "and the autograph of Giles's 'Scechina,' begun in 1530 at the request of Clement VII." The notation is not readily visible. Martin's biography of the cardinal only mentions that François Secret has made "a major advance toward an

understanding of Giles" (151n84). It appears that Martin did not consult Viterbo's *Scechina* while writing *Friar, Reformer.*

127. Secret, "Le Symbolisme de la Kabbale," 149.

128. The light in this case is the Divine Illumination given by the Shekhinah. Javary, "Recherches," 28–29.

129. Secret, "Le Symbolisme de la Kabbale," 143.

130. Javary cites Antonini's *Scechina*, fol. 319v. Javary, "Recherches," 322.

131. Secret, "Le Symbolisme de la Kabbale," 141. Secret cites *Scechina*, fol. 276.

132. Escorial will be discussed in the following chapter.

133. Karl Kottman notes that Luis de León "owed an intellectual debt to . . . Egidio da Viterbo." Karl Kottman, *Law and Apocalypse: The Moral Thought of Luis de León 1527?–1591* (The Hague: Martinus Nijhoff, 1972), ix. De León wrote *The Names of Christ* while he was imprisoned on charges of heresy. He was accused of practicing Judaism. Catherine Swietlicki states in *Spanish Christian Cabala* that "Luis de León had a 'Hebrew soul,'" citing George Tichnor, *History of Spanish Literature* (Boston: Houghton-Mifflin, 1863), 2: part 1, 104. Secret, "Le Symbolisme de la Kabbale," 149; and Swietlicki, *Spanish Christian Cabala*, 158. Swietlicki also cites Georges Morel, *Le sense de l'existence selon Saint Jean de la Croix* (Paris: Aubier, 1960), 1:203–205; and Alberto Colunga, "San Juan de la Cruz, intérprete de la Santa Escritura," *Ciencia Tomista* 63 (1942): 275–276.

Chapter 5   The Sphinx

1. In this situation, a *capellán* would be a priest in the employment of the king.

2. José de Sigüenza, *Historia de la Orden de San Jerónimo* (Madrid: Bailly//Bailliére é Hijos Editores, 1909), 2:660.

3. Henry Kamen, *The Escorial: Art and Power in the Renaissance* (New Haven, CT: Yale University Press, 2010), xii. Kamen writes, "Uniquely among the buildings of early modern Europe, the Escorial seems to challenge us with its Sphinx-like immobility. It raises questions to which there appear to be no simple answers."

4. The Counter-Reformation was a reform movement of the Roman Catholic Church created in response to the rise of Protestantism.

5. The Council of Trent was a gathering of Roman Catholic prelates in the mid-sixteenth century. Its main purpose was to clarify and strengthen the dogma of the Church.

6. The main entrance in 2013 is what had been considered the original back entrance.

7. San Lorenzo de Escorial is 207 meters long, 161 meters wide, and 95 meters at its highest point. I thank Dr. Juan Rafael de la Cuadra Blanco for this information.

8. Bernard Rekers, *Benito Arias Montano* (London: Warburg Institute, 1972), 105.

9. Philippe Erlenger, *Carlos V*, trans. Jesús Fernández Zulaica (Barcelona: Salvat Editores, 1985), 49.

10. Ibid., 129.

11. Fernand Braudel, *The Mediterranean and the Mediterranean World in the Age of Philip II*, trans. Siân Reynolds (Berkeley: University of California Press, 1995), 2:674.

12. José Antonio Maravall, *Carlos V y el pensamiento político del Renacimiento* (Madrid: Boletín Oficial del Estado Centro de Estudios Políticos y Constitucioncionales, 1999), 90. Letter from Cardinal Carcia de Loayssa to Carlos V, November 18, 1530. Maravall adds, "If the heretics cannot remain converted Christians, at least they can be vassals and servants of the Emperor."

13. Américo Castro, Aspectos del Vivir Hispanico: Espiritualismo, Mesianismo, Actitude Personal en los Siglos XIV al XVI (Santiago de Chile: Editorial Cruz del Sur, 1949), 126.

14. Ibid.

15. The Jewish Kabbalah is spelled "Cabala" when studied by Christians.

16. Gaspar Morocho Gayo, "Hermetismo y cábala cristiana en la corte de Carlos V: Egidio de Viterbo, Dionisio Vázquez, Cipriano de la Huerga," La Ciudad de Dios 213 (December 2000): 814. These included Dionisio Vazquez, Cipriano de la Huerga, and Italian Egidio da Viterbo.

17. Castro, Aspectos del Vivir Hispanico, 125, 126. Castro cites Marcel Bataillon, Erasme et l'Espagne: recherches sur l'historie spirituelle du XVIe siècle (Paris: Librairie E. Droz, 1937), 747–748. Castro quotes the emperor's envoy to Rome, Hugo of Moncada, in Alfonso de Valdéz, Diálogo de cosas ocurridas en Roma , ed. J. F. Montesinos (Madrid: Ediciones "La Lectura," 1928), 50–53.

18. Ibid., 135. Renaissance Humanism is a form of religious and philosophical study that focuses "on the human (as opposed to the divine) side of biblical texts." See Magne Saebo, Michael Fishbane, and John Louis Ska, Hebrew Bible/Old Testament: The History of Its Interpretation, from the Renaissance to the Enlightenment (Göttingen: Vandenhoeck & Ruprecht, 2008), 2:203.

19. Juan Rafael Cuadra Blanco, "King Philip of Spain as Solomon the Second: The Origins of Solomonism of the Escorial in the Netherlands," in The Seventh Window: The King's Window Donated by Philip II and Mary Tudor to Sint Janskerk in Gouda (1557) (Hilversum, Neth: Uitgeverij Verloren, 2005), 171. Cuadra Blanco cites Archiv des Ordens vom Goldenen Vlies als Deport im Österreichischen Staatsarchiv, Valenciennes 1556, fols. 14v–15r.

20. Cuadra Blanco, "King Philip of Spain."

21. Ibid., 170.

22. Juan Rafael Cuadra Blanco, "El Escorial y el Templo de Salomón," en Anales de arquitectura, no. 7, Valladolid, ESTSAUV (1996), 11.

23. François Secret, La Kabbala Cristiana del Renacimiento, trans. Ignacio Gómez de Liaño and Tomás Pollán (Madrid: Taurus, 1979), 141. Secret cites Egidio Antonini (da Viterbo), Scechina e Libellus de litteris hebraicis: Inediti a cura di François Secret, ed. F. Secret, (Rome: Centro Internazionale di Studi Umanistic, 1959), 68, 89.

24. Maravall, Carlos V y el pensamiento, 90; and Guido Marnef, "Charles V's Religious Policy and the Antwerp Market: A Confrontation of Different Interests?," in Charles V in Context: The Making of a European Identity (Brussels: VUB Brussels University Press, 2003), 21–33.

25. Mandell Creighton, A History of the Papacy: From the Great Schism to the Sack of Rome (New York: Longmans, Green, 1903), 6:123.

26. Under the name Carlos I, he was king of Spain (1516–1556) and its dominions in the East and West Indies, archduke of Austria (1516–1521), and king of Naples. As Carlos V he was elected Holy Roman emperor in 1516 and served until his death in 1556.

27. Maravall, Carlos V y el pensamiento, 46. Maravall cites Prudencio de Sandoval, Historia de la vida y hechos del Emperador Carlos V (Barcelona: Sebastian de Cormellas, 1625), 1:372.

28. Maravall, Carlos V y el pensamiento, 46.

29. Manuel Romero Carrión, "Vision Que Tuvo Felipe II de Mano de Domenico Greco" (lecture, 1972–73), 94.

30. Marcel Bataillon, *Erasmo y España: Estudios sobre la historia espiritual del siglo xvi*, trans. Antonio Alatorre (México City: Fondo de Cultural Economica, 1950), 281. Bataillon cites *Acta Tomiciana*, t. IX, 217; and Lu Ann Homza, "Erasmus as Hero, or Heretic? Spanish Humanism and the Valladolid Assembly of 1527," *Renaissance Society of America* 50, no. 1 (Spring 1997): 78. Homza states a different purpose to the meeting. The participants in the meeting in Valladolid were "to judge a variety of suspicious passages culled from Erasmus's works."

31. Bataillon, *Erasmo y España*, 1:92.

32. Ibid., 278. As noted in a previous footnote, Erasmus dedicated *Intitutio Principis Christiani* to Carlos V.

33. Homza, "Erasmus as Hero," 78.

34. Creighton, *History of the Papacy*, 6:320. Creighton cites Antonio Rodriguez Villa in *Memorias para la historia del asalto y saqueo di Roma en 1527 por el ejercito imperial* (Madrid: Imprenta de la Biblioteca de Instruccion y Recreo, 1875), 21.

35. Bataillon, *Erasmo y España*, 272–274.

36. Ibid., 274. Batallion cites Fermín Caballero, *Alonso y Juan de Valdés* (Madrid: Oficina tipográfica del hospicio, 1875), 324.

37. Ibid. Batallion cites Andrea Navagero alla Signoría, Valladolid, March 8, 1527.

38. Alonso de Santa Cruz, *Crónica del Emperador Carlos V* (Madrid: Real Academia de la Historia, Imprenta del Patronato de Huérfanos de Intendencia é Intervención Militares, 1920), 291.

39. William H. Prescott, *History of the Reign of Philip II, King of Spain* (Boston: Phillips, Sampson, and Company, 1855), 28.

40. Antonio Rodriguez Villa, *Memorias para la historia del asalto y saqueo de Roma en 1527 por el ejercito imperial* (Madrid: Imprenta de la Biblioteca de Instruccion y Recreo, 1875), 119.

41. Ibid., 119–121. Curiously, Rodriguez Villa states: "Assuredly, Jacobo Buonaparte says in his *Relación* that the Spanish respected those sacred places and holy relics, it was the Germans who were the most cruel and treacherous." The details of the letters the author states are so vivid and intense that it seems unlikely that the Spaniards played no part in the sacking of religious spaces or objects. Interestingly, he does not deny that the Spanish soldiers attacked the clergy.

42. Ibid., 135–136. Cited from a manuscript of the Biblioteca Nacional de España, Cc-59, dated ca. seventeenth century.

43. Ludwig Pastor, *The History of the Popes, from the Close of the Middle Ages: Drawn from the Secret Archives of the Vatican and Other Original Sources* (London: Kegan Paul, Trench, Trübner & Co., 1910), 9:400. Pastor adds that the Italians and the Neapolitans were just as ingenious at finding treasure and exacting torture. He doubts the information on the Jews and *conversos* is accurate, yet he cites three authors who report this to be true: Luigi Guicciardini, *Il Sacco di Roma*, ed. Carlo Milanesi (Florence: Barbéra, 1867), 229; Eustachio Celebrino, *La presa di Roma: Con breve narrazione di tuttili magni fatti di Guerre successi, net tēpo che lo Exercito Imperiale statte in viaggio da Milano a Roma* (Rome: Tip. Romana, 1872), 15; and Caesar Grolierius, *Historia Expvgnatæ et Direptæ Vrbis Romæ per Exercitvm Caroli V. Imp. Die VI. Maii M. D. XXVII. Clemente VII. Pontifice* (Paris: Cramoisy, 1637), 24.

44. Ibid., 9:460. Cited from the account book of Paolo Montanari, expeditor of Clement VII, Roman State Archives.

45. Rawdon Brown, ed., *Calendar of State Papers and Manuscripts Relating to English Affairs Existing in the Archives and Collections of Venice and in Other Libraries of Northern Italy* (London: Longman & Co., and Trubner & Co., 1871), 4:76, sec. 1527, no. 142, cited from dispatch Andrea Navagero to Signory, July 27, 1527. Cicogna Copy in the Correr Museum, http://www.archive.org/stream/calendarstatepaoounkngoog#page/n0/mode/2up.

46. Pastor, *History of the Popes*, 9:450, citing Nunziatura di Francia I., fol. 34.

47. Santa Cruz, *Crónica del Emperador Carlos V*, 293.

48. Rodriguez Villa, *Memorias para la historia.*

49. Santa Cruz, *Crónica del Emperador Carlos V*, 293.

50. Kathleen Bollard de Broce, "Authorizing Literary Propaganda: Alfonso de Valdés' Diálogo de las cosas acaecidas en Roma (1527)," *Hispanic Review* 68, no. 2 (Spring 2000): 132.

51. Henry Kamen, *Philip of Spain* (New Haven, CT: Yale University Press, 1997), 168.

52. Olwen Hufton, "Altruism and Reciprocity: The Early Jesuits and Their Female Patrons," *Renaissance Studies* 15, no. 3 (2001): 335, doi:10.1111/1477-4658.00373. Hufton uses the spelling "Mascareñas"; however, a number of other authors use "Mascarenhas."

53. Ibid., 335–336.

54. Felix Labrador Arroyo, Manuel Rivero Rodriguez, and Carlos Javier de Morales, "En busca del equilibrio en la corte de Carlos V (1522–1529)," in *Corte de Carlos V*, ed. José Martínez Millán (Madrid: Sociedad Estatal para la Conmemoración de los Centenarios de Felipe II y Carlos V, 2000), 239.

55. Carlos-Eugenio Mascareñas, "Sobre Doña Leonor Mascareñas, aya de Don Felipe II y Del Principe Don Carlos," *Hispania* 7, no. 26 (March 1947): 10.

56. Selma Stern, *The Court Jew: A Contribution to the History of the Period of Absolutism in Central Europe* (Philadelphia: Jewish Publication Society, 1950), 102.

57. Hufton, "Altruism and Reciprocity," 335–336. Leonor Mascareñas was instrumental in providing financial and emotional support to Ignatius Loyola during the time he established the Jesuit Order. She was known to have been a close friend of Ignatius of Loyola and Saint Teresa of Avila. Avila is known to be from a converso family; her grandfather was put on trial by the Spanish Inquisition.

58. Christine Göttler, "Securing Space in a Foreign Place: Peter Paul Ruben's 'Saint Teresa' for the Portuguese Merchant-Bankers in Antwerp," *Journal of the Walters Art Gallery* 57 (1999): 134–136.

59. David S. Katz, "Menasseh ben Israel's Mission to Queen Christina of Sweden, 1651–1655," *Jewish Social Studies* 45, no. 1 (Winter 1983): 67.

60. Kamen, *Philip of Spain*, 5. Both Calvet and Sepúlveda were instrumental in the development of monarchial policies toward the Indies (America).

61. Kamen, *Escorial*, 26, 139, 149. He spent 1548–1551 in Europe, where he stayed one year in Germany and lived among numerous Lutherans. He resided in England with his second wife, Mary Tudor, from July 1554 to September 1555. He also lived in Portugal from 1581 to 1584 after he was named king. As Kamen notes, Felipe spent time in "northern Italy, the Alps, southern Germany, the Rhineland, the Netherlands, parts of France, and southern England" (26).

62. Kamen, *Philip of Spain*, 38.

63. Bataillon, *Erasmo y España*, 2:432.

64. Catherine Swietlicki describes the *alumbrados* as controversial for "their interest in interiorized religion and their less-than-orthodox inclinations"; see Swietlicki, *The Spanish Christian Cabala* (Columbia: University of Missouri Press, 1986), 36.

65. Kamen, *Philip of Spain*, 178–179.

66. Sigüenza, *Historia de la Orden de San Jerónimo*, 2:403, 401.

67. Rene Taylor, "Architecture and Magic: Considerations on the Idea of the Escorial," in *Essays in the History of Architecture Presented to Rudolf Wittkower* (New York: Phaidon, 1967), 83.

68. Gaspar Morocho Gayo, "Trayectoria humanística de Benito Arias Montano II: Años de plentitude (1568–1598)," in *El Humanismo Extremeño, III Jornadas* (Trujillo: Real Academia de Extremadura, 1999), 273.

69. The Bible was produced by the Antwerp printer Christopher Plantin.

70. Sergio Fernández López, *El Cantar de los Cantares en el humanismo español: La tradición judía* (Huelva, Spain: Universidad de Huelva, 2009), 115.

71. The "court converso" is a variation on the term "court Jew" used by Selma Stern; see *Court Jew*.

72. Guy Lazure, "To Dare Fame: Constructing a Cultural Elite in Sixteenth- Century Seville" (PhD diss., Johns Hopkins University, 2003), 159.

73. Stafford Poole, *Juan de Ovando: Governing the Spanish Empire in the Reign of Philip II* (Norman: University of Oklahoma Press, 2004), 21, 24. El Consejo de Indias (Council of the Indies) was the most powerful administrative branch of the Spanish monarchy with regards to its colonies. Poole cites Robert Paddon, "The Ordenanza de Padronazgo: An Interpretive Essay," in *The Church in Colonial Latin America*, edited by John Frederick Schwaller, 27–47 (Wilmington, DE: Scholarly Resources, 2000), 36.

74. Paddon, "Ordenanza de Padronazgo," 36.

75. Fernando Navarro Antolín, Luis Gómez Canseco, and Baldomero Macías Rosendo, "Fronteras del Humanismo: Arias Montano y el Nuevo Mundo," in *Orbis incognitvs: Avisos y legajos del Nuevo Mundo: homenaje al profesor Luis Navarro García* (Huelva: Universidad de Huelva, 2007), 1:102.

76. Gaspar Morocho Gayo, "Trayectoria humanística de Benito Arias Montano I: Sus cuarenta primeros años (1526–27–1567)," in *El Humanismo Extremeño, III Jornadas* (Trujillo: Real Academia de Extremadura, 1998), 180. Montano was released a few days later.

77. Poole, *Juan de Ovando*, 35.

78. Navarro Antolín, Gómez Canseco, and Macías Rosendo, "Fronteras del Humanismo," 110.

79. Kamen, *Philip of Spain*, 235.

80. Baldomero Macías Rosendo, *La correspondencia de Benito Arias Montano con el Presidente de Indias Juan de Ovando: Cartas de Benito Arias Montano convervadas en el Instituto de Valencia de Don Juan* (Huelva, Spain: Universidad de Huelva, 2008), 243.

81. Jesús Paniagua Pérez, "La obra y las relaciones de Arias Montano con las Indias," in *El humanismo español entre el viejo mundo y el nuevo* (Salamanca, Spain: Universidad de Jaén, 2008), 416.

82. Cornelia von der Osten Sacken, *El Escorial estudio iconologico*, trans. Maria Dolores Abalos (Bilbao: Xarait Ediciones, 1984), 130. From left to right, the statues are Josephat, Ezekiel, David, Solomon, Josiah, and Manasas.

83. Kamen reports that Montano commissioned the statues while Felipe was in Portugal. See Kamen, *Escorial*, 95; and Poole, *Juan de Ovando*, 195.

84. Kamen explains that Felipe was an "unswerving supporter of the spiritual authority of the papacy" yet "within Spain Philip felt himself completely free to act as he liked

in Church matters ... he did not hesitate to sanction the use of troops against monasteries and convents" and "had total control over appointment of bishops." Kamen,
Philip of Spain, 235.

85. Marcelino Meléndez y Pelayo, *Historia de los heterodoxos españoles* (Madrid:
Librería católica de San José, 1880), 376–377; and Kamen, *Philip of Spain*, 152.

86. For more information on Montano's political involvements, see Luis Durán Guerra,
"Benito Arias Montano: Emblemas para una Biblización de la Política," *Cuadernos
sobre Vico* 21–22 (2008): 237–262.

87. Pedro Urbano González de la Calle, "Arias Montano, humanista. (Apuntes y notas
para un ensayo)," *Revista de Centro de Estudios Extremeños* 2 (1928): 1.

88. Sáenz-Badillos, "Benito Arias Montano: Hebraísta," *Thélème: Revista complutense
de estudios franceses* 12 (1997): 352n31.

89. Rekers, *Benito Arias Montano*, 46.

90. Ibid., 140n40.

91. Ibid., 54; and Fernández López, *El Cantar de los Cantares*, 15.

92. Fray Luis de Estrada was a fellow student of Arias Montano at the University of
Alcalá in 1546. Benito Arias Montano, *Prefacios de Benito Arias Montano a la Biblia
Regia de Felipe II*, ed. Sánchez Manzano and María Asunción (León: Junta de
Castilla y León, Consejería de Cultura y Turismo: Universidad de León, Servicio de
Publicaciones, 2006), xliv, lii.

93. Ángel Valbuena Prat, *Historia de la literatura española*, 4th ed. (Barcelona: G. Gili,
1953), 1:613; and Morocho Gayo, "Trayectoria humanística I," 156.

94. Tomás González Carvajal, "Elogio histórico del Doctor Benito Arias Montano,
leído en la Real Academia de la Historia," *Memorias de la Real Academia de la
Historia* (1832) 2:32. González Carvajal states that Josef (or José) de Sigüenza and
Cipriano de Valera were both Jerónimos. Sigüenza studied with Montano at Escorial and took the position of librarian after Montano retired. Valera is known for his
editing of the bible *Reina Valera*. He was persecuted for his Calvinist leanings.

95. Fernández López, *El Cantar de los Cantares*, 28.

96. Morocho Gayo, "Trayectoria humanística I," 158. A number of texts written by
Montano are included in the appendix of Morocho Gayo's document. In one titled
"Testimony of Arias regarding his progenitor," he writes, "No one had a voice like his,
not a song so sweet ... whatever he intended ... he realized with facile execution."

97. Ibid., 159. Morocho Gayo cites a document published by González de Carvajal,
however no date is given. A copy of a very similar document was published by
Miguel Artigas in *Catálogo de los manuscritos de la Biblioteca de Menendez y Pelayo*
(Santander: s.n., 1930), 230.

98. Fernández López, *El Cantar de los Cantares*, 24; and Morocho Gayo, "Trayectoria
humanística I," 158n9.

99. Linda Martz, *A Network of Converso Families in Early Modern Toledo: Assimilating
a Minority* (Ann Arbor: University of Michigan Press, 2003), 280–285.

100. Daviken Studnicki-Gizbert, "La Nación among the Nations: Portuguese and Other
Maritime Trading Diasporas in the Atlantic, Sixteenth to Eighteenth Centuries,"
in *Atlantic Diasporas: Jews, Conversos, and Crypto-Jews in the Age of Mercantilism,
1500–1800*, ed. Richard L. Kagan and Philip D. Morgan (Baltimore: Johns Hopkins
University Press, 2008), 87.

101. Morocho Gayo, "Trayectoria humanística I," 163–171; see also Jesús Luis Paradinas
Fuentes, "Dos cartas atribuidas a Arias," in *El Humanismo extremeño: Estudios
presentados a las I". Jornadas organizadas por la Real Academia de Extremadura*, ed.

Marqués de la Encomienda, M. Terrón, and A. Viudas (Trujillo: Real Academia de Extremadura de las Letras y las Artes, 1997), 77–82.

102. Tobias Green, "Masters of Difference: Creolization and the Jewish Presence in Cabo Verde, 1497–1672" (PhD diss., University of Birmingham, 2007), 30.

103. Morocho Gayo, "Trayectoria humanística I," 162.

104. Ibid., 161.

105. Ibid., 159.

106. Manuel Pecellín Lancharro, "Benito Arias Montano, íntimio de judeoconversos, familiastas y procesados por la Inquisición," in *Del candelabro a la encina: raíces hebreas en Extremadura: Actas*, ed. Fernando Cortés Cortés (Bajadoz, Spain: Junta de Extremadura, Consejería de Cultura y Patrimonio: Diputación de Badajoz, 1995), 355. Pecellín Lancharro cites a poem written by the famous Golden Age poet, Lope de Vega.

107. Fernández López, *El Cantar de los Cantares*, 109–110.

108. Sáenz-Badillos, "Benito Arias Montano," 346.

109. Fernández López, *El Cantar de los Cantares*, 115.

110. Arias Montano, *Prefacios de Benito Arias Montano*, xlv.

111. Ibid.

112. As mentioned in a previous chapter, Rabadé Obradó discusses the ubiquity of known conversos and crypto-Jews in service of the Spanish monarchs in the late fifteenth century.

113. Fernández López, *El Cantar de los Cantares*, 16.

114. Ibid.

115. Ibid.

116. Ibid., 75.

117. The concern was that secret Jews would use the Old Testament of the Bible written in Spanish to maintain their religious beliefs and practice their rites. For the most part, only the clergy was able to read Latin.

118. Rekers, *Benito Arias Montano*, 9.

119. Fernández López, *El Cantar de los Cantares*, 75.

120. Ibid.

121. Ibid.

122. Ruth Pike, *Aristocrats and Traders: Sevillian Society in the Sixteenth Century* (Ithaca, NY: Cornell University Press, 1972), 1.

123. Poole, *Juan de Ovando*, 30.

124. The censored texts that reached the colonies significantly influenced clerics such as Manuel Espinosa de los Monteros (who will be discussed in a later chapter). In a manuscript dated 1825, Monteros cites Montano regarding the Old Testament narrative of the diadem worn by the high priest of the Jewish Temple in Jerusalem. See Manuel Espinosa de los Monteros, *Interpretacion de la Imagen Guadalupana y Confirmacion del Systema Milenario*, fol. 7a. *Monumentos Guadalupanos*, Obadiah Rich Collection, New York Public Library (hereafter cited as Guadalupe manuscript).

125. Miguel López Perez and Mar Rey Bueno, "Simón de Tovar (1528–1596): Redes familiares, naturaleza americana y comercio de maravillas en la Sevilla del XVI," *Dynamis* 26 (2006): 70.

126. Macías Rosendo, *La correspondencia de Benito Arias Montano*, 243.

127. Ibid.

128. López Perez and Rey Bueno, "Simon de Tovar," 72. Tovar's three books on botany were published in Antwerp by Montano's friend Christopher Plantin. The books are

titled *De compositorum medicamentorum examine: Nova methodus, qua medicamentorum compositorum omnium temperamenta ad unguem examinari, ac rursus propositae cuiuscunque temperaturae medicamenta compini facillime queant*, Antuerpiae, ex officina Christophori Plantini, 1586; *Hispalensium pharmacopoliorum recognitio*, Hispali, exofficina Andreae Pescionis et Ioannis Leonis, 1587; and *El tercer escrito de Tovar nada tiene que ver con la práctica médica, situándose de lleno en el terrenode la cosmografía: Examen i censura, por el doctor Simón de Tovar, del modo deaveriguar las alturas de las tierras, por la altura de la estrella del norte, tomada con la ballestilla*, Sevilla, Rodrigo de Cabrera, 1595.

129. López Perez and Rey Bueno, "Simon de Tovar," 74n9.

130. Ibid., 76.

131. Ibid., 73; and Gil, *Arias Montano y su Entorno*, 149.

132. Gil, *Arias Montano y su Entorno*, 149.

133. Jonathan Israel, "Jews and Crypto-Jews in the Atlantic World systems, 1500–1800," in *Atlantic Diasporas: Jews, Conversos, and Crypto-Jews in the Age of Mercantilism, 1500–1800* (Baltimore: Johns Hopkins University Press, 2009), 11.

134. Daviken Studnicki-Gizbert, *A Nation upon the Ocean Sea: Portugal's Atlantic Diaspora and the Crisis of the Spanish Empire, 1492–1640* (Oxford: Oxford University Press, 2007), 41.

135. Jonathan Israel, "Preface," in *Atlantic Diasporas: Jews, Conversos, and Crypto-Jews in the Age of Mercantilism, 1500–1800*, ed. Richard L. Kagan and Philip D. Morgan (Baltimore: Johns Hopkins University Press, 2009), viii.

136. Ibid.

137. Among the works by Arias Montano shipped to the colonies were *Comentarios a los doce profetas*, published in 1571, which was sent to the Indies in 1576, and *Historia del género humano* (History of the Human Species, published in 1593), which was shipped in 1600. *Comentario al libro de Josue* (Comment on the Book of Joshua, published in 1583), was also shipped with no date specified. See Navarro Antolín, Gómez Canseco, and Macías Rosendo, "Fronteras del Humanismo," 124.

138. Paniagua Pérez, "La obra y las relaciones," 415–416.

139. Studnicki-Gizbert, *Nation upon the Ocean Sea*, 15.

140. Francisco Fernández del Castillo, *Libros y libreros en el Siglo XVI* (México City: Publicaciones del Archivo General de la Nación, 1914), 6:584.

141. Macías Rosendo, *La correspondencia de Benito Arias Montano*, 121–135.

142. Fernández del Castillo, *Libros y libreros*, 6:254, 260.

143. Luis de Carvajal, "Memorias de Luis de Carvajal," in *Procesos de Luis de Carvajal (El Mozo)* (México City: Publicaciones del Archivo General de la Nación, 1935), 28:432. It is reported that a man named Juan de Cassal, living in Pachuca, México, requested a book by Luis de Granada titled *Simbolo de Fe* so that he could learn to be a better Jew. This occurred sometime during the last two decades of the sixteenth century. The book had been censored by the Spanish Inquisition.

144. Fernández del Castillo, *Libros y libreros*, 6:263–281.

145. Ibid., 6:315, 317.

146. Irving A. Leonard, "On the Mexican Book Trade, 1683," *Hispanic American Historical Review* 27, no. 3 (August 1947): 412.

147. Espinosa de los Monteros, *Interpretacion de la Imagen*, Guadalupe manuscript.

148. W. Michael Mathes, *The Americas' First Academic Library: Santa Cruz De Tlatelolco* (Sacramento: California State Library Foundation, 1985), 51–74; and W. Michael

Mathes, "Humanism in Sixteenth- and Seventeenth-Century Libraries of New Spain," *Catholic Historical Review* 82, no. 3 (1996): 427. Mathes's article in the *Catholic Historical Review* states that two unnamed libraries in México City contained Montano's writings.

149. Arias Montano, *Prefacios de Benito Arias Montano*, lxxxvi.

150. Mathes, "Humanism in Sixteenth- and Seventeenth-Century Libraries," 422, 427. Mathes does not name the libraries that contained Montano's writings.

Chapter 6   Miguel Sánchez, Guadalupe, and the Inquisition

1. Leo Strauss, *Persecution and the Art of Writing* (Chicago: University of Chicago Press, 1988), 90.

2. Solange Alberro, *Inquisición y sociedad en México: 1571–1700* (México City: Fondo de Cultura Economica, 1988), 580. In this essay, the terms "Santa Inquisición" and "Santo Oficio" (Holy Office, Holy Tribunal) are used to describe the Mexican Inquisition. A *reconciliado* (reconciled person) is an individual who has returned to the Church after having gone against its doctrines, generally referring to a person tried and found guilty by the Inquisition.

3. Antonio de Robles, *Diario de sucesos notables (1665–1703)* (México City: Editorial Porrúa, 1946), 1:144. Robles states that Sánchez was "was greatly admired in our America for his sermons[;] it was commonly thought by many educated men that Sánchez knew all of St. Augustine's writings from memory."

4. Alberro, *Inquisición y sociedad*, 580.

5. Cayetana Alvarez de Toledo, *Politics and Reform in Spain and Viceregal Mexico: The Life and Thought of Juan de Palafox, 1600–1659* (Oxford: Oxford University Press, 2004), 117–118.

6. Alberro, *Inquisición y sociedad*, 580; and Serge Gruzinski, *Images at War: Mexico from Columbus to Blade Runner (1492–2019)* (Durham, NC: Duke University Press, 2001), 123.

7. Miguel Sánchez, "Sermon S. Felipe de Jesus" (México: Juan Ruiz, 1640), intro.; and Jonathan I. Israel, *Race, Class and Politics in Colonial Mexico: 1610–1670* (Oxford: Oxford University Press, 1975), 214–215. Miguel Sánchez notes in the second page of his introduction, "I remain with the hope for another major manuscript, the second Eve in our Sanctuary of Guadalupe."

8. Alvarez de Toledo, *Politics and Reform*, 50.

9. Ibid., 51.

10. Ibid., 56. Alvarez cites "Advertimentos sobre algunos puntos del gobierno de la Nueva España que el marqués de Montesclaros envió a S.M. cuando dejó el ser virrey de aquel reino." Acapulco, August 3, 1607, in *Instrucciones que los virreyes de Nueva España dejaron a sus sucesores* (México, 1873), 79–96.

11. Alvarez de Toledo, *Politics and Reform*, 64–65.

12. Ibid., 122.

13. Ibid., 125.

14. Alberro, *Inquisición y sociedad*, 158–159.

15. Luis de Carvajal, *The Enlightened: the Writings of Luis de Carvajal, el Mozo* (Coral Gables, FL: University of Miami Press, 1967), 235.

16. Israel, *Race, Class and Politics*, 215.

17. Vicente Riva Palacio, *Memorias de un impostor: Don Guillen de Lampart, Rey de Mexico* (México City: Editorial Porrúa, 1908), 1:xv.

18. Donald G. Castanien, *A Seventeenth-Century Mexican Library and the Inquisition* (Ann Arbor: University of Michigan Press, 1951), 25–26. In 1640 the Calderóns maintained more than one thousand books on their list.

19. Joaquin García Izcazbalceta, *Carta acerca del origen de la Imagen Nuestra Señora de Guadalupe de México* (México City: Imprenta de Luis G. Gonzalez, 1896), 30; David A. Brading, *Mexican Phoenix: Our Lady of Guadalupe: Image and Tradition Across Five Centuries* (Cambridge: Cambridge University Press, 2001), 54. García Izcazbalceta states that there was only one copy of Guadalupe's image in the city. David Brading reports that her cult was so popular in 1629 that she was taken to the cathedral during one of México City's floods.

20. Brading, *Mexican Phoenix*, 55; and Timothy Matovina, "Theologies of Guadalupe: From the Spanish Colonial Era to Pope John Paul II," *Theological Studies* 70, no. 1 (2009): 71.

21. Timothy Matovina, "Guadalupe at Calvary: Patristic Theology in Miguel Sanchez's *Imagen de la Virgen Maria* (1648)," *Theological Studies* 64, no. 4 (2003): 796.

22. Ernesto de la Torre Villar and Ramiro Navarro de Anda, *Testimonios históricos guadalupanos* (México City: Fondo de Cultura Economica, 1982), 152.

23. Israel, *Race, Class and Politics*, 54.

24. García Izcazbalceta, *Carta acerca del origen*, 30.

25. Miguel Sánchez, *Imagen de la virgen Maria Madre de Dios de Gvadalvpe, milagrosamente aparecida en la civdad de Mexico* (México City: Imprenta Biuda de Bernardo Calderon, 1648), fol. 2a.

26. Recent studies have noted the possibility of Revelations being a Jewish, not Christian, book. John W. Marshall argues this in *Parables of War: Reading John's Jewish Apocalypse* (Waterloo, Ont.: Wilfrid Laurier University Press, 2001), 2; More recently Elaine Pagels (who was a graduate advisor to Marshall) states that John of Patmos "sees himself as a Jew" and "regards being Jewish as an honor." John "consistently sees himself *as a Jew who acknowledges Jesus as Israel's messiah*—not someone who has converted to a new 'religion.'" See Elaine Pagels, *Revelations: Visions, Prophecy, and Politics in the Book of Revelation* (New York: Penguin, 2012), 60.

27. Marie-Theresa Hernández, *Delirio—The Fantastic, the Demonic, and the Réel: The Buried History of Nuevo León* (Austin: University of Texas Press, 2002), 4.

28. Ibid., 63–67. Luis Carvajal y de la Cueva was the first Spanish governor of Nuevo León. In 1589 he was arrested by the Inquisition for harboring Jews. Although it is reported that he was a sincere Christian, his immediate family were still practicing Jews at the time of their imprisonment. He died in prison. Most of his family members were burned at the stake in 1596. Also, as mentioned in the previous chapter, Carvajal y de la Cueva had ties to Benito Arias Montano.

29. Miguel Angel Muñoz Borrego, interviewed by the author, 2006.

30. Brading, *Mexican Phoenix*, 74.

31. Ibid., 71.

32. Sánchez, *Imagen de la virgen*, fol. 13a.

33. Ibid., fols. 12b–13a.

34. Solange Alberro, "Crypto-Jews and the Mexican Holy Office in the Seventeenth Century," in *The Jews and the Expansion of Europe to the West, 1400–1800*, ed. Paolo Bernardini and Norman Fiering (New York: Berghahn Books, 2001), 183. Although it is termed a great conspiracy, it appears that the Inquisition had information on Jewish activity for some time, yet decided to act as a result of other political influences.

35. Alberro, *Inquisición y sociedad*, 49.

36. Sánchez, *Imagen de la virgen*, fol. 16b.

37. Ibid., fol. 17a.

38. Augustine, Saint Bishop of Hippo, *Expositions of the Psalms: The Works of Saint Augustine. A Translation for the 21st Century* (New City Press, 2000), 1:185–187; Benito Arias Montano, *Comentarios a los Trienta y un Primeros Salmos de David* (León: Secretariado de Publicaciones de la Universidad de León, 1999), 1:351. Montano's exegesis of Psalm 16 parallels Saint Augustine's assessment of the psalm, including the idea of persecution: "They have slapped me like a lion ready to go for the kill, as if I am a small animal that inhabits hidden spaces."

39. Alberro, *Inquisición y sociedad*, 43.

40. Luisa Schell Hoberman, "Merchants in Seventeenth-Century Mexico City: A Preliminary Portrait," *Hispanic American Historical Review* 57, no. 3 (August 1977): 497.

41. Sánchez, *Imagen de la virgen*, fol. 13b.

42. The common Bible translations do not include "confound" in the text. The only Bible that includes the word "confound" in David's Psalm 8:3 in the French *Biblia Louis Segond* (1910), "From the lips of children and infants You have established your praise so that you may confound your adversaries, and silence the enemy and the vengeful." A number of versions place this verse as second instead of third in the psalm. I thank my colleague Claudine Giacchetti for her assistance in translating this passage.

43. Luis de Carvajal, "Memorias de Luis de Carvajal," in *Procesos de Luis de Carvajal, El Mozo*, ed. Luis González Obregón (México City: Publicaciones del Archivo General de la Nación, 1935), 28:485. Carvajal was a *judaizante* who was burned by the Mexican Inquisition in 1596.

44. Luis González Obregón, ed., *Procesos de Luis de Carvajal (El Mozo)*, Publicaciones del Archivo General de la Nacion (México City: Talleres Graficos de la Nacion, 1935), 28:244.

45. Carvajal, "Memorias de Luis de Carvajal," 485.

46. Carvajal, *Enlightened*, 34.

47. Américo Castro, *Aspectos del Vivir Hispanico: Espiritualismo, Mesianismo, Actitude Personal en los Siglos XIV al XVI* (Santiago de Chile: Editorial Cruz del Sur, 1949), 24n11. Castro notes Bernáldez's citation of Psalm 8. Bernáldez was a priest of the court of King Fernando and Queen Isabel.

48. Andrés Bernáldez, *Historia de los reyes católicos C. Fernando y Doña Isabel* (Impr. que fué de J. M. Geofrin, 1870), 25.

49. Ibid., 24–25.

50. Ibid., 25.

51. Strauss, *Persecution and the Art of Writing*, 30.

52. Castro, *Aspectos del Vivir Hispanico*, 24n. 11.

53. Shima Ohara, "La Propaganda Politica Entorno al Conflicto Sucesorio de Enrique IV (1457–1474)" (PhD diss., Universidad de Valladolid, 2004), n.p.

54. Scholars have presented differing opinions on the genealogy of Bernáldez. Ruth Pike believes he was the descendant of conversos. Miriam Bodian says he was not. Norman Roth notes the punitive anti-Semitism of Bernáldez's writings. This attitude, however, was often seen in conversos, exemplified in Johannes Pfefferkorn (1469–1523), a converted Jew who later joined the Dominican Order. Pfefferkorn studiously blasted Johannes Reuchlin (1455–1522) for the latter's interest in Hebrew studies. See Ruth Pike, *Aristocrats and Traders: Sevillian Society in the Sixteenth Century* (Ithaca, NY: Cornell University Press, 1972), 103; Miriam Bodian, *Hebrews*

of the Portuguese Nation: Conversos and Community in Early Modern Amsterdam (Bloomington: Indiana University Press, 1997), 16; and Norman Roth, *Conversos, Inquisition, and the Expulsion of Jews from Spain* (Madison: University of Wisconsin Press, 1995), 228.

55. Augustine, *Expositions of the Psalms*, (Hyde Park, NY: New City Press), 6:132.

56. Alberro, *Inquisición y sociedad*, 31.

57. Ibid., 49.

58. Alberro, *Inquisición y sociedad*, 35–36.

59. Ibid., 42. Alberro cites Archivo Historico Nacional, Legajo 1737, Visíta de Medina Rico, num. 12, Cargo num 54.

60. Ibid., 37.

61. Two centuries after Sánchez, Manuel Espinosa de los Monteros, archivist of the Basilica of Guadalupe in México City, wrote a number of texts that exhibit strong references to Judaism. Monteros's work will be discussed in the next chapter.

62. Sánchez, *Imagen de la virgen*, fols. 25a, 8a; Jewish conversos were known to use the term "*santo*" (saint) when speaking or writing about revered personages from the Old Testament. Sánchez uses the terms "Santo Patriarcha Moises" and "Santo Abraham." See Herman P. Salomon, "Spanish Marranism Re-examined," *Sefarad* 68, no. 1 (January–June 2008): 144; and Renee Levine Melammed, *A Question of Identity: Iberian Conversos in Historical Perspective* (Oxford: Oxford University Press, 2004), 144–145. Melammed describes "the Jewish heroine," Esther, being "transformed into Saint Esther."

63. Brading, *Mexican Phoenix*, 21.

64. Ibid., 75.

65. Seymour Liebman, *The Jews in New Spain: Faith, Flame, and the Inquisition* (Coral Gables, FL: University of Miami Press, 1970), 62.

66. Seymour Liebman, ed., *Jews and the Inquisition of Mexico: The Great Auto de Fe of 1649 as Related by Mathias de Bocanegra, S.J.* (Lawrence, KS: Coronado Press, 1974), 169.

67. Ibid., 191.

68. Bruce Rosenstock, *New Men: Conversos, Christian Theology, and Society in Fifteenth-Century Castille* (London: Department of Hispanic Studies, Queen Mary, University of London, 2002), 94. Rosenstock cites Carlos Carrete Parrondo, *Proceso inquisitorial contra los Arias Dávila segovianos: Un enfrentamiento social entre judíos y conversos* (Salamanca, Spain: Universidad Pontificia de Salamanca, 1986), 73.

69. Janet Liebman Jacobs, *Hidden Heritage: The Legacy of the Crypto-Jews* (Berkeley: University of California Press, 2002), 94–95.

70. Arthur Green, "Shekhinah, the Virgin Mary, and the Song of Songs: Reflections on a Kabbalistic Symbol in its Historical Context," *AJS Review* 26, no. 1 (April 2002): 15, 50. Green cites the book of Zohar, from the Kabbalah, as describing the Shekhinah as "that of nourisher; motherly shekhinah is naturally depicted as the source of sustenance for the lower worlds. Here the imagery of female fullness and of humans nursing at the divine breast." She is also the "divine female," a figure within the divine-symbolic realm who serves as consort to the blessed Holy One, God of Israel. See Green for an in-depth analysis of the relationship between the Virgin Mary and the Shekhinah.

71. Ibid., 13.

72. During the early modern period, a century before Sánchez, an image of the Virgin Mary "symbolized by the seven-branched candlestick of Zacharias 4:2" was

published in a French Book of Hours, the *Bedford Book of Hours* commissioned by "John of Lancaster, Duke of Bedford and regent of France," produced "between 1423 and 1430 as a wedding gift from the duke to his wife Anne." Maurice Vloberg, "The Iconography of the Immaculate Conception," in *The Dogma of the Immaculate Conception*, ed. E. D. O'Connor (Notre Dame, IN: University of Notre Dame Press, 1958), pl. VII.

73. Sánchez, *Imagen de la virgen*, fol. 86a; and Zacharias 4:2.

74. Ibid., fol. 86b. Sánchez cites András II "Salut. ad Virg."

75. Nora Berend, *At the Gate of Christendom: Jews, Muslims and "Pagans" in Medieval Hungary, c. 1000–c. 1300* (Cambridge: Cambridge University Press, 2001), 158–159.

76. Ibid., 160.

77. Francisco de Siles, "Afterword," in *Imagen de la virgen Maria Madre de Dios de Guadalupe, milagrosamente aparecida en la ciudad de Mexico* (México City: Viuda de B. Calderon, 1648), n.p.

78. Nathan Wachtel, "Una América Subterránia: Redes y Religiosidades Marranas," in *Para una Historia de América II. Los nudos 1*, ed. Marcello Carmagnani, Ruggiero Romano, and Alicia Hernández Chavez (México City: Fondo de Cultura Economica, 1999), 52.

79. Michel de Certeau, *The Writing of History*, trans. Tom Conley (New York: Columbia University Press, 1988), 87. De Certeau explains that historical writing (*Imagen* can be classified as such) "functions as an inverted image, it gives way to lack and hides it; it creates these narratives of the past which are the equivalent of cemeteries within cities; it exorcises and confesses a presence of death amidst the living."

80. Gruzinski, *Images at War*, 123.

81. A third commentary added to *Imagen* is by "El Licenciado," Luis Lasso de la Vega, "Vicarios de la S. ermita de Guadalupe," in *Imagen de la virgen Maria Madre de Dios de Guadalupe, milagrosamente aparecida en la ciudad de México* (México City: Viuda de B. Calderon, 1648), n.p. Vega is known for having written the first description of the Mexican Guadalupe written in Nahua, an indigenous language, the *Nican Mopohua*. Luis Lasso de la Vega presents a completely different position than Barcenas and Siles. He begins his commentary with praise for the chief inquisitor, Juan de Mañozca, for having named Lasso de la Vega vicar of the Guadalupe sanctuary. The rest of what he writes is praise for Guadalupe, except where he writes that "I understate when I say that he [Sánchez] is the most daring *criollo* of all our nation."

82. Francisco de Bárcenas, "Afterword," in *Imagen de la virgen Maria Madre de Dios de Guadalupe, milagrosamente aparecida en la ciudad de Mexico* (México City: Viuda de B. Calderon, 1648), n.p.

83. Siles, "Afterword," in *Imagen*, n.p.

84. Castanien, *Seventeenth-Century Mexican Library*, 15.

85. Alberro, *Inquisición y sociedad*, 64.

86. Carmen Menéndez Onrubia, "Hacia la Biografia de un Iluminado Judio: Felipe Godíñez (1585–1659)," *Segismundo*, no. 25–26 (1977): 101–102.

87. Mateo de la Cruz, *Original profético de la Santa Imagen: Relacion de la milagrosa aparicion de la Santa Imagen de la Virgen de Guadalupe de Mexico, sacada de la historia que compuso el Br. Miguel Sánchez*, in *Testimonios históricos guadalupanos*, ed. E. Torre Villar and R. Navarro de Anda (México City: Fondo de Cultura Economica, 1982), 267–281.

88. Torre Villar and Navarro de Anda, *Testimonios históricos guadalupanos*, 152.

89. Brading, *Mexican Phoenix*, 190.

Chapter 7   Madre Sion

1. Manuel Espinosa de los Monteros, *Interpretacion de la Imagen Guadalupana y Confirmacion del Systema Milenario* (unpublished manuscript, 1825), in *Monumentos Guadalupanos*, Obadiah Rich Collection, New York Public Library (hereafter cited as Guadalupe manuscript), fol. 104a.
2. Richard Popkin, "Intellectual Biography: Warts and All," in *The Sceptical Mode in Modern Philosophy: Essays in Honor of Richard Popkin*, ed. Richard Watson and James E. Forth (Dordrecht, Neth.: Nijhoff, 1988), 116–117.
3. Popkin is not referring to evangelical Messianic Jews.
4. Richard H. Popkin, "Jewish Christians and Christian Jews in Spain, 1492 and After," *Judaism* 41, no. 3 (1992): 248–267.
5. Francisco Cantera y Burgos, "El 'Purim' del rey Don Sebastián," *Sefarad* 6, no. 1 (1946): 37–61. Ironically, Vieira, who was closely associated with Portuguese conversos, supported the idea of Sebastián's return, even though among the Jewish community it was said that if King Sebastián would have been victorious at Alcacerquivir, the king would have made all the Jews in the Portugal convert to Catholicism. A festival of Purim was established in Tangiers to commemorate Sebastián's defeat.
6. Yirmiyahu Yovel notes that Menassah ben Israel was Spinoza's teacher; however, other scholars disagree. See Yovel, *Spinoza and Other Heretics: The Marrano of Reason* (Princeton, NJ: Princeton University Press, 1989), 4, 8.
7. Jacob Alting, *Opera omnia theologica* (Amsterdam: Gerardus Borstius, 1685), 5:121, cited in Geneviève Javary, "Recherches sur l'utilisation du theme de la sekina dans l'apologetique Chretienne du XV éme au XVIII éme siecle" (PhD diss., Université de Paris, 1976), 478.
8. Geneviève Javary studied with François Secret, who is well-known for his work on the Christian Cabbala.
9. Javary, "Recherches sur l'utilisation," 478.
10. David A. Brading, *Mexican Phoenix: Our Lady of Guadalupe: Image and Tradition across Five Centuries* (Cambridge: Cambridge University Press, 2001), 201–212.
11. Presbitero Pio Saens (Manuel Espinosa de los Monteros?), *El Observador Guadalupano: En el que se contexta al argumento negativo contrario a la tradicion, y hace observar la santa pintura por los aspectos de historica y profetica* (unpublished manuscript, n.d.), no. 120, Guadalupe manuscript. This document shows the author as Presbitero Pio Saens, yet Monteros indicates in the manuscript that Monteros himself is the author. This document is written in Monteros's handwriting and writing style.
12. "Historia de Chiautla," *Municipio de Chiautla*, November 21, 2011, http://www.chiautladetapia.com/historia/.
13. Manuel Espinosa de los Monteros, *Interpretacion de la Pintura Guadalupana* (unpublished manuscript, 1825), n.p., Guadalupe manuscript.
14. Brian F. Connaughton, "Introduction," in *Miscelánea de varias doctrinas morales, costumbres, observaciones y otras noticias pertenecientes al curato de Iztacalco*, by Manuel Espinosa de los Monteros, ed. Brian F. Connaughton (México City: UNAM, 2012), 50. Connaughton cites Archivo Histórico de la Basilica de Guadalupe (hereafter AHBG) Fondo Secretaría Capitular, Serie Relaciones de méritos, Caja 405, exp. 72, "Relación de méritos del Cura propio de Ixtapaluca, Bachiller Manuel Espinosa de los Monteros, en el concurso del año 1818," 1818, 3 fols.
15. Espinosa de los Monteros, *Interpretacion de la Pintura*, n.p.

16. Connaughton, "Introduction," in *Miscelánea*, 50. Connaughton cites AHBG, Fondo Secretaria Capitular, Serie Correspondencia, Caja 382, esp. 11, "Apuntes históricos sacados de los que dejo entre sus papeles don Mariano Espinosa de los Monteros, y de las partidas de bautismo y de lo que su hijo el Bachiller don Manuel Espinosa de los Monteros oyó decir de sus padres." Acolman, junio 24 de 1821, 6 fols.

17. Espinosa de los Monteros, *Interpretacion de la Imagen*, fol. 2b.

18. The documents I found by Monteros in the Obadiah Rich Collection at the New York Public Library contained a number of "books" on the Virgin of Guadalupe. However, upon close inspection, some appeared to be different sections of the same book, even though each title was slightly altered.

19. Monteros lists his assignments in Nexticpac (1800–1802); Coyoacán (1802–1806); Tlanchinol, Sierra Alta (1806–1810); Chiautla, Texcoco (1810–1814); Ixtapaluca (1814–1819); Acolman (1819–1830); Iztacalco (1830–1831); and Santuario de Nuestra Señora de Guadalupe (1832–1838). His list ends as he is given a position at Guadalupe, where he remained until his death in 1838. Espinosa de los Monteros, *Miscelánea de varias doctrinas morales*, 6. The original text of *Miscelánea* is located at the Archivo Histórico del Arzobispado de México. Colocación CL 51.

20. Gustavo Watson Marrón, "Catedral de México," Basílica de Santa María de Guadalupe, http://www.virgendeguadalupe.org.mx/academicos/Archi_Historico/guia_sec5.htm.

21. His various unpublished manuscripts are located at the Basilica of Guadalupe in México City and the New York Public Library. It is not clear whether additional writings exist.

22. For a comprehensive anthology of writings on Guadalupe, see Ernesto Torre Villar and Ramiro Navarro de Anda, *Testimonios históricos guadalupanos* (México City: Fondo de Cultura Economica, 1982).

23. Stafford Poole, *The Guadalupan Controversies* (Stanford, CA: Stanford University Press, 2006), 24.

24. Brading, *Mexican Phoenix*, 240–241.

25. Poole, *Guadalupan Controversies*, 25. Poole details the resistance scholars encounter if they pursue Guadalupan narratives that are not officially sanctioned by the Mexican Church.

26. Connaughton notes that Monteros temporarily taught philosophy at the University of México as a replacement for Dr. Pedro Foronda. Connaughton, "Introduction," to *Miscelánea*, 50.

27. Espinosa de los Monteros, *Interpretacion de la Imagen*, pt. 3, sec. 4, no. 7, fol. 3a.

28. Popkin, "Jewish Christians and Christian Jews," 248–249.

29. Manuel Lacunza, *La venida del Mesías en gloria y majestad* (London: R. Ackerman, 1826), 1:xxxv–xxvi.

30. Ibid., 3:5.

31. Espinosa de los Monteros, *Interpretacion de la Imagen*, no. 192, p. 69. This section does not have folios. Instead Monteros has given the text page numbers.

32. Espinosa de los Monteros, *Interpretacion de la Pintura*, fol. 45b, Discurso 2, no. 138.

33. Manuel Espinosa de los Monteros, *La interpretacion del misterio Guadalupano: Obervaciones preparatorias contrahidas preciamente a los material de la Imagen*, fol. 1a (unpublished manuscript, 1830). *Monumentos Guadalupanos*, Obadiah Rich Collection, New York Public Library, Guadalupe manuscript.

34. Espinosa de los Monteros, *Miscelánea*, 162.

35. Saens, *El Observador Guadalupano*, art. 1, sec. 10, no. 76.

36. For a detailed study of the monastery of Acolman, see Rebecca Joy Holzworth, "The Apse Murals in San Agustín de Acolman: Augustinian Friars as the Foundation of the Roman Church in New Spain" (master's thesis, University of Arizona, 2007).

37. Jaime Lara, *City, Temple, Stage: Eschatological Architecture and Liturgical Theatrics in New Spain* (Notre Dame, IN: University of Notre Dame Press, 2004), 45; and Holzworth, "Apse Murals," 35. Holzworth suggests that the Acolman frescos were probably whitewashed in 1830, after Monteros had already left Acolman. This was shortly after México's independence from Spain.

38. Espinosa de los Monteros, *Miscelánea*, 50.

39. Espinosa de los Monteros, *Interpretacion de la Imagen*, 3a.

40. Espinosa de los Monteros, *La interpretacion del misterio Guadalupano*.

41. Espinosa de los Monteros, *Interpretacion de la Imagen*, fol. 2a.

42. Thomas N. Cohen, *The Fire of Tongues: Antonio Vieira and the Missionary Church in Brazil and Portugal* (Palo Alto, CA: Stanford University Press, 1998), 5.

43. Espinosa de los Monteros, *Interpretacion de la Imagen*, discurso 2, no. 216, fol. 79b. Monteros uses the phrase "*esperanza de Israel*" (hope of Israel). He does not list it as title of Menassah ben Israel's book. Although he writes of Antonio Vieira, it is not clear whether this was deliberate or an accidental omission.

44. Cohen, *Fire of Tongues*, 137; and José van den Besselaar, "Erudição, espírito crítico e escriba na Historia do Futuro de António Vieira," *Alfa: Revista de Lingüística* 20–21 (1975).

45. Espinosa de los Monteros, *Interpretacion de la Imagen*, fol. 2b.

46. Alfredo Félix Vaucher, *Lacunza, un Heraldo de la Segunda Venida de Cristo* (Barcelona: Aula7activa-AEGUAE, 2005), 9, http://aula7activa.org/edu/libros/documentos/lacunza.pdf.

47. Ibid., 9–10.

48. Fortuno Hipólito Vera, *Colección de documentos eclesiásticos de México* (México City: Amecameca, Impr. del Colegio Católico, 1887), 44–46, http://cdigital.dgb.uanl.mx/la/1080015731_C/1080015735_T3/1080015735_T3.html.

49. Espinosa de los Monteros, *Interpretacion de la Imagen*, fol. 2b.

50. Espinosa de los Monteros, *Interpretacion de la Pintura Guadalupana*, fol. 2b.

51. Espinosa de los Monteros, *Interpretacion de la Imagen*, fol. 2b.

52. Ibid., fol. 5b.

53. Emil G. Hirsch et al., "Urim and Thummin," *Jewish Encyclopedia* (Conshohocken, PA: Kopelman Foundation, 2002).

54. Nicolas Sylvestre Bergier, "Racional del Juicio," *Diccionario de teologia*, ed. Antolin Monescillo (Madrid: D. Primitivo Fuentes, 1846), 542.

55. Monteros spells the terms "Umin" and "Tumin." For the purposes of this book, I will use the spelling from the *Jewish Encyclopedia*. See Hirsch et al., "Urim and Thummin."

56. Ibid.

57. Cornelis Van Dam, *The Urim and Thummim: A Means of Revelation in Ancient Israel* (Winona Lake, IN: Eisenbrauns, 1997), 157.

58. Espinosa de los Monteros, *Interpretacion de la Imagen*, fol. 7a; and Hirsch et al., "Urim and Thummin," 386.

59. Hirsch et al., "Urim and Thummin," 386.

60. Espinosa de los Monteros, *Interpretacion de la Imagen*, fol. 7a.

61. Ibid., fol. 7b.

62. Ibid., fol. 8a.

63. For a comprehensive analysis on the Lost Tribes in the Americas, see Menasseh ben Israel, *The Hope of Israel* (Oxford: Littman Library, 1987).

64. Espinosa de los Monteros, *Interpretacion de la Imagen*, fol. 45b.
65. Ibid. Monteros continues with great emotion: "The Indian, incapable of his own will, or treated by the Laws like a child, this miserable person, marked with the seal of slavery was treated more cruelly than a beast of burden, and he was placed in the mines, the Indian in the end, whose color, whose language, whose misery and clothing make him despicable, he does not find a place in decent society, if I say that Indian is superior to the more prominent nations, more knowledgeable and powerful that are known in the world, I will be taken for a silly person, capable of a large paradox. The idea would be not tolerated well. P. Lacunza says the Jews will attain the glories of the millennial system, and it will no longer be despised, as I understand even to the Indians." Ibid., fol. 45a, 46a. It is interesting that Monteros had this attitude considering the indigenous languages were his specialty, and his major focus was to work with the native people of México. This brings to mind the munificent slave owner who treats his slaves very well but does not think they are human.
66. Espinosa de los Monteros, *Interpretacion del misterio*, fol. 5b, no. 13. Monteros immediately asks if the rich clothing she wears is proper if she truly represents the indigenous people.
67. Espinosa de los Monteros, *Interpretacion de la Imagen*, fol. 59b.
68. "Strong women," known as "ESHET HAYIL" (Heb. לַיִח תֶּשֵׁא; "a woman of valor"), are the opening words praising the virtuous woman in Proverbs 31:10–31. This poem enumerates the qualities of the ideal wife in a sequential alphabetic acrostic of twenty-two verses, one for each of the letters of the Hebrew alphabet. She is lauded as provident, economically successful, working hard for husband and household, and charitable to the needy. She possesses optimism, faces life with confidence, and speaks in wisdom and kindness. Her efforts enable her husband to function as a prominent communal leader, "As he sits among the elders of the land." Yael Levine, "Eshet Hayil," in *Encyclopaedia Judaica*, 2nd ed., ed. Michael Berenbaum and Fred Skolnick, vol. 6, *Gale Reference Library*; and Espinosa de los Monteros, *Interpretacion de la Pintura Guadalupana*, fol. 73b. Monteros spells *"mujer"* (woman) with a "g"—"muger." He cites Proverbs 31.
69. Espinosa de los Monteros, *Interpretacion de la Pintura Guadalupana*, fol. 73b.
70. Espinosa de los Monteros, *Interpretacion de la Imagen*, fol. 73b, no. 205. Miguel Sánchez also uses the phrase *"La Señora"* in his *Imagen de la virgen Maria Madre de Dios de Guadalupe, milagrosamente aparecida en la civdad de Mexico* (Mexico City: Imprenta Biuda de Bernardo Calderon, 1648).
71. Espinosa de los Monteros, *Interpretacion de la Imagen*, fol. 101a, no. 263.
72. Kaufmann Kohler and Henry Malter, "Purim," *Jewish Encyclopedia* (Conshohocken, PA: Kopelman Foundation, 2002).
73. Espinosa de los Monteros, *Interpretacion de la Imagen*, fol. 104a, no. 270.
74. Espinosa de los Monteros, *Interpretacion del misterio*, fol. 2a, no. 4.
75. Ibid., fol. 4b, no. 12.
76. Ibid., fol. 14b, no. 35.
77. Ibid., fol. 19a, no. 48, 20a, no. 51.
78. Ibid., fol. 2a, no. 4.
79. Espinosa de los Monteros, *Interpretacion de la Imagen*, fol. 88b, sec. 233.
80. The actual document states he had no last name and was only the given name of Jose Manuel. His godmother was Anna Maria Castillo. There is no mention of Monteros. He is the only male child christened on the day indicated at that particular church. The ledger account of Monteros's sisters christening shows the mother's complete name to be Maria Gertrudis Ferrer Velasco. "Christening Record of

Manuel Espinosa de los Monteros"; and Iglesia Santa Catarina, Ciudad de México; "Christening Record Gertrudis Margarita Espinosa Ferel," both from the collection of the Genealogy Library of Church of Jesus Christ of Latter Day Saints.

81. See Espinosa de los Monteros, *Miscelánea*, 248–249.

82. Vicente Ferrer was canonized a saint by the Catholic Church in 1455.

83. See Francisca Vendrell, "La actividad proselitista de San Vicente Ferrer durante el reinado de Fernando I de Aragón," *Sefarad* 13, no. 1 (1953): 87–105.

84. Ibid., 88.

85. In August 2008 a Catholic priest by the name of Glyn Jemmott, who oversees a parish in Costa Chica, Guerrero, México, told me that one of his parishioners had found an old coin with the inscription "Judea Libera."

86. Espinosa de los Monteros, *Interpretacion de la Imagen*, fol. 54a, sec. 123; and Isaiah 52:1, 2.

87. Espinosa de los Monteros, *Interpretacion del misterio*, pt. 2, fol. 43b, no. 124. These include (in the order that he cites them) Isaiah 62, 60:15, 43:4, 60:17, 62:3, 49:16, 33:20; Baruch 5:5, Isaiah 58:14, 54, 52:13.

88. Saens, *El Observador Guadalupano*, part II, sec. 1, no. 216.

89. Ibid., art. 2, sec. 1, no. 216.

90. Antoine Guénée, *Cartas de unos Judios alemanes y polacos à M. de Voltaire: Con un comentario sacado de otro mayor para el uso que leen sus obras,y cuatro memorias sobre la fertilidad de la Judea*, trans. Francisco Pablo Vazquez (Brussels: A. Wahlen, 1827), 1.

91. Brading, *Mexican Phoenix*. For Guadalupe's role in Mexican independence, see chapters 9, 10.

92. Solange Alberro, *Inquisición y Sociedad en México 1571–1700* (México City: Fondo de Cultural Economica, 1988), 583. Alberro cites the Archivo General de la Nación, vol. 416, fol. 536, Carta del Santo Oficio de Méxicoal Consejo de Indias.

93. Lacunza, *La venida del Mesías*, 107.

94. Popkin, "Intellectual Biography," 117.

95. There are a number of his signatures on his manuscripts with the location of Acolman and the same date, October 2, 1825.

96. Espinosa de los Monteros, *Interpretacion de la Imagen*, fol. 136a. Monteros read this information in the newspaper article "Restablecimiento de la Nacion Hebrea," *Aguila Mexicana*, no. 292, January 31, 1826. He writes that the *Aguila* is citing a New York newspaper named the *Star*. The name of the newspaper was actually the *Evening Star* and was founded by Mordecai Noah, who was descended from Portuguese Jews who escaped the Inquisition. It is likely that Monteros was not aware of this information.

97. Michael Weingrad, "Messiah, American Style: Mordecai Manuel Noah and the American Refuge," *AJS Review* 31, no. 1 (2007): 95.

98. Ibid., 75. Weingrad also reports that Noah "influenced presidential elections through his editorship of major newspapers, and served as judge and port surveyor of New York City.

99. Richard H. Popkin, "Mordecai Noah, the Abbe Gregoire, and the Paris Sanhedrin," *Modern Judaism* 2, no. 2 (1982): 133, citing Joseph L. Blau and Salo W. Baron, ed. *The Jews of the United States, 1790–1840: A Documentary History* (New York: Columbia University Press, 1963), 1:82. Noah was speaking at the inauguration of the synagogue Kahal Kadrah Shearith Israel.

100. Espinosa de los Monteros, *Interpretacion de la Imagen*, fol. 109a, no. 285, fol. 117b, no. 303; and Espinosa de los Monteros, *Interpretacion de la Pintura Guadalupana*, fol. 132a, no. 337.

101. Espinosa de los Monteros, *Interpretacion de la Imagen*, fol. 136b.

Conclusion

1. "Prision De Un Judio En La Capital," *La Prensa* (San Antonio, TX), August 13, 1932.
2. "El Dr. Nachbin Partio de la Republica," *La Prensa* (San Antonio, TX), November 22, 1932.
3. Rafael Lopez, "Introduction," in *Procesos de Luis de Carvajal (el Mozo)*, vol. 28 (México City: Talleres Graficos de la Nacion, 1935), 10, no. 1.
4. J. Horace Nunemaker, review of *La Familia Carvajal*, by Alfonso Toro, *Pacific Historical Review* 15, no. 1 (March 1946): 103.
5. Vito Alessio Robles, "Los Arrechuchos de Don Alfonso Toro," *La Prensa* (San Antonio, TX), January 9, 1936.
6. Nunemaker, review of *La Familia Carvajal*, 103; and Robles, "Los Arrechuchos de Don Alfonso Toro."
7. Ibid. Robles is citing a letter from Toro (sent to the Archivo). I was not able to obtain a copy of Toro's letter. The Porfirian dictatorship (*dictadura porfiriana*) refers to thirty-five-year presidency of José de la Cruz Porfirio Diaz. Porfirio Diaz's administration led México to unprecedented economic stability and a significant presence of an upper class "cultured" society. His leadership was ultimately undermined by his dictatorial policies and the continued extreme poverty of most of the population. Curiously, it was during his administration (mostly through the efforts of his wife) that the Virgin of Guadalupe became the official patroness of México. See David A. Brading, *Mexican Phoenix: Our Lady of Guadalupe: Image and Tradition across Five Centuries* (Cambridge: Cambridge University Press, 2001), 312.
8. Ibid.
9. Marie-Theresa Hernández, *Delirio—the Fantastic, the Demonic, and the Réel: The Buried History of Nuevo León* (Austin: University of Texas Press, 2002), 186–189, 170.
10. Vito Alessio Robles, "La Juderia de Monterrey," in *Bosques historicos* (México City: Editorial Polis, 1938), 95–107. This is a reprinting of the work. The original appeared in various Mexican newspapers. Robles writes that the people of Monterrey "regularly and strictly adhere to the law of Moses and wait for the promised Messiah, they observe Saturdays (the Sabbath) . . . and rigidly avoid pork . . . and do not eat fish with scales" (106).
11. Hernández, *Delirio*, 188.
12. Robles, "Juderia de Monterrey," 97–98.
13. Hernández, *Delirio*, 186–189.
14. Luis de Carvajal, "Memorias de Luis de Carvajal," in *Procesos de Luis de Carvajal (el Mozo)*, ed. Luis González Obregón (México City: Publicaciones del Archivo General de la Nación, 1935), 463.
15. Semuel Temkin, "Luis Carvajal and His People," *AJS Review* 32, no. 1 (2008): 79, 84. Temkin discusses how Carvajal y de la Cueva negotiated this astounding agreement with Felipe II.
16. Luis González Obregón, ed., *Procesos de Luis de Carvajal (el Mozo)*, (México City: Talleres Graficos de la Nacion, 1935), 28:10, no. 1. The original document has been lost, but a copy that was published by the Mexican National Archives in the twentieth century is available.
17. Two scholars discussing these possibilities were Gaspar Morocho Gayo, "Trayectoria humanística de Benito Arias Montano I. Sus cuarenta primeros años (1526–27–1567) I," in *El Humanismo Extremeño, III Jornadas* (Trujillo: Real Academia de Estremadura, 1998), 161–162; and Norman Roth, *Conversos, Inquisition, and the Expulsion of Jews From Spain* (Madison: University of Wisconsin Press, 1995), 114–202.

18. Robles, "Judería de Monterrey," 99.
19. Temkin, "Luis Carvajal," 81.
20. Ibid., 86.Temkin cites a document from los Archivos General de las Indias (AGI), Contratación, 5538.L.11478 recto–48. This citation appeared in English in Temkin's article.
21. Ibid., 85.
22. Martin A. Cohen, *The Martyr: Luis de Carvajal, a Secret Jew in Sixteenth-Century Mexico* (Albuquerque: University of New Mexico Press, 2001), xix.
23. Luis de Carvajal, *The Enlightened: the Writings of Luis de Carvajal, el Mozo* (Coral Gables, FL: University of Miami Press, 1967), 36.
24. This is exceedingly significant to most Jewish scholars. The ongoing question of who is really Jewish chafes at the question of Jewish authenticity in regions where converso populations took on Christian traditions (out of necessity) in order to avoid discovery.
25. Carvajal, "Memorias de Luis de Carvajal," 463.
26. Cohen, *Martyr*, 21–22. Carvajal's parents were Francisca Nuñez Carvajal and Francisco Rodriguez de Matos. Considering that he was baptized a Christian and was educated in a Jesuit school, it is doubtful that he would be technically considered a Jew in today.
27. Ibid., 63.
28. Temkin, "Luis Carvajal," 87. Temkin cites AGI, Contratación, 5538.L.11478 recto–483 recto.
29. Cohen, *Martyr*, 202. Dominican Jerome Oleaster, who wrote the commentary, used the work of Maimonides in his study but did not cite the original author.
30. Ibid., 202–203. Ironically, three books from the Old Testament—Psalms, Prophets, and Genesis—that Carvajal had with him when he was arrested the second time, were confiscated.
31. Ibid., 204
32. Carvajal, "Memorias de Luis de Carvajal," 472.
33. Ibid., 473.
34. Brading, *Mexican Phoenix*, 111; and Francisco de Florencia, *Estrella del Norte*, 2nd ed. (México City: Por doña Maria de Benavides, viuda de Juan de Ribera, 1688), 666–667. Brading's translation.
35. Pio Saens [Manuel Espinosa de los Monteros?], *El observador Guadalupano*, pt. 3, art. 1, sec. 1, no. 96. (unpublished manuscript, no date). *Monumentos Guadalupanos*, Obadiah Rich Collection, New York Public Library (hereafter cited as Guadalupe manuscript).
36. Ernesto Torre Villar and Ramiro Navarro de Anda, *Testimonios históricos guadalupanos* (México City: Fondo de Cultural Economica, 1982), 76; and Epigmenio Gonzalez, ed., "La Virgen del Tepeyac, patrona principal de la nación mexicana: Compendio histórico-crítico / por un sacerdote residente en esta arquidiócesis," in *Miscellaneous Mexican publications* (Guadalajara, 1884), n.p.
37. Torre Villar and Navarro de Anda, *Testimonios históricos guadalupanos*, 76–77n4.
38. Saens, *El observador Guadalupano*, art. 1, no. 95.
39. Matt Goldish, "Patterns of Converso Messianism," in *Jewish Messianism in the Early Modern World*, Millenarianism and Messianism in Early Modern European Culture 1 (Dordrecht, Neth.: Kluwer Academic Publishers, 2001), 41–42.
40. Rodolfo Aguirre Salvador. "Las informaciones de legitimidad y limpieza de sangre en la Real Universidad de México, Siglo XVIII," in *Teoría y práctica archivística II, Cuadernos del Archivo Histórico de la UNAM 12*, ed. Gustavo Villanueva Bazán

(México City: Universidad Nacional Autónoma de México, Coordinación de Humanidades, Centro de Estudios sobre la Universidad, 2000), 2:132–133. Aguirre Salvadore cites Margarita Menegus Bornemann, "La Real y Pontificia Universidad de México y los expedientes de limpieza de sangre," in *La Real Universidad de México. Estudios y textos I. Historia de la Universidad Colonial avances de investigación*, ed. Lorenzo Mario Luna Diaz (México City: CESU-UNAM, 1987), 81–82.

41. Sánchez's character, as presented in contemporary biographical sketches, is the opposite of the how *criollos* in New Spain were described. Ilona Katzew, *Casta Painting: Images of Race in Eighteenth-Century Mexico* (New Haven: Yale University Press, 2005), 57.

42. Jonathan Israel, *Race, Class and Politics in Colonial Mexico: 1610–1670* (Oxford: Oxford University Press, 1975), 217.

43. Cayetana Alvarez de Toledo, *Politics and Reform in Spain and Viceregal Mexico: The Life and Thought of Juan de Palafox, 1600–1659* (Oxford: Oxford University Press, 2004), 246.

44. Ibid., 53.

45. Antonio de Robles, *Diario de sucesos notables (1665–1703)* (México City: Editorial Porrúa, 1946), 1:145.

46. Manuel Espinosa de los Monteros, *Interpretacion de la Imagen Guadalupana y Confirmacion del Systema Milenario*, Discourse 2, fol. 45b, no. 138 (unpublished manuscript, 1830), Guadalupe manuscript.

47. Manuel Espinosa de los Monteros, *Interpretacion de la Pintura Guadalupana*, fol. 9a, no. 30 (unpublished manuscript, 1825), Guadalupe manuscript.

48. Espinosa de los Monteros, *Interpretacion de la Imagen*, fol. 109, no. 283.

49. Ibid., fol. 106b, part 3, no. 277.

50. Goldish, "Patterns of Converso Messianism," 42.

51. According to numerous historical accounts, after the death of Governor Carvajal in the Inquisition jail, a group of the original Carvajal group traveled through Del Rio on their way to New México, headed by Gaspar Castaño de Sosa. The late Diana Zertuche directed me to the cemetery while informing me about the Latino history of the Del Rio area.

Glossary

alumbrado. Mystical sect popular in sixteenth-century Spain. Also known as the Iluminati. Often associated with the teachings of Erasmus.

audiencia. A high court in the colonies.

auto-da-fe. Public sentencing and punishment of Inquisition prisoners.

capellán. Chaplain.

Consejo de las Indias. Highest-ranking administrative arm of the Spanish Empire.

criollo. Individual born in the colonies of Spanish parents.

cura. Parish priest.

Devotio Moderna. Fourteenth-century religious movement given to meditation and prayer.

Escorial. Palace/monastery of Felipe II, San Lorenzo de Escorial, constructed in the last half of the sixteenth century. Considered in its time to be the Eighth Wonder of the World.

godo. A Visigoth, a population of Germanic origin inhabiting the Iberian peninsula in the first millennium. The Visigoth Kingdom ruled much of Iberia from the sixth to the ninth centuries of the Common Era.

Inmaculada. Literally meaning "without stain," the name given to the Virgin Mary of the Immaculate Conception who is said to have been born without Original Sin.

judaizante. Judaizer—usually associated with someone who has converted to Christianity yet continues to practice Judaism.

Kabbalah. Esoteric Jewish teachings.

limpieza de sangre. Literally means "purity of blood," associated with individuals not having Jewish or Muslim ancestors.

macula. Associated with having the "impure blood" of Jews or Muslims in one's ancestry.

maravedi. Unit of Spanish currency.

marrano. A professed Christian who secretly practices Jewish rites. The term literally means "pig."

puebla. Spanish village

peninsular. Spaniard born on the Iberian peninsula.

proceso. Records of an inquisition trial or hearing.

Santo Oficio. Holy Office of the Inquisition.

Shekhinah. Literally meaning "dwelling" or "setting," associated with the feminine aspect of the Hebrew God and often represented as a brilliant light.

Suprema. Highest governing council of the Spanish Inquisition.

tornadizo. One who vacillates between Judaism and Christianity.

visitador. A representative of the king who visits the colonies for the purpose of examining the colony's governmental state of affairs.

Bibliography

Aguirre Salvador, Rodolfo. "La informaciones de legitimidad y limpieza de sangre in la Real Universidad de Mexico, Siglo XVIII." In *Teoría y práctica archivística II*, 2:131–140. Cuadernos del Archivo Histórico de la UNAM 12, México City: Universidad Nacional Autónoma de México, Coordinación de Humanidades, Centro de Estudios sobre la Universidad, 2000.

Alberro, Solange. "Crypto-Jews and the Mexican Holy Office in the Seventeenth Century." In *The Jews and the Expansion of Europe to the West, 1400–1800*, edited by Paolo Bernardini and Norman Fiering, 172–185. New York: Berghahn Books, 2001.

———. *Inquisición y Sociedad en Mexico 1571–1700*. México City: Fondo de Cultura Economica, 1988.

Allen, Michael J. B. "Introduction." In *Marsilio Ficino: His Theology, His Philosophy, His Legacy*. Leiden: Brill, 2002.

Alting, Jacob. *Opera omnia theologica*. Amsterdam: Gerardus Borstius, 1685.

Álvarez Álvarez, Arturo. "Cuatro Hermanos, Sabios y Santos." *Historia* 16, no. 371 (2007): 40–55.

———. *La Virgen de Guadalupe en el Mundo: Culto e Imágenes Antiguas*. Madrid: Viña Extremeña, S.A., 2000.

Alvarez de Toledo, Cayetana. *Politics and Reform in Spain and Viceregal Mexico: The Life and Thought of Juan de Palafox, 1600–1659*. Oxford: Oxford University Press, 2004.

Antonini, Egidio [Egidio da Viterbo]. *Scechina e Libellus de litteris hebraicis: Inediti a cura di François Secret*. Edited by François Secret. Rome: Centro Internazionale di Studi Umanistic, 1959.

Arango y Escandon, Alejandro, ed. *Proceso del P. M. Fray Luis de Leon: Doctor Teologo del Claustro y Gremio de la Universidad de Salamanca*. México City: Imprenta de Andrade y Escalante, 1856.

Artigas, Miguel. *Catálogo de los manuscritos de la Biblioteca de Menendez y Pelayo*. Santander: s.n., 1930.

Augustine, Saint, Bishop of Hippo. *Expositions of the Psalms: The Works of Saint Augustine. A Translation for the 21st Century*, vol. 6. Hyde Park, NY: New City Press.

Baer, Yitzhak. *The History of the Jews in Christian Spain*. Translated by Louis Schoffman. Philadelphia: Jewish Publication Society, 1992.

Bancroft, Hubert. *History of Mexico: 1824–1661*, vol. 5. San Francisco: A. L. Bancroft, 1885.

Bárcenas, Francisco de. "Afterword." In *Imagen de la virgen Maria Madre de Dios de Guadalupe, milagrosamente aparecida en la ciudad de México*, by Miguel Sanchez. México City: Viuda de B. Calderon, 1648.

Barthes, Roland. *Camera Lucida: Reflections on Photography*. New York: Hill and Wang, 1981.

Bataillon, Marcel. *Erasme et l'Espagne: recherches sur l'historie spirituelle du XVIe siècle* (Paris: Librairie E. Droz, 1937)

———. *Erasmo y España: Estudios sobre la historia espiritual del siglo xvi*. Translated by Antonio Alatorre. México City: Fondo de Cultural Economica, 1950.

Beinart, Haim. "The Spanish Inquisition and a Converso Community in Extremadura." *Mediaeval Studies* 43 (1981): 445–471.

Beitchman, Philip. *Alchemy of the Word: Cabala of the Renaissance*. Albany: State University of New York Press, 1998.

Bell, Aubrey F. G. "Notes on Luis de Leon's Lyrics." *Modern Language Review* 21, no. 2 (April 1926): 168–177.

Berend, Nora. *At the Gate of Christendom: Jews, Muslims, and "Pagans" in Medieval Hungary, c. 1000—c. 1300*. Cambridge: Cambridge University Press, 2001.

Bergier, Nicolas Sylvestre. "Racional del Juicio." In *Diccionario de teologia*, edited by Antolin Monescillo. Madrid: D. Primitivo Fuentes, 1846. Library of Catalonia.

Bernáldez, Andrés. *Historia de los reyes católicos C. Fernando y Doña Isabel*. Impr. que fué de J. M. Geofrin, 1870.

Besselaar, José van den. "Erudição, espírito crítico e escriba na Historia do Futuro de António Vieira." *Alfa: Revista de Lingüística* 20/21 (1975).

Bibliotheca Mexicana or a Catalogue of the Library of Rare Books and Important Manuscripts relating to Mexico and other parts of Spanish America Formed by the Late Señor Don José Fernando Ramirez. London: G. Norman and Son, printers, 1880.

Blau, Joseph L., and Salo W. Baron, ed. *The Jews of the United States, 1790–1840: A Documentary History*. New York: Columbia University Press, 1963.

Bodian, Miriam. *Hebrews of the Portuguese Nation: Conversos and Community in Early Modern Amsterdam*. Bloomington: Indiana University Press, 1997.

Bollard de Broce, Kathleen. "Authorizing Literary Propaganda: Alfonso de Valdés' Diálogo de las cosas acaecidas en Roma (1527)." *Hispanic Review* 68, no. 2 (Spring 2000): 131–145.

Bonser, Wilfrid. "The Cult of Relics in the Middle Ages." *Folklore* 74, no. 4 (Winter 1962): 234–256.

Bornemann, Margarita Menegus. "La Real y Pontificia Universidad de México y los expedientes de limpieza de sangre." In *La Real Universidad de México: Estudios y textos I. Historia de la Universidad Colonial avances de investigación*, edited by Lorenzo Mario Luna Diaz. México City: CESU-UNAM, 1987.

Brading, David A. *Mexican Phoenix: Our Lady of Guadalupe: Image and Tradition across Five Centuries*. Cambridge: Cambridge University Press, 2001.

Braudel, Fernand. *The Mediterranean and the Mediterranean World in the Age of Philip II*, vol. 2. Translated Siân Reynolds. Berkeley: University of California Press, 1995.

Brown, Rawdon, ed. *Calendar of State Papers and Manuscripts Relating to English Affairs Existing in the Archives and Collections of Venice and in Other Libraries of Northern Italy*, vol. 6. London: Longman & Co, and Trubner & Co., 1871.

Burgos, Abner de. *Mostrador de justicia*. Opladen: Westdeutscher Verlag, 1994.

Caballero, Fermín. *Alonso y Juan de Valdés*. Madrid: Oficina tipográfica del hospicio, 1875.

Cantera y Burgos, Francisco. "El 'Purim' del rey Don Sebastián." *Sefarad* 6, no. 1 (1946): 37–61.

Caro Baroja, Julio. *Las formas complejas de la vida religiosa: Religión, sociedad y carácter en la España de los siglos XVI y XVII.* Madrid: SARPE, 1985.

Carrete Parrondo, Carlos. "Los conversos Jeronimos ante el estatuto de limpieza de sangre." *Helmantica: Revista de filología clásica y hebrea* 26, no. 79–81 (1975): 97–116.

———. *Proceso inquisitorial contra los Arias Dávila segovianos: Un enfrentamiento social entre judíos y conversos.* Salamanca, Spain: Universidad Pontificia de Salamanca, 1986.

Carvajal, Luis de. *The Enlightened: The Writings of Luis de Carvajal, el Mozo.* Edited by Seymour B. Liebman. Coral Gables, FL: University of Miami Press, 1967.

———. "Memorias de Luis de Carvajal." In *Procesos de Luis de Carvajal (el Mozo)*, edited by Luis González Obregón, 28:461–496. México City: Publicaciones del Archivo General de la Nación, 1935.

Castanien, Donald G. *A Seventeenth-Century Mexican Library and the Inquisition.* Ann Arbor: University of Michigan Press, 1951.

Castro, Américo. *Aspectos del vivir hispanico: Espiritualismo, mesianismo, actitude personal en los Siglos XIV al XVI.* Santiago de Chile: Editorial Cruz del Sur, 1949.

———. *España en su historia; cristianos, moros y judíos*, 1st ed. Buenos Aires: Editorial Losada, 1948.

Celebrino, Eustachio. *La presa di Roma: Con breve narrazione di tuttili magni fatti di Guerre successi, net tēpo che lo Exercito Imperiale statte in viaggio da Milano a Roma.* Rome: Tip. Romana, 1872.

Certeau, Michel de. *The Mystic Fable: The Sixteenth and Seventeenth Centuries.* Translated by Michael B. Smith. Chicago: University of Chicago Press, 1992.

———. *The Writing of History.* Translated by Tom Conley. New York: Columbia University Press, 1988.

Cervantes, Fernando. *The Devil in the New World: The Impact of Diabolism in New Spain.* New Haven, CT: Yale University Press, 1994.

[Cervantes, Miguel?]. *Comedia de la Soberana Virgen de Guadalupe, y sus Milagros, y Grandezas de Espana.* Sevilla: Bartolome Gomez de Pastrana, 1617.

Cervantes, Miguel. *Persiles y Sigismunda.* Madrid: Imprenta Bernardo Rodriguez, 1914.

Cohen, Martin A. *The Martyr: Luis de Carvajal, a Secret Jew in Sixteenth-Century Mexico.* Albuquerque: University of New Mexico Press, 2001.

Cohen, Thomas N. *The Fire of Tongues: Antonio Vieira and the Missionary Church in Brazil and Portugal.* Palo Alto, CA: Stanford University Press, 1998.

Connaughton Hanley, Brian Francis. "Introduction." In *Miscelánea (1831–1832) Tomos I y II de varias doctrinas morales, costumbres, observaciones y otras noticias pertenecientes al curato de Iztacalco*, by Manuel Espinosa de los Monteros, edited by Brian Francis Connaughton Hanley, 21–76. México City: Universidad Autónoma Metropolitana, 2012.

Coussemacker, Sophie. "L'Ordre of Saint Jerome en Espagne, 1373–1516." PhD diss., Université de Paris X—Nanterre, 1994.

Creighton, Mandell. *A History of the Papacy: From the Great Schism to the Sack of Rome*, vol. 6. Longmans, Green, and Co., 1903.

Cruz, Mateo de la. "Original Profético de la Santa Imagen Relacion de la Milagrosa Aparicion de la Santa Imagen de la Virgen de Guadalupe de Mexico, Sacada de la Historia Que Compuso el Br. Miguel Sánchez." In *Testimonios históricos guadalupanos*, edited by Ernesto Torre Villar and Ramiro Navarro de Anda, 267–281. México City: Fondo de Cultura Economica, 1982 (1660).

Cuadra Blanco, Juan Rafael. "King Philip of Spain as Solomon the Second. The Origins of Solomonism of the Escorial in the Netherlands." In *The Seventh Window: The King's Window Donated by Philip II and Mary Tudor to Sint Janskerk in Gouda (1557)*, edited by William de Groot. Hilversum: Uitgeverij Verloren, 2005.

Cuevas, Mariano. *Historia de la Iglesia en Mexico*, vol. 3. El Paso, TX: Editorial "Revista Catolica," 1923.

Ecija, Diego de, and Arcángel Barrado Manzano. *Libro de la invención de esta Santa Imagen de Guadalupe; y de la erección y fundación de este monasterio; y de algunas cosas particulares y vidas de algunos religiosos de él.* Cacares, Spain: Departamento Provincial de Seminarios de F.E.T y de las J.O.N.S., 1953.

Eco, Humberto. *Foucault's Pendulum.* New York: Harcourt Brace Jovanovich, 1988.

Egido, Aurora. "Poesia y Peregrinacion en el Persiles el Templo de la Virgen de Guadalupe." In *Actas del Tercer Congreso Internacional de la Asocación de Cervantistas*, edited by Antonio Bernat Vistarini, 13–29. Palma, Spain: Servei de Publicacions i Intercanvi Científic, Universitat de les Illes Balears, 1998.

Eliade, Mircea. *The Forge and the Crucible: The Origins and Structures of Alchemy*, 2nd ed. Chicago: University of Chicago Press, 1978.

———. *Myths, Rites, Symbols: A Mircea Eliade Reader.* New York: Harper & Row, 1976.

Emmerson, Richard K., and Bernard McGinn, eds. *The Apocalypse in the Middle Ages.* Ithaca, NY: Cornell University Press, 1992.

Erlenger, Philippe. *Carlos V.* Translated by Jesús Fernández Zulaica. Barcelona: Salvat Editores, 1985.

Espinosa de los Monteros, Manuel. *Interpretacion de la Imagen Guadalupana y Confirmacion del Systema Milenario*, unpublished manuscript, 1825. *Monumentos Guadalupanos*, Obadiah Rich Collection, New York Public Library.

———. *Interpretacion de la Pintura Guadalupana*, unpublished manuscript, 1825. *Monumentos Guadalupanos*, Obadiah Rich Collection, New York Public Library.

———. *La interpretacion del misterio Guadalupano: Obervaciones preparatorias contrahidas preciamente a los material de la Imagen*, unpublished manuscript, 1830. *Monumentos Guadalupanos*, Obadiah Rich Collection, New York Public Library.

———. *Miscelánea (1831–1832) Tomos I y II de varias doctrinas morales, costumbres, observaciones y otras noticias pertenecientes al curato de Iztacalco.* Edited by Brian F. Connaughton. México City: UNAM, 2012.

Estow, Clara. *Pedro the Cruel of Castile: 1350–1369.* Leiden, Neth.: Brill, 1995.

Evans, Julie A. "Heresy as an Agent of Change: Inquisition in the Monastery of Guadalupe." PhD diss., Stanford University, 1998.

Fernández, Quirino. "Fray Dionisio Vázquez de Toledo orador sagrado del Siglo de Oro." *Archivo Agustiniano* 60, no. 178 (1976): 105–198.

Fernández del Castillo, Francisco. *Libros y Libreros en el Siglo XVI*, vol. 6. México City: Publicaciones del Archivo General de la Nación, 1914.

Fernández López, Sergio. *El Cantar de los Cantares en el humanismo español: La tradición judía.* Huelva, Spain: Universidad de Huelva, 2009.

Ficino, Marsilio. *Marsilio Ficino.* Edited by Angela Voss. Berkeley, CA: North Atlantic Books, 2006.

Fita Colomé, Fidel. "La Inquisición en Guadalupe." *Boletín de la Real Academia de la Historia* 23 (1893): 283–343.

———. "La Inquisición Toledana: Relación Contemporánea de los Autos y Autillos Que Celebro Desde el Ano 1485 hasta el de 1501." *Boletín de la Real Academia de la Historia* 11 (1887): 289–322.

Florencia, Francisco de. *Estrella del Norte*, 2nd ed. México City: Por doña Maria de Benavides, viuda de Juan de Ribera, 1688.

Forsyth, Ilene H. *The Throne of Wisdom: Wood Scultptures of the Madonna in Romanesque France.* Princeton, NJ: Princeton University Press, 1972.

Foucault, Michel. *The Order of Things: An Archaeology of the Human Sciences.* New York: Vintage Books, 1970.

Fraker, Charles F. "Gonçalo Martínez de Medina, the Jerónimos, and the Devotio Moderna." *Hispanic Review* 34, no. 4 (July 1966): 197–217.

Friedman, Jerome. "Sixteenth-Century Christian-Hebraica: Scripture and the Renaissance Myth of the Past." *Sixteenth Century Journal* 11, no. 4 (1980): 67–85.

Fuchs, Barbara. *Exotic Nation: Maurophilia and the Construction of Early Modern Spain.* Philadelphia: University of Pennsylvania Press, 2009.

———. *Passing for Spain: Cervantes and the Fiction of Identity.* Hispanisms. Urbana: University of Illinois Press, 2003.

Fulcanelli. *El Misterio de las Catedrales: La Obra Maestra de la Hermetica en el Siglo XX.* México City: Random House Mondadori, 1926.

García, Sebastian. *Guadalupe: Siete siglos de fe y cultura.* Guadalupe Extremadura, Spain: Ediciones Guadalupe, 1993.

———. *Guadalupe de Extremadura en America.* Guadalupe Extremadura, Spain: Comunidad Franciscana de Guadalupe, 1990.

———. "Medicina y cirugía en los Reales Hospitales de Guadalupe," *Revista de estudios extremeños* 59, no. 1 (2003): 11–77

García Izcazbalceta, Joaquin. *Carta acerca del origen de la Imagen Nuestra Señora de Guadalupe de México.* México City: Imprenta de Luis G. Gonzalez, 1896.

Gil, Juan. *Arias Montano y su Entorno.* Bajadoz, Spain: Junta de Extremadura, Consejería de Cultura y Patrimonio: Diputación de Badajoz, 1998.

———. "De Sevilla a Fregenal." In *Benito Arias Montano y Los Humanistas de su Tiempo,* edited by José María Maestre Maestre, 547–615. Merida, Spain: Junta de Extremadura, Consejería de Cultura y Patrimonio: Diputación de Badajoz, 2006.

Gill, Meredith J. *Augustine in the Italian Renaissance: Art and Philosophy from Petrarch to Michelangelo.* Cambridge: Cambridge University Press, 2005.

Giovio, Paolo. *An Italian Portrait Gallery: Being Brief Biographies of Scholars Illustrious within the Memory of Our Grandfathers for the Published Monuments of Their Genius.* Translated by Florence Alden Gragg. Boston: Chapman and Grimes, 1935.

Gitlitz, David M. *Secrecy and Deceit: The Religion of the Crypto-Jews.* Albuquerque: University of New Mexico Press, 2002.

Godínez, Felipe. "Auto Sacramental de La Virgen de Guadalupe." In *Autos sacramentales, y al Nacimiento de Christo, con sus loas y entremesses,* 145–177. Madrid: Juan Fernandez, 1675.

Goldberg, Alice. "Una vida de santos extrana: O el fraile ha de ser ladron o el ladron ha de ser fraile, de Felipe Godinez." *AIH ACTAS* (1983): 624–629.

Goldish, Matt. "Patterns of Converso Messianism." In *Millenarianism and Messianism in Early Modern European Culture,* edited by Richard Popkin and Matt Goldish, 41–63. Dordrecht, Netherlands: Kluwer Academic Publishers, 2001.

Gómez Menor, José. *Cristianos Nuevos y Mercaderes de Toledo: Notas y documentos para el estudio de la sociedad castellana en el siglo XVI.* Toledo: Imprenta Gómez Menor, 1970.

Gongora Argote, Luis de. "Religion. Justicia." In *Obras de Luis de Góngora y Argote. [Varias poesias. Fabula de Polifemo y Galatea. Las Soledades. Panegiciro] [Dadas a luz por Geronymo de Villegas],* edited by Geronymo de Villegas, 417–436. Brussels: Imprenta de Francisco Foppens, 1659.

González, Epigmenio, ed. "La Virgen del Tepeyac, patrona principal de la nación mexicana: Compendio histórico-crítico / por un sacerdote residente en esta arquidiócesis." In *Miscellaneous Mexican publications.* Guadalajara, México, 1884.

González de la Calle, Pedro Urbano. "Arias Montano, humanista. (Apuntes y notas para un ensayo)." *Revista de Centro de Estudios Extremeños* 2 (1928): 17–170.

González Carvajal, Tomás. "Elogio histórico del Doctor Benito Arias Montano, leído en la Real Academia de la Historia." *Memorias de la Real Academia de la Historia* 2 (1832): 1–199.

González Obregón, Luis, ed. *Procesos de Luis de Carvajal (el Mozo)*, vol. 28. Publicaciones del Archivo General de la Nacion. México City: Talleres Graficos de la Nacion, 1935.

Göttler, Christine. "Securing Space in a Foreign Place: Peter Paul Ruben's 'Saint Teresa' for the Portuguese Merchant-Bankers in Antwerp." *Journal of the Walters Art Gallery* 57 (1999): 133–151.

Green, Arthur. "Shekhina, the Virgin Mary, and the Song of Songs: Reflections on a Kabbalistic Symbol in Its Historical Context." *AJS Review* 26, no. 1 (April 2002): 1–52.

Green, Tobias. "Masters of Difference: Creolization and the Jewish Presence in Cabo Verde, 1497–1672." PhD diss., University of Birmingham, 2007.

Greenfield, Jonas C. "Book Review of Élie Lévita, Humaniste et Massoréte." *Journal of the American Oriental Society* 88, no. 3 (1968): 529–531.

Gregorov, Ferdinand. *History of the City of Rome in the Middle Ages*, vol. 8. Translated by Annie Hamilton. London: George Bell and Sons, 1902.

Grolierius, Caesar. *Historia Expvgnatæ et Direptæ Vrbis Romæ per Exercitvm Caroli V. Imp. Die VI. Maii M. D. XXVII. Clemente VII. Pontifice*. Paris: Cramoisy, 1637.

Gruzinski, Serge. *Images at War: Mexico from Columbus to Blade Runner (1492–2019)*. Durham, NC: Duke University Press, 2001.

Guénée, Antoine. *Cartas de unos Judios alemanes y polacos à M. de Voltaire: Con un comentario sacado de otro mayor para el uso que leen sus obras,y cuatro memorias sobre la fertilidad de la Judea*. Translated by Francisco Pablo Vazquez. Brussels: A. Wahlen, 1827.

Guerra, Luis Durán. "Benito Arias Montano: Emblemas para una Biblización de la Política." *Cuadernos sobre Vico* 21–22 (2008): 237–262.

Guicciardini, Luigi. *Il Sacco di Roma*, ed. Carlo Milanesi. Florence: Barbéra, 1867.

Hagstrom, Aurelie A. "The Symbol of the Mandorla in Christian Art: Recovery of a Feminine Archetype." *Month-London-Longman's Magazine of Lite* 29, no. 5 (1996): 190–194.

———. "The Symbol of the Mandorla in Christian Art: Recovery of a Feminine Archetype." *Arts: The Arts in Religious and Theological Studies* 10, no. 2 (1998): 25–29.

Halevy, Schulamith. "Descendents of the Anusim (Crypto-Jews) in Contemporary México." PhD diss., Hebrew University, 2009.

Harris, E. "Mary in the Burning Bush: Nicolas Froment's Triptych at Aix-en-Provence." *Journal of the Warburg Institute* 1, no. 4 (April 1938): 281–286.

Hemptinne, Thérèse de. "Jeanne de Castille, une reine entre folie et pouvoir (1479–1555)." In *Charles V in Context: The Making of a European Identity*, edited by Marc Boone and Marysa Demoor, 235–248. Brussels: VUB Brussels University Press, 2003.

Hernán, Vicente Mendez. "Una Nueva Obra del Entallador y Escultor Placentino Alonso Hipólito: La Piedad de la Iglesia de el Salvador, de Plasencia (Cácares)." *Norba-Arte* 22–23 (2003 2002): 61–71.

Hernández, Marie-Theresa. *Delirio—The Fantastic, the Demonic, and the Réel: The Buried History of Nuevo León*. Austin: University of Texas Press, 2002.

Hernández Morejón, Antonio. *Historia bibliográfica de la medicina española*. Madrid: Impr. de la viuda de Jordan e hijos, 1842.

Herrero, José Sánchez. "Fundación y desarrollo de la Orden de los Jerónimos, 1360–1561." *Codex Aqvilarensis: Cuadernos de investigación del Monasterio de Santa María la Real* 10 (December 1994): 73.

Herrero del Collado, Tarsicio. "El proceso inquisitorial por delito de herejía contra Hernando de Talavera." *Anuario de historia del derecho español* 39:671–706.

Hoberman, Luisa Schell. "Merchants in Seventeenth-Century Mexico City: A Preliminary Portrait." *Hispanic American Historical Review* 57, no. 3 (August 1977): 497.

Holzworth, Rebecca Joy. "The Apse Murals in San Agustín de Acolman: Augustinian Friars as the Foundation of the Roman Church in New Spain." Master's thesis, University of Arizona, 2007.

Homza, Lu Ann. "Erasmus as Hero, or Heretic? Spanish Humanism and the Valladolid Assembly of 1527." *Renaissance Society of America* 50, no. 1 (Spring 1997): 78–118.

Hufton, Olwen. "Altruism and Reciprocity: The Early Jesuits and Their Female Patrons." *Renaissance Studies* 15, no. 3 (2001): 335. doi:10.1111/1477-4658.00373.

Huynen, Jacques. *El enigma de las Virgenes Negras.* Translated by R. M. Bassols. Barcelona: Plaza y Janes Editorial, 1972.

Idel, Moshe. *Kabbalah and Eros.* New Haven, CT: Yale University Press, 2005.

Ingram, Kevin. *The Conversos and Moriscos in Late Medieval Spain and Beyond.* Leiden, Neth.: Brill, 2009.

Israel, Jonathan. *Enlightenment Contested: Philosophy, Modernity, and the Emancipation of Man 1670–1752.* Oxford: Oxford University Press, 2006.

———. "Jews and Crypto-Jews in the Atlantic World Systems, 1500–1800." In *Atlantic Diasporas: Jews, Conversos, and Crypto-Jews in the Age of Mercantilism, 1500–1800*, edited by Richard L. Kagan and Philip D. Morgan, 3–17. Baltimore, MD: Johns Hopkins University Press, 2009.

———. *Race, Class, and Politics in Colonial Mexico: 1610–1670.* Oxford: Oxford University Press, 1975.

Israel, Menasseh ben. *The Hope of Israel.* Oxford: Littman Library, 1987.

Ivy, Marilyn. *Discourses of the Vanishing: Modernity, Phantasm, Japan.* Chicago: University of Chicago Press, 1999.

Jacobs, Janet Liebman. *Hidden Heritage: The Legacy of the Crypto-Jews.* Berkeley: University of California Press, 2002.

Jacobs, Lynn F. "The Triptychs of Hieronymus Bosch." *Sixteenth Century Journal* 31, no. 3 (Autumn 2000): 1009.

Javary, Genevieve. "Recherches sur l'utilisation du theme de la sekina dans l'apologetique Chretienne du XV éme au XVIII éme siecle." PhD diss., Université de Paris, 1976.

Jiménez Sánchez, Antonio Jesús. "Beatriz de Silva y la Inmaculada Concepción: Orígenes de una orden." In *La Inmaculada Concepción en España: Religiosidad, historia y arte: Actas del simposium*, edited by Francisco Javier Campos y Fernández de Sevilla, 691–709. San Lorenzo de El Escorial, 2005.

Jung, Carl. *Collected Works.* Vol. 12, *Psychology and Alchemy*, 2nd ed. Princeton, NJ: Princeton University Press, 1968.

Kagan, Richard, and Philip D. Morgan, eds. *Atlantic Diasporas: Jews, Conversos, and Crypto-Jews in the Age of Mercantilism, 1500—1800.* Baltimore, MD: Johns Hopkins University Press.

Kamen, Henry. *The Escorial: Art and Power in the Renaissance.* New Haven, CT: Yale University Press, 2010.

———. *Philip of Spain.* New Haven, CT: Yale University Press, 1997.

Katz, David S. "Menasseh ben Israel's Mission to Queen Christina of Sweden, 1651–1655." *Jewish Social Studies* 45, no. 1 (Winter 1983): 57–72.

Katzew, Ilona. *Casta Painting: Images of Race in Eighteenth-Century Mexico.* New Haven, CT: Yale University Press, 2005.

Kottman, Karl A. *Law and Apocalypse: The Moral Thought of Luis de Leon (1527?–1591)*. The Hague: Martinus Nijhoff, 1972.

Kristeva, Julia, and Arthur Goldhammer. "Stabat Mater." *Poetics Today* 6, no. 1–2 (1985): 133–152.

Labrador Arroyo, Felix, Manuel Rivero Rodriguez, and Carlos Javier de Morales. "En busca del equilibrio en la corte de Carlos V (1522–1529)." In *Corte de Carlos V*, edited by José Martínez Millán, 207–259. Madrid: Sociedad Estatal para la Conmemoración de los Centenarios de Felipe II y Carlos V, 2000.

Lacunza, Manuel. *La venida del Mesías en gloria y majestad*. London: R. Ackerman, 1826.

Lafaye, Jacques. *Quetzalcóatl y Guadalupe: La formación de la conciencia nacional*, 2nd ed. México City: Fondo de Cultura Economica, 2002.

Lara, Jaime. *City, Temple, Stage: Eschatological Architecture and Liturgical Theatrics in New Spain*. Notre Dame, IN: University of Notre Dame Press, 2004.

Lazar, Moshe. "Alfonso de Zamora, copiste." *Sefarad* 14, no. 2 (1958): 314–327.

Lazure, Guy. "To Dare Fame: Constructing a Cultural Elite in Sixteen Century Seville." PhD diss., Johns Hopkins University, 2003.

Lea, Henry Charles. *A History of the Inquisition of the Middle Ages*. New York, 1958.

Leftley, Sharon Ann. "Millenarian Thought in Renaissance Rome with Special Reference to Pietro Galatino (c. 1464–c. 1540) and Egidio da Viterbo (c. 1469–1532)." University of Bristol, 1995.

Lehfeldt, Elizabeth A. "Ruling Sexuality: The Political Legitimacy of Isabel of Castile." *Renaissance Quarterly* 53, no. 1 (Spring 2000): 31–56.

León, Luis de. "A Nuestra Señora." In *Obras del Maestro Fray Luis de León*, vol. 2, edited by Gregorio Mayans y Siscar, Biblioteca de Autores Espanoles. Madrid: M. Rivadeneyra, 1855.

———. "Protestacion de fe que hizo Fray Luis de León estando en la carcel del Santo Oficio de Valladolid, temiendo morir en la prision." In *Proceso del P. M. Fray Luis de Leon: Doctor Teologo del Claustro y Gremio de la Universidad de Salamanca*, edited by Alejandro Arango y Escandon. México City: Imprenta de Andrade y Escalante, 1856.

Leonard, Irving A. "On the Mexican Book Trade, 1683." *Hispanic American Historical Review* 27, no. 3 (August 1947): 403–435.

Lerner, Robert E. *The Heresy of the Free Spirit in the Later Middle Ages*. Berkeley: University of California Press, 1972.

Liebman, Seymour B. "Hernando Alonso: The First Jew on the North-American Continent." *Journal of Inter-American Studies* 5, no. 2 (1963): 291–296.

———. *Jews and the Inquisition of Mexico: The Great Auto de Fe of 1649 as Related by Mathias de Bocanegra, S.J.* Lawrence, KS: Coronado Press, 1974.

———. *The Jews in New Spain: Faith, Flame, and the Inquisition*. Coral Gables, FL: University of Miami Press, 1970.

Linehan, Peter. "The Beginnings of Santa Maria de Guadalupe en the Direction of the Fourteenth-Century Castile." *Journal of Ecclesiastical History* 36, no. 1 (1985): 284–304.

Liss, Peggy K. *Isabel the Queen: Life and Times*. New York: Oxford University Press, 1992.

Llavia, Ramón de. *Cancionero de Ramón de Llavia*. Edited by Rafael Benitez Claros. Madrid: Sociedad de Bibliófilos Españoles, 1945.

Llopis Agelán, Enrique. "Milagros, Demandas y Prosperidad: El Monasterio Jerónimo de Guadalupe, 1389–1571." *Revista de Historia Económica* 16, no. 2 (Spring–Summer 1998).

Long, J. C. "Botticelli's 'Birth of Venus' as Wedding Painting." *Aurora* 9 (2008): 1–27.

Lope de Vega Carpio, Félix Arturo. *La Limpieza No Manchada*. Cervantes Virtual, 1618.

López, Rafael. "Introduction." In *Procesos de Luis de Carvajal (el Mozo)*, vol. 28, edited by Luis González Obregón, vii–xii. México City: Talleres Graficos de la Nacion, 1935.

López Perez, Miguel, and Mar Rey Bueno. "Simón de Tovar (1528–1596): Redes familiares, naturaleza americana y comercio de maravillas en la Sevilla del XVI." *Dynamis* 26 (2006): 69–91.

López Piñero, José María. "La disección y el saber anatómico en la España de la primera mitad del siglo xvi." *Cuadernos de Historia de la Medicina Española* 13 (1974): 51–110.

Lugo, Antonio de. "El monacato 'sui generis,' de lo Jerónimos. Desde los origenes hasta la desamortización." *Cistertium* 23 (1970): 230–238.

Lyell, James P. *Cardinal Ximenes, Statesman, Ecclesiastic, Soldier, and Man of Letters, with an Account of the Complutensian Polyglot Bible.* London: Grafton & Co., 1917.

Macías Rosendo, Baldomero, ed. *La correspondencia de Benito Arias Montano con el Presidente de Indias Juan de Ovando: Cartas de Benito Arias Montano convervadas en el Instituto de Valencia de Don Juan.* Huelva, Spain: Universidad de Huelva, 2008.

Maravall, José Antonio. *Carlos V y el pensamiento político del Renacimiento.* Madrid: Boletín Oficial del Estado Centro de Estudios Políticos y Constitutioncionales, 1999.

Marnef, Guido. "Charles V's Religious Policy and the Antwerp Market: A Confrontation of Different Interests?" In *Charles V in Context: The Making of a European Identity*, edited by Marc Boone and Marysa Demoor, 21–33. Brussels: VUB Brussels University Press, 2003.

Marshall, John W. *Parables of War: Reading John's Jewish Apocalypse.* Waterloo, Ont.: Wilfrid Laurier University Press, 2001.

Martin, F. X. *Friar, Reformer, and Renaissance Scholar: Life and Work of Giles of Viterbo 1469–1532.* Villanova, PA: Augustinian Press, 1992.

———. "The Problem of Giles of Viterbo: A Historiographical Survey." *Augustiniana* IX (1959): 357–379.

Martz, Linda. *A Network of Converso Families in Early Modern Toledo: Assimilating a Minority.* Ann Arbor: University of Michigan Press, 2003.

Mascareñas, Carlos-Eugenio. "Sobre Doña Leonor Mascareñas, aya de Don Felipe II y Del Principe Don Carlos." *Hispania* 7, no. 26 (March 1947): 3–23.

Mathes, W. Michael. *The Americas' First Academic Library: Santa Cruz de Tlatelolco.* Sacramento: California State Library Foundation, 1985.

———. "Humanism in Sixteenth- and Seventeenth-Century Libraries of New Spain." *Catholic Historical Review* 82, no. 3 (1996): 412–435.

Matovina, Timothy. "Guadalupe at Calvary: Patristic Theology in Miguel Sanchez's Imagen de la Virgen Maria (1648)." *Theological Studies* 64 (2003): 795–812.

———. "Theologies of Guadalupe: From the Spanish Colonial Era to Pope John Paul II." *Theological Studies* 70 (2009): 61–91.

Mayberry, Nancy. "The Controversy over the Immaculate Conception in Medieval and Renaissance Art, Literature, and Society." *Journal of Medieval and Renaissance Studies* 21, no. 2 (Fall 1991): 207–224.

Melammed, Renee Levine. *A Question of Identity: Iberian Conversos in Historical Perspective.* Oxford: Oxford University Press, 2004.

Meléndez y Pelayo, Marcelino. *Historia de los heterodoxos españoles.* Madrid: Librería católica de San José, 1880.

Menéndez Onrubia, Carmen. "Hacia la Biografía de un Iluminado Judio: Felipe Godíñez (1585–1659)." *Segismundo*, no. 25–26 (1977): 90–130.

Monfasani, John. "Hermes Trismegistus, Rome, and the Myth of Europa: An Unknown Text of Giles of Viterbo." *Viator* 22 (1991): 311–342.

Montano, Benito Arias. *Comentarios a los Trienta y un Primeros Salmos de David.* León: Secretariado de Publicaciones de la Universidad de León, 1999.

————. *Prefacios de Benito Arias Montano a la Biblia Regia de Felipe II*. Edited by Sánchez Manzano and María Asunción. León, España: Junta de Castilla y León, Consejería de Cultura y Turismo, Universidad de León, Servicio de Publicaciones, 2006.

Morocho Gayo, Gaspar. "Hermetismo y cábala cristiana en la corte de Carlos V: Egidio de Viterbo, Dionisio Vázquez, Cipriano de la Huerga." *La Ciudad de Dios* 213 (December 2000): 813–854.

————. "Trayectoria humanística de Benito Arias Montano, I. Sus cuarenta primeros años (1526–27–1567)." In *El Humanismo Extremeño, III Jornadas,* 4–97. Trujillo: Real Academia de Estremadura, 1998.

————. "Trayectoria humanística de Benito Arias Montano, II. Años de plentitude (1568–1598)." In *El Humanismo Extremeño, III Jornadas,* 227–304. Trujillo: Real Academia de Extremadura, 1999.

Moss, Leonard W., and Stephen C. Cappannari. "The Black Madonna: An Example of Culture Borrowing." *Scientific Monthly* 76, no. 6 (June 1953): 319–324.

Navarro Antolín, Fernando, Luis Gómez Canseco, and Baldomero Macías Rosendo. "Fronteras del Humanismo: Arias Montano y el Nuevo Mundo." In *Orbis incognitvs: Avisos y legajos del Nuevo Mundo: Homenaje al profesor Luis Navarro García*, vol. 1, edited by Fernando Navarro Antolín, 101–136. Huelva: Universidad de Huelva, 2007.

Newman, Zelda Kahan. "Elye Levita: A Man on the Cusp of Modernity." *Shofar: An Interdisciplinary Journal of Jewish Studies* 24, no. 4 (2006): 90–109.

Noriega y Pubul, J. Diaz de. *La Blanca de la carne en Sevilla*, tomo IV. Hidalguía: Instituto Salazar y Castro, 1977.

Nowak, William J. "Virgin Rhetoric: Fray Luis de Leon and Marian Piety in Virgen, que el sol mas pura." *Hispanic Review* 73, no. 4 (Autumn 2005): 491–509.

Nunemaker, J. Horace. Review of *La Familia Carvajal* by Alfonso Toro. *Pacific Historical Review* 15, no. 1 (March 1946): 102–104.

Oberman, Heiko A. Preface to *Devotio moderna: Basic Writings*. Ed. John Van Engen (Paulist Press: New York, 1988).

Ohara, Shima. "La Propaganda Politica Entorno al Conflicto Sucesorio de Enrique IV (1457–1474)." PhD diss., Universidad de Valladolid, 2004.

O'Malley, John. *Giles of Viterbo on Church and Reform*. Leiden: Brill, 1968.

Ordax, Salvador A. "Las artes plasticas de Guadalupe." In *Guadalupe: Siete siglos de fe y cultura*, edited by Sebastian García (Guadalupe Extremadura, Spain: Ediciones Guadalupe, 1993), 287–325.

Pacheco, Francisco. *Libro de descripción de verdaderos retratos de ilustres y memorables varones.* Edited by Pedro M. Piñero Ramírez and Rogelio Reyes Cano. Sevilla: Diputación Provincial de Sevilla, 1985.

Paddon, Robert. "The Ordenanza de Padronazgo: An Interpretive Essay." In *The Church in Colonial Latin America*, edited by John Frederick Schwaller, 27–47. Wilmington, DE: Scholarly Resources, 2000.

Pagels, Elaine. *Revelations: Visions, Prophecy, and Politics in the Book of Revelation*. New York: Penguin, 2012.

Paniagua Pérez, Jesús. "La obra y las relaciones de Arias Montano con las Indias." In *El humanismo español entre el viejo mundo y el nuevo*, edited by Jesús Maria Nieto Ibáñez, 409–444. Salamanca: Universidad de Jaén, 2008.

Paradinas Fuentes, Jesús Luis. "Dos cartas atribuidas a Arias." In *El Humanismo extremeño: Estudios presentados a las I^{as}. Jornadas organizadas por la Real Academia de Extremadura*, edited by Marqués de la Encomienda, M. Terrón, and A. Viudas. Trujillo: Real Academia de Extremadura de las Letras y las Artes, 1997.

Pastor, Ludwig. *The History of the Popes from the Close of the Middle Ages: Drawn from the Secret Archives of the Vatican and Other Original Sources*, vol. 4, 3rd ed. London: Kegan Paul, Trench, Trübner & Co., 1906.

———. *The History of the Popes from the Close of the Middle Ages: Drawn from the Secret Archives of the Vatican and Other Original Sources*, vol. 9. Edited by Ralph Francis Kerr. London: Kegan Paul, Trench, Trübner & Co., 1910.

Pecellín Lancharro. "Benito Arias Montano, íntimio de judeoconversos, familiastas y procesados por la Inquisición." In *Del candelabro a la encina: raíces hebreas en Extremadura: Actas*, edited by Fernando Cortés Cortés, 351–374. Bajadoz, Spain: Junta de Extremadura, Consejería de Cultura y Patrimonio: Diputación de Badajoz, 1996.

Pérez, Joseph. *Los judios en España*. Madrid: Marcial Pons, 2005.

Pérez Castro, Federico. "Semblanza Bio-Bibliografico de Alfonso de Zamora." In *El manuscrito apologético de Alfonso de Zamora: Traduccion y estudio del Séfer Hokmat Elohim*, edited by Federico Pérez Castro, xi–ci. Madrid: Instituto Benito Arias Montano, 1950.

Perez de Tudela y Velasco, Maria Isabel. "Alfonso XI y el Santuario de Santa Maria de Guadalupe." In *Estudios en memoria del profesor D. Salvador de Moxó*, edited by Miguel Angel Ladero Quesada, 271–286. Madrid: Universidad Complutense de Madrid, 1982.

Persson, Ana Lorena Ericson. *La crisis del guadalupanismo: Cerca de cien años de silencio a través de los textos del arzobispo Montúfar*. Mexico City: Ediciones Navarra, 2006.

Peterson, Jeanette Favrot. "Creating the Virgin of Guadalupe: The Cloth, the Artist, and Sources in Sixteenth-Century New Spain." *Americas* 61, no. 4 (April 2005): 571–610.

Pidal, Ramón Menéndez. *Estudios Literarios*. Buenos Aires: Espasa-Calpe Argentina, 1938.

Pike, Ruth. *Aristocrats and Traders: Sevillian Society in the Sixteenth Century*. Ithaca, NY: Cornell University Press, 1972.

Pinta Llorente, Miguel de la, ed. *Procesos inquisitoriales contra los catedráticos hebraistas de Salamanca: Gaspar de Grajal, Martínez de Cantalapiedra y Fray Luis de León / estudio y transcripción paleográfica por Miguel de la Pinta Llorente*. Madrid: Monasterio de Escorial, 1935.

Poole, Stafford. *The Guadalupan Controversies*. Stanford, CA: Stanford University Press, 2006.

———. *Juan de Ovando: Governing the Spanish Empire in the Reign of Philip II*. Norman: University of Oklahoma Press, 2004.

———. "The Politics of Limpieza de Sangre: Juan de Ovando and His Circle in the Reign of Philip II." *Americas* 55, no. 3 (January 1999): 359–389.

Popkin, Richard H. "Christian Jews and Jewish Christians in the 17th Century." In *Jewish Christians and Christian Jews: From the Renaissance to the Enlightenment*, edited by Richard Popkin and Gordon Weiner, 57–72. Dordrecht: Kluwer Academic Publishers, 1994.

———. "Intellectual Biography: Warts and All." In *The Sceptical Mode in Modern Philosophy: Essays in Honor of Richard Popkin*, edited by Richard Watson and James E. Forth, 116–117. Dordrecht, Neth.: Nijhoff, 1988.

———. "Jewish Christians and Christian Jews in Spain, 1492 and After." *Judaism* 41, no. 3 (1992): 248–267.

———. "Mordecai Noah, the Abbe Gregoire, and the Paris Sanhedrin." *Modern Judaism* 2, no. 2 (1982): 131–148.

———. "Savonarola and Cardinal Ximines: Millenarian Thinkers and Actors at the Eve of the Reformation." In *Catholic Millenarianism: From Savonarola to Abbé Grégoire*, edited by Karl Kottman, 15–26. Dordrecht, Neth.: Kluwer Academic Publishers, 2001.

Prescott, William H. *History of the Reign of Ferdinand and Isabella the Catholic*, vol. 2, 4th ed. Boston: Charles C. Little and James Brown, 1838.

———. *History of the Reign of Philip II, King of Spain.* Boston: Phillips, Sampson, and Company, 1855.

Quiroz, Alonso W. "*The Expropriation of Portuguese* New Christians in Spanish America, 1635–1649." *Ibero-Amerikanisches Archiv* 11, no. 1 (1985): 407–465.

Rábade Obradó, María del Pilar. "El entorno judeoconverso de la Casa y Corte de Isabel la Católica." In *Las relaciones discretas ente las monarquías hispana y portuguesa: las casas de las reinas (siglos XV–XIX),* edited by José Martínez Millán and Maria Paula Marçal Lourenço. Madrid: Ediciones Polifemo, 2008.

———. "Judeoconversos y monarquía: Un problema de opinión pública." In *La monarquía como conflicto en la Corona castellano-leonesa (c. 1230–1504),* edited by José Manuel Nieto Soria. Madrid: Silex Ediciones, 2006.

———. *Un elite de poder en la corte de los Reyes Catolicos: Los Judeoconversos.* Madrid: Sigilo, 1993.

Ramirez, José Fernando. *Obras del Lic: Don José Fernando Ramirez,* vol. 1. México City: Imp. de V. Agüeros, Editor, 1898.

Rekers, Bernard. *Benito Arias Montano.* London: Warburg Institute, 1972.

Revuelta Somalo, José Maria. *Los Jerónimos: Una orden religiosa nacida en Guadalajara.* Guadalajara, Spain: Institucion Provincial de Cultura Marques de Santillana, 1982.

Ricard, Robert. "Pour une étude de judaisme portugais au Mexique pendant période coloniale." *Revue d' Histoire Moderne,* August 14, 1939, 522.

Riva Palacio, Vicente. *Memorias de un Impostor: Don Guillen de Lampart, Rey de México.* Vol. 1. México City: Editorial Porrúa, 1908.

Robles, Antonio de. *Diario de sucesos notables (1665–1703).* Vol. 1. México City: Editorial Porrúa, 1946.

Robles, Vito Alessio. "La Juderia de Monterrey." In *Bosquejos históricos,* 94–107. México City: Editorial Polis, 1938.

———. "Los Arrechuchos de Don Alfonso Toro," *La Prensa* (San Antonio, TX), January 9, 1936.

Rodriguez Marín, Francisco. "Nuevos datos para las biografias de algunos excritores españoles de los siglos XVI y XVII: Benito Arias Montano." *Boletín de la Real Academic Española* 5 (1918): 447–455.

Rodriguez Villa, Antonio. *Memorias para la historia del asalto y saqueo de Roma en 1527 por el ejercito imperial.* Madrid: Imprenta de la Biblioteca de Instruccion y Recreo, 1875.

Romero Carrión, Manuel. "Vision Que Tuvo Felipe II de Mano de Domenico Greco." n.d., 94.

Rosenstock, Bruce. *New Men: Conversos, Christian Theology, and Society in Fifteenth-Century Castille.* London: Department of Hispanic Studies, Queen Mary, University of London. 2002.

Roth, Norman. *Conversos, Inquisition, and the Expulsion of Jews from Spain.* Madison: University of Wisconsin Press, 1995.

Rubio, Fray German. *Historia de Ntra. Sra. de Guadalupe.* Barcelona: Thomas, 1926.

Rucquoi, Adeline. "Mancilla y Limpieza: La Obsesión por el Pecado en Castilla a Fines del Siglo XV." Os *"Últimos Fins" Na Cultura Ibérica (XV–XVIII)* Anexo VIII (1997): 113–135.

Ruiz-Gálvez Priego, Estrella. "'Sine Labe': El inmaculismo en la España de los siglos XV a XVII: la proyección social de un imaginario religioso." *Revista de dialectología y tradiciones populares* 63, no. 2 (2008): 197–241.

Rummel, Erika. *The Case against Johann Reuchlin: Religious and Social Controversy in Sixteenth-Century Germany.* Toronto: University of Toronto Press, 2002.

Saebo, Magne, Michael Fishbane, and John Louis Ska. *Hebrew Bible/Old Testament: The History of Its Interpretation: From the Renaissance to the Enlightenment,* vol. 2. Göttingen: Vandenhoeck & Ruprecht, 2008.

Saens, Pio [Manuel Espinosa de los Monteros?]. *El Observador Guadalupano: En el que se contexta al argumento negativo contrario a la tradicion, y hace observar la santa pintura por los aspector de historica y profetica,* unpublished manuscript, n.d. *Monumentos Guadalupanos,* Obadiah Rich Collection, New York Public Library.

Sáenz-Badillos, Angel. "Benito Arias Montano, Hebraísta." *Thélème: Revista complutense de estudios franceses* 12 (1997): 345–359.

Sagerman, Robert. "A Kabbalistic Reading of the Sistine Chapel Ceiling." *Acta ad archaeologiam et artium historiam pertinentia* 16 (2002): 93–177.

———. "The Syncretic Esotericism of Egidio da Viterbo and the Development of the Sistine Chapel Ceiling Program." *Acta ad archaeologiam et artium historiam pertinentia* 19 (2005): 37–76.

Saillens, E. *Nos Vierges Noires: Leurs origines.* Paris: Les Editions Universelles, 1945.

Salomon, Herman P. "Spanish Marranism Re-examined." *Sefarad* 68, no. 1 (January–June 2008): 131–158.

Sánchez, Miguel. *Imagen de la virgen Maria Madre de Dios de Guadalupe, milagrosamente aparecida en la ciudad de Mexico.* México City: Imprenta Biuda de Bernardo Calderon, 1648.

———. "Sermon S. Felipe de Jesus." México: Juan Ruiz, 1640.

Sánchez Herrero, José. *Historia de la Iglesia en España e Hispanoamérica: Desde sus inicios hasta el siglo XXI.* Madrid: Silex Ediciones, 2008.

Sandoval, Prudencio de. *Historia de la vida y hechos del Emperador Carlos V.* Barcelona: Sebastian de Cormellas, 1625.

Santa Cruz, Alonso de. *Crónica del Emperador Carlos V.* Madrid: Real Academia de la Historia, Imprenta del Patronato de Huérfanos de Intendencia é Intervención Militares, 1920.

Scheer, Monique. "From Majesty to Mystery: Change in the Meanings of Black Madonnas from the Sixteenth to Nineteenth Centuries." *American Historical Review* 105, no. 5 (December 2002): 1412–1442.

Scholem, Gershom. *Kabbalah.* New York: Dorset Press, 1974.

———. *Origins of the Kabbalah.* Edited by R. I. Zwi Werblowsky. Translated by Allan Arkush. Princeton, NJ: Princeton University Press, 1987.

Secret, François. *La Kabbala Cristiana del Renacimiento.* Translated by Ignacio Gómez de Liaño and Tomás Pollán. Madrid: Taurus, 1979.

———. "Le Symbolisme de la Kabbale Chretienne dans la 'Scechina' de Egidio da Viterbo." *Umanesimo e Machiavellismo: Archivio di Filosofia* 2–3 (1958): 131–154.

Shatzmiller, Joseph. *Jews, Medicine, and Medieval Society.* Berkeley: University of California Press, 1994.

Sicroff, Albert. "Clandestine Judaism in the Hieronymite Monastery of Nuestra Senora de Guadalupe." In *Studies in Honor of M. J. Bernadete (Essays in Hispanic and Sephardic culture),* 89–125. New York: Las Americas, 1965.

———. "The Jeronymite Monastery of Guadalupe in 14th and 15th Century Spain." In *Collected Studies in Honour of Americo Castro's Eightieth Year,* edited by M. P. Hornik. Oxford: Lincombe Lodge Research Library, 1965.

Sigüenza, José de. *Historia de la Orden de San Jerónimo,* vol. 2. Madrid: Bailly//Bailliére é Hijos Editores, 1909.

———. *Vida de San Gerónimo doctor máximo de la Yglesia.* Madrid: Imprenta de la Esperanza, 1853.

Siles, Francisco de. "Afterword." In *Imagen de la virgen Maria Madre de Dios de Guadalupe, milagrosamente aparecida en la ciudad de México,* by Miguel Sanchez. México City: Viuda de B. Calderon, 1648.

Starr-Lebeau, Gretchen. *In the Shadow of the Virgin: Inquisitors, Friars, and Conversos in Guadalupe, Spain.* Princeton, NJ: Princeton University Press, 2003.

Stern, Elsie R. "Esther and the Politics of Diaspora." *Jewish Quarterly Review* 100, no. 1 (Winter 2010): 25–53.

Stern, Selma. *The Court Jew: A Contribution to the History of the Period of Absolutism in Central Europe.* Philadelphia: Jewish Publication Society, 1950.

Stoler, Ann Laura. *Along the Archival Grain: Epistemic Anxieties and Colonial Common Sense.* Princeton, NJ: Princeton University Press, 2009.

Stratton, Suzanne L. *The Immaculate Conception in Spanish Art.* Cambridge: Cambridge University Press, 1994.

Strauss, Leo. *Persecution and the Art of Writing.* Chicago: University of Chicago Press, 1988.

Studnicki-Gizbert. 2008. "La Nación among the Nations: Portuguese and Other Maritime Trading Diasporas in the Atlantic, Sixteenth to Eighteenth Centuries." In *Atlantic Diasporas: Jews, Conversos, and Crypto-Jews in the Age of Mercantilism, 1500–1800,* edited by Richard L. Kagan and Philip D. Morgan, 75–98. Baltimore: Johns Hopkins University Press.

———. *A Nation upon the Ocean Sea: Portugal's Atlantic Diaspora and the Crisis of the Spanish Empire, 1492–1640.* Oxford: Oxford University Press, 2007.

Swietlicki, Catherine. *The Spanish Christian Cabala.* Columbia: University of Missouri Press, 1986.

Taylor, Rene. "Architecture and Magic: Considerations on the Idea of the Escorial." In *Essays in the History of Architecture Presented to Rudolf Wittkower,* edited by Douglas Fraser, Howard Hibbard, and Milton J. Lewine, 81–109. New York: Phaidon, 1967.

Temkin, Semuel. "Luis de Carvajal and His People." *AJS Review* 32, no. 1 (2008): 79–100.

Thompson, Colin P. *The Strife of Tongues: Fray Luis de Leon and the Golden Age of Spain.* Cambridge: Cambridge University Press, 1988.

Torre Villar, Ernesto, and Ramiro Navarro de Anda. *Testimonios históricos guadalupanos.* México City: Fondo de Cultura Economica, 1982.

Turel, Sara. "The Annunciation to Esther: Felipe Godíñez' Dramatic Vision." In *Jews, Christians, and Muslims in the Mediterranean World after 1492,* edited by Alisa Meyuhas Ginio, 44–52. London: Taylor and Francis, 1992.

Valbuena Prat, Ángel. *Historia de la literatura española,* vol. 1, 4th ed. Barcelona: G. Gili, 1953.

Valdéz, Alfonso de. *Diálogo de cosas ocurridas en Roma.* Edited by J. F. Montesinos. Madrid: Ediciones "La Lectura," 1928.

Van Dam, Cornelis. *The Urim and Thummim: A Means of Revelation in Ancient Israel.* Winona Lake, IN: Eisenbrauns, 1997.

Vaucher, Alfredo Félix. *Lacunza, un Heraldo de la Segunda Venida de Cristo.* Barcelona: Aula7activa-AEGUAE, 2005.

Vega, Pedro de la. *Cronica de los frayles de la orden del bienaventurado Fant Hieronymo.* Alcala de Henares: Casa de Juan de Brocer, 1539.

Vendrell, Francisca. "La actividad proselitista de San Vicente Ferrer durante el reinado de Fernando I de Aragón." *Sefarad* 13, no. 1 (1953): 87–105.

Vera, Fortuno Hipólito. *Colección de documentos eclesiásticos de México.* México City: Amecameca, Impr. del Colegio Católico, 1887.

Vloberg, Maurice. "The Iconography of the Immaculate Conception." In *The Dogma of the Immaculate Conception,* edited by E. D. O'Connor, plate VII. Notre Dame, IN: University of Notre Dame Press, 1958.

von der Osten Sacken, Cornelia. *El Escorial Estudio Iconologico.* Translated Maria Dolores Abalos. Bilbao: Xarait Ediciones, 1984.

Wachtel, Nathan. *La fe del recuerdo: Laberintos marranos.* Translated by Sandra Garzonio. México City: Fondo de Cultura Economica, 2007.

———."Una América Subterránia: Redes y Religiosidades Marranas." In *Para una Historia de América II. Los nudos 1,* edited by Marcello Carmagnani, Ruggiero Romano, and Alicia Hernández Chavez. México City: Fondo de Cultura Economica, 199.

Warner, Marina. *Alone of All Her Sex: The Myth and the Cult of the Virgin Mary.* New York: Vintage Books, 1983.

Weingrad, Michael. "Messiah, American Style: Mordecai Manuel Noah and the American Refuge." *AJS Review* 31, no. 1 (2007): 75–108.

Wilkinson, Robert J. *Orientalism, Aramaic, and Kabbalah in the Catholic Reformation: The First Printing of the Syriac New Testament.* Leiden, Neth.: Brill, 2007.

Wolfson, Elliot R. *Through a Speculum That Shines: Vision and Imagination in Medieval Jewish Mysticism.* Princeton, NJ: Princeton University Press, 1994.

Yovel, Yirmiyahu. *Spinoza and Other Heretics: The Marrano of Reason.* Princeton, NJ: Princeton University Press, 1989.

Index

57; studies, 77–78, 85–86; text, 61, 77, 113–114, 129; teachers, 79, 86; translation, 61, 77, 82

Hebrew truth. *See Hebraica veritas*

Hebrew University, 9

heresy/heretics, 9, 26, 34, 38, 43, 54, 102; accusations of, 43, 83, 87; *Antwerp Polyglot Bible* ruled as, by Roman Inquisition, 110; Arianism as, 68; Beghards and Beguines accused of, 192n107; Carlos V's policy toward, 95, 205n12; condemnation of, by Miguel Sánchez, 130; creation of the world, 82; at Escorial, 35; Godíñez as, 34; at the Guadalupe Monastery, 21, 35, 38; heretical nature of *Imagen de la virgen* [book], 163; Jewish doctrines as, 117; Luis de León imprisoned on charges of, 205n133; Lutheran doctrines, 117; mosaic, 129; in New Spain, 26; policy of Felipe II on, 102, 109; and pre-Jerónimos, 43; in the puebla of Guadalupe, 190n66; reading Hebrew as, 110; recommendations of Viterbo to Carlos V on, 97; Los Reyes Católicos policy toward, 129; semi-heretical nature of Felipe II's monarchy, 104; Spain as being full of, 128; Vásquez charged with, 83; and writings of Manuel Espinosa de los Monteros, 139, 146; Zapata de Toledo burned at the stake for, 54

Hieronymite Order, 35, 41, 43, 53, 56; pre-Hieronymites, 45. *See also* Jerónimos, Order of

Holiest Conception, Order of the [Concepción Santísima, Orden de la], 68

Holy Ghost, 59

Holy of Holies [Santa Sanctorum], 142, 143

Holy Office [México]: Barrientos Lomelin as official of, 181n32; censorship of *La venida del mesías* [book], 145, dissolution of, 145; and the great conspiracy, 119, 123; intense scrutiny of, 125, 127; irregularities at, 126, 130–131, 135–136; Luis de Carvajal (el Mozo)'s arrest by, 158, 159; Miguel Sánchez on, 9, 125, 127; official arrival, 11; relationship with Palafox y Mendoza, 122–123, 163; restrictions on travel, 123; text(s), 9; ubiquity of writing on, 123, and Váez Sevilla, 127; vigilance of, 125, 127. *See also* Inquisition [México]

Holy Office [Spain]: and Álvarez de Toledo family, 80; as book censor, 16; censorship of *La venida del mesías* [book], 145, and *limpieza de sangre*, 65; and Luis de León, 60–61; and Ovando, 106; relationship with Arias Montano, 16. *See also* Inquisition [Spain]

Holy Tribunal for the Inquisition. *See* Holy Office; Inquisition

Hospedería Real, 49

Huerga, Cipriano de la, 15, 84, 92, 105, 182n58

humanism, 82, 96, 206n18, 207n30

Iberia: concern about *macula* [stain], 67; devotion to the Virgin of the Immaculate Conception [Inmaculada]; 64; devotion to the Virgin Mary 13; identity, 68, medicine as a Jewish profession in, 48; obsession with *limpieza de sangre*, 67, 68; Portuguese merchant network in, 116; presence of conversos in, 15; Sephfarad in, 94

identity: of Castilla, 41; of Christian Jew, 143; *criollo*, 123; *criollo* Jew, 155; hybrid, 40; Jewish, 70, 116; Jewish, in México, 157, 158; and Manuel Espinosa de los Monteros, 146, 153; Mexican, 9, 142, 146; national, 8; New Spain's, 121; Spain's, 64, 67–69, 71, 75; symbolic, 157; Virgin of Guadalupe as a representation of Mexican, 142, 154

Illustrious Brotherhood of Our Blessed Lady, 43

Imagen de la Virgen Maria [Sánchez]: as a foundation myth of México, 10; censored, 136; enthralled the *criollo* elite, 124; most significant publication, 17, 124; as a nation-building text, 134; Old Testament references, 125; publication coinciding with active period for the Inquisition, 74, 120, 122, 134; published by Imprenta Viuda de Bernardo Calderon, 123; recounts the Guadalupe apparitions, 124; references the Inquisition, 125, 126; revised, 136–137; risk of censure, 134, 135; sanctioned by highest level of church officials, 9, 120; as syncretic converso theology, 135

About the Author

MARIE-THERESA HERNÁNDEZ is a professor of world cultures and literatures and the director of Jewish Studies at the University of Houston. She is the author of *Delirio—The Fantastic, the Demonic, and the Reel: The Buried History of Nuevo León* and *Cemeteries of Ambivalent Desire: Unearthing Deep South Narratives from a Texas Graveyard.*